Iowa State Fair
COOKBOOK

18th EDITION

PRIZE WINNING RECIPES FROM THE 2014 & 2015 FAIRS

Copyright 2016 by Iowa State Fair Authority. ISBN 978-0-930463-10-6
All rights reserved. No part of the book may be reproduced or transmitted in any form or by any means without written permission from the Iowa State Fair Board.

Artwork by Rachel Moylan

TO ORDER, WRITE: IOWA STATE FAIR COOKBOOK
PO Box 57130 | Des Moines, IA 50317-003 or call 515.262.3111

WWW.IOWASTATEFAIR.ORG

IowaStateFair | NOTHING COMPARES

We are proud to present the eighteenth edition of ribbon-winning Iowa State Fair recipes. Inside, you'll find classic family comfort foods and indulgent desserts, as well as mouth-watering new flavors and unique combinations.

The Iowa State Fair published the first award winning recipe cookbook in 1983 and in the decades since, its purpose has remained the same: to showcase the Iowa State Fair Food Department and the unique talent that makes it the largest competitive food department of any state fair. The 2016 competition will feature 203 divisions and 809 classes with more than $72,000 in premiums and prizes.

This collection of recipes is among the very best from 2014 and 2015 food competitions and ranges from main dishes and appetizers to breads and desserts and everything in-between. Edited for clarity, in general, the recipes are presented as submitted for judging. Although they have not been tested in a laboratory kitchen, they have been judged and awarded a first-place ribbon at the Iowa State Fair.

We applaud all exhibitors for their time, effort and dedication to perfecting their entries; they truly are what make the Food Department and the Iowa State Fair the best. We hope you enjoy the 18th edition of the Iowa State Fair cookbook.

The Editors: Jean Koss, Jean Lucas, Mindy Williamson and Jenna Beary

April 2016

TABLE OF CONTENTS

APPETIZERS, SIDE DISHES AND SALADS

APPETIZERS

A Honey of A BBQ Sauce 7
Appetizer Meatballs 22
Applesauce Salsa 21
Best Meat Dipping Sauce – Raspberry Chipotle Sauce 8
Best Tailgate Dip 14
BLT Bites 9
Bourbon Whiskey BBQ Sauce 2
Buffalo Chicken Cheese Balls 9
Caesar Mayonnaise Dressing 50
Cheesy Bacon Party Mix 10
Cheesy Chili Dip 10
Cocoa-Coconut Coffee Cooler 50
Coconut Chutney Wings 6
Coffee Liqueur Dip 21
Creamy Parmesan Dressing 29
Edamame Cheese Ball 26
Flaming Balls 11
Fresh Corn and Chorizo Salsa 15
Fresh from My Mom's Garden – Don't Tell Salsa 22
Fruit Pizza 18
Grilled Sweet and Spicy Chicken Wings 13
Guacamole 18
Gyoza 20
Honey Dip 13
Honey Mango Dip 11
Jalapeno Pizza Empanadas with Jalapeno Pesto
       Dipping Sauce 16
Little Queen Bee Honey BBQ Sauce 4
Madam Mary Small Batch Shrimp Appetizer 3
Mango Fire Wing Sauce 5
Mini Bruschetta Toppers 3
Overnight Rhubarb Slush 37
Parmesan Pesto Arancini 19
Pico De Gallo 8
Polenta Sweet Corn Edamame Bites with
       Edamame Sour Cream Spread 1
Pumpkin Pie Layered Dip 2

I

Robin's Cheesy Nacho Dip 6
Rosemary, Almond and Parmesan Shortbread
    Cocktail Cookies 25
Salsa Cruda 16
Sam's Stuffed Spicy Shrooms 17
Sausage Pretzel Bites 14
Sausage Taquitos.. 4
Shrimp Rice Cakes with Chili Plum Sauce 23
Spinach & Artichoke Cream Cheese Dip 5
Summer's Garden Sauerkraut Salsa 23
Sunshine Spicy Peach Salsa 20
Sweet Honey Sangria.... 44
Sweet N' Spicy Bits 12
Sweet N' Spicy Boom Boom Dipping Sauce 33
Sweet, Hot, Chopped Cherry Salsa 28
Teriyaki Hawaiian Appetizers 12
Tortilla, Corn and Sausage Fritter Appetizers 24
Tropical Honey Mocktail 41
Waiting for the Turkey Cranberry Salsa 7

SIDE DISHES AND SALADS
All-American Bacon Cheeseburger Soup 43
Bean & Kale Soup... 42
Carrot Noodles in Chimichurri Sauce.............................. 32
Charlie's Salad 35
Cheesy Hash Brown Potato Soup 36
Chicken Salad 31
Chicken Salad 38
Chipotle Cherry Salmon Salad 29
Cinnamon Mango Deviled Eggs 46
Classic Ukrainian Borscht 26
Corn Pudding 49
Crab Pasta Salad 40
Crab Pasta Salad 46
Creamy Double Corn Chowder 31
Fruit Cream.. 34
Hamburger Soup.. 37
Hamburger Soup with A Kick 39
Hot Potato Salad.. 47
Kale, Caesar! 27
Layered Salsa Salad 48
Low-Fat Tortilla Soup.. 45

Mom's Beet Salad 44
Picnic Baked Beans 47
Potato Tartlets... 32
Real Russian Borscht 41
Roasted Butternut Squash Soup............................... 42
Rockin' Rowan Baked Beans 34
Sicilian Deviled Eggs 28
Simply Carrots Soup.. 48
Smoked Maple-Wine Salmon Salad 35
Spicy Southwest Corn-Cheese Soup.......................... 30
Stuffed Twice Baked Potatoes 36
Super Seven Spinach Salad.. 44
Sweet Potato Salad.. 30
Thai Curry Shrimp Soup.. 38
Twice Baked Potato Casserole................................... 49
Vibrant Vegan Bean Soup.. 39
Wild Rice Salad 40
Zippy Zucchini Zuppa with Asparagus and
   Cannellini Beans 33

MAIN DISHES

MAIN DISHES
Alfredo Garlic Thai Pizza...................................... 102
Bacon Baked Potatoes... 68
Basil Cream Cheese Turkey Panini.......................... 60
BBQ Steak Wrap 104
Beef Curry in Sweet Peanut Sauce with Coconut Rice 84
Bessie's Chicken and Noodles................................. 74
Breakfast Burrito 59
Calla Lily Sandwiches 97
Candy Corn Bacon Mac-N-Cheese 70
Caramelized Onion and Garlic Pasta 66
Cheesy Pasta and Italian Sausage Patties 72
Cheesy Zucchini Quiche 98
Chicken Enchilada Mac N' Cheese.......................... 91
Chicken Rub.. 94
Chili Con Carne.. 68
Chocolate Fried Chicken... 80
Chorizo and Corn Empanadas................................. 59
Citrus Glazed Grilled Chicken with Mixed-Grain Salad.. 90
Classic Strata with Crispy Bacon and Cheeses 69

III

Classic Stroganoff with Ostrich.. 53
Cranberry Apple Spicy Meatballs.. 88
Curry Egg Wrap 51
Dill Pickle Cheeseburger Pockets 66
Dreams Are Made Of Penne.. 64
Egg Salad for Sandwiches... 65
Enchilada Pie 89
Farmer Meatloaf 83
Fresh Pasta with Sausage and Butternut Squash in
    Roasted Red Pepper Sauce 62
Flarin' Southwest Style Taco 82
Game Day Chili... 83
Garden Girl's Pep and Veggie Sandwich 101
Garden Sandwiches 87
Garlic Butternut Squash Chicken Casserole........................ 57
Garlic Chicken Quinoa Al Fresco 61
German Apple Pancake.. 74
Glazed Salmon with Crispy Topping.................................... 86
Gluten Free French Onion Salisbury Steak........................ 114
Gluten Free Taco Casserole 99
Grandma Ostendorf's Meatloaf 84
Grandma's Chicken and Noodles.. 69
Grandpa Bob's Favorite Farm Field Egg Salad
    Sandwich... 93
Grown-Up Grilled Cheese 105
Ham Loaf Cupcakes with Sweet Potato Tops...................... 85
Harvest Braid.. 75
Hearty Potato Bake 72
Iowa State Fair Corny Crabby Quiche 65
Iowa Sweet Corn Chili.. 100
Italian Pita 103
Italian Zucchini Pie with Venison Salami.......................... 106
Jamaican Jerk Chicken Lettuce Wraps 78
La "Causa" De Tita Denegri 77
Lobster Fra Diavolo 86
Lunch Wraps Of Love 61
Mac N' Cheese with Beer Bread Crumbs & Bacon!............ 67
Mac N' Cheese with A Zing! 71
Meat Loaf 60
Moroccan Merguez Meatballs with Spiced
    Yogurt Sauce 110

My Best Sauerkraut Recipe 56
My Favorite Chili 88
My Grandma's Whole Hearty Spaghetti
    and Meatballs 107
Onion Pie with Country Sausage 108
Peaches and Cream French Toast Bake 79
Pickle Pizza Pie 52
Pineapple Rum Chicken Kabobs 92
Pizza Rice Pie 53
Pork Rub 109
Portobello Mushroom Pizza 52
Potato-Covered Ham and Swiss Loaf Surprise 100
Provolone and Pork Tacos 94
Queen Bee's Honey Do This… BBQ Sauce 97
Rice and Black Bean Burgers 95
Ricotta Meatballs with Chianti Sauce 112
Rockin' Rowan Kielbasa Casserole 58
Rubbed Beef Tenderloin 73
Sausage Gravy Biscuit 108
Seafood Alfredo Lasagna 113
Shrimp and Pickle Tea Sandwich 51
Smokey Meatloaf 76
Sour Cream & Onion Turkey Meatballs 102
Spiced Pasta Sausage Casserole 58
Spicy Iowa Pork Loin with Ginger-Maple Sauce 78
Steak Rub 92
Stuffed Pork Loin 64
Stuffed Puff Pastry 76
Sweet & Spicy Tuna Burgers with Peanut Butter Sauce ... 80
Sweet Corn Cob Sandwiches 63
Taco Salad 98
Tamarind Pork Tacos with Grilled Corn Crema
    and Corn & Bacon Slaw 54
Tex-Mex Meatball Pie 81
Walnut Burger 70
Weekend Eggs 94
White Lasagna 104
Wild Game Pot Pie 111
Yummy Party Pizza 96

V

YEAST BREADS AND QUICK BREADS

YEAST BREADS AND ROLLS

Anadama Bread.. 115
Artisan Italian Bread.. 125
Beer Bread 117
Beer Bread 120
Black Olive Pesto Bread 118
Braided Coffee Cake 145
Braided Egg Bread 137
Brewer's Rye Bread... 117
Butterhorns 133
Butterscotch Rolls.. 152
Cheesy Potato Bread 129
Cherry Raspberry Almond Danish................................... 134
Cherry Rhubarb Cream Cheese Braid.............................. 130
Christmas Stöllen 138
Cinnamon Bear Claws with Milk and Honey Glaze........ 140
Cinnamon Bread 130
Cinnamon Raisin Bread 142
Cinnamon Raisin Bread 153
Croissants.. 151
Crusty Italiano Bread... 129
English Muffin Bread 116
Fluffy Honey Dinner Rolls.. 148
Foccacia 144
Frosted Cinnamon Rolls... 136
Glazed Raisin Bread... 139
Halle's Honey Crescent Rolls 146
Honey Butter Rolls... 128
Honey Dinner Yeast Rolls... 150
Honey-Mustard Oatmeal Bread...................................... 143
Honey Wheat Bread... 118
Honey Wheat Bread... 133
Kolaches 120
Magic Christmas Wreath 124
Multigrain Sunflower Bread.. 148
New York Deli Rye Bread 127
Oat Sunflower Millet Bread 128
Oatmeal Bread 119
Old Order Amish Bread.. 141

Pinwheel Bread.. 121
Potato Bread... 147
Potato Buns 123
Raspberry Kolaches 115
Sandwich Bread... 132
Sesame Cheddar Bread 124
Spelt Sourdough.. 122
Summer Squash Seven Grain Rolls 132
Swedish Rye Bread 135
Tomato, Basil & Garlic Filled Pane Bianco 122
White French Bread 126
Whole Wheat Bread 116
Whole Wheat Harvest Grain Rolls 126

QUICK BREADS
Almond Cinnamon Nut Bread.. 160
Almond Poppy Seed Bread 166
Apple-Nut Coffee Cake.. 172
Apricot Bread... 165
Apricot Mango Scones... 176
Apricot Nut Bread.. 164
Baking Powder Biscuits.. 175
Banana Bread 156
Banana Nut and Ginger Bread 157
Best Ever Banana Bread... 154
Blueberry-Lemon Muffins 175
Butter Pecan Bread.. 144
Buttermilk Biscuits... 155
Caramel Apple Buttermilk Muffins.................................. 158
Cheddar Cheese Cornbread 174
Chipotle Cheddar Corn Bread 153
Chocolanutty Banana Coffee Cake 169
Chocolate Chip and Coconut Banana Bread 157
Chocolate Zucchini Bread.. 159
Coconut Muffins 151
"Corn"Ucopia Muffins.. 170
Cranberry Whole Wheat Bread.. 154
Cream Cheese Banana Nut Bread.................................... 166
Date-Nut Loaf.. 161
Grandmother's Buttermilk Cornbread.............................. 147
Holiday Fruit Bread 164
Honey Banana Nut Bread 142

VII

Honey-Blueberry Muffins 159
Honey Gingerbread 160
Honey Glazed Buttermilk Coffee Cake 171
Honey Oatmeal Coffee Cake 173
Honeycomb Coffee Cake 168
Lavender Walnut Scones 177
Lemon-Chai Cranberry Orange Scones 162
Lemon Ginger Scones 162
Maple-Drizzle Apple Muffins 168
Nutty Banana Bread 178
Onion Herb Biscuits 155
Orange Pecan Tea Bread 172
Piña Colada Zucchini Bread 165
Pumpkin Nut Bread 176
Raspberry Corn Muffins 174
Rustic Pumpkin Bread 167
Salsa Corn Muffins 163
Savory Cheddar Bread 143
Sour Cream Pumpkin Coffee Cake 170
Star-Spangled Honey Scones 161
Strawberry Banana Walnut Bread 156
Sweet Potato Corn Bread 146
Taco Cheese Bread 150

PIES, CAKES AND DESSERTS

PIES
Apple Crumb Pie 186
Apricot Pie 180
Berry Custard Pie 191
Blueberry Cream Pie 202
Browned Butterscotch Pie 189
Buttermilk Pie 199
Butternut Squash Pie 184
Cherry Pie 203
Chocolate Cream Pie 187
Coconut Cream Haupia Pie 190
Coconut Cream Pie 202
Cranberry Pie 186
Cranberry-Raspberry Pie 204
Double Strawberry Pie 180
Eggnog Pumpkin Pie 196

VIII

Five Layer Lemon-Raspberry Pie 198
German Chocolate Pie 181
Gooseberry Pie 200
Honey Pie 179
Key Lime Pie 205
Key Lime Coconut Pie 188
Lemon Meringue Pie 188
Lemon Sponge Pie with Limoncello Crust 196
Maple Nut Cream Pie 190
Maple Pecan Pie 197
Mocha Rum Chiffon Pie 200
Nothing Compares Iowa State Fair Corn Pie 185
Oatmeal Pecan Raisin Pie 179
Orange and Spice Mincemeat Pie 182
Peach Raspberry Pie 201
Peanut Butter Pie 182
Pineapple Cream Pie 198
Precious Peach Pie 193
Prize-Winning Pie Crusts 206-208
Rhubarb Custard Pie 183
Spiced Up Sour Cream Raisin Pie 192
Strawberry Chiffon Pie 192
Strawberry Lemonade Chiffon Pie with Donut
      Crumb Crust 204
Strawberry Rhubarb Pie 184
Sweet Corn Pie 194
Sweet Potato Pie 187
Triple Cherry Pie 195
Zucchini Pie 194

CAKES
Apple Pie Cupcakes 232
Best Chocolate Cake with Chocolate Buttercream 236
Blueberry Cream Cake 210
Boozy Bourbon Pound Cake 232
Chocolate Sour Cream Applesauce Bundt Cake 228
Chocolate Sour Cream Cake 222
Czech Coffee Cake 214
Fabulous, Fresh Raspberry Cake 215
German Chocolate Cake 224
Gluten Free Sponge Cupcakes with
      Buttercream Frosting 209

Harvest Apple Cake 212
Honey Oatmeal Cake.. 214
Hummingbird Cake.. 226
Jelly Roll 213
Kanzi's Fruit Cake... 240
Lemon Bundt Cake 226
Lemon-Lime Filled Cake Roll... 236
Lime Dream Angel Food Cake... 238
Marble Cake with Chocolate Buttercream Frosting 216
Mocha Chia Cake 221
Molten Chocolate Lava Cakes... 233
Piña Colada Cupcakes.. 242
Rhubarb Upside-Down Cake 219
Sour Cream Carrot Cake... 212
Sour Cream Pumpkin Spice Cake.. 220
Spice Cake with Apple Filling.. 217
Strawberry Angel Food Cake 223
Stuffed Carrot Cake with Orange Cream Cheese Glaze. 230
Toffee Crunch Cupcakes.. 218
Walnut Mocha Sour Cream Cake 211
Walnut Torte with Coffee Whipped Cream 229

DESSERTS
Almond Cheesecake 240
Almond Venetian Dessert.. 252
Black & White Chocolate Cheesecake 235
Black Forest Crepes.. 248
Buttermilk Pumpkin Doughnuts with Brown
    Butter Maple Glaze... 244
Chocolate Cherry No-Bake Cheesecake............................. 257
Chocolate Mousse Cheesecake... 234
Chocolate Orange Cheesecake 246
Chocolate Truffle Cheesecake 256
Dark Chocolate Raspberry Sauce.. 237
Double Chocolate Mint Choux Pastry 250
Harissa Espresso Ice Cream... 238
Honey Pecan Tassies 225
Jammin' Apple Crostata 248
Lemon Mousse Crepes with Blueberry Sauce................... 254
Lomalagi Cheesecake 246
Margarita Dessert... 243
Mocha Mousse... 227

Not Your Basic Panna Cotta 255
Peach Cobbler 250
Peach Crepes 260
Peach Ice Cream 230
Peaches and Cream Cheesecake 258
Peaches and Cream Parfait 244
Praline Sundae Topping 231
Pumpkin Cheesecake 252
Sea Salt and Honey Ice Cream 228
Smokin' Cinnamon Ice Cream 241
Spiced Banana Ice Cream 245
Sweet Espresso Tapioca 242
Un-Fried Mexican Fried Ice Cream 224

COOKIES, CANDIES AND SNACKS

COOKIES
Almond Butter – Jam Thumbprints 263
Apple Hazelnut Blondies 302
Applesauce Bars with Pecan Praline Topping 275
Blonde Brownies 264
Blue Cheese Sugar Cookies 290
Blueberry Bars 268
Butterscotch Bars 261
Cherry Brownie Cookies 300
Chewy Fruit & Oatmeal Bars 271
Chocolate Almond Bars 274
Chocolate Almond Biscotti 271
Chocolate Chip and Butterscotch Gluten Free Cookies .. 273
Chocolate Chip Oatmeal Chia Cookies 268
Chocolate Crackle Cookies 293
Chocolate Mint Brownies 294
Coconut Key Lime Macaroons 266
Cranberry Streusel Shortbread Bars 284
Dark Chocolate & Mint Ganache Stout Brownies 281
Dark Chocolate Brownies 280
Dark Chocolate Espresso Cookies 298
Divine Chocolate Toffee Cookies 266
Donna and Linda's Pumpkin Bars 273
Dutch Letter Circles 287
Fall Fantasy Flavored Cookies 297
Five Layer Bars 261

French Macaroons 304
Fudgy Chocolate Chunk Brownies 262
Gluten Free Dutch Letter Bars 283
Grandma's Italian Cookies 292
Honey Barzzzz 265
Jacked-Up Jalapeno Cookies 294
Jam Bars 299
Key Lime Cookies 296
Lemon Pie Sandwich Cookies 286
Little Almond Bites 284
Luscious Lemon Bars 276
Molasses Crackles 282
Mom's Sugar Cookies with A Lemon Twist 288
No-Bake Peanut Butter Cup Bars 292
Old Fashioned Sour Cream Cookies 283
Orange and Almond Coconut Macaroons 265
Orange & Cranberry Ginger Oat Bars 276
Orange Brownies 278
Peanut Butter Bars 264
Peanut Butter Crunch Bars 282
Peanut Butter Shortbread Cookies 286
Pecan Pie Bars 279
Pineapple Drop Cookies 288
Pineapple Jewels 291
Pumpkin Chocolate Chip Bars 262
Raspberry Almond Thumbprints 272
Raspberry Chocolate Bars 267
Raspberry Mascarpone-Filled Brownies 274
Rich Butterscotch Bars 280
Salted Caramel Brownies 267
Scandinavian Almond Bars 289
Soft Molasses Cookies 269
Spiced Rosemary Chocolate Chip Cookies (Vegan) 270
Spritz 263
Sugar Cookies 272
Triple Chocolate Brownie Delight 278
Ultimate Double Chocolate Cookies 269
White Chocolate Cranberry Blondies 290
White Chocolate Orange Drop Cookies 277
White Chocolate Ruby Roads 285

XII

CANDIES AND SNACKS

Almond Rum Truffles 309
Apple Pie Candied Apple 318
Apple Surprise Bites 316
Bacon & Chocolate Brittle Bites............................. 306
Baked Buttermilk Corn Donuts.............................. 307
Brown Sugar Crispy Ice Cream Topping................. 317
Caramels.. 314
Cashew Cereal Snack Mix...................................... 327
Chipotle Peanut Clusters 297
Chocolate Covered Caramels 303
Chocolate Dipped Cherries 313
Chocolate Fudge.. 306
Chocolate Fudge with Nuts 318
Chocolate Spice Snack Mix 319
Cinnamon Apple Harvest Snack Mix..................... 323
Cinnamon Bun Popcorn... 320
Cinnamon Vanilla Sugar Nuts 296
Creamy Caramels... 311
Creamy Dark Chocolate Mocha Fudge................... 295
Granola 325
Granola Bars 270
Honey and Nuts Granola.. 328
Kickin' and Krunchy Snack Mix 322
Maple Nut Fudge 313
Maple Pecan Fudge... 310
Maple Sugar Chai Macadamia Nuts 323
Milk Chocolate Almond Toffee.............................. 305
My Favorite Chocolate Fudge 315
Nutty Toffee Popcorn 312
Old Fashioned Fudge 311
Old Fashioned Peanut Brittle 308
On the Go Snack Mix.. 315
Peanut Butter Fudge 319
Pumpkin Pie Spice Mix 322
Quick Salted Caramel Rolls................................... 321
Raspberry Lemon Cream Cheese Whoopie Pies 326
Salted Honey Crispy Cereal Treats........................ 310
Salty Churro Toffee Snack Mix 302
Sicilian Lemon & Fig Truffles............................... 301
Sorghum Granola... 320
Sour Cream Fudge 315

Special Dark Fudge.. 312
Spicy Sugar Corn... 321
Sugared Nuts 326
Sunbutter Crunch Shell 298
Surprise Chocolate Fudge with Nuts 316
Sweet & Spicy Pecans 300
Sweetened Nuts... 325
Toffee 305
Toffee 310
Toffee Pecan Cream Fudge 309
Toffee Popcorn 324
Truffle Fudge 317
Truffles 308
Vanilla Fudge... 314
White Chip Snack Mix.. 324

Iowa State Fair
COOKBOOK

POLENTA SWEET CORN EDAMAME BITES WITH EDAMAME SOUR CREAM SPREAD

For SALSA:

6 ears Iowa sweet corn
4 tbsp. olive oil
12-oz. pkg. edamame, shelled
1 large red onion, peeled
   and diced

3 medium multi-colored sweet
   peppers, diced
1/4 c. finely chopped cilantro
2 tsp. granulated sugar
Juice from 1/2 lime
1/4 tsp. coriander

Cut kernels from ears of corn. In a skillet, sauté corn kernels in olive oil until golden brown. Steam edamame 5 minutes; coarsely chop and add to corn. In separate skillet, sauté onions until softened and golden. Add to corn. Sauté sweet peppers 2 to 3 minutes; add to corn mixture. Add cilantro, sugar, lime juice and coriander; mix well.

For EDAMAME/SOUR CREAM SPREAD:

1 c. shelled edamame
1/4 c. tofu sour cream
1 tbsp. lime juice

1 tbsp. cumin
1 tbsp. cayenne pepper

In a food processor, combine all ingredients. Process on high 15 to 20 seconds or until spread is smooth in consistency.

For POLENTA:

14-oz. can chicken broth
2 c. water
1/4 tsp. cumin

1/2 tsp. salt
1 c. polenta
Tofu sour cream

In medium saucepan combine chicken broth, water, cumin and salt. Bring to a boil. Slowly mix in polenta, whisking quickly and continuously 3 to 4 minutes until polenta is smooth. Pour into greased square or round 8-inch baking pan. Let stand 15 to 20 minutes until formed and firm. Remove polenta from baking pan. Spread 1 tablespoon edamame sour cream spread onto polenta. Top sour cream spread with 2 tablespoons salsa mix. Top salsa with dollop of tofu sour cream.

Joshua Calhoun, *Des Moines*
First Place, 2014 It's Soy Amazing – Appetizers/Sides

PUMPKIN PIE LAYERED DIP

For DIP:

2/3 c. honey
1 c. natural peanut butter
15-oz. can pumpkin puree
15-oz. can chickpeas, drained
    and rinsed

2 tbsp. water
2 tbsp. pumpkin pie spice
2 tbsp. vanilla
1/8 tsp. sea salt

Add all ingredients to a food processor or high-powered blender; blend until smooth. Refrigerate at least 30 minutes.

For WHIPPED TOPPING:

1 c. heavy cream
1 tsp. vanilla

1 tbsp. honey

Whip cream with a chilled whisk in a chilled bowl until stiff peaks form. Slowly add vanilla and honey; whip to mix. In a glass container, alternate layers of dip with whipped topping. Serve with celery sticks.

Holly Houg, *Urbandale*
First Place, 2015 Taste of Honey Challenge – Honey Challenge

BOURBON WHISKEY BBQ SAUCE

1/2 onion, minced
4 cloves garlic, minced
3/4 c. bourbon
2 c. catsup
1/2 c. honey
1/3 c. cider vinegar

1/4 c. Worcestershire sauce
1/4 c. tomato paste
1 tbsp. liquid smoke
1 tsp. salt
1/2 tsp. black pepper
1/4 tsp. hot pepper sauce

Combine onion, garlic and bourbon in a deep saucepan. Simmer over medium heat 10 minutes or until onion is translucent, being careful not to ignite the alcohol. If it does ignite, cover with a lid to extinguish flames. Mix in catsup, honey, vinegar, Worcestershire, tomato paste, liquid smoke, salt, pepper and hot pepper sauce. Bring to a boil. Reduce heat to medium low; simmer 20 minutes.

Marjorie Rodgers, *Indianola*
First Place, 2014 Mine is the Best BBQ Sauce

MINI BRUSCHETTA TOPPERS

For BASIL CREAM CHEESE DIP:

6 to 8 leaves fresh basil
16 oz. softened cream cheese
2 tsp. minced garlic

1 c. grated Parmesan cheese
1 c. chopped walnuts
3/4 c. olive oil

Combine basil, cream cheese and garlic in food processor. Process until smooth. Remove from processor and stir in Parmesan cheese, walnuts and olive oil.

For MINI BRUSCHETTA TOPPERS:

12 butter-flavored crackers
1 c. diced Roma tomatoes

4 leaves fresh basil, chopped
1 tbsp. grated Parmesan cheese

Spread crackers with a thin layer of basil cream cheese dip. Sprinkle with diced tomatoes, basil and Parmesan cheese.

Trent Gilbert, *West Des Moines*
First Place, 2014 Sleepy Hollow Appetizers

MADAM MARY SMALL BATCH SHRIMP APPETIZER

18 cooked peeled tail-on shrimp
1 tbsp. finely chopped candied
   ginger
1 1/2 tsp. celery salt, divided
1 tbsp. light corn syrup
3/4 c. rye whiskey

2 1/2 c. bloody mary mix
1/2 tsp. soy sauce
1/2 tsp. grated fresh ginger
2 tbsp. lime juice
12 olives
6 radishes

Thaw, rinse and dry shrimp; set aside in refrigerator. In bowl, combine candied ginger and 1 teaspoon celery salt. Lightly rub corn syrup on rim of 6 small glasses. Dip into candied ginger mixture to coat edge of glass; set aside. In glass pitcher mix rye whiskey and bloody mary mix with remaining celery salt, soy sauce, grated ginger and lime juice. Refrigerate until ready to serve. When ready to serve, place 3 shrimp, 2 olives and 1 radish in each glass. Add mix to cover shrimp. Garnish as desired.

Bridget Lottman, *Norwalk*
First Place, 2014 Best Templeton Rye Appetizer

SAUSAGE TAQUITOS

1 lb. spicy hot breakfast
   sausage
1 small onion, finely chopped
2, 6-oz. cans diced tomatoes
   with green chilies, divided
1/2 tsp. ground cumin

10 flour tortilla shells
1 c. shredded cheddar cheese
1/2 c. oil
4 oz. processed American
   cheese
1 tbsp. milk

In large skillet cook sausage and onions until sausage is completely cooked; drain. Add 1 can of diced tomatoes and cumin; simmer 1 hour stirring occasionally. Remove from heat. To make taquitos, place 1/8 cup meat mixture down center of tortilla shell; sprinkle cheddar cheese on top. Roll up very tightly; repeat with remainder of shells and meat. In skillet, heat oil on medium/high heat, place taquitos in skillet turning when golden brown. Remove from skillet; place on paper towels to drain. Cut on a diagonal, place on a serving dish. In microwave-safe bowl or dish, combine processed cheese, remaining tomatoes and milk. Microwave, checking every 15 to 20 seconds, stirring until melted. Serve with taquitos.

Connie Schaffer-Sherman, *Pleasant Hill*
First Place, 2015 Purnell Old Folks' Sausage Cook-Off – Appetizers

---

LITTLE QUEEN BEE HONEY BBQ SAUCE

1 tsp. chili powder
1 tsp. restaurant black pepper
1 tsp. kosher flake salt
1 tsp. red chipotle powder
2 tsp. smoked paprika
1/2 tsp. granulated garlic
1/2 tsp. ground mustard

1/2 tsp. onion powder
1/2 tsp. cayenne pepper
1/4 c. apple cider vinegar
1 1/2 c. catsup
1 1/4 c. honey
1 1/2 tsp. liquid smoke

In saucepan, combine all ingredients. Heat, stirring often, until mixture begins to boil. Reduce heat; simmer approximately 20 minutes. Pour into jars and let cool to room temperature before refrigerating. Allow sauce to refrigerate overnight allowing flavors to blend.

Emlin Schnathorst, Jr., *Norwalk*
First Place, 2015 Foods Made with Honey – Honey BBQ Sauce

APPETIZERS, SIDE DISHES AND SALADS

MANGO FIRE WING SAUCE

3 habanero peppers
1 tbsp. olive oil
3 ripe mangoes, peeled, pitted
   and diced
1/2 c. diced yellow onion
1 tsp. garlic powder

3/4 c. white wine vinegar
1 tsp. yellow curry powder
1 c. packed brown sugar
2 tsp. salt
1/4 c. honey

Lightly coat habanero peppers with olive oil. Roast on grill until charred. Place in plastic bag for 10 minutes. Remove skin, seed and finely dice. Combine all ingredients except olive oil in 3-quart saucepan. Bring to boil; boil 5 minutes. Puree until smooth. Simmer 20 minutes. Strain mixture. Serve warm or chilled.

Mark Pleis, *Des Moines*
First Place, 2015 Best Wing Sauce

SPINACH & ARTICHOKE CREAM CHEESE DIP

10-oz. box frozen spinach,
   thawed and squeezed dry
8.5-oz. can artichoke hearts
1/2 c. mayonnaise
1/2 c. sour cream
8 oz. jalapeno cream cheese
1/2 c. shredded mozzarella
   cheese
1/2 c. shredded gouda cheese
1/2 c. grated Parmesan cheese

2/3 c. pepperoni (1/4-inch cubed)
1 1/2 c. coarsely chopped
   mushrooms
1 tsp. garlic powder
1/2 tsp. onion powder
1/2 tsp. celery salt
1/2 tsp. garlic salt
1/4 tsp. chili powder
1/4 tsp. smoked paprika
1 small jalapeno-cheddar
   bread bowl

In a saucepan on medium heat, combine spinach, artichoke hearts, mayonnaise, sour cream and cream cheese. Bring to a low boil; reduce heat. Add cheeses, pepperoni, mushrooms and spices. Simmer on low about 20 minutes. Add heated dip to bread bowl; garnish and serve with crackers.

Kyle Barton, *West Des Moines*
First Place, 2015 Allspice Party Dip – Hot Dip

APPETIZERS, SIDE DISHES AND SALADS

ROBIN'S CHEESY NACHO DIP

For DIP:
1/2 lb. Italian sausage
1/2 lb. ground pork
1 small onion, finely chopped
4-oz. can chopped green chili
    peppers, drained

1/3, 1.25-oz. env. taco
    seasoning
2 tomatoes, chopped
2 lbs. processed American
    cheese, cubed

Brown sausage, pork and onion; drain. Place all ingredients in a crockpot and heat until cheese melts (or microwave until cheese begins to melt and then transfer to a crockpot). Serve with homemade taco chips.

For HOMEMADE NACHO CHIPS:
Oil
Tortillas, refrigerated

Salt

Heat 1 to 2 inches of oil to 375°. Cut chilled tortillas into wedges. Fry wedges in hot oil, turning occasionally, 2 to 3 minutes until brown. Remove to paper towels and sprinkle with salt.

Diane Rauh, *Des Moines*
First Place, 2014 Kraft Kreations with Velveeta – Side Dish
Second Place Overall, 2014 Kraft Kreations with Velveeta

COCONUT CHUTNEY WINGS

1 tsp. coriander seeds
1 tsp. cumin seeds
1 tsp. fennel seeds
3/4 c. shredded unsweetened
    coconut
3/4 c. fresh cilantro
Juice from 1 lime

Grated lime zest
1 small fresh green Thai chili,
    seeded
1/2 c. coconut milk
2 dozen chicken wings
Salt
Pepper

Toast spices on low heat until fragrant. Pulse in food processor with coconut, cilantro, lime juice, lime zest, chili and coconut milk to desired consistency. Toss the wings with salt and pepper. Bake in 375° oven 15 minutes until done. Toss with coconut mixture while warm and serve.

Carrie Kupka, *Walford*
First Place, 2015 Goldie's Chicken Lickin' Wings

A HONEY OF A BBQ SAUCE

4 qts. tomato juice
4 c. tomato paste
3 large red onions, finely
　　chopped
1 1/2 c. honey
2 c. apple cider vinegar
2 tsp. liquid smoke
2 tsp. stoneground mustard
2 tsp. Worcestershire sauce

3 tsp. red pepper sauce
1 c. strong black coffee
3 cloves garlic, mashed
4 tsp. black pepper
4 tsp. chili powder
2 tsp. pickling spice
2 tsp. celery seed
Whiskey

In very large Dutch oven, place tomato juice, tomato paste, onions, honey, vinegar, liquid smoke, mustard, Worcestershire sauce, red pepper sauce, coffee and garlic. Tie spices in cheesecloth bag. When mixture in Dutch oven comes to boil, add spice bag. Reduce heat; simmer until thickened, 2 to 3 hours. Remove from heat; remove spice bag and discard. Put through food sieve; add whiskey to taste. Return to heat; bring to boil. Place in jars and store in refrigerator.

Joyce Larson, *New Market*
First Place, 2014 Foods Made with Honey – Honey BBQ Sauce

WAITING FOR THE TURKEY
CRANBERRY SALSA

12-oz. bag cranberries (fresh or
　　frozen)
1 Granny Smith apple, peeled
　　and chopped
1 medium red bell pepper
1 medium red onion
3/4 c. granulated sugar

1/2 c. apple juice
3 tbsp. fresh cilantro
1 small jalapeno
1 tsp. grated lime zest
2 tbsp. lime juice
Salt to taste
Pepper to taste
Tortilla chips

In a blender or a food processor add all ingredients except chips. Pulse ingredients until blended but chunky. Season with salt and pepper. Pour salsa into a bowl; garnish with cilantro. Serve with tortilla chips.

Kenzie Piper, *Waukee*
First Place, 2015 Thanksgiving Favorites

APPETIZERS, SIDE DISHES AND SALADS

PICO DE GALLO

1 large tomato, seeded and
    diced
1 tbsp. diced red onion
1 tsp. diced jalapeno
1 tsp. minced garlic

Juice from 1/2 lime
1/2 tbsp. chopped fresh cilantro
    leaves
Salt
Pepper

Combine all ingredients in a bowl; season to taste with salt and pepper.
Garnish with additional cilantro, if desired.

Charlotte Bowden, *Monroe*
First Place, 2015 Adventureland Resort Intermediate – Salsa

BEST MEAT DIPPING SAUCE – RASPBERRY CHIPOTLE SAUCE

2 tbsp. butter
1 tbsp. freeze dried garlic
1 tbsp. freeze dried onion
1 tbsp. fresh lime juice
2 chipotle peppers in adobo
    sauce, chopped
1 tbsp. minced garlic (2 to 3
    cloves)
15-oz. can tomato sauce

24-oz. bottle catsup
1/2 c. Worcestershire sauce
1 c. water
3 tbsp. red wine vinegar
1 tbsp. raspberry chipotle
    hot sauce
1 c. pureed fresh raspberries
Salt to taste
Pepper to taste

In large heavy-bottom saucepan, melt butter over medium heat. Add
freeze dried ingredients and lime juice. Sauté about 3 minutes until soft;
add chipotle peppers and fresh garlic. Continue sautéing additional 5
minutes until well blended. Add tomato sauce, catsup, Worcestershire
sauce and water. Stir well to combine; bring sauce to a boil. Reduce heat;
simmer 5 minutes. Add vinegar, hot sauce and raspberries. Continue
simmering on low 30 minutes, stirring frequently. Carefully pour sauce
through a strainer into another pot; discard solids. Season remaining
sauce to taste with salt and pepper. Let sauce cool; store in refrigerator
up to 1 week.

Jacqueline Riekena, *West Des Moines*
First Place, 2014 The Best Dipping Sauce Ever

BUFFALO CHICKEN CHEESE BALLS

Vegetable oil for frying
1 cooked rotisserie chicken
1/4 c. plus 1/2 tsp. hot sauce,
    divided
1 tsp. ground black pepper
1 3/4 c. shredded sharp
    cheddar cheese
1/4 c. finely sliced scallions

1 c. all-purpose flour
3 eggs, lightly beaten
2 c. panko bread crumbs
1 c. blue cheese salad dressing
2 tsp. Worcestershire sauce
Juice from 1/2 lemon
1 tsp. chopped garlic

Pour oil into frying pan to a depth of 1/2-inch; heat oil to 350°. Remove meat from bones; discard skin and bones. Coarsely chop chicken; place in large bowl. Add 1/4 cup hot sauce, pepper, cheese and scallions; toss to combine. Roll chicken into 2 ounce balls, about the size of a golf ball. Place flour, eggs and breadcrumbs in 3 separate bowls. Roll each ball in flour, then egg and then bread crumbs; set aside. When oil is hot, fry chicken balls in batches, turning to brown evenly. Do not crowd pan. Cook about 2 minutes per batch. Remove chicken to a paper towel-lined plate to drain excess oil. To make the sauce, combine blue cheese salad dressing, remaining hot sauce, Worcestershire sauce, lemon juice and garlic in a large bowl. Adjust seasoning if necessary. Serve chicken alongside dipping sauce.

Amy Smith, *Winterset*
First Place, 2015 Sleepy Hollow Appetizers – Youth Appetizers
First Place, 2015 Adventureland Resort Intermediate – Appetizers

BLT BITES

16 to 20 cherry tomatoes
1 lb. bacon, cooked and
    crumbled
1/2 c. mayonnaise

1/3 c. chopped green onions
3 tbsp. grated Parmesan cheese
2 tbsp. snipped fresh parsley

Cut a thin slice off of each tomato top; scoop out and discard pulp. Invert tomatoes onto paper towel to drain. In a small bowl, combine remaining ingredients; mix well. Spoon into tomatoes; refrigerate several hours.

Emma Whitlock, *Indianola*
First Place, 2014 Bacon, Bacon, Bacon with Greyson

CHEESY CHILI DIP

For CHILI:
2 lbs. ground beef
1 large onion, chopped
2 tsp. allspice
2 tsp. chili seasoning
40-oz. can chili beans
2, 15-oz. cans spicy hot chili
   beans

2, 14.5-oz. cans diced tomatoes
2, 14.5-oz. cans diced tomatoes
   with green chilies
6-oz. can tomato paste
2 tbsp. sweet and spicy
   barbeque sauce

Cook ground beef and onion in skillet until beef is brown; drain. Add allspice and seasoning. Combine all ingredients in large pot. Simmer 30 to 45 minutes.

For CHEESY CHILI DIP:
1 lb. processed Mexican
   cheese, cubed

2 c. chili (recipe above)

In large microwave-safe bowl, combine cheese and chili. Heat until cheese is melted, about 2 minutes. Stir and continue microwaving, stirring every 30 seconds until melted. Serve with chips.

Debbie Wise, *Des Moines*
First Place, 2015 Kraft Kreations with Velveeta – Side Dish
Second Place Overall, 2015 Kraft Kreations with Velveeta

CHEESY BACON PARTY MIX

1 c. corn or rice cereal squares
1 c. wheat cereal squares
1 c. pretzels
1 c. bacon cheddar pretzels
1/2 c. peanuts

1/2 c. butter, melted
1/2 c. minced garlic
1 tbsp. onion powder
2 1/2 tbsp. smoked bacon salt
4 tbsp. Worcestershire sauce

Mix cereals, pretzels and nuts in large bowl. Melt butter; add garlic. Add onion powder, bacon salt and Worcestershire. Pour over cereal mixture; stir to coat well. Place in large baking pan; bake in 250° oven until dry.

Natalie Ridgway, *Johnston*
First Place, 2015 Allspice Snack Mix – Salty
First Place Overall, 2015 Allspice Snack Mix

FLAMING BALLS

For FLAMING BALLS:

1 1/2 lbs. ground chicken
1/3 c. cream cheese, softened
1 large clove garlic, minced
1/3 c. grated Parmesan cheese
2 tbsp. spicy seasoning
1 tbsp. dried parsley
2 eggs, lightly beaten
1 1/2 tsp. black pepper
1 1/2 tbsp. Semolina flour or fine
  bread crumbs
1 1/2 tbsp. olive oil
1/2 tsp. garlic chili paste

Mix all ingredients in a bowl until well combined. Form into 1 1/2-inch balls and place on baking sheet lined with nonstick foil or parchment paper. Bake in 450° oven 14 to 16 minutes. Toss hot meatballs in warm sauce until well covered. Serve warm.

For SPICY WHISKEY SAUCE

1/4 c. rye whiskey
1/4 c. packed brown sugar
1/3 c. catsup
1 tbsp. apple cider vinegar
1 tbsp. hot sauce
1/4 tsp. cayenne pepper
1/4 tsp. garlic pepper
1 tbsp. honey
2 tbsp. unsalted butter

Place all ingredients in small saucepan. Heat over medium heat until bubbly; reduce heat to low. Cook sauce until consistency of molasses.

Jennifer Bartles, *Des Moines*
First Place, 2015 You're Gonna Want Mo'! – Mo' Appetizer
First Place Overall, 2015 You're Gonna Want Mo'!

HONEY MANGO DIP

2 mangos, peeled and chopped
3 green onions, chopped
1/4 c. honey
2 tbsp. cider vinegar
2 tbsp. lime juice
2 tsp. pepper flakes
1/2 tsp. cumin
3 cloves garlic, peeled

Place all ingredients in blender and process until smooth.

Natalie Ridgway, *Johnston*
First Place, 2015 Allspice Party Dip – Cold Dip
First Place Overall, 2015 Allspice Party Dip

TERIYAKI HAWAIIAN APPETIZERS

12-oz. can Teriyaki canned meat product, sliced, grilled and cubed
1 c. crushed pineapple
8 oz. cream cheese
1 1/2 c. unsweetened shredded coconut
2 tbsp. Teriyaki baste and glaze
1/4 c. cream of coconut
1/8 tsp. cayenne pepper
Shredded coconut for topping
Chopped macadamia nuts for topping

Mix all together except topping ingredients; set aside.

For PIE DOUGH:
2 c. all-purpose flour
1 tsp. salt
3/4 c. butter-flavored shortening
8 to 9 tbsp. water

Mix flour, salt and shortening with pastry blender. Add enough water to make dough come together. Roll out on floured surface. Using cookie or biscuit cutter cut 3-inch circles. Place in mini tart pans or mini muffin pans. Fill with meat mixture. Bake in 375° oven 20 minutes. Top with shredded coconut and macadamia nuts.

Anita Van Gundy, *Des Moines*
First Place, 2014 The Great American Spam Championship (Adult)

SWEET N' SPICY BITS

Soft tortilla shells
Salami (1 1/2 to 2-inch diameter)
8 oz. cream cheese, room temperature
2 tbsp. chopped roasted red peppers
2 tbsp. chopped sweet jalapenos
1/2 c. sweet and spicy barbeque sauce

Cut circles from the tortilla the size of the salami. Place salami circles on top of tortilla circles; press together into small tart cup. Bake in 350° oven 10 minutes, until tortilla is toasted; set aside. In small bowl mix cream cheese, peppers, jalapenos and barbecue sauce; mix well. Fill the shells with cream cheese mixture. Garnish with jalapeno if desired.

Bridget Lottman, *Norwalk*
First Place, 2015 Cooking with Cookies' Sauces & Seasonings

GRILLED SWEET AND SPICY CHICKEN WINGS

2 1/2 tbsp. black pepper
1 tbsp. onion powder
1 tbsp. chili powder
1 tbsp. garlic powder
1 tbsp. seasoned salt

5 lbs. chicken wings, rinsed and dried
1 c. honey
1/2 c. hot barbecue sauce
3 tbsp. apple ale

Mix together the pepper, onion powder, chili powder, garlic powder and seasoned salt in a small bowl. Place chicken wings in a large resealable bag. Pour in spice mixture; shake to coat wings well. Marinate at least 30 minutes (at room temperature) or as long as 24 hours (in the refrigerator). Light a chimney three-fourths full of charcoal. When charcoal is fully lit and covered in gray ash, pour coals out and arrange on either side of charcoal grate, keeping the middle empty. Add 1 small piece of apple wood to both piles of charcoal. When wood is lit and producing smoke, place wings in middle of grill (not over the coals), cover and cook 25 minutes. Turn and cook additional 20 to 25 minutes. While wings are cooking, mix honey, barbecue sauce and apple ale together in small saucepan. Heat over medium heat until warm. Place wings in foil pan; pour warm sauce over wings. Toss to coat evenly. Cover and cook another 20 to 30 minutes, stirring occasionally. Remove from grill and serve on a bed of Nasturtium leaves, topping wings with extra sauce and cut up Nasturtium leaves.

Mark McCaffrey, *Red Oak*
First Place, 2014 Goldie's Chicken Lickin' Wings

HONEY DIP

1 c. powdered peanut butter
1/2 c. honey
4 oz. cream cheese

1 tsp. vanilla
1 tsp. cinnamon

Blend all ingredients with electric mixer. Chill and serve with fruit.

Nicole Woodroffe, *Des Moines*
First Place, 2014 Foods Made with Honey – Honey Dips

BEST TAILGATE DIP

8-oz. pkg. cream cheese
10-oz. can Mexican lime and
    cilantro diced tomatoes
    and green chilies, undrained
1 c. cooked brown rice
1 c. bacon pieces
1 small jalapeno, diced

In saucepan, combine all ingredients except jalapenos; stir on medium heat until cream cheese has melted. Add jalapenos; serve with tortilla chips or crackers.

Jacqueline Riekena, *West Des Moines*
First Place, 2014 My Kind of Appetizers

SAUSAGE PRETZEL BITES

2 tbsp. butter
3 tbsp. diced onion
1/4 c. diced green pepper
1 lb. spicy country sausage
1/2, 16.5-oz. pkg. pretzel mix
1 tsp. active dry yeast
6 tbsp. warm water (120°)
2 tbsp. vegetable oil
1/2 tbsp. grated Parmesan
    cheese
1/4 tsp. garlic powder
1 large egg
2 tbsp. cool water

Melt the butter in a medium skillet, add onions and green pepper; cook until tender. Remove from heat; set aside and let cool. In large mixing bowl add sausage, peppers and onions; stir until well blended. Divide sausage mixture into 4 equal sections; roll into ropes about 10 inches long. Bake in 350° oven 10 minutes. Cut each rope into 2-inch sections; set aside. In medium bowl, combine 1 1/2 cups plus 2 tablespoons pretzel mix and yeast. Stir in warm water, oil, cheese and garlic powder until well combined. Cover bowl with towel; let stand in warm area 30 minutes. Dough will rise slightly, but not double. Line 2 baking sheets with parchment paper. In small bowl, lightly beat egg with cool water until well combined. Divide dough into 6 equal pieces; shape each piece of dough into a 24-inch rope. Cut each rope into 6 pieces. Cover dough pieces with plastic wrap to prevent drying. Wrap pretzel dough around cooked sausage sections; pinch dough edges together and place seam down on baking sheets. Brush pretzel dough with egg wash; sprinkle with 1/2 of the salt from pretzel mix package. Bake in 350° oven 15 minutes or until golden brown.

(CONTINUED)

For HONEY MUSTARD DIP:

1/4 c. mayonnaise	1/4 c. prepared mustard
1/4 c. Dijon mustard	1/3 c. honey

In a small bowl, whisk together all ingredients. Cover and chill up to 5 days.

Connie Schaffer-Sherman, *Pleasant Hill*
First Place, 2014 Purnell Old Folks' Sausage Cook Off – Appetizer
First Place Overall, 2014 Purnell Old Folks' Sausage Cook Off

FRESH CORN AND CHORIZO SALSA

2 c. corn kernels (2 to 3 ears Serendipity corn)	1 jalapeno pepper, finely chopped
1 bay leaf	4 oz. chorizo sausage
10 whole cloves	1 tsp. chopped fresh thyme
1 cinnamon stick	2 tbsp. fresh squeezed lime juice
3/4 c. chicken broth	Salt
2 tbsp. olive oil	Freshly ground black pepper
1 medium onion, finely chopped	Additional fresh thyme for garnish
1/2 red bell pepper, diced	
2 cloves garlic, finely chopped	

Combine corn with bay leaf, cloves, cinnamon stick and broth in a medium saucepan; bring to a boil. Reduce heat; simmer about 5 minutes, until corn is tender. Set aside. Heat oil in a frying pan. Add onion, red bell pepper, garlic and jalapeno. Cook, stirring often, about 3 minutes. Add chorizo sausage; cook 3 more minutes. Mix in thyme and remove from heat. Remove bay leaf, cinnamon and cloves from the corn. Add corn to chorizo mixture in the frying pan. Bring to a simmer; simmer 1 to 2 minutes to evaporate any excess liquid. Mixture should not be runny. Remove from heat; transfer to a bowl. Mix in lime juice and season to taste with salt and pepper. If not serving immediately, refrigerate. Reheat before serving. Best served warm. Garnish with fresh thyme.

Joyce Krause, *Johnston*
First Place, 2014 Fresh Corn Cuisine – Salads/Appetizers
First Place Overall, 2014 Fresh Corn Cuisine

SALSA CRUDA

1 1/2 c. diced Roma or plum
    tomato
1 tbsp. seeded and diced
    jalapeno pepper
1/3 c. diced red onion
1/3 c. diced green bell pepper

1/3 c. diced red bell pepper
1 to 2 garlic cloves, peeled and
    minced
1/4 to 1/2 tsp. ground cumin
1/2 tsp. salt
1 tbsp. fresh cilantro

Mix together all ingredients, tossing until thoroughly combined. To make a little smoother, use blender or food processor and blend until desired texture.

Kira Conlan, *Pleasant Hill*
First Place, 2014 Adventureland Resort Intermediate – Salsa

JALAPENO PIZZA EMPANADAS WITH JALAPENO PESTO DIPPING SAUCE

For JALAPENO PIZZA EMPANADAS:

1 lb. Italian sausage
15-oz. can tomato sauce
1 white onion, chopped
1 c. coarsely chopped
    mushrooms
4.25-oz. can black olives
3 jalapenos, chopped
1/2 tbsp. pizza seasoning
1/2 tbsp. Italian seasoning
1 tsp. ground oregano
1 tsp. garlic powder

1/2 tsp. garlic salt
2 tbsp. maple syrup
2 slices toasted Italian bread,
    crushed
1 c. shredded mozzarella cheese
1 c. shredded Swiss cheese
2 to 3 refrigerated pie crusts
3 tbsp. butter, softened or
    melted
1 tbsp. garlic bread and jalapeno
    powder topping

Cook sausage in a skillet; place in saucepan with tomato sauce. Add onions, mushrooms, olives and seasonings; simmer 15 minutes. Reduce heat; add syrup and bread crumbs. Simmer 10 additional minutes. Add cheeses, stirring very quickly. Cut each pie crust into four pieces. Place 1 to 2 tablespoons sausage mixture on one half of each piece; fold crust over. Pinch edges to seal. Brush butter on top of empanadas. Sprinkle with garlic bread topping. Bake in 350° oven 15 to 20 minutes.

(CONTINUED)

For PESTO:

1/4 c. pine nuts	1/2 tsp. cumin
1/4 c. coarsely chopped walnuts	1 1/2 c. olive oil
5 cloves garlic, peeled	1/2 c. shredded Fontina cheese
4 to 5 c. fresh basil	1/2 c. shredded Gruyere cheese
1 tsp. salt	

Combine all ingredients in food processor and process until desired consistency.

For JALAPENO DIPPING SAUCE:

1 c. pesto (recipe above)	1/4 tsp. cumin
1/2 c. mayonnaise	1/4 tsp. salt
3 jalapenos, seeded and minced	

Combine all ingredients. Whisk together or process in food processor to desired consistency. Serve with empanadas.

Kyle Barton, *West Des Moines*
First Place, 2015 Something Hot

SAM'S STUFFED SPICY SHROOMS

15 to 20 button mushrooms	5 oz. diced tomatoes with
12 oz. canned meat product	green chilies
3 oz. smoked hickory bacon bits	2 tsp. Mexican seasoning
8 oz. cream cheese	6 oz. grated Mexican cheese
	Parsley for garnish

Clean mushrooms; dice 3 mushrooms. Dice meat product; add bacon bits and stir together. Place in warm skillet on low. Heat 10 minutes or until golden brown. In small bowl, mix cream cheese, tomatoes and Mexican seasoning until creamy. Add diced mushrooms and meat mixture; stir until blended. Place remaining mushrooms in 10x13-inch glass baking dish. Add thin layer of grated cheese to bottom of mushroom cap. Add 1 to 3 teaspoons cream cheese mixture. Bake in 350° oven 10 minutes. Add grated cheese to top of mushroom in last minute of cooking and heat until melted.

Samantha Hilbert, *Urbandale*
First Place, 2014 The Great American Spam Championship (Kid Chef)

APPETIZERS, SIDE DISHES AND SALADS

GUACAMOLE

2 Haas avocados, halved,
  seeded and peeled
Juice from 1 lime
1/2 tsp. kosher salt
1/2 tsp. ground cumin
1/2 tsp. cayenne pepper

1/2 medium onion, diced
1/2 jalapeno pepper, seeded
  and minced
2 Roma tomatoes, seeded and
  diced
1 tbsp. chopped cilantro
1 clove garlic, minced

In large bowl, combine avocado halves and lime juice; toss to coat. Drain and reserve lime juice. Add salt, cumin and cayenne; mash with potato masher or fork. Fold in onions, jalapeno, tomatoes, cilantro and garlic. Add 1 tablespoon of reserved lime juice. Let stand at room temperature 1 hour before serving.

Charlotte Bowden, *Cedar Rapids*
First Place, 2014 Adventureland Resort Intermediate – Dip for Chips

FRUIT PIZZA

For CRUST:
1 1/4 c. granulated sugar
1 c. butter, softened
3 egg yolks
1 tsp. vanilla

2 1/2 c. all-purpose flour
1 tsp. baking soda
1/2 tsp. cream of tartar

Mix sugar and butter until creamy; add egg yolks and vanilla. Stir in dry ingredients. Pour into 9x13-inch pan and press down. Bake in 350° oven 20 minutes until golden brown; cool.

For TOPPING:
8 oz. cream cheese
1/2 c. granulated sugar
1 tsp. vanilla

Sliced strawberries, blueberries,
  Mandarin oranges, or other
  fruits of choice

Stir together cream cheese, powdered sugar and vanilla until smooth; spread over cooled crust. Top with strawberries, blueberries, Mandarin oranges, or other fruits of choice.

Mackenzie Becker, *Pella*
First Place, 2014 Adventureland Resort Intermediate – Fruit Dessert

PARMESAN PESTO ARANCINI

4 c. water
1 3/4 c. uncooked rice
3/4 tsp. salt, divided
2 tbsp. olive oil
1/2 c. chopped yellow onion
2 small cloves garlic, minced
1/2 c. half and half
1/4 c. heavy cream
2 beaten egg yolks
1 c. grated Parmesan cheese,
   divided
1/8 tsp. pepper
3/4 c. basil pesto, divided
Oil for frying
1 1/2 c. panko crumbs, divided
1/2 c. all-purpose flour
1/2 tbsp. seasoned salt
36 small bocconcini (fresh
   mozzarella pearls)
2 eggs, beaten
Marinara sauce for serving
   or dipping

In a stockpot, boil 4 cups water; add rice and 1/2 teaspoon salt. Reduce to simmer; simmer 15 to 20 minutes. Fluff with fork; set aside. In medium saucepan over medium heat, add oil and onion. Sauté 5 minutes until onions are soft and translucent. Add garlic; cook 2 minutes. Add cooked rice, half and half and cream. Cook until simmering. Temper egg yolks by adding some of the hot liquid while whisking. Add tempered yolks to cream mixture. Simmer 2 minutes more. Add half the Parmesan cheese, remaining salt and pepper; cool to warm. Stir in 1/4 cup of basil pesto. Refrigerate until well chilled and stiff. When ready to assemble and fry, pour 3 inches depth oil into a heavy large saucepan. Heat the oil over medium heat to 350°. Fold chilled rice mixture with remaining Parmesan and 1/2 cup of panko crumbs in a large bowl to combine. Place remaining panko crumbs in medium bowl with flour and seasoned salt. Using approximately 2 tablespoons of rice mixture for each, form into 1 3/4-inch diameter balls. Insert 1 bocconcini into center of each ball. Drizzle 1 teaspoon pesto in after inserting cheese. Seal ball. Chill 30 minutes until balls are firm. When ready to fry, roll the balls in beaten eggs, then panko crumbs to coat. Working in batches, add rice balls to hot oil. Cook until golden and heated through, turning as necessary, about 2 to 3 minutes. Using a slotted spoon, transfer rice balls to paper towels to drain. Let rest 2 minutes. Serve hot, sprinkled with additional freshly grated Parmesan and marinara sauce for dipping.

Cristen C. Clark, *Runnells*
First Place, 2014 Rice Creations – Appetizer
First Place Overall, 2014 Rice Creations

SUNSHINE SPICY PEACH SALSA

4 peaches, peeled and sliced
2 cloves garlic
1 habanero pepper
1/2 jalapeno pepper
1/2 Serrano pepper
1 tomatillo

1/2 c. chopped red onion
2 tbsp. peach preserves
1 1/2 tbsp. raspberry jam
1 1/2 tsp. kosher salt
Juice from 1/2 lime
1/2 tsp. fresh basil
8 oz. cream cheese

Carefully chop peaches, garlic, peppers, tomatillo and onion. Stir together all ingredients except cream cheese. Spoon over a block of cream cheese; serve with chips and crackers.

Jamie Buelt, *Polk City*
First Place, 2015 Salsa Sensations – Fruit Salsa

GYOZA

For GYOZA:
12-oz. can reduced sodium
    canned meat product
8 oz. water chestnuts
6 green onions, chopped
2 eggs, lightly beaten
4 oz. canned pineapple, drained
1/2 tsp. pepper
1 tsp. garlic chili sauce

1 tbsp. dried parsley
1 tsp. sesame oil
2 tsp. hoisin sauce
1/2 tsp. grated fresh ginger
2, 12-oz. pkgs. round gyoza
    wrappers or wonton
    wrappers
Water for sealing wrappers
Oil for frying

In a food processor, pulse all ingredients (except wrappers) until chopped fine and well combined, but not pasty; set aside. On clean flat surface, lay out 4 to 6 wrappers. Place rounded teaspoon of filling in center of wrapper. Moisten one half of outer circumference with a wet finger. Quickly fold in half and pinch 5 to 6 pleats along edge. Keep filled gyoza covered with moist paper towel to prevent drying while others are made. Heat deep fryer with oil according to manufacturer's directions (375° oil). Fry until golden brown. Remove to heatproof platter lined with a paper towel; place in warm oven. Repeat; serve immediately with dipping sauce or sweet chili sauce.

(CONTINUED)

APPETIZERS, SIDE DISHES AND SALADS

For GYOZA DIPPING SAUCE:

1/2 c. rice vinegar
1/2 c. low-sodium soy sauce
1/2 tsp. crushed red pepper
 flakes

1 clove garlic, minced
1/2 tsp. minced fresh ginger root
1/3 c. thinly sliced green onions
1 tsp. sesame oil

Whisk together rice vinegar, soy sauce, red pepper flakes, garlic, ginger, green onions and sesame oil in a bowl; allow to sit 15 minutes before serving. Store in refrigerator up to 1 week.

Jennifer Bartles, *Des Moines*
First Place, 2015 The Great American Spam Championship – Adult

COFFEE LIQUEUR DIP

8 oz. cream cheese
3/4 c. honey

1 tbsp. coffee liqueur

Soften cream cheese, add honey and liqueur; mix well. Serve with choice of berries or apple slices.

Marjorie Rodgers, *Indianola*
First Place, 2015 Foods Made with Honey – Honey Dips

APPLESAUCE SALSA

1 c. chunky applesauce
1 1/2 c. chopped dried
 cranberries
4-oz. can green chilies, chopped
 and well drained
1/4 c. chopped red onion

Juice from 2 limes
Juice from 1 orange
2 tbsp. chopped cilantro
4 tbsp. honey
1/4 tsp. salt

In small bowl, combine applesauce, cranberries, chilies, red onion, lime juice, orange juice and cilantro. Add honey and salt. Cover and refrigerate at least 1 hour to blend flavors. Garnish with fresh parsley or cilantro. Serve with tortilla chips.

Kevin Greiman, *Haverhill*
First Place, 2015 Applesauce Creation

FRESH FROM MY MOM'S GARDEN – DON'T TELL SALSA

7 Roma tomatoes, cut into
    1/4-inch cubes
1 red onion, cut into 1/4-inch
    cubes
1 each green, yellow and orange
    bell pepper, cut into
    1/4-inch cubes
2 jalapenos, diced
1/2 c. Italian salad dressing
3 cloves garlic, minced
Juice from 1/2 lime

12 cloves garlic pickled nuggets
1 bunch cilantro, stemmed and
    chopped (about 1/2 cup)
15 oz. tomato sauce
1 tbsp. honey
2 tsp. garlic powder
2 tsp. chili powder
1/2 tsp. cumin
1/2 tsp. garlic salt
1/2 tsp. salt
1/4 tsp. cayenne pepper

Place tomatoes, onions, peppers and jalapenos into container with salad dressing. Cover and refrigerate overnight. Add garlic, lime juice, garlic pickled nuggets, cilantro, tomato sauce, honey and spices. Stir, then refrigerate at least 30 minutes. Serve with tortilla chips.

Kyle Barton, *West Des Moines*
First Place, 2015 Garden Fresh Salsa
First Place, 2015 Salsa Sensations – Vegetable Salsa

APPETIZER MEATBALLS

1 lb. 85% ground beef
1 egg, beaten
1/8 tsp. pepper
1/4 c. cherry chipotle barbeque
    sauce

2 tbsp. brown sugar
3/4 c. crispy rice cereal
1/4 tsp. salt
1 tbsp. finely chopped onion
Additional barbeque sauce

Combine all ingredients except additional barbeque sauce, roll into balls. Place in baking dish. Bake in 400° oven 15 minutes. Remove from oven; cover with additional barbeque sauce. Cook 15 minutes more. Serve with toothpicks or place on mini toasted buns for barbecue meatball sliders.

Clarissa Ridgway, *Johnston*
First Place, 2014 Adventureland Resort Intermediate – Appetizers

SUMMER'S GARDEN SAUERKRAUT SALSA

1/2 c. fresh corn kernels
1 pt. sauerkraut canned with
   caraway seed, drained
1 small onion, chopped
1/2 red bell pepper, diced
1/2 green bell pepper, diced
1 jalapeno pepper, finely diced
1 clove garlic, finely diced

1 carrot, peeled and shredded
2 tbsp. freshly squeezed lime
   juice
2 tsp. chopped fresh cilantro
Freshly ground black pepper
   to taste
Additional fresh cilantro for
   garnish

In saucepan, cover corn kernels with water. Bring to a boil; reduce to simmer and cook 3 minutes. Drain; mix all ingredients in a large bowl. Season to taste with pepper. Cover tightly; refrigerate at least 3 hours to allow flavors to blend. Serve with tortilla chips.

Joyce Krause, *Johnston*
First Place, 2014 Iowa's Best Sauerkraut – Most Creative Sauerkraut Recipe

SHRIMP RICE CAKES WITH CHILI PLUM SAUCE

1/2 lb. raw shrimp, peeled
   and deveined
1/4 c. chopped green onions
1 tsp. fresh ginger
2 tbsp. plus 1 tsp. olive oil,
   divided
1 clove garlic, minced
1/4 tsp. salt

1/4 tsp. pepper
2 c. cooked jasmine rice
1 egg, beaten
1 c. panko crumbs
1/2 c. plum sauce
1/2 c. sweet Thai chili sauce
2 tbsp. lime juice

Pulse shrimp with green onions, ginger, 1 teaspoon olive oil, garlic, salt and pepper in food processor until finely chopped. Transfer to large bowl; mix in rice and egg. Pack into 1/4 measuring cup and turn out. Shape into patties; coat patties with panko crumbs. Brush lightly with oil. Cook 3 minutes on each side in skillet over medium heat. Stir plum sauce, chili sauce and lime juice together; serve with shrimp rice cakes.

Anita Van Gundy, *Des Moines*
First Place, 2015 Rice Creations – Appetizer
First Place Overall, 2015 Rice Creations

APPETIZERS, SIDE DISHES AND SALADS

TORTILLA, CORN AND SAUSAGE FRITTER APPETIZERS

For CREAM CHEESE SPREAD:

8 oz. cream cheese, softened
4 tbsp. corn kernels, reserved
    from can below, divided
1 green onion, chopped
1/2 tbsp. fresh cilantro

2 tbsp. diced celery
2 tbsp. softened butter
4-oz. can diced green chilies,
    drained
2 tbsp. heavy cream

Process cream cheese, 2 tablespoons corn kernels, green onion, cilantro, celery, butter, green chilies and cream in food processor until smooth. Stir in 2 additional tablespoons corn; mix well. Refrigerate at least 2 hours.

For SAUSAGE FRITTERS:

15-oz. can whole kernel corn,
    drained
1/3 c. plus 2 tbsp. skim milk,
    divided
2 green onions, chopped
1/3 c. extra virgin olive oil
1/2 tsp. white pepper

1/8 tsp. hot pepper sauce
1/4 tsp. red pepper flakes
1/4 tsp. sea salt
3/4 c. sifted self-rising flour
1 large egg, lightly beaten
1/3 c. heavy cream
1/2 lb. ground sausage, cooked
Olive oil cooking spray

Reserve 6 tablespoons of corn; set aside. In food processor, combine remainder of corn with 2 tablespoons milk and process until combined. Pour into bowl. Add green onions, olive oil, pepper, hot pepper sauce, red pepper flakes and sea salt; set aside. Place flour in large mixing bowl. Make a well in center of flour; add egg, cream and remaining milk; stir with a wooden spoon. Stir in corn mixture and sausage. Spray skillet with olive oil; use a small scoop to make fritters in batches. Flatten mixture out a bit. Fry over medium-high heat 2 minutes per side or until golden brown. Drain on paper towels.

For TORTILLA BOTTOM:

8 burrito size flour tortillas
2 tbsp. olive oil
1 tbsp. chipotle lime rub

1/2 c. hot pepper jelly
Fresh cilantro leaves
2 tbsp. corn kernels, reserved
    from can above

(CONTINUED)

Cut tortillas into circles slightly larger than fritters. Fry tortilla rounds in olive oil in nonstick fry pan. Sprinkle each tortilla with chipotle lime rub. Assemble by spreading cream cheese mixture on tortilla base; add a fritter and top with hot pepper jelly, cilantro leaves and reserved corn kernels.

Pamela Reynolds, *Norwalk*
First Place, 2015 It's A "Wrap" with Azteca Tortillas

ROSEMARY, ALMOND AND PARMESAN SHORTBREAD COCKTAIL COOKIES

1/2 c. slivered almonds
2 tbsp. finely chopped rosemary
3 tbsp. granulated sugar
2 c. all-purpose flour
1/2 tsp. salt

1/3 c. freshly grated Parmigiano-
    Reggiano cheese (1 oz.)
1 c. cold unsalted butter, diced
2 large egg yolks, beaten

Spread almonds in a pie plate and toast in 350° oven 10 minutes or until golden brown; set aside to cool. In a bowl, gently bruise rosemary with sugar using a pestle or back of spoon. In food processor, combine rosemary sugar with almonds, flour, salt and cheese; pulse until almonds are coarsely chopped. Add butter; pulse until mixture resembles coarse meal. Add egg yolks and pulse until large clumps of dough form. Transfer dough to a work surface; knead gently until it just comes together. Divide dough in half; press each piece into a circle. Roll out each circle between 2 sheets of wax paper to about 1/4-inch thick. Slide circles onto a baking sheet and freeze at least 1 hour, until very firm. Line 2 large baking sheets with parchment paper. Working with one piece of dough at a time, peel off top sheet of wax paper. Using small round cookie cutter, stamp out cookies as close together as possible. Arrange cookies about 1 inch apart on prepared baking sheets. Sprinkle lightly with salt. Bake in 350° oven 20 minutes, until lightly golden. Shift baking sheets from top to bottom and front to back halfway through. Let cookies cool on baking sheets 3 minutes and then transfer to wire rack to cool.

Sharon Krause, *Waukee*
First Place, 2015 Midwest Living & Gold Medal Flour Cookies –
Shortbread, Flavored
Second Place Overall, 2015 Midwest Living & Gold Medal Flour Cookies

CLASSIC UKRAINIAN BORSCHT

10 c. water
3 to 4 medium beets, washed
   and trimmed
10 small potatoes, sliced into
   bite-sized pieces
4 tbsp. cooking oil
1/2 c. grated baby carrots
1 medium onion, finely chopped
5 tbsp. catsup

6 c. chicken broth
4 tbsp. lemon juice
1/4 tsp. freshly ground pepper
2 bay leaves
15.5-oz. can kidney beans,
   undrained
1 tsp. chopped dill
1/2 head cabbage, thinly
   chopped

Fill large soup pot with water; add beets. Cover and boil about 1 hour. Remove beets from water; retain water. Add sliced potatoes to same water; cook 15 to 20 minutes. Add oil to a skillet; add carrots and onion. Stir in catsup when carrots are tender. Peel and slice beets into matchsticks; add to pot. Add chicken broth, lemon juice, pepper, bay leaves and kidney beans to pot. Add carrots, onion, dill and cabbage. Cook another 5 to 10 minutes until cabbage is tender. Serve with dollop of sour cream if desired.

Matthew Greazel, *Boone*
First Place, 2015 Best Borscht

EDAMAME CHEESE BALL

For EDAMAME CHEESE BALL:
4 oz. soy cheddar cheese
4 oz. cheddar cheese
3 oz. soy cream cheese
6 oz. cream cheese
1 tsp. soy sauce
1 tsp. Worcestershire sauce

1 tsp. garlic powder
1/2 tsp. onion powder
3/4 tsp. Beau Monde seasoning
3 tbsp. chopped water chestnuts
3/4 c. chopped edamame
Parsley for garnish

Combine soy cheddar cheese and cheddar cheese; set aside 3/4 cup. Place remainder of cheese in mixing bowl; add all remaining ingredients. Mix with electric mixer. Shape cheese mixture as desired. Roll in reserved cheese. Garnish with parsley. Serve with crackers.

(CONTINUED)

For EDAMAME CRACKERS:

1/2 c. plus 2 tbsp. butter-
    flavored vegetable shortening
1 tbsp. soy oil
3 to 4 tbsp. warm water
2 c. plus 3 tbsp. all-purpose flour
1 tbsp. soy flour
1/4 c. nonfat dry milk
4 tsp. granulated sugar
1 1/2 tsp. salt
1 tbsp. chopped chives
1/4 c. finely chopped edamame
1/2 tsp. garlic powder
1/2 tsp. onion powder

Place shortening and oil in bowl of stand mixer fitted with paddle attachment. Pour warm water over shortening and oil; let stand 5 minutes. Mix all other ingredients together in a medium bowl. Add 3/4 cup of flour mixture to shortening mixture. Add enough flour mixture to form ball. Knead dough 3 minutes, adding flour if needed. Cover dough with plastic wrap; let stand 1 hour. Place dough on floured surface; roll out and cut into shapes. Bake in 350° oven 12 minutes.

Deanna Smith, *Des Moines*
First Place, 2015 It's Soy Amazing – Appetizers/Sides

KALE, CAESAR!

1 bunch Tuscan kale
1 slice country bread
1/2 garlic clove, finely chopped
1/4 c. finely grated pecorino
    (Romano) cheese, more for
    garnish
Juice from 1 lemon
1/4 tsp. salt
1/8 tsp. red pepper flakes
Freshly ground black pepper, to
    taste
3 tbsp. extra virgin olive oil,
    more for garnish

Trim bottom 2 inches off kale stems and discard. Slice kale, including ribs, into 3/4-inch-wide ribbons. You should have 4 to 5 cups. Place kale in a large bowl. Toast bread slice until golden on both sides. Grind bread in a food processor until coarse. Pound garlic into a paste with the back of a knife. Transfer garlic to a small bowl. Add cheese, lemon juice, salt, pepper flakes, black pepper and olive oil. Whisk to combine. Pour dressing over kale; toss to thoroughly combine (dressing is thick and needs a lot of tossing to coat leaves). Let salad sit 10 minutes. Serve topped with breadcrumbs, additional cheese and a drizzle of oil.

Jackie Garnett, *Des Moines*
First Place, 2014 Healthy Creations (Featuring Kale)

SICILIAN DEVILED EGGS

6 eggs
1 baguette, thinly sliced
2 tbsp. butter
1/4 tsp. minced garlic
3 tbsp. shredded Parmesan
   cheese

1/4 c. mayonnaise
1/4 tsp. dry mustard
1/2 tsp. Sicilian salad seasoning
1/2 tsp. vinegar
1/4 tsp. salt

Place eggs in a pan; cover with cold water. Bring to a boil for 8 minutes. Remove from heat; run under cold water. Using a cookie cutter, cut 1-inch hole in center of baguette slices. Melt butter; add the garlic. Brush on the baguette slices and rounds, reserving remainder of butter. Broil until light brown. Sprinkle with half the Parmesan cheese; set aside. When eggs are cool, peel and cut in half. Remove yolks; place yolks in resealable plastic bag. Add the remainder butter garlic mix, mayonnaise, mustard, salad seasoning, vinegar and salt. Seal bag and mash together. Place each half of egg in center of baguette. Snip off end of bag; pipe yolk mixture into the egg. Place the round on the yolk; top with remaining Parmesan.

Bridget Lottman, *Norwalk*
First Place, 2014 Egg-ceptional Eggs – Deviled Eggs
Second Place Overall, 2014 Egg-ceptional Eggs

SWEET, HOT, CHOPPED CHERRY SALSA

1 c. coarsely chopped black
   sweet cherries
1 clove garlic, minced
1 1/2 tbsp. granulated sugar
1 tsp. kosher salt
1 apple, cored and coarsely
   chopped

1/2 jalapeno, finely chopped
1 tbsp. chopped red bell pepper
1/3 red onion, chopped
3 sprigs cilantro, finely chopped
2 tsp. balsamic vinegar
8 oz. cream cheese
Tortilla or pita chips

Combine all ingredients except cream cheese and chips. Spoon over cream cheese and serve with tortilla or pita chips. Can also be used to complement white fish such as halibut.

Jamie Buelt, *Polk City*
First Place, 2014 Salsa Sensations – Fruit Salsa

APPETIZERS, SIDE DISHES AND SALADS

CHIPOTLE CHERRY SALMON SALAD

For SALMON SALAD:

1 lb. fresh Atlantic salmon filet
3 tbsp. cherry chipotle
   barbeque sauce
3 tbsp. sesame oil
1 tbsp. minced garlic
2 tbsp. minced onion

1/4 c. reduced sodium soy sauce
8 oz. veggie pasta rotini
1 red bell pepper, seeded and
   chopped
1 small onion, chopped
12 cherry tomatoes, halved

Place salmon in a shallow dish; cover with barbeque sauce, oil, garlic, onion and soy sauce. Cover and refrigerate at least 1 hour. Grill salmon at 400 to 450° for 7 minutes or until easily flakes with fork. Remove from grill and cool. Break into bite size chunks. Cook pasta according to package directions; drain and cool. Add pepper, onion and tomatoes.

For CHIPOTLE CHERRY SALMON SALAD DRESSING:

1/2 c. mayonnaise
1/2 c. sour cream
3 tbsp. cherry barbeque sauce
1 tsp. lime juice

1 tsp. honey
1 tbsp. chopped fresh basil
Salt and pepper to taste
Dash of ground chipotle
   peppers

Mix all ingredients and fold into pasta. Add salmon chunks. Arrange on individual plates over field greens. Garnish with fresh basil.

Pamela Cooper, *Mount Ayr*
First Place, 2014 Spice It Up with Pampered Chef

CREAMY PARMESAN DRESSING

2 c. mayonnaise or mayonnaise-
   style salad dressing
3/4 c. finely grated Parmesan
   cheese
1/4 c. granulated sugar

1/2 c. heavy cream
1 tbsp. white vinegar
1/2 tsp. smoked Spanish paprika
1/4 tsp. garlic powder

Mix all ingredients until well incorporated. For best flavor, refrigerate overnight.

Linda Spevak, *Urbandale*
First Place, 2014 Dress It Up

APPETIZERS, SIDE DISHES AND SALADS

SPICY SOUTHWEST CORN-CHEESE SOUP

10-oz. pkg. frozen whole
   kernel corn, thawed and
   drained
1 clove garlic, minced
1 tbsp. butter
8 oz. processed American
   cheese, cut up
4-oz. can chopped green
   chilies, undrained
3/4 c. chicken broth
3/4 c. milk
2 tbsp. chopped cilantro
1/2 c. crushed tortilla chips

In large saucepan, cook and stir corn and garlic in butter on medium high heat until garlic is tender. Reduce heat to medium. Add all remaining ingredients except chips. Cook until cheese is completely melted and soup is heated through, stirring occasionally. Serve topped with crushed chips.

Daphane Trevillyan, *Urbandale*
First Place, 2014 Kraft Kreations with Velveeta – Soup
First Place Overall, 2014 Kraft Kreations with Velveeta

SWEET POTATO SALAD

2 lbs. sweet potatoes, peeled
   and cut into 1-inch cubes
2 tbsp. lemon juice
1 c. mayonnaise-style
   salad dressing
2 tbsp. orange juice
1 tbsp. honey
1 tsp. grated orange zest
1/2 tsp. ground ginger
1/4 tsp. salt
1/8 tsp. nutmeg
1/4 c. chopped celery
1/2 c. chopped dates
1/2 c. chopped pecans
11-oz. can mandarin oranges,
   drained
Lettuce leaves

In saucepan, cover potatoes with water. Cook potatoes until tender, 5 to 8 minutes. Drain; toss with lemon juice. In large bowl, combine salad dressing, orange juice, honey, orange zest, ginger, salt and nutmeg. Add potatoes, celery, dates and pecans; toss to coat. Cover and chill. Spoon salad onto lettuce lined platter. Arrange orange slices around salad.

Rita Johannsen, *Des Moines*
First Place, 2014 Show Me Your Salad
First Place, 2015 Show Me Your Salad

CREAMY DOUBLE CORN CHOWDER

1 1/4 c. whole milk, divided
1 1/4 c. heavy cream, divided
6 slices thin cut bacon, cut into
    small pieces
5 c. popped butter flavored
    microwave popcorn

2 ears sweet corn
1 tbsp. jalapeno juice from jar
1/2 c. potato flakes
Salt
Pepper
1/4 c. chopped chives
1/4 c. chopped dill

Place 5/8 cup whole milk, 5/8 cup heavy cream and bacon in a freezer resealable bag, removing as much air as possible before sealing. Cook in a sous vide water bath machine 2 hours at 82° C. Allow to cool (with bag open), then seal and place in refrigerator until ready to use. Place popped corn in a food processor or blender with remaining cream and whole milk. Pulse a few times to coarsely chop popcorn. Place in resealable bag; refrigerate overnight. In large saucepan, boil corn in water 3 minutes; cut kernels off ears. Strain bacon mixture; set aside. Strain popped corn mixture, squeezing out liquid from swollen kernels. Place both strained liquids and corn kernels (from boiled ears) in saucepan. Heat until just simmering. Remove from heat; place in food processor or blender along with jalapeno juice and potato flakes. Blend until smooth and airy, approximately 2 minutes. Season to taste with salt and pepper. Warm soup in a saucepan being careful not to boil. Garnish with chives and dill.

Sharon Krause, *Waukee*
First Place, 2014 Chef Baru's Gourmet Corn Chowder

CHICKEN SALAD

1 1/2 lbs. cooked chicken,
    chopped
1 c. mayonnaise-style salad
    dressing

1/2 c. chopped celery
1/2 c. pineapple tidbits
1/4 c. chopped toasted pecans
1/2 tsp. poppy seeds

Combine all ingredients; serve on a bed of lettuce or on a croissant.

Rose Ridgway, *Johnston*
First Place, 2015 Miracle Whip Salads

APPETIZERS, SIDE DISHES AND SALADS

POTATO TARTLETS

1 c. prepared instant mashed
  potatoes
1/2 c. sour cream
1 c. shredded cheddar cheese
1 c. crushed crispy fried onions
2 tbsp. finely chopped chives

1/2 tsp. garlic powder
2 tbsp. all-purpose flour
1/2 of a 17.3-oz. pkg. puff
  pastry sheets (1 sheet),
  thawed

In medium bowl, combine potatoes, sour cream, cheese, onions, chives and garlic powder. Sprinkle flour on work surface; unfold pastry sheet. Roll pastry sheet to 12-inch square. Cut into 36, 2-inch squares. Press pastry squares into 1 1/2-inch mini muffin pan cups. Spoon approximately 1 tablespoon potato mixture into each tartlet shell. Sprinkle with additional crushed crispy fried onions, if desired. Bake in 400° oven 15 minutes or until pastries are golden brown. Let pastries cool in pans on wire racks 10 minutes.

Peri Halma, *West Des Moines*
First Place, 2015 Spotlighting Spuds – Convenience Potatoes
Third Place Overall, 2015 Spotlighting Spuds

CARROT NOODLES IN CHIMICHURRI SAUCE

1 c. fresh parsley
1/2 c. fresh basil
1/4 c. chopped fresh green
  onions
3 large cloves garlic, roughly
  chopped

1/4 c. white vinegar
2/3 c. vegetable oil
4 tbsp. crushed red chili
  pepper flakes
Salt to taste
5 medium carrots

Place parsley, basil, onions, garlic, vinegar, oil and chili pepper flakes in food processor; process until thick paste. Add salt to taste; set aside. Bring a large pot of water to a boil. Peel and shred carrots into noodles. Blanch carrot noodles in boiling water 1 to 2 minutes until soft and cooked. Mix carrot noodles with chimichurri sauce; divide equally into two bowls. Garnish with sprig of parsley and a bit more crushed red chili pepper flakes.

Lynn Jeffers, *Jesup*
First Place, 2015 Stan's Spicy Stringy Carrots

ZIPPY ZUCCHINI ZUPPA WITH ASPARAGUS AND CANNELLINI BEANS

2 tbsp. olive oil
1 large red onion, diced
2 stalks celery, diced
1 large carrot, diced
1 large zucchini, quartered
   lengthwise and sliced
3 cloves garlic, minced
3 sprigs thyme, stemmed and
   minced
2 bay leaves

4 c. vegetable stock
3 1/2 c. cooked cannellini beans
   (2, 15-oz. cans undrained)
1/4 c. garlic chili paste
1 bunch asparagus, trimmed
   and quartered crosswise
1 tsp. grated lemon zest
Juice from 1 lemon
1 tsp. salt
1/2 tsp. black pepper

Heat oil in large Dutch oven or soup pot over medium-high heat. Add onion, celery and carrot; sauté until vegetables start to soften and brown slightly, about 8 minutes. Add zucchini, garlic, thyme and bay leaves; sauté until garlic is fragrant, about 30 seconds. Pour in 1 cup of stock to deglaze the pan with a wooden spoon. Stir in remaining stock, beans and garlic chili paste. Bring to a boil; immediately lower the heat, cover and simmer gently 15 minutes. Stir in asparagus, stirring occasionally, until soup has thickened and beans and vegetables are soft, about 5 minutes. Discard bay leaves. Stir in lemon zest and juice; season with salt and pepper to taste. Serve immediately.

Linda Asbille, *Indianola*
First Place, 2014 Vegetarian Soup

SWEET N' SPICY BOOM BOOM DIPPING SAUCE

16 oz. Thousand Island dressing
2 tbsp. buffalo wing sauce
2 tsp. Worcestershire sauce
1 tsp. prepared mustard

1/2 onion
2 tbsp. cilantro
3 cloves garlic
1/2 tsp. garlic salt

Combine all ingredients in food processor. Blend well, about 10 minutes. Chill and serve with your favorite appetizer or main dish for dipping.

Kyle Barton, *West Des Moines*
First Place, 2015 The Best Dipping Sauce Ever

ROCKIN' ROWAN BAKED BEANS

1/2 lb. smoked bacon, cut into
    1/2-inch pieces
1 large sweet onion, finely
    chopped
4 cloves garlic, minced
1 red bell pepper, seeded and
    finely chopped
1 poblano pepper, seeded and
    finely chopped
3 jalapeno peppers, seeded
    and diced

15-oz. can black beans
15-oz. can dark red kidney beans
15-oz. can great Northern beans
2, 15-oz. cans pork and beans
2 c. barbeque sauce
1 1/2 c. firmly packed brown
    sugar
1/2 c. Dijon mustard
1 tsp. salt
1/2 tsp. fresh ground pepper

In large electric skillet, fry bacon and onion until bacon is crisp and onions are translucent; add garlic. Add red pepper, poblano pepper and jalapeno peppers; sauté until peppers soften. Rinse and drain black, red and Northern beans; add to pepper mixture. Add undrained pork and beans and heat until beans are warm. Stir in barbeque sauce, brown sugar and mustard; mix well. Season with salt and pepper as needed. Simmer on low 30 minutes.

Diane Rauh, *Des Moines*
First Place, 2014 Something Hot

FRUIT CREAM

16 oz. fat-free cream cheese
1/4 c. artificial sweetener
1/2 tsp. vanilla
1/2 tsp. almond extract
2 c. fat-free frozen whipped
    topping, thawed

2 c. blueberries
2 c. red raspberries
2 c. blackberries
1 c. sliced strawberries

In medium bowl, beat cream cheese, sweetener, vanilla and almond extract until fluffy. Fold in whipped topping. Gently mix berries together. Layer in trifle bowl half of cream mixture and half of berry mixture. Repeat layers; refrigerate until ready to serve.

Cindie Robinette-Anderson, *Des Moines*
First Place, 2015 Healthy Creations (Berry Blast)

CHARLIE'S SALAD

2, 3-oz. boxes lemon-flavored
    gelatin, divided
2 c. boiling water, divided
2 tbsp. mayonnaise-style
    salad dressing
2 tbsp. vegetable cottage
    cheese, mashed

2.6-oz. pouch lemon-pepper
    flavored tuna
2 tbsp. chopped red onion
2 tbsp. sweet pickle relish,
    juice squeezed off
2 tsp. prepared mustard

In a medium sized bowl, dissolve 1 box gelatin with 1 cup boiling water. Whisk in salad dressing and mashed cottage cheese. Pour into gelatin mold; chill to set. Stir together tuna, onion, relish and mustard; mix well. In a 2 cup measuring cup dissolve remaining box of gelatin in remaining boiling water. Stir into tuna mixture. Gently pour over set layer; chill to set. Dip mold in hot water 30 to 60 seconds to loosen; invert onto serving platter.

Sharon Gates, *Des Moines*
First Place, 2015 Jell-O – Salads
First Place Overall, 2015 Jell-O

SMOKED MAPLE-WINE SALMON SALAD

5 to 6 oz. smoked salmon, flaked
1 tbsp. brown sugar
1 tbsp. soy sauce
1/4 c. cooking wine
1 tbsp. maple syrup
1 1/2 c. mayonnaise-style
    salad dressing
1/2 onion, minced
1/2 green pepper, minced

1/3 c. shredded carrots
2 tbsp. parsley
1/2 c. grated Parmesan cheese
1 tsp. dried garlic flakes
1 tsp. dried onion flakes
1/2 tsp. garlic powder
Pinch of salt
Cayenne pepper, garlic salt
    and parsley for garnish

Combine salmon, brown sugar, soy sauce, wine and maple syrup; refrigerate overnight. Combine salmon mixture and salad dressing. Add onion, pepper, carrot, parsley, cheese, garlic and onion flakes and spices; stir. Refrigerate 30 minutes. Place on bed of lettuce. Sprinkle with cayenne and garlic mixture. Serve with crackers.

Kyle Barton, *West Des Moines*
First Place, 2014 Miracle Whip Salads

APPETIZERS, SIDE DISHES AND SALADS

STUFFED TWICE BAKED POTATOES

5 large baking potatoes
1 tbsp. olive oil
2 c. shredded sharp cheddar
   cheese
1 c. sour cream
6 tbsp. unsalted butter

8 slices crispy cooked bacon,
   crumbled
1 3/4 tsp. salt
1/2 tsp. fresh ground black
   pepper

Wash potatoes and dry; rub with olive oil. Place on foil-lined baking sheet; bake in 400° oven until potatoes are tender, about 1 hour. Remove potatoes from oven; cut top quarter from each potato. Scoop out potatoes into medium size bowl. Return potato skins to foil-lined baking sheet. Mash potatoes until smooth. Add 1 cup of cheese, sour cream, butter, bacon, salt and pepper; mash until smooth. Spoon potato mixture back into potato skins; top with remaining cheese. Bake until hot and cheese is melted, about 10 to 15 minutes. Serve immediately.

Taylor Conlan, *Pleasant Hill*
First Place, 2014 Adventureland Resort Intermediate – Twice Baked Potatoes

CHEESY HASH BROWN POTATO SOUP

1/2 lb. bacon
1 small carrot, chopped
1 stalk celery, finely chopped
1 small white onion, finely
   chopped
1 small red onion, finely
   chopped

1 tbsp. butter
4 c. chicken broth
24-oz. bag frozen hash browns
1/2 lb. processed American
   cheese, cubed
2 c. heavy cream
Pepper to taste

Cut bacon into small chunks; cook in skillet until crisp. Drain well on paper towels. Sauté carrots, celery and onions in skillet with butter. Bring chicken broth to a boil in a Dutch oven; add sautéed vegetables and frozen hash browns. Cook until hash browns are tender. Add cubed cheese and bacon. Stir until cheese is melted; add cream. Add pepper to taste; serve hot.

Susan Schultz, *Haverhill*
First Place, 2015 Cooking with Mr. Dee's – Shredded Hash Browns

OVERNIGHT RHUBARB SLUSH

8 c. sliced rhubarb
8 c. water
3 tbsp. black cherry gelatin
1/2 c. lemon juice

Juice from 1/2 lime
2 c. granulated sugar
Lemon/lime flavored soft drink

Place rhubarb in water; bring to boil. Reduce heat; let simmer 20 minutes. Drain rhubarb through cheesecloth reserving liquid. Squeeze to remove all juice; discard rhubarb. Heat reserved liquid on low heat; add gelatin, lemon juice, lime juice and sugar. Stir until dissolved. Pour into plastic or glass container. Place in freezer until frozen. Remove from freezer; let stand a few minutes. Fill a glass with rhubarb slush then add splash of lemon/lime soft drink. Garnish with lime and/or a rhubarb stick. Serve chilled.

Kyle Barton, *West Des Moines*
First Place, 2015 Coach's Favorite Rhubarb

HAMBURGER SOUP

1 1/2 lbs. lean ground beef
1 tsp. minced garlic
2 c. diced carrots
1/2 medium onion, minced
3, 14-oz. cans beef broth
2 beef bouillon cubes
14.5-oz. can Italian tomatoes

1 tsp. Italian seasoning
2 tbsp. Worcestershire sauce
1/2 tsp. hot pepper sauce
3 tbsp. margarine
2 tbsp. all-purpose flour
Shredded Parmesan cheese

In large soup pot, brown beef; add garlic, carrots and onions. Cook and stir 2 minutes. Drain grease. Add broth, bouillon cubes and tomatoes. Cook and stir 2 more minutes. Add Italian seasoning, Worcestershire sauce and hot pepper sauce. Bring to a boil; reduce heat and simmer 15 minutes. In small saucepan on medium heat, melt margarine. Add flour; cook and stir on medium heat until mixture begins to brown. Carefully mix into soup. Cover and simmer 15 additional minutes, stirring occasionally. Garnish with shredded Parmesan cheese if desired.

Charlotte Bowden, *Monroe*
First Place, 2015 Adventureland Resort Intermediate Hamburger Soup

THAI CURRY SHRIMP SOUP

1 tbsp. coconut oil
2 tbsp. fresh minced ginger
1 red bell pepper, sliced
2 tbsp. red curry paste
2 cloves garlic, minced
1 tsp. lemon pepper
1 tsp. turmeric
1 tsp. curry
1 tsp. coriander
1/2 tsp. paprika
1/2 tsp. cayenne pepper
3 c. chicken stock
13.5-oz. can unsweetened
   coconut milk
3 tbsp. lime juice
1 tbsp. brown sugar
Salt to taste
8.8-oz. pkg. rice noodles
1 lb. cooked shrimp
1/2 c. fresh cilantro
Chili peppers
Wedge of lime

In stockpot heat oil. In a bowl, combine ginger, red pepper, red curry paste and garlic. In separate bowl, combine lemon pepper, turmeric, curry, coriander, paprika and cayenne. Add first bowl with ginger to oil; stir for 1 minute. Add second bowl; stir for 1 minute. Add 1/2 cup chicken stock; heat until almost boiling. Reduce heat to medium low; add coconut milk, lime juice, brown sugar and salt. Heat through. Prepare rice noodles following package directions. When ready to serve, add shrimp and noodles to stockpot; heat through. Garnish with cilantro, chili peppers and lime.

Bridget Lottman, *Norwalk*
First Place, 2015 Can You Curry That? – Main or Side Dish

CHICKEN SALAD

2 c. diced cooked chicken
1 1/2 c. chopped celery
1 1/2 c. mayonnaise
1 tsp. minced onion
1/4 tsp. salt
1/4 tsp. black pepper
1/3 c. sliced almonds
Lettuce or spinach for garnish
Tomatoes for garnish
Black olives for garnish
Croutons for garnish

Mix together all ingredients; chill. Serve on lettuce or spinach. Garnish with tomatoes, black olives and croutons.

Daphane Trevillyan, *Urbandale*
First Place, 2014 Trust Your Recipe to Gurleys – Non-Baked

HAMBURGER SOUP WITH A KICK

1 lb. 93% ground beef
Salt
Pepper
2 tbsp. butter
2 tbsp. all-purpose flour
2 1/2 c. milk, divided

1 c. shredded cheddar cheese
1.25-oz. pkg. taco seasoning
10-oz. can tomatoes and green
   chilies
15-oz. can tex mex chili beans
Crushed tortilla chips

Brown ground beef in Dutch oven over medium heat; add salt and pepper to taste. Melt butter in small saucepan over medium heat; whisk in flour and cook 1 minute. Slowly whisk in 1 cup of milk; season with salt and pepper. Stir until thickened, about 3 to 4 minutes. Remove from heat; stir in shredded cheese until smooth. Set aside. Stir taco seasoning, tomatoes and chilies, chili beans and remaining milk into cooked ground beef; stir well to combine. Add cheese sauce. Bring to boil; reduce heat to medium and simmer 10 minutes, stirring occasionally. Serve with crushed tortilla chips and additional shredded cheese.

Taylor Conlan, *Pleasant Hill*
First Place, 2014 Adventureland Resort Intermediate – Hamburger Soup

VIBRANT VEGAN BEAN SOUP

2, 15-oz. cans navy beans
1 1/4 c. water
2 tsp. dried sweet basil
4 tbsp. vegan butter
3/4 c. chopped onion
1 to 2 tsp. dried parsley
1/2 c. chopped celery

1 tsp. salt
1 tsp. black pepper
1 tbsp. garlic powder
3 tsp. applesauce
1 medium white potato, baked
   skin on
1/4 to 1/3 c. plain soy creamer

In soup pot combine navy beans, water, sweet basil, butter, onion, parsley, celery, salt, pepper, garlic powder and applesauce. Bring to boil; simmer while potato bakes. Rough chop potato and place in blender. Add to blender 1 to 2 cups of liquid from bean mixture. Blend on low to medium until potato is pureed; add to soup. Add soy creamer as desired to thin soup. Serve with sea salt straws.

Sheryl Davis, *Ames*
First Place, 2014 Vibrant Vegan – Vegan Main Dish

CRAB PASTA SALAD

For CRAB PASTA SALAD:

6 oz. tri-color rotini pasta
8-oz. pkg. flaked crab
1/2 red bell pepper, chopped

1/2 orange bell pepper, chopped
1 c. chopped carrot chips
1 Roma tomato, chopped
Chopped cilantro

Cook pasta according to package directions; drain. Mix in crab and vegetables except cilantro. Stir dressing into salad; chill. Garnish with chopped cilantro.

For DRESSING:

1 c. mayonnaise-style
salad dressing

1/2, 1-oz. pkg. dry ranch mix
3 tbsp. grated Parmesan cheese

Stir together all ingredients; mix well.

Sheryl Davis, *Slater*
First Place, 2015 Barilla Pasta & Sauce – Salad
First Place Overall, 2015 Barilla Pasta & Sauce

WILD RICE SALAD

For WILD RICE SALAD:

1 c. uncooked wild rice
6 c. water
1 tsp. salt
Juice from 1/2 lemon
2 stalks celery, chopped

3 green onions, sliced
1 red bell pepper, diced
Lettuce
1 c. cashews, roasted

Place rice, water and salt in medium saucepan; bring to rapid boil. Adjust heat to simmer; cook approximately 45 minutes until grains begin to open. Drain rice; transfer to bowl. Toss with lemon juice and cool. Add celery, onions and red pepper to cooled rice. Toss with dressing; refrigerate 2 to 4 hours. Place on bed of lettuce. Add cashews when serving.

(CONTINUED)

For DRESSING:

2 cloves garlic, minced
1 tbsp. Dijon mustard
1/2 tsp. salt
1/4 tsp. pepper
1/4 c. balsamic vinegar
1/2 c. vegetable oil

Whisk all ingredients in bowl or place in food processor.

Terry Heinichen, *Marengo*
First Place, 2015 Vibrant Vegan – Vegan Main Dish

TROPICAL HONEY MOCKTAIL

1 mint leaf
1 c. pineapple juice
1/4 c. lime juice
3/4 c. coconut milk, well shaken
2 tbsp. honey
Ice cubes
Seltzer to taste
Lime wedges, sprigs of mint or
    sliced fresh pineapple for
    garnish

In the bottom of a cocktail shaker, lightly muddle mint to release flavor. Add pineapple juice, lime juice, coconut milk, honey and a few ice cubes; shake well. Pour over ice cubes in glasses. Finish with a splash of seltzer and lime wedge, pineapple or mint sprig.

Natalie Ridgway, *Johnston*
First Place, 2015 Foods Made with Honey – Honey Drinks

REAL RUSSIAN BORSCHT

1 1/2 lbs. bread and butter pot
    roast
1 large onion, chopped
2 carrots, diced
2 stalks celery, chopped
2 c. shredded red cabbage
1 large potato, diced
4 large beets, grated
Salt to taste
8-oz. can tomato sauce
2 tbsp. granulated sugar
2 cloves garlic, mashed

Brown pot roast on both sides in large soup pot; add 3 quarts water. Add onion, carrots, celery, red cabbage and potato. Add beets and salt to taste. Cook over low heat approximately 1 1/2 hours or until meat is tender. Add tomato sauce, sugar and garlic; cook 30 additional minutes.

Gail Stricker, *Des Moines*
First Place, 2014 Best Borscht

BEAN & KALE SOUP

2 cloves garlic, minced
6 c. chicken broth
4 c. roughly torn kale, discard
    all stems and tough veins
1 tsp. seasoning blend
15-oz. can organic tan
    soybeans, drained and
    rinsed
15-oz. can organic black
    soybeans, drained and
    rinsed
10-oz. pkg. organic shelled
    edamame, cooked per
    package directions
4, 3-oz. soy based Italian
    sausages

Spray saucepan with soybean oil cooking spray and heat garlic about 1 minute until aromatic. Add broth; bring to boil. Add kale and seasoning. Cover pot; cook on low until kale is wilted. Add soybeans and edamame. In separate pan, brown sausage over medium heat about 5 minutes. Let stand 2 minutes; slice diagonally and add to soup.

Jan Trometer, *Jamaica*
First Place, 2015 It's Soy Amazing – Entrees

ROASTED BUTTERNUT SQUASH SOUP

2 lbs. whole butternut squash
2 tbsp. butter
Salt
Pepper
1 medium Granny Smith apple
1/2 medium yellow onion
4 cloves garlic
1/2 tsp. sage
1/4 tsp. nutmeg
1/4 tsp. ginger
1/8 tsp. cayenne pepper
Dash of cinnamon
1 1/4 c. low sodium
    chicken broth
1 1/4 c. water
Scant 1/4 c. plain, no sugar
    almond milk
Sour cream thinned with almond
    milk to desired consistency
Roasted squash seeds for
    garnish

Cut squash in half lengthwise, scoop out seeds; place on foil lined baking pan. Rub 1 tablespoon butter over insides of squash. Salt and pepper both halves. Cut apple in half; place on roasting pan along with onion and garlic. Roast in 425° oven. Remove garlic after 10 minutes, apples and onion after 20 minutes or until softened. Continue roasting squash additional 30 minutes or until softened. Remove skins from onion and

(CONTINUED)

garlic and skin and core from apple; coarsely chop. Scoop out squash pulp. Melt 1 tablespoon butter in Dutch oven; add squash, apples, onion and garlic. Add spices, chicken broth, water, salt and pepper. Bring to boil over medium-high heat; reduce to simmer and cook to meld flavors 10 to 15 minutes. Remove from heat; stir in almond milk. Puree in blender to desired consistency. Add salt and pepper if needed. Spoon into bowls. Garnish with sour cream and sprinkle with squash seeds.

Amy Fuson, *Indianola*
First Place, 2014 Cooking with Winter Squash

ALL-AMERICAN BACON CHEESEBURGER SOUP

1 lb. ground beef	14.5-oz. can diced tomatoes,
1 medium onion, chopped	drained
1 stalk celery, chopped	2, 8-oz. pkgs. shredded
2 cloves garlic, minced	processed American cheese
2 tbsp. all-purpose flour	6-oz. can tomato paste
2, 14-oz. cans lower sodium	1/4 c. catsup
beef broth	2 tbsp. prepared mustard
2 medium potatoes, scrubbed	1 c. whole milk
and coarsely chopped	1/2 lb. bacon, fried, drained
	and crumbled

Form 5 hamburger patties for grilling on barbecue grill; grill burgers until pink inside. Remove from grill; cut meat into bite-size pieces. Keep warm and set aside. In a Dutch oven, sauté onion, celery and garlic over medium heat until vegetables are tender. Return hamburger pieces to Dutch oven. Sprinkle flour on beef mixture; cook and stir 2 minutes. Stir in broth and potatoes. Bring to boil, stirring occasionally. Reduce heat; simmer covered, 10 minutes or until potatoes are tender. Stir in tomatoes, cheese, tomato paste, catsup and mustard. Cook and stir until cheese is melted and smooth and soup comes to gentle boil. Stir in milk; heat through. Add bacon pieces before serving. If desired, serve with pickle, onion and tomato.

Diane Rauh, *Des Moines*
First Place, 2015 Kraft Kreations with Velveeta – Soup
First Place Overall, 2015 Kraft Kreations with Velveeta

MOM'S BEET SALAD

3/4 c. beet juice
3 tbsp. vinegar
3-oz. pkg. sugar-free or regular
   lemon gelatin
1/2 tsp. salt
2 tsp. onion juice or finely
   minced onions
3/4 c. chopped celery
1 c. diced beets
1 tbsp. horseradish

Combine beet juice and vinegar in measuring cup. Add water to make 1 1/2 cups. Dissolve gelatin in liquids. Add salt, onion juice, celery, beets and horseradish. Pour into gelatin mold; refrigerate until firm.

Starr Hinrichs, *Johnston*
First Place, 2014 Jell-O – Salads
First Place Overall, 2014 Jell-O

SWEET HONEY SANGRIA

3 c. white cranberry peach juice
1/2 c. honey
1 c. Moscato wine
4 tbsp. coconut rum
1/2 c. strawberries and orange
   slices, for garnish

In a large pitcher, mix juice and honey. Add wine, rum and fruit. Refrigerate at least 2 hours.

Jenna Brady, *Runnells*
First Place, 2014 Foods Made with Honey – Honey Drinks

SUPER SEVEN SPINACH SALAD

For SUPER SEVEN SPINACH SALAD:
6-oz. pkg. baby spinach leaves
1/3 c. cubed cheddar cheese
1 apple, peeled, cored and diced
1/3 c. finely chopped red onion
1/4 c. fresh raspberries
1/4 c. sweetened dried
   cranberries
1/3 c. blanched slivered almonds
3 tbsp. poppy seed salad
   dressing (recipe below)

In large bowl, combine spinach, cheese, apple, red onion, raspberries, cranberries and slivered almonds. Toss with poppy seed dressing just before serving.

(CONTINUED)

APPETIZERS, SIDE DISHES AND SALADS

For POPPY SEED SALAD DRESSING:

1 1/2 c. honey	**2 tsp. salt**
2 tsp. dry mustard	**3/4 c. white vinegar**
2 c. vegetable oil	**3 tbsp. onion juice**
3 tbsp. poppy seeds	

In 1-quart jar with lid, mix together honey, mustard, vegetable oil, poppy seeds, salt, vinegar and onion juice. To make onion juice, finely chop an onion in a blender; pour onion onto a piece of cheesecloth or fine strainer. Allow juice to drip into a bowl. Squeeze cloth to get more juice. Serve on greens.

Lana Shope, *Indianola*
First Place, 2015 Puckerbrush Potluck – Salad/Entrée

LOW-FAT TORTILLA SOUP

4 c. chicken stock	**2 or 3 tomatoes, cut in bite size**
1 tsp. chili powder	**pieces**
1 tsp. cumin	**Cilantro leaves, washed and**
1 jalapeno pepper, finely diced	**coarsely chopped**
1/2 onion, chopped (approx. 1 c.)	**Tortilla chips**
3 boneless, skinless chicken	
breasts	

In large pot bring stock, chili powder and cumin to boil. Add jalapeno, onion and chicken. Reduce heat to low; cook gently 15 to 20 minutes until breasts are cooked (165°). Remove chicken; let cool slightly then shred. Add chicken, tomatoes and cilantro to taste. Garnish with crushed tortilla chips and additional cilantro.

Jan Trometer, *Jamaica*
First Place, 2014 Souper Soups

APPETIZERS, SIDE DISHES AND SALADS

CINNAMON MANGO DEVILED EGGS

8 eggs
3 tbsp. cream cheese, softened
2 tbsp. Greek yogurt

4 tbsp. mango preserves
1/2 tsp. cinnamon

Cover eggs with an inch of cold tap water in a pot. Bring to boil. Cover, remove from heat; let stand 13 to 14 minutes. Drain water; place eggs in ice water. When cool, crack eggshells; carefully peel under cool running water. Gently dry with paper towels. Slice eggs in half lengthwise, removing yolks to a medium bowl and placing whites on a serving platter. Using a fork, mash yolks into a fine crumble. Add cream cheese, Greek yogurt, mango preserves and cinnamon; mix well. Blend mixture in a blender until smooth and creamy. Pipe yolk mixture into egg whites. Sprinkle with dash of cinnamon and serve.

Holly Houg, *Urbandale*
First Place, 2015 Egg-ceptional Eggs – Deviled Eggs

CRAB PASTA SALAD

1/2 lb. farfalle noodles
1/2 lb. crabmeat, chopped
1 red bell pepper, chopped
1 yellow bell pepper, chopped
1/2 c. chopped carrots
1/2 c. chopped cauliflower

1/2 c. chopped broccoli
1 c. mayonnaise-style
   salad dressing
1/2, 1-oz. pkg. ranch dry
   seasoning
2 tbsp. grated Parmesan cheese

Cook noodles per package directions; drain. Mix noodles, crabmeat, peppers, carrots, cauliflower and broccoli. In separate bowl mix salad dressing, seasoning and Parmesan cheese. Pour dressing over salad and mix; refrigerate.

Sheryl Davis, *Ames*
First Place, 2014 Barilla Pasta & Sauce – Salad
Second Place Overall, 2014 Barilla Pasta & Sauce

HOT POTATO SALAD

16-oz. bag shredded hash browns
4 hard cooked eggs, peeled and chopped
1 small onion, finely diced
2 tsp. prepared mustard
Fresh black pepper
8 oz. sour cream
1 c. mayonnaise
1/4 c. milk
1 lb. processed American cheese, diced
1 tsp. celery seed
3 tbsp. cider vinegar
1/2 lb. bacon, chopped, cooked and drained

Mix all ingredients. Spoon into 9x13-inch baking pan or 2 smaller casserole dishes. Bake in 350° oven 45 minutes. Garnish with sliced hard cooked egg and green onions.

Lynn Jeffers, *Jesup*
First Place, 2014 Cooking with Mr. Dee's

PICNIC BAKED BEANS

4 slices bacon, quartered
1/4 c. minced onion
1 large tart apple, peeled and chopped
1/2 c. packed brown sugar
1/2 c. molasses
1/2 c. catsup
1 tsp. salt
1/4 tsp. pepper
1 tsp. dry mustard
1/4 c. water
3 c. dry navy beans, soaked and cooked as directed on bag

Fry bacon. Add onion and apple; sauté until tender. Add brown sugar; stir until dissolved. Mix in molasses, catsup, salt, pepper, dry mustard and water. Place beans in 2-quart casserole dish. Pour sauce over beans; mix well. Bake in 375° oven 60 to 90 minutes.

Patty Hummel, *Allison*
First Place, 2015 Nostalgic Comfort Food – Side Dish/Appetizer
Second Place Overall, 2015 Nostalgic Comfort Food

SIMPLY CARROTS SOUP

1/2 c. butter, divided
1 lb. carrots, peeled and sliced
1/4 c. granulated sugar
1 tsp. salt
6 c. chicken stock

1/2 c. all-purpose flour
2 tbsp. heavy cream
1/2 tsp. ginger
1/4 tsp. coriander
Squeeze of lemon juice

Heat 6 tablespoons of butter in stockpot; add carrots, sugar and salt. Sauté uncovered until very soft; puree in blender, adding a bit of chicken stock if necessary to make smooth. Return to pot; blend in flour. Add remaining chicken stock; bring to a boil and simmer 10 minutes. Strain; return to pan. Remove from heat; add cream, remainder of butter, seasonings and lemon juice.

Susan Hanke, *Clive*
First Place, 2015 Souper Soups

LAYERED SALSA SALAD

1/4 lb. ostrich steak
All-purpose flour
All-purpose seasoning
Olive oil
1 1/2 c. shredded green cabbage
1 c. mild salsa, divided

1 Granny Smith apple, chopped
1/4 c. sour cream
2 tbsp. bacon bits
3 tbsp. chopped green onion
Parsley
Sour cream
Sliced almonds

Cut ostrich into strips; dredge ostrich in flour and seasoning. Stir-fry in olive oil to medium rare. Remove from heat; set aside. Layer in serving bowl cabbage, 1/2 cup salsa, apple, sour cream, bacon bits, green onion, remaining salsa and ostrich steak strips. Garnish with parsley, sour cream and sliced almonds.

Helen Wall, *Alden*
First Place, 2015 Cookies' Salsa Creation

TWICE BAKED POTATO CASSEROLE

4 Russet potatoes, unpeeled
   and baked
16 oz. chive dip
2 c. shredded Colby jack
   cheese

2 bunches green onion, sliced
1/4 tsp. salt
1/4 tsp. black pepper
6 slices bacon, cooked, drained
   and crumbled

Cut baked potatoes into 1 inch cubes; leave skins on. Place into 2-quart greased baking dish. In medium bowl, combine chive dip, cheese, green onion, salt, pepper and half the crumbled bacon. Pour over potatoes. Bake in 350° oven 30 minutes. Top with other half of bacon; bake 10 minutes to brown and crisp bacon.

Cindie Robinette-Anderson, *Des Moines*
First Place, 2015 Spotlighting Spuds – Side Dishes
Second Place Overall, 2015 Spotlighting Spuds

CORN PUDDING

5 eggs
2/3 c. milk
2/3 c. heavy cream
1 tsp. salt

1/4 tsp. pepper
1/4 tsp. cayenne pepper
4 c. frozen corn
4 scallions, chopped
Butter

In large bowl, beat together eggs, milk, cream, salt, pepper and cayenne pepper. Stir in corn and scallions. Pour into buttered 1 1/2-quart baking dish. Dot top with butter. Bake in 350° oven 45 minutes or until a knife inserted in the center comes out clean.

Marianne Carlson, *Jefferson*
First Place, 2014 Our Iowa Church Cookbook Favorites – Sweet Corn

COCOA-COCONUT COFFEE COOLER

4 c. strong brewed espresso
   coffee
1/2 c. granulated sugar
1/4 c. unsweetened cocoa
   powder

2 c. half and half
13.5-oz. can coconut milk
2 tsp. vanilla
1/4 tsp. coconut extract

Whisk hot coffee, sugar and cocoa in large pitcher until dissolved. Whisk in half and half, milk, vanilla and coconut extract until blended. Chill 1 to 24 hours. Pour over ice cubes.

Rose Ridgway, *Johnston*
First Place, 2015 Cooking with Coffee – Beverages
Second Place Overall, 2015 Cooking with Coffee

CAESAR MAYONNAISE DRESSING

2 cloves garlic, minced
1/4 tsp. kosher salt
1 1/2 tsp. anchovy paste
2 tbsp. fresh lemon juice
1 tsp. Dijon-style mustard

1 tsp. Worcestershire sauce
1 c. mayonnaise
1/2 c. freshly grated Parmesan
   cheese
Fresh ground pepper

In small bowl, mash garlic with salt to form a paste. Combine garlic paste and remaining ingredients in medium-mixing bowl, mixing well. Add pepper to taste. Toss with salad greens or serve as a dip with veggies.

Sally Kilkenny, *Granger*
First Place, 2015 Dress It Up

SHRIMP AND PICKLE TEA SANDWICH

2 lbs. medium shrimp
1 clove garlic, minced
1 c. mayonnaise
1/4 c. sour cream
2 tbsp. chili sauce
2 to 4 dashes hot sauce
2 1/2 tbsp. finely chopped dill
   pickle

3/4 tsp. celery seed
1/2 tsp. kosher salt
2 stalks celery, coarsely
   chopped
1/2 medium onion, coarsely
   chopped

Cook shrimp in boiling salted water, stirring once or twice, until pink and just cooked through. Drain and cool completely. Peel, devein and coarsely chop. Blend garlic, mayonnaise, sour cream, chili sauce, hot sauce, pickles, celery seed and salt in a food processor until smooth. Add celery and onion; pulse until finely chopped. Transfer to serving bowl; stir in shrimp. Cover and chill at least 1 hour. Spread on choice of bread. Garnish as desired.

Sally Kilkenny, *Granger*
First Place, 2014 Let's Have Tea – Tea Sandwich
First Place Overall, 2014 Let's Have Tea

CURRY EGG WRAP

6 eggs
1/4 c. mayonnaise
1/4 tsp. dry mustard
1/2 tsp. curry
1/2 tsp. vinegar
1/4 tsp. salt

1 tbsp. shredded Parmesan
   cheese
Salad greens
6 tortilla wraps
11-oz. can Mandarin oranges,
   drained

Place eggs in pan; cover with cold water. Bring to a boil for 8 minutes; remove from heat. Run eggs under cold water. Peel eggs and slice. In bowl, combine eggs with mayonnaise, mustard, curry, vinegar, salt and Parmesan cheese; mix gently. Place salad greens on tortillas; add scoop of curry egg mixture. Top with Mandarin orange pieces. Roll up tortilla; slice in half.

Bridget Lottman, *Norwalk*
First Place, 2014 Egg-ceptional Eggs, Sandwiches – Salads & Sides
First Place Overall, 2014 Egg-ceptional Eggs

MAIN DISH

PICKLE PIZZA PIE

5 dill pickles, finely chopped
15-oz. can tomato sauce
1/2 lb. Italian sausage, browned
    and drained
2 tbsp. dried basil
1 tsp. oregano
2 tbsp. brown sugar
2 tsp. prepared mustard

4 cloves garlic, minced
1 refrigerated pizza crust
4 c. shredded mozzarella cheese
1/2 c. sliced cherry tomatoes
Pickles and cherry tomatoes
    for garnish
1 c. shredded lettuce

In saucepan, combine pickles, tomato sauce, sausage, basil, oregano, brown sugar, mustard and garlic. Simmer on medium heat. While simmering, roll out pie crust on round pan. Bake in 400° oven 8 to 10 minutes. Place meat-tomato mixture on crust; top with cheese and tomatoes. Garnish with thinly sliced pickles and cherry tomato halves. Bake 8 minutes more in 340° oven or until cheese is golden brown. Remove from oven; top with lettuce.

Kyle Barton, *West Des Moines*
First Place, 2014 Picklicious Recipes with Gedney Pickles

PORTOBELLO MUSHROOM PIZZA

2 Portobello mushrooms
2 tbsp. olive oil
1 c. pizza sauce
1/2 c. chopped onion
1/3 c. chopped red bell pepper
1/3 c. chopped green bell pepper

1 c. vegan soy protein crumbles
1 c. dairy free shredded cheese
4 to 5 red and yellow cherry
    tomatoes, sliced
Basil leaves and tomatoes
    for garnish

Wash and remove stems from mushrooms. Spray glass baking dish with olive oil. Turn mushrooms upside down and place into dish. Add pizza sauce to middles of each. Add onion, peppers and protein crumbles, dividing evenly between each mushroom. Add cheese; top with tomatoes and basil. Bake in 350° oven 50 minutes or until mushrooms are soft. Garnish plate and serve. Pizza toppings can be varied to include other vegetables.

Nicole Woodroffe, *Des Moines*
First Place, 2014 Versatile Vegetarian Creations

CLASSIC STROGANOFF WITH OSTRICH

2 to 3 tbsp. all-purpose flour	1 clove garlic, minced
1/4 tsp. salt to taste	1/2 c. ostrich or beef broth
6-oz. ostrich filet, cut into	2 tbsp. tomato paste
1/4-inch slices	1/2 c. sour cream
3 tbsp. butter, divided	Egg noodles, cooked according
2 tbsp. chopped onion	to package directions
2 to 3 button mushrooms, sliced	Parsley for garnish

Mix together flour and salt; dredge ostrich in flour mixture and set aside. Melt 1 to 2 tablespoons butter in a skillet. When butter reaches a medium temperature quickly brown ostrich slices. Add onions, mushrooms and garlic to skillet. Remove ostrich and mushrooms when browned. Allow onions and garlic to cook a few minutes longer. Add remaining butter and flour. Stir in broth and tomato paste; boil until sauce thickens. Just before serving add sour cream, ostrich and mushrooms to sauce and heat gently until heated through. Do not overcook ostrich. Spoon meat and sauce over noodles. Garnish with parsley.

Helen Wall, *Alden*
First Place, 2014 Ostrich: The Smart Choice

PIZZA RICE PIE

2 2/3 c. cooked rice	1/4 tsp. oregano
1/3 c. minced onion	1/4 tsp. basil
2 eggs, beaten	1 c. shredded mozzarella cheese
2 tbsp. butter, melted	4.5-oz. pkg. sliced pepperoni
8-oz. can tomato sauce	1/2 c. sliced stuffed olives

Mix together rice, onion, eggs and melted butter. Line a 12-inch pizza pan with rice mixture. Bake in 350° oven 12 minutes or until set. Spread tomato sauce over rice crust. Sprinkle with spices and cheese. Top with pepperoni and olives. Bake 20 to 25 minutes more. Remove from oven; let stand a few minutes before serving.

Phyllis Olson, *Newton*
First Place, 2014 Rice Creations – Main Dish
Third Place Overall, 2014 Rice Creations

TAMARIND PORK TACOS WITH GRILLED CORN CREMA AND CORN & BACON SLAW

For SUGARCANE MARINADE WITH TAMARIND:

1 1/2 c. dark molasses	3/4 tsp. cayenne pepper
3/4 c. Spanish sherry vinegar	1 1/2 tsp. peeled and minced
6 tbsp. fresh lemon juice	ginger
3/4 c. Creole mustard	1 1/2 tsp. grated orange zest
1 1/2 c. canned tomato sauce	1/8 tsp. minced fresh thyme
3 cloves garlic, minced	1/8 tsp. grated nutmeg
2 jalapenos, stemmed, seeded	1/2 c. tamarind pulp or paste
and minced	

In a food processor, combine all ingredients except tamarind pulp; pulse until smooth. Combine 1 1/4 cups sugarcane marinade with 1/2 cup tamarind pulp in small pot. Heat over medium-low heat, stirring to dissolve tamarind. When mixture just begins to simmer, remove from heat and pass through coarse strainer. Let cool.

For GRILLED CORN CREMA:

3 ears fresh sweet corn	Kosher salt
1 guajillo chili	Freshly ground black pepper
1 tbsp. Spanish sherry vinegar	1 tsp. annatto seeds
6 oz. smokey bacon, diced	1/2 tsp. smoked paprika
1 tbsp. olive oil	1 bay leaf, broken in half
1 poblano, stemmed, seeded	1 tsp. ground cumin seeds
and minced	1 tsp. pepper
1/2 large red onion, diced	1/2 c. fresh orange juice
1 carrot, peeled and diced	1/2 c. chicken stock
2 cloves garlic, sliced	2 c. heavy cream
1 jalapeno, stemmed, seeded	1 vanilla bean, split lengthwise
and minced	

Rub corn with a little olive oil; cook on preheated grill until nicely charred. Remove from grill and set aside to cool. When cool, cut kernels from cobs. Reserve one-third kernels for corn and bacon slaw. Toast chili in a small skillet over medium heat; remove stem and seeds. Combine vinegar and toasted chili in a small bowl; set aside to soften. In a medium pot, cook bacon in olive oil over medium-low heat until beginning to crisp. Remove two-thirds of bacon and set aside. Increase

(CONTINUED)

heat to medium; add poblano, onion, carrot, garlic, remaining corn and jalapeno. Season with salt and pepper. Cook until vegetables begin to soften, about 4 minutes. Add annatto seeds and stir. Add chili-vinegar mixture, smoked paprika, bay leaf, cumin and 1 teaspoon pepper; simmer until nearly all liquid has evaporated, 2 to 3 minutes. Add orange juice and simmer until a small amount of liquid remains, 4 to 6 minutes. Add chicken stock; reduce to a glaze, about 7 minutes. Add heavy cream and vanilla bean; stir, simmer 8 to 10 minutes, until cream is thick. Pass mixture through a fine-mesh strainer; discard solids. Reserve liquid. Refrigerate until needed; will keep 4 to 5 days.

For CORN & BACON SLAW DRESSING:

1/2 c. fresh orange juice	**2 tbsp. honey**
2 tbsp. rice vinegar	**1/2 c. blood orange olive oil**
2 tbsp. ground chipotle pepper	**Salt**
	Freshly ground pepper

Whisk together orange juice, vinegar, chipotle pepper and honey in a bowl. Whisk in oil; season to taste with salt and pepper. The dressing can be made a day in advance, covered, and kept refrigerated. Bring to room temperature before using.

For SLAW:

1 c. jicama, peeled and cut into matchsticks	**1/4 c. chopped red onion**
1 c. red cabbage, cored and shredded	**Reserved corn kernels and bacon**
1 carrot, grated	**2 tbsp. finely chopped fresh cilantro leaves**

Combine jicama, cabbage, carrot, onion, reserved corn and bacon in a large bowl. Pour dressing over jicama mixture and toss to coat well. Mix in cilantro. Let stand at room temperature 15 minutes before serving.

For CORN TORTILLAS:

2 c. masa harina (corn masa)	**1 1/4 to 1 1/3 c. water**

Mix masa harina and water; knead to form dough. Pinch off a golf-ball sized piece of masa; roll into a ball. Set masa on a piece of plastic in tortilla press; cover with another piece of plastic. Press masa in tortilla

(CONTINUED)

press. Transfer tortilla to a hot, dry skillet. Cook about 30 seconds on one side; gently turn. Cook about 60 seconds (it should puff slightly); turn back to first side. Cook another 30 seconds on first side. Remove and keep the tortilla warm.

For TACOS:

1 pork tenderloin, silver skin and fat removed
Sugarcane marinade with tamarind

Grilled corn crema
Corn & bacon slaw
Corn tortillas

Place pork tenderloin in large resealable plastic bag; pour in marinade. Seal bag and refrigerate overnight, turning bag occasionally. Using a charcoal grill prepare a medium-hot fire. When coals are ready, lightly oil grill rack. Remove pork from marinade, allowing excess marinade to fall away. Place on grill. Grill 15 to 20 minutes turning halfway until internal temperature of 145°. Allow pork to rest a few minutes on a platter. Cut crosswise into thin slices. Place a portion of sliced pork in each tortilla. Top with corn and bacon slaw and grilled corn crema. Serve additional slaw and crema on side.

Rebecca Howe, *Des Moines*
First Place, 2014 Des Moines Register's Hog (And Corn) Heaven

MY BEST SAUERKRAUT RECIPE

Salt to taste
Pepper to taste
3 lbs. pork shoulder roast, cut into 3-inch chunks
1 medium yellow onion, peeled and diced
3 c. apple juice

1 Granny Smith apple, peeled, cored and diced
1 Braeburn apple, peeled, cored and diced
3 tbsp. brown sugar
3, 14-oz. cans Bavarian style sauerkraut

Salt and pepper pork; brown in Dutch oven. Add onion; cook until onion is translucent. Add remaining ingredients to Dutch oven; cover and cook in 350° oven 3 1/2 hours. You may also cook it in a slow cooker 6 to 7 hours on high.

Scott Andreas, *Ankeny*
First Place, 2014 Iowa's Best Sauerkraut – Best Sauerkraut Recipe

GARLIC BUTTERNUT SQUASH CHICKEN CASSEROLE

For BUTTERNUT SQUASH CHICKEN CASSEROLE:

1 butternut squash
2 tbsp. orange juice
2 tbsp. butter
1 small roasted chicken
1 medium onion, chopped
1 green bell pepper, chopped
1 c. crushed crackers
Garlic cream sauce
   (recipe below)
1 egg, beaten
2 refrigerated pie crusts
2 c. shredded mozzarella cheese
Bell pepper for garnish

Cut squash in half lengthwise; remove seeds. Place in baking dish. Brush with orange juice and butter. Bake in 350° oven 70 to 80 minutes. Remove chicken from bone; place in a large mixing bowl. Once squash is cooled, remove squash from skin and add to chicken. Add onion, green pepper and cracker crumbs; set aside. Add sauce to chicken mixture and stir. Add egg and stir again. To assemble, place one crust in bottom of casserole dish and bake in 350° oven 12 minutes. Pour chicken mixture into crust and top with second crust. Bake 30 minutes or until crust is golden brown. When crust starts to brown, top with mozzarella cheese and garnish with bell peppers

For GARLIC CREAM SAUCE:

1 c. heavy cream
4 cloves garlic, minced
1/2 c. chicken broth
1/2 tsp. ground mustard
1/2 tsp. Worcestershire sauce
2 tbsp. butter
2 tbsp. sherry wine
1/2 c. shredded Swiss cheese
1/2 c. shredded sharp cheddar
   cheese
2 tbsp. all-purpose flour
1 tsp. garlic salt
2 tsp. brown sugar
1/2 tsp. cayenne pepper

In a saucepan on medium heat, combine cream, garlic, broth, mustard, Worcestershire sauce and butter. Cook and stir until smooth. Add sherry; reduce heat. Add cheeses while stirring. Next add flour, garlic salt, brown sugar and cayenne pepper. Whip vigorously until mixture thickens.

Kyle Barton, *West Des Moines*
First Place, 2015 Sunday Dinner at Mom's (Grandma's) – Main Dish
Third Place Overall, 2015 Sunday Dinner at Mom's (Grandma's)

SPICED PASTA SAUSAGE CASSEROLE

1 tsp. oregano
1 tsp. garlic powder
1 tsp. rubbed sage
1/2 tsp. onion powder
1/2 tsp. salt
1/2 tsp. pepper
1/2 tsp. chili powder
2 lbs. sage sausage
2, 15-oz. cans tomato sauce
2, 10-oz. boxes penne noodles
4 c. shredded mozzarella
　　cheese, divided

Mix spices together. Separate out about one-fourth of spice mixture and use to season sausage as you brown it. Drain and set aside. Simmer tomato sauce with remainder of the spices for 20 minutes. Add drained sausage to sauce. Cook noodles according to package instructions. Combine noodles and sauce mixture; add half the cheese. Spoon in casserole dish; top with remainder of the cheese. Bake in 350° oven just until cheese is melted; serve hot.

Deanna Wright, *Colfax*
First Place, 2014 Purnell Old Folks' Sausage Cook Off Casserole

ROCKIN' ROWAN KIELBASA CASSEROLE

1 small onion, chopped
14 oz. kielbasa, cut into bite-
　　size pieces
3 c. baked beans
3 c. pancake and baking mix
2 eggs
1 1/2 c. buttermilk
1 c. shredded sharp cheddar
　　cheese, divided

In large skillet, sauté onion until crisp-tender. Stir in kielbasa pieces; sauté 3 to 4 minutes longer or until lightly browned. Stir in baked beans; heat through. Combine baking mix, eggs and buttermilk; spread half the batter into a greased 8x8-inch baking dish. Set aside 5 minutes. Gently spoon warm meat mixture on top of batter. Sprinkle 1/2 cup of cheese on top of meat mixture. Mix remaining cheese into remaining batter. Spread gently to completely cover meat mixture. Garnish with a few kielbasa pieces. Bake uncovered in 350° oven 28 to 32 minutes. Let stand 5 minutes before serving.

Diane Rauh, *Des Moines*
First Place, 2014 Bisquick Quick Creations

CHORIZO AND CORN EMPANADAS

For FILLING:

1 c. textured soy protein
1 c. water
8 oz. soy chorizo
1 1/2 c. cooked corn kernels
8 oz. soy cream cheese

8 oz. shredded soy mozzarella
1 clove garlic, chopped
1 tsp. cumin
3/4 c. chopped roasted pepper

Put textured soy in water; let stand 10 minutes. Mix all ingredients together.

For DOUGH:

3 c. all-purpose flour
1/2 c. soy flour
1 tsp. salt

1 c. vegetable shortening
1/4 c. soy margarine
3/4 c. cold water
Paprika

Mix flours and salt; cut in shortening and soy margarine. Add enough water to moisten dough. Form dough into balls; roll to 8-inch circles. Place filling in middle; fold dough over and press edges with fork. Sprinkle with paprika. Bake in 375° oven 20 to 25 minutes.

Anita Van Gundy, *Des Moines*
First Place, 2014 It's Soy Amazing – Entrees

BREAKFAST BURRITO

10 oz. chorizo
6 eggs, beaten
Salt
Pepper
Tortilla shells

Sour cream
Salsa
Shredded cheddar cheese
Chives

Cook chorizo in skillet. When chorizo is partially cooked, add eggs, salt and pepper; cook until eggs are set. Fill tortilla with egg mixture; top with sour cream, salsa, cheese and roll up. Serve with sour cream and chives on the side.

Jasey Olson, *Des Moines*
First Place, 2014 Five Alive – Ages 6-10

MEAT LOAF

1 1/2 lbs. 85% ground beef
1/2 tsp. salt
2 eggs
1 c. bread crumbs

1 c. medium salsa, divided
6 to 9 tbsp. Mexican style
shredded cheese

In large bowl combine ground beef, salt, eggs, bread crumbs and 3/4 cup salsa. Shape into 3 oblong loaves. Create an indentation down the center of each loaf. Place in baking pans or on a rack set on baking sheet. Spoon remaining salsa into indentations. Bake in 350° oven about 1 hour. Sprinkle 2 to 3 tablespoons cheese on each loaf. Return to oven until cheese is melted.

Rita Johannsen, *Des Moines*
First Place, 2014 Cookies' Salsa Creation

BASIL CREAM CHEESE TURKEY PANINI

For BASIL CREAM CHEESE TURKEY PANINI:
Basil cream cheese spread
(recipe below)
Loaf of French bread, sliced
horizontally

1/4 lb. turkey, sliced
1/4 lb. Colby Jack cheese, sliced

Generously spread basil cream cheese spread on top and bottom halves of bread, reserving remainder of spread for other uses such as a dip with crackers. Lay turkey and cheese slices evenly over bottom half of loaf and replace top. Grill sandwich about 4 minutes in panini maker or heat in oven until cheese is melted.

For BASIL CREAM CHEESE SPREAD:
16 oz. cream cheese, softened
3 tsp. squeezable fresh basil
2 tsp. minced garlic

1 c. grated Parmesan cheese
3/4 c. olive oil
1/4 c. finely chopped walnuts

Combine cream cheese, basil and garlic in mixing bowl of stand mixer. Add Parmesan cheese, olive oil and walnuts; mix well.

Trent Gilbert, *West Des Moines*
First Place, 2014 Adventureland Resort Intermediate – Panini

GARLIC CHICKEN QUINOA AL FRESCO

1 1/4 c. quinoa
2 1/2 c. chicken broth
2 c. cherry tomatoes, quartered
2 tbsp. olive oil
7 fresh garlic cloves, peeled and
    thinly sliced
1 tsp. coconut oil
4 boneless, skinless chicken
    breasts

Pink Himalayan sea salt to
    taste
Coarsely ground black pepper
    to taste
3/4 c. freshly grated Percorino
    Romano cheese, 1 to 2 tbsp.
    reserved for garnish
1/2 c. fresh basil leaves, 1 to 2
    leaves reserved for garnish

Run water through fine mesh strainer so dry quinoa doesn't stick to it. Thoroughly rinse and drain quinoa. Pour chicken broth and quinoa into medium pot; bring to boil. Turn heat on low, cover and cook 15 minutes; let cool 5 minutes. Add tomatoes, olive oil and garlic to small pot. Cover; cook on medium-low 5 to 7 minutes or until tomatoes are very soft. Crush tomatoes to release juices. Put coconut oil in skillet. Cut chicken breasts into 3 strips and sprinkle each side with salt and pepper. Cover and cook about 4 minutes per side. Once internal temperature reaches 165°, remove from skillet. Chop into bite-size pieces. Spoon quinoa into large serving dish; pour in tomatoes. Add chicken, salt, pepper and grated cheese. Stir to melt cheese. Finely chop basil; stir in and garnish with remaining cheese and basil. Serve hot or chilled.

Holly Houg, *Urbandale*
First Place, 2015 Chicken Cuisine – Adult

LUNCH WRAPS OF LOVE

2 Romaine lettuce leaves
4 slices oven roasted turkey

6 pieces smokey bacon cheddar
    cheese
4 kosher baby dill pickles

Lay out lettuce leaves; place 2 slices of turkey on each leaf. Put 3 pieces of cheese on turkey with space between for pickles. Place 2 pickles in spaces between cheese. Roll up leaves to create wrap.

Grace Whitlow, *Johnston*
First Place, 2014 My Grandparent's Favorite Food – Main Dish/Side Dish
First Place Overall, 2014 My Grandparent's Favorite Food

FRESH PASTA WITH SAUSAGE AND BUTTERNUT SQUASH IN ROASTED RED PEPPER SAUCE

For FRESH PASTA WITH SAUSAGE AND BUTTERNUT SQUASH:

3 tbsp. olive oil, divided
1 lb. hot Italian sausage
1 c. chopped onion
5 garlic cloves, thickly sliced
1 tbsp. chopped basil
1 tbsp. chopped fresh sage
1/2 c. white wine
1 1/2 c. butternut squash,
   peeled, seeded and cut into
   1/2-inch dice

1/2 c. chicken stock
2 c. roasted red pepper sauce
   (recipe below)
2 tbsp. salt
1 recipe fresh pasta
6 tbsp. Parmesan cheese
2 tbsp. softened butter

Pour 1 tablespoon olive oil into large skillet; cook over high heat 2 minutes. Remove casing from sausage; add sausage to hot oil. Cook about 3 minutes until brown. Using back of a wooden spoon, break sausage into small, bite-size pieces while browning. Remove from heat. Using slotted spoon, place sausage in a bowl; cover and set aside. Keep about 1 tablespoon oil left in the pan; discard remainder. Add remaining 2 tablespoons olive oil to the pan; cook over medium heat 3 minutes. Add onion, garlic, basil and sage; cook 4 minutes, stirring well, until onion and garlic start to brown. Add reserved sausage; cook 2 more minutes, stirring well. Add wine and deglaze the pan. Cook 5 minutes more, stirring well to dislodge brown bits at bottom of pan. Add butternut squash; cook 2 minutes, stirring well. Add chicken stock, bring to a boil over high heat. Reduce heat and allow to simmer 30 minutes until squash is tender. Stir in roasted red pepper sauce; heat through. While sauce is cooking, bring a large pot of water to a boil; add salt. When water reaches rolling boil, add pasta and cook until al dente (2 to 3 minutes). When pasta is cooked, drain well. Pour pasta back into pot, add sauce; cook over medium heat 3 to 5 minutes, stirring constantly. Remove pan from heat; add Parmesan cheese and softened butter. Serve.

(CONTINUED)

MAIN DISH

For ROASTED RED PEPPER SAUCE:

3 whole roasted red bell peppers
1/2 c. chopped onion
2 cloves garlic, minced

2 to 3 tbsp. minced fresh herbs
of choice
1 c. tomato puree
3/4 c. heavy cream

Puree peppers with onion, garlic and herbs; add tomato puree. Cook on top of stove 10 to 15 minutes. Add cream; cook over low heat additional 10 to 15 minutes. Do not boil.

For FRESH PASTA:

3 c. Semolina flour

4 large eggs

Place flour in bowl, make well in center. Break eggs into well. Beat eggs with fork; gradually start working in flour, a little at a time. When dough becomes sticky, begin kneading, working in more flour as necessary, until dough is smooth and pliable. Cover and let rest at least 30 minutes. Roll out dough until thin. You can use a pasta machine or a rolling pin. Cut dough into desired shapes. If not cooking immediately, toss with a little flour to keep pasta from sticking together.

Rebecca Howe, *Des Moines*
First Place, 2014 Perfect Pasta

SWEET CORN COB SANDWICHES

1/2 c. melted butter
1/2 c. granulated sugar
2 eggs
1 c. buttermilk
1 c. cornmeal
1 c. all-purpose flour

1/2 tsp. baking soda
1/2 tsp. salt
2 c. frozen corn
1/3 c. cream cheese
1/3 c. pepper jelly

Combine butter and sugar in bowl with whisk. Add eggs then buttermilk. Combine dry ingredients; gradually add to wet mixture. Mix in corn. Pour into greased corn cob pans. Bake in 375° oven 8 to 12 minutes. When cool, spread cream cheese on half of corn cobs and spread pepper jelly on other half. Place together to form sandwiches.

Clarissa Ridgway, *Johnston*
First Place, 2015 Locally Grown - Iowa Fresh – Teens (ages 13-17)

DREAMS ARE MADE OF PENNE

1 1/2 lbs. Italian sausage
1 large yellow onion, chopped
1 large clove garlic, minced
1/2 large red sweet bell pepper, diced
1/2 green bell pepper, diced
13.25-oz. box pasta, cooked
3 tbsp. olive oil
1/2 c. water, reserved from cooking pasta
1 1/2 tsp. salt-free spicy seasoning
1/2 tsp. black pepper
1/3 c. grated Parmesan cheese

In large skillet, brown sausage. Add onions, garlic, red and green peppers. Cook, stirring until onion and peppers are softened. Add hot pasta; mix well. Drizzle olive oil over top; mix to blend. Add pasta water and seasonings; mix well. Sprinkle with Parmesan cheese; gently mix. Serve with extra Parmesan cheese. Garnish with parsley and cherry tomatoes if desired.

Marianne Carlson, *Jefferson*
First Place, 2014 My Best Dreamfield's Pasta Dish

STUFFED PORK LOIN

4 lbs. pork loin
1 c. packed dark brown sugar
1/2 to 1 c. Cajun seasoning
2 tbsp. crushed red pepper
3 large onions, peeled and sliced
1/2 lb. bacon, cut in 1-inch pieces
2 Granny Smith apples, finely chopped
1 c. diced onions
1/2 c. coarsely chopped pecans
1/2 c. raisins
3 tbsp. butter

Cut slit length of loin on fat side. Mix brown sugar, Cajun seasoning and red pepper together in large resealable plastic bag. Place loin in bag; refrigerate 12 to 24 hours. Place onions and bacon in bottom of Dutch oven. Mix apples, onions, pecans and raisins with butter. Stuff into slit on loin. Place loin fat side up on top of onions and bacon in Dutch oven. Roast in 350° oven 1 1/2 to 2 hours or until internal temperature of pork loin reaches 140° to 150°.

Ron Groenendyk, *Cedar*
First Place, 2014 Dutch Oven Cooking – Main Dish/Side Dish
Second Place Overall, 2014 Dutch Oven Cooking

IOWA STATE FAIR CORNY CRABBY QUICHE

1 1/4 c. all-purpose flour
1/2 c. cold butter
3 tbsp. cold water
6 eggs
2 1/2 c. light cream
1/4 tsp. nutmeg
1 c. shredded hard cheese

5 slices bacon, cooked crisp
  and chopped
2 c. cooked fresh peaches and
  cream sweet corn
1/2 c. coarsely chopped jumbo
  lump crab
2 tbsp. chopped red bell pepper

Sift flour and cut in butter until mixture has consistency of cornmeal. Move mixture to one side of bowl; using fork, rake approximately one-sixth of mixture into other half. Add 1 tablespoon water and combine. Repeat with remainder of water. Roll out piecrust; place in 9-inch pie plate. Beat eggs until frothy. Add cream and nutmeg; beat well. Layer ingredients into pie shell starting with cheese, then bacon, corn, crab and chopped pepper. Pour egg mixture over the layers. Bake in 375° oven 45 minutes or until knife inserted near center comes out clean.

Jamie Buelt, *Polk City*
First Place, 2014 Fresh Corn Cuisine – Main Dishes
Third Place Overall, 2014 Fresh Corn Cuisine

EGG SALAD FOR SANDWICHES

2 oz. cream cheese, softened
1/3 c. mayonnaise
1 to 2 tbsp. mayonnaise-style
  salad dressing
1/4 tsp. salt
1/4 tsp. pepper
1/4 tsp. curry powder

6 hard cooked eggs, finely diced
1/4 c. very finely chopped celery
1/4 c. very thinly sliced green
  onion
1/3 c. very thinly chopped red
  bell pepper
1 clove garlic, very finely
  chopped

Mix together cream cheese, mayonnaise, salad dressing, salt, pepper and curry powder. Fold in eggs, celery, green onion, red bell pepper and garlic. Serve on bread of your choice.

Louise Piper, *Garner*
First Place, 2015 Egg-ceptional Eggs – Sandwiches, Salads and Sides
Third Place Overall, 2015 Egg-ceptional Eggs

CARAMELIZED ONION AND GARLIC PASTA

1/4 c. butter, cubed
2 large sweet onions, thinly sliced
1/4 tsp. crushed red pepper flakes
1/8 tsp. salt
8 cloves garlic, minced
2 c. grape tomatoes, halved
1/4 c. red wine
1/4 c. olive oil, divided
16-oz. pkg. uncooked angel hair pasta
9 strips bacon, cooked, drained and crumbled
2/3 c. shredded Parmesan cheese
1/2 tsp. ground pepper
Fresh basil leaves for garnish

In a large skillet, over medium-high heat, melt butter. Add onions, pepper flakes and salt; sauté until onions are tender. Stir in garlic. Reduce heat to medium-low; cook, stirring occasionally, 30 to 40 minutes or until onions are deep golden brown. Add grape tomatoes, red wine and 2 tablespoons olive oil to skillet. Cook pasta according to package directions. Drain pasta; toss with onion mixture. Drizzle with remaining olive oil. Sprinkle with bacon, Parmesan cheese and pepper; heat through. Garnish with fresh basil.

Linda Asbille, *Indianola*
First Place, 2014 Barilla Pasta & Sauce – Entrée

DILL PICKLE CHEESEBURGER POCKETS

For FILLING:
1 lb. ground beef
1/2 c. chopped onion
1/2 tsp. garlic salt
1/4 tsp. salt
1/4 tsp. pepper
1/4 c. all-purpose flour
1/2 c. catsup
1 tbsp. mustard
1/3 c. pickle juice
2 tbsp. Worcestershire sauce
1 1/2 c. baby dill pickles, chopped in 1/2-inch pieces
6 oz. shredded cheddar cheese
1 egg, beaten

Brown ground beef with onion and garlic salt. Add salt and pepper to taste. Add flour, catsup, mustard and pickle juice; cook 2 minutes. Add Worcestershire sauce and pickles; remove from heat. Add cheese and egg; stir well. Cool slightly.

(CONTINUED)

For PASTRY:

2 c. all-purpose flour	2 eggs, divided
1 tsp. salt	3/4 c. cold water
2/3 c. shortening	1 tsp. vinegar

Mix flour and salt; cut in shortening. Combine 1 egg, water and vinegar. Add enough liquid to make dough stick together. Make 10 balls; chill 30 minutes. Roll out each ball to 6-inch circle. Beat remaining egg; brush around edge of circle. Place 1/4 cup filling on circle. Fold in half and seal edges with fork. Brush with egg. Bake in 350° oven 25 minutes until golden brown.

Anita Van Gundy, *Des Moines*
First Place, 2015 Picklicious Recipes with Gedney Pickles
First Place Overall, 2014 Barilla Pasta & Sauce

MAC N' CHEESE WITH
BEER BREAD CRUMBS & BACON!

1 lb. macaroni noodles	8 oz. Monterey Jack cheese,
8 tbsp. butter, divided	grated
1/2 c. all-purpose flour	2 oz. gouda, grated
2 c. beer of choice	1 tsp. white pepper
2 c. half and half	1 tsp. ground mustard
8 oz. cream cheese, cubed	1 tsp. Worcestershire sauce
8 oz. sharp cheddar cheese,	1 tsp. salt
grated	4 slices thick cut bacon
	2 c. beer bread crumbs

Cook macaroni according to package directions; drain and set aside. Melt 6 tablespoons butter in large pot. Slowly add flour while whisking. Allow to cook 2 minutes while whisking. Add beer, half and half and cream cheese; whisk until melted. Add other cheeses, one at a time; whisk until melted. Add pepper, mustard, Worcestershire and salt to sauce. Pour macaroni into sauce; stir to combine. Pour into 3-quart dish; set aside. Fry bacon; drain and dice. Sprinkle on top of macaroni and cheese. Melt remaining butter; stir in bread crumbs. Sprinkle over bacon. Bake in 375° oven 30 minutes.

Amy Kruzich, *Ankeny*
First Place, 2015 Cooking with Iowa Craft Beer

BACON BAKED POTATOES

8 potatoes
8-oz. pkg. cream cheese
1 c. sour cream
1/2 c. butter
1/2 tsp. minced fresh garlic
1/2 tsp. pepper

1 1/4 c. shredded Monterey
   Jack cheese, divided
1/4 c. buttermilk
1/8 c. chopped parsley
1 lb. bacon, fried and drained
Parsley for garnish

Bake potatoes in 350° oven 60 to 70 minutes. Remove from oven; let cool briefly. Cut in half and carefully scoop out potato from skin; place potato in a mixing bowl. Set aside potato skins. Beat together all ingredients except 1/4 cup of cheese; mix until well blended. Place potato filling back into potato shells. Place on baking sheet. Top with reserved 1/4 cup cheese; cover loosely with foil and bake in 350° oven 20 minutes. Uncover; bake 10 minutes more.

Lana Ross, *Indianola*
First Place, 2014 Puckerbrush Potluck – Salad/Entrée

CHILI CON CARNE

1 onion, chopped
1 red bell pepper, chopped
2 jalapenos, chopped
2 cloves garlic, minced
Oil or bacon fat
1 lb. ground beef
1 lb. sausage
3 lbs. smoked brisket
3, 15-oz. cans diced tomatoes
8 oz. beef broth

8 oz. beer
2 oz. crushed tortilla chips
15-oz. can kidney beans
1/2 c. medium chili powder
1 tsp. ground cumin
1 tsp. oregano
1 tsp. whole coriander, ground
1 tsp. smoked black
   peppercorns, ground
2 bay leaves

Sauté onion, pepper, jalapenos and garlic in oil or bacon fat 2 to 3 minutes. Place in slow cooker. In same skillet, brown ground beef and sausage. Combine with ingredients in slow cooker. Cook on high 6 hours. Remove bay leaves before serving.

Matthew Phoenix, *Ankeny*
First Place, 2015 Allspice Chili
First Place, 2015 Mrs. Grimes Chili Cook Off

GRANDMA'S CHICKEN AND NOODLES

2 eggs
2 tbsp. milk
1 to 2 c. all-purpose flour

3 c. chicken broth
1 c. cooked chicken
Dash of salt and pepper

Mix together eggs and milk; add enough flour so dough is easy to handle and not sticky. Roll dough out on floured surface in a rectangle. Roll up from long side; cut slices to make noodles about 1/4-inch thick. When finished, shake noodles out on a sheet pan; dust with flour so they do not stick to each other. Set aside. In a large pan, bring chicken broth to boil. Add noodles, a handful at a time, while stirring. Once all noodles are in pot, add chicken. Let noodles simmer 15 to 20 minutes until tender and broth has thickened. Salt and pepper to taste.

Quinn Harbison, *Ames*
First Place, 2015 My Grandparents' Favorite Foods – Main Dish/Side Dish
First Place Overall, 2015 My Grandparents' Favorite Foods

CLASSIC STRATA WITH CRISPY BACON AND CHEESES

2 c. shredded Swiss cheese
6 strips bacon, cooked and
    crumbled
3 tbsp. sliced green onion
4 eggs, slightly beaten
1 1/2 c. light cream
1/2 tsp. salt

Dash of pepper
Dash of nutmeg
2 tbsp. grated Parmesan cheese
2 small tomatoes, peeled and
    sliced
1/2 c. bread crumbs

Sprinkle Swiss cheese, bacon and onion on bottom of greased pan. Beat together eggs, cream, salt, pepper and nutmeg. Pour over bacon mixture; sprinkle with Parmesan cheese. Bake in 375° oven 15 to 18 minutes until slightly set. Cover sliced and peeled tomatoes in bread crumbs; place on top of strata. Return to oven 15 to 20 minutes more or until knife inserted near center comes out clean. Cool slightly; serve warm.

Lisa Dekowski, *Cedar Rapids*
First Place, 2015 Cockadoodle-Do Casserole – Breakfast/Brunch Casserole

CANDY CORN BACON MAC-N-CHEESE

3/4 c. packed dark brown sugar
3/4 tsp. crushed red pepper
1 lb. bacon
8 oz. macaroni noodles, cooked
1 c. peaches and cream fresh
    sweet corn
14.75-oz. can cream style corn
1/2 lb. cheddar cheese, grated

Kosher salt, to taste
Coarse ground black pepper,
    to taste
1/4 c. butter
3 tbsp. all-purpose flour
2 c. whole milk, room
    temperature
1/2 lb. young gouda, grated and
    room temperature

Grease baking rack with vegetable oil; place inside a rimmed baking sheet. Combine brown sugar and red pepper in a bowl. Coat one side of bacon with sugar mixture; place sugar side up, flat on rack. Sprinkle remaining sugar on top. Bake in 350° oven 30 minutes or until crisp. Chill 5 to 10 minutes before chopping. Grease 9x13-inch baking dish. In a large bowl combine chopped bacon, noodles, fresh corn, cream corn, cheddar cheese, salt and pepper. In a saucepan, melt butter on medium-low heat; whisk in flour. Whisk in milk; slowly add gouda until melted and smooth. Do not overheat. Add cheese sauce to mixture; pour into baking dish. Bake in 350° oven 50 to 60 minutes or until golden brown.

Deb Bolfik, *Des Moines*
First Place, 2014 Beginner's Contest – Main Dish
Third Place Overall, 2014 Beginner's Contest

WALNUT BURGER

For WALNUT BURGER:
5 eggs, beaten
1 c. cottage cheese
2 tbsp. fresh basil
1 tsp. kosher salt
1/2 tsp. pepper
3/4 c. chopped onion

1 c. grated mozzarella cheese
2 c. bread crumbs
1/2 c. regular rolled oats
1 tsp. Italian seasoning
1 c. ground walnuts

Mix all ingredients in a bowl; let rest 15 minutes. Form into patties; place in freezer. When ready to bake, remove from freezer, place on greased broiler pan. Bake in 350° oven 35 to 45 minutes. Serve with walnut spread.

(CONTINUED)

For WALNUT SPREAD:

2 tbsp. mayonnaise or
    mayonnaise-style salad
    dressing

1 tbsp. catsup
2 tbsp. toasted walnuts

Blend in food processor.

Lana Shope, *Indianola*
First Place, 2015 Create a Winner with Gurley's – Other Baked Items

MAC N' CHEESE WITH A ZING!

3 c. elbow macaroni noodles
5 tbsp. butter, divided
1 white onion, chopped
1 jalapeno, chopped
5 cloves garlic, minced
1 c. heavy cream
1 c. whole milk
1 tsp. prepared mustard
1/2 tsp. Worcestershire sauce
2 tbsp. all-purpose flour
2 c. shredded cheddar cheese,
    divided

1 1/2 c. shredded young gouda,
    divided
2 c. shredded bacon cheese
1 1/2 c. shredded chili pepper
    cheddar cheese
2 tsp. chili powder
1/2 tsp. cumin
1 1/2 tsp. brown sugar
1 1/2 tsp. salt, divided
1 c. panko bread crumbs

Boil macaroni in water 8 minutes; remove from heat and rinse with cold water. In a saucepan, combine 3 tablespoons butter, onion, jalapeno, garlic, cream, milk, mustard and Worcestershire sauce. Simmer on medium heat 10 to 15 minutes. Transfer to food processor; puree and pour back into saucepan. Stir in flour, 1 cup cheddar cheese, 1/2 cup gouda, bacon cheese, chili pepper cheese, chili powder, cumin, brown sugar, 1/2 teaspoon salt and noodles to the sauce mixture and stir. Place in a baking dish; bake in 350° oven 15 minutes. While baking, melt remaining butter in skillet. Add bread crumbs and remaining salt. Stir until crumbs and butter are well combined. Remove dish from oven; add remaining cheddar and gouda to top. Top with bread crumb mixture. Bake 10 to 15 minutes more.

Kyle Barton, *West Des Moines*
First Place, 2014 All Iowa Raised Mac N' Cheese
First Place, 2015 All Iowa Raised Mac N' Cheese

CHEESY PASTA AND ITALIAN SAUSAGE PATTIES

4 oz. jumbo pasta shells
Olive oil
9 oz. sharp cheddar processed
    American cheese, cubed and
    divided
1/3 c. half and half

1/2 tsp. minced garlic
1/4 c. chopped onion
1/4 tsp. ground pepper
Pinch of salt
2/3 lb. Italian sausage

Boil jumbo shells until tender; drain. Toss with olive oil; set aside. Melt 8 ounces of cubed cheese with half and half. When creamy, add garlic, onion, ground pepper and salt. Pour over shells; mix well. Set aside and keep warm. Finely dice remaining cheese; mix with Italian sausage. Form patties; cook covered in skillet over medium heat 5 to 7 minutes. Turn and continue cooking another 5 to 7 minutes or until juices run clear. Serve patties with pasta.

Bryon Preminger, *Runnells*
First Place, 2015 Kraft Kreations with Velveeta – Entrée
Third Place Overall, 2015 Kraft Kreations with Velveeta

HEARTY POTATO BAKE

For FILLING:
3 slices bacon, cut into 1-inch
    pieces
1 large orange sweet potato
1 tbsp. butter
Freshly grated nutmeg to taste
1/2 lb. strawberry potatoes,
    thinly sliced

2 oz. butterkase cheese (or
    hard cheese such as gouda
    or cheddar), grated
1 yellow sweet potato,
    thinly sliced
1/4 c. chopped Genoa salami

Cook bacon in skillet until crispy. Drain and set aside; reserve drippings. Peel, slice and cook large orange sweet potato in water. When potato is tender, remove from water; place in pie plate. Mash with butter and freshly grated nutmeg. Place bacon on top of sweet potatoes; layer with strawberry potatoes. Cover with sauce; sprinkle grated cheese on top. Layer yellow sweet potato over grated cheese. Sprinkle with chopped salami. Cover with more sauce and more cheese.

(CONTINUED)

MAIN DISH

For SAUCE:

1 clove garlic, chopped	1/4 c. quick mixing flour
2 shallots, finely chopped	1/2 c. heavy cream
3 fresh sage leaves, chopped	1 tsp. coarse salt
1 sprig fresh rosemary, chopped	2 1/2 c. chicken stock

Sauté garlic, shallots and fresh herbs in bacon drippings until shallot is translucent. Add flour, cream and salt to form paste. Quickly stir in chicken stock. Simmer until thick. If sauce gets too thick, add more stock or water.

For CRUST:

1/4 c. cold lard	1/2 tsp. salt
1/4 c. cold unsalted butter	1 tsp. minced garlic
1 1/4 c. all-purpose flour	3 tbsp. cold water
	1 beaten egg

Work lard and butter into flour, salt and garlic. Add cold water; knead dough into a ball. Flatten and roll out. Place on top of potatoes; brush beaten egg over top. Bake in 350° oven 50 to 60 minutes.

Jamie Buelt, *Polk City*
First Place, 2014 Spotlighting Spuds – Main Dishes
Second Place Overall, 2014 Spotlighting Spuds

RUBBED BEEF TENDERLOIN

2 tsp. kosher salt	1 tbsp. Worcestershire powder
1 tbsp. coarsely ground black pepper	2 tbsp. vegetable oil
2 tsp. smoked hot paprika	2 lbs. beef tenderloin roast, trimmed and tied
1 tsp. garlic powder	

Mix all spices together. Rub oil over beef. Rub spice mix into the beef. Wrap in plastic wrap; refrigerate several hours or overnight. Cook over hot coals, turning frequently, to an internal temperature of 128°. Let rest 20 minutes. Slice and serve warm. Will be rare to medium rare.

Cheryl Rogers, *Ankeny*
First Place, 2014 Allspice Rub – Beef Rub Blend
First Place Overall, 2014 Allspice Rub

MAIN DISH

GERMAN APPLE PANCAKE

4 eggs
1/2 c. unbleached all-purpose
    flour
1/2 tsp. baking powder
1/2 c. plus 1 tbsp. granulated
    sugar, divided
Pinch of salt
1 c. milk
1 tsp. vanilla

2 tbsp. unsalted butter,
    melted
1 tsp. ground nutmeg,
    divided
1/4 c. unsalted butter
1/2 tsp. ground cinnamon
1 large tart apple, peeled,
    cored and sliced

In large bowl, blend eggs, flour, baking powder, 1 tablespoon sugar and salt. Gradually mix in milk, stirring constantly. Add vanilla, melted butter and 1/2 teaspoon nutmeg. Let batter stand 30 minutes or overnight. Melt 1/4 cup butter in 10-inch oven-proof skillet, brushing butter up on sides of pan. In small bowl, combine 1/4 cup sugar, cinnamon and 1/2 teaspoon nutmeg. Sprinkle mixture over butter. Line pan with apple slices. Sprinkle remaining sugar over apples. Place pan over medium-high heat until mixture bubbles. Gently pour batter mixture over apples. Bake in 425° oven 15 minutes. Reduce heat to 375°; bake 10 minutes more. Slide pancake onto serving platter; cut into wedges.

Rebecca Howe, *Des Moines*
First Place, 2015 Eggs Around the World, Breakfast
First Place Overall, 2015 Eggs Around the World

BESSIE'S CHICKEN AND NOODLES

For CHICKEN AND CHICKEN STOCK:
1 fresh chicken
1 to 2 tsp. salt
2 carrots, sliced

1/2 medium onion, chopped
2 to 3 stalks celery, chopped

Cook chicken in water with 1 to 2 teaspoons salt. When fully cooked (180° internal temperature), remove from water and remove meat from bone; set aside. After removing chicken, add vegetables to make stock. Boil until vegetables are fully cooked. Either discard cooked vegetables or puree and return to stock.

(CONTINUED)

For NOODLES:

3 c. all-purpose flour, sifted	2 tsp. rubbed sage
3 eggs, beaten	1/2 tsp. marjoram
3 to 4 tbsp. water	1/2 tsp. ground thyme
1/2 tsp. kosher salt	1 tsp. dried rosemary
	1/2 c. heavy cream

Make noodles by sifting flour into a bowl. Make a well; place beaten eggs and water in well. Work mixture together with a fork. Place on floured surface; knead dough about 15 minutes. Cover with bowl; allow dough to rest 10 minutes. Cut dough into four sections and roll out flat. Once flat, roll dough and trim ends. Cut into 1/8 to 1/4-inch slices. These noodles are more like dumplings and will be thick. Bring stock to boil. Add noodles and stir. Reduce heat and simmer at least 20 minutes. Add chicken back to pot along with spices and cream. Bring back to boil; reduce heat and simmer 45 minutes longer. Serve over mashed potatoes.

Jamie Buelt, *Polk City*
First Place, 2014 Old Threshers Family Reunion

HARVEST BRAID

2 1/4 c. all-purpose flour	2/3 c. orange marmalade,
1/4 tsp. salt	divided
1/4 c. butter	1 c. sliced apples
1 tbsp. baking powder	6 slices Havarti cheese
1 c. milk	1/3 c. chopped pecans
1 lb. sweet apple chicken	1/3 c. dried cranberries
sausage	

Combine flour, salt, butter, baking powder and milk in a mixer with dough hook until ball forms; roll out dough. Remove casing from sausage and brown in skillet. Spread 1/3 cup marmalade down center of dough; top with apples, cheese and sausage. Add half of pecans and cranberries. Make 3/4-inch diagonal slices along the sides of filling. Fold the strips over filling, alternating sides, until whole loaf is braided. Seal the ends. Bake in 375° oven 15 minutes; brush with remaining marmalade and top with remaining pecans and cranberries. Bake an additional 20 minutes or until nicely browned.

Natalie Ridgway, *Johnston*
First Place, 2015 Locally Grown - Iowa Fresh – College/Adult

STUFFED PUFF PASTRY

12 large eggs, divided
1 tsp. salt
1 tsp. black pepper
1 1/2 lbs. sausage
1/4 c. olive oil, divided
1 red pepper, chopped
1 green bell pepper, chopped

1 onion, chopped
8 oz. shredded mild cheddar
  cheese
17.3-oz. pkg. frozen puff pastry
1 tsp. garlic powder
1 tsp. parsley

In a medium bowl, whisk together 11 eggs, salt and pepper; set aside. In large skillet, cook sausage over medium heat, stirring occasionally, until browned and crumbled. Drain and set aside. Using same skillet, heat 2 tablespoons olive oil over medium heat. Add peppers and onion, stirring occasionally until tender. Remove from pan; set aside. Heat remaining oil; add egg mixture and cook, stirring often, until eggs are set but not dry. Remove from heat; spoon into a large bowl. Add sausage mixture and cheese, mixing to combine. On a lightly floured surface, roll each pastry sheet into a 12x10-inch rectangle. Using a sharp knife, trim pastry, cutting slits 1-inch apart and 1-inch from filling on both sides. Spoon half the egg mixture down center of each sheet leaving 1-inch border. Starting at one end fold pastry strips over sausage mixture, alternating sides to cover filling. Place on parchment paper-lined baking sheet. In a small bowl, beat remaining egg and brush tops of pastry. Sprinkle each with garlic powder and parsley. Bake in 400° oven 25 to 30 minutes. Cut into eight slices and serve.

Connie Schaffer-Sherman, *Pleasant Hill*
First Place, 2014 Purnell Old Folks' Sausage Cook Off – Breakfast

---

SMOKEY MEATLOAF

For GLAZE:
1 c. catsup
1/2 c. cider vinegar
6 tbsp. brown sugar

2 tsp. hot sauce
1 tsp. coriander

Combine all glaze ingredients in a saucepan; simmer 5 to 10 minutes.

(CONTINUED)

For MEATLOAF:

3/4 c. glaze, divided
   (recipe above)
1/4 c. catsup
3 tbsp. Worcestershire sauce
1 tbsp. soy sauce
30 saltines, finely crushed
2 lbs. bacon, divided
1 onion, chopped
1 jalapeno, chopped

3 cloves garlic, minced
4 eggs
1 tbsp. spicy brown mustard
1/3 c. chopped parsley
1/2 tsp. salt
1/2 tsp. pepper
3/4 lb. ground beef
3/4 lb. ground pork

Combine 1/4 cup glaze, catsup, Worcestershire, soy sauce and saltines to form a panade; set aside. Dice 1/2 lb. bacon; brown diced bacon in skillet. Drain, reserving bacon fat. Sauté onion, jalapeno and garlic in reserved bacon fat; drain. Add browned bacon, cooked vegetables, eggs, mustard, parsley, salt and pepper to panade. Mix in beef and pork; form into loaf shape. Weave remaining 1 1/2 lbs. bacon into a lattice on a baking pan. Brush with 1/4 cup glaze. Place loaf on bacon lattice and roll up until completely covered. Smoke 60 to 90 minutes at 350° to an internal temperature of 165°, brushing on 1/4 cup glaze during final 10 minutes. Serve with remaining glaze.

Matthew Phoenix, *Ankeny*
First Place, 2015 My Favorite Meat Loaf

LA "CAUSA" DE TITA DENEGRI

5 lbs. yellow potatoes
2 tbsp. salt
4 fresh squeezed limes
2 tbsp. aji Amarillo paste
   (Peruvian yellow pepper)

2 tbsp. canola oil
4 avocados
2 c. chicken salad
2 tbsp. mayonnaise
2 hard boiled eggs

Boil potatoes until soft; peel and mash. Thoroughly mix potatoes, salt, lime juice, aji Amarillo paste and oil. In a 4-inch deep pan, layer half the potato mash, avocado, chicken salad and remaining potato. Spread mayonnaise on top. Grate hardboiled eggs over mayonnaise.

Matthew Chapman, *Ankeny*
First Place, 2015 Spotlighting Spuds – Main Dishes
First Place Overall, 2015 Spotlighting Spuds

JAMAICAN JERK CHICKEN LETTUCE WRAPS

1 tsp. coconut oil
1 1/2 tbsp. Jamaican jerk rub, divided
4 boneless, skinless chicken breasts
1 1/2 c. finely shredded Monterey Jack cheese
1/4 c. sour cream
1 small red bell pepper, finely diced
1/4 c. coarsely chopped fresh cilantro, several leaves reserved for garnish
1 lime, divided, several slices reserved for garnish
12 small romaine lettuce leaves

Put oil in bottom of 10-inch skillet. Sprinkle 1 tablespoon Jamaican jerk rub on both sides of chicken breasts. Cook chicken about 4 minutes per side, until internal temperature is 165°; finely chop chicken. In a medium bowl, combine chicken, cheese and remaining 1/2 tablespoon of rub; stir until cheese is melted. Add sour cream, red pepper and cilantro. Cut lime in half; juice half the lime and add to chicken mixture. Lay out lettuce leaves on serving platter. Spoon about 3 tablespoons chicken mixture into each leaf. Slice remaining lime half and use to garnish. Use remaining cilantro to garnish. Serve slightly warm or chilled.

Carson Houg, *Urbandale*
First Place, 2015 Chicken Cuisine – Youth

SPICY IOWA PORK LOIN
WITH GINGER-MAPLE SAUCE

For PORK LOIN:
2 tsp. chili powder
1 tsp. ground cinnamon
1 tsp. black pepper
1/2 tsp. salt
1/4 tsp. ground allspice
1 lb. pork tenderloin
1/2 tsp. olive oil

In small bowl, combine chili powder, cinnamon, pepper, salt and allspice. Rub over pork loin. In large skillet, brown pork on all sides in olive oil. Transfer to an 11x17-inch baking dish coated with cooking spray. Bake uncovered in 375° oven 15 minutes; add sauce. Bake 10 to 15 minutes longer or until meat thermometer reads at least 160° throughout entire loin. Let cool 5 to 10 minutes prior to slicing.

(CONTINUED)

For SAUCE:

1/2 c. chopped onion	1/2 c. chicken broth
1 tbsp. butter	1/2 tbsp. maple extract
1 tsp. minced fresh gingerroot	1 tbsp. diced crystalized ginger

In small skillet sauté onion in butter until tender. Add gingerroot; sauté 1 to 2 minutes longer stirring in chicken broth, maple extract and ginger. Bring to boil; cook sauce until reduced to approximately 1/2 cup. Pour over pork.

Joshua Calhoun, *Des Moines*
First Place, 2014 My Favorite Tone's Recipe – Everyday Family Recipe

PEACHES AND CREAM FRENCH TOAST BAKE

4 firm ripe peaches	12 large eggs
1 c. packed brown sugar	1 1/2 c. half and half
1/2 c. butter, cut up	1 tsp. vanilla
2 tbsp. pure maple syrup	1/2 c. slivered almonds, toasted
16-oz. loaf day-old French	1 tbsp. powdered sugar
bread, cut in 1-inch cubes	1/4 tsp. ground nutmeg
8-oz. pkg. cream cheese	

Score the bottom of each peach with a paring knife, making an "x" on bottom of each one. Fill a medium saucepan half full with water; bring to a boil. Add peaches; return to boiling and then reduce heat. Gently simmer 5 minutes. Remove peaches, peel and cut into slices (you should have 2 cups). In a medium saucepan, combine brown sugar, butter and maple syrup. Cook and stir over medium heat until brown sugar is dissolved. Pour brown sugar mixture into greased 9x13-inch baking dish. Arrange cooked, sliced peaches on top of brown sugar mixture. Place half the bread cubes over peaches. Layer with cream cheese and remaining bread cubes. In a large bowl, whisk together eggs, half and half and vanilla; pour over bread layers in dish. Cover and refrigerate overnight. Remove from refrigerator; let stand 30 minutes at room temperature before baking. Top with slivered almonds. Bake, uncovered, in 350° oven 50 to 60 minutes, or until top is golden and filling is set. Combine powdered sugar and nutmeg; sprinkle over top before serving.

Teresa Nolte-Pinkert, *Stuart*
First Place, 2014 Cockadoodle-Do Casserole

SWEET & SPICY TUNA BURGERS WITH PEANUT BUTTER SAUCE

For SWEET & SPICY TUNA BURGERS:

5-oz. can chunk light tuna
  in water, drained
1 egg
1/2 slice white bread, crumbled

4 slices hot and sweet pickle
  chips, chopped
1/8 tsp. ground black pepper
1/8 tsp. garlic salt

Mix all ingredients well; form into 2 patties. Cook in frying pan sprayed with nonstick spray over medium-low heat until lightly browned.

For SAUCE:

1 tbsp. creamy peanut butter

2 tbsp. juice from hot and sweet
  pickles

Warm for about 30 seconds in microwave; spread over tuna patties.

Brenda Becker, *Pella*
First Place, 2014 Quality, Not Quantity

CHOCOLATE FRIED CHICKEN

2/3 c. kosher salt
2 tbsp. brown sugar
2 heaping tbsp. chocolate
  spread
1/2 tbsp. instant coffee
4 c. water
4 c. ice cubes
Salt to taste
1 whole fresh chicken
2 c. buttermilk
Oil for frying

2 c. all-purpose flour
1/2 c. unsweetened cocoa
  powder
1 tbsp. instant coffee granules
2 tbsp. salt
1 1/2 tbsp. black pepper
1/2 tsp. cayenne pepper
2 tsp. garlic powder
2 tsp. onion powder
3 eggs

In a 4-quart Dutch oven, mix kosher salt, brown sugar, chocolate spread, instant coffee and water. Bring to a boil; boil until chocolate spread melts completely, 5 to 10 minutes. Remove from heat. Place ice in large container; add chocolate mixture and stir to cool. Cut chicken into 10 pieces: 2 wings, 2 legs, 2 thighs and 4 breast pieces (cut breast in half).

(CONTINUED)

Place chicken in the chocolate mixture; cover and refrigerate overnight. Drain and rinse chicken under cold water; rinse container. Pour buttermilk into container; add chicken. Toss to coat the pieces. Cover and refrigerate for another overnight. Place oil in electric fryer/skillet and heat to 375°. In a large bowl mix flour, cocoa, coffee granules, salt, pepper, cayenne, garlic powder and onion powder until well combined. In separate bowl, beat eggs. Remove chicken from buttermilk and drain excess. Dredge chicken in flour mixture. Dip chicken in beaten egg then back into flour mixture. Place chicken on a cookie sheet; let stand 10 minutes. Fry chicken in hot oil 12 to 15 minutes or until the internal temperature reaches 180°. Chicken will look dark from the cocoa in the crust. Remove chicken from fryer; drain on a rack.

Lisa Alessandro, *Winterset*
First Place, 2014 Innovative Chocolate

TEX-MEX MEATBALL PIE

For PIE CRUST:

1 1/2 c. all-purpose flour	**1 egg**
1/2 tsp. salt	**1 tsp. vinegar**
1/2 c. shortening	**1/2 c. cold water**

Mix flour and salt; cut in shortening. In separate bowl, mix egg, vinegar and water. Add enough liquid mixture to flour mixture to make dough stick together. Chill 30 minutes; roll out and place on baking sheet.

For FILLING:

12-oz. pkg. tomato basil chicken meatballs	**3/4 c. shredded Mexican cheese**
1 c. fresh corn	**1 c. shredded lettuce**
3/4 c. salsa	**1/2 c. sour cream**

Place meatballs in center of pie crust. Mix corn and salsa; pour over meatballs. Fold crust over filling. Bake in 375° oven 35 to 40 minutes. Sprinkle with cheese; bake 5 minutes more. Top with lettuce and sour cream.

Anita Van Gundy, *Des Moines*
First Place, 2015 Best Al Fresco Dish – Chicken Sausage Entrée,
Appetizer, or Breakfast

FLARIN' SOUTHWEST STYLE TACO

For MEAT:
2 lbs. ground beef
3/4 c. Italian sausage
29 oz. tomato sauce
10 oz. salsa
12-oz. can creamy tomato soup
2, 15-oz. cans chili beans
1 onion, finely chopped
1 green pepper, finely chopped
1 jalapeno, finely chopped
10-oz. can diced tomatoes with
    green chilies

4 tbsp. chili powder
1 tbsp. pasilla chili powder
1 tbsp. Ancho chili powder
1 tbsp. minced garlic
1 tbsp. dextrose powder
2 tbsp. brown sugar
1 tsp. chipotle powder
1 tsp. ground celery
1 tsp. ground oregano
1 tsp. salt

Combine all ingredients in a stockpot; cook on a low boil 2 hours. Stir every 5 to 10 minutes. Drain meat mixture.

For TACO:
2 tbsp. oil
3 flour tortillas
1/2 c. shredded Colby Jack
    cheese
1/2 c. shredded Monterey Jack
    cheese

3/4 c. garlic sour cream
    (recipe below)
1 1/2 c. shredded lettuce
1 c. chopped onions
1/2 c. chopped tomatoes
1/3 c. chives

Heat oil in skillet. Cook tortillas on each side 1 to 2 minutes until golden brown. Place in a taco rack; add a small layer of cheese on bottom of tortilla shell to prevent meat from making tortilla soggy. Place approximately 1/2 cup meat mixture in each shell. Add sour cream and lettuce. Place onions on lettuce and top with a small amount of tomatoes and chives. Garnish as desired.

For GARLIC SOUR CREAM TOPPING:
1 c. sour cream
1 c. mayonnaise
1 tbsp. dried onion flakes
1 tbsp. dried garlic chunks

1 tsp. jalapeno powder
1/4 c. chopped jalapeno and
    onion, mixed
Pinch hot chili powder

Combine all ingredients; mix well.

Kyle Barton, *West Des Moines*
First Place, 2014 World's Greatest Taco

GAME DAY CHILI

2 tbsp. ground cumin
1 tbsp. ground ancho chili
    pepper
2 tsp. hot chili pepper
2 tsp. cayenne pepper
1 tsp. crushed red pepper flakes
1 tbsp. ground black pepper
2 tsp. salt
1 lb. beef ribs
2 c. chopped white onion

1 tbsp. minced garlic
1 tbsp. olive oil
1 1/2 lbs. ground beef
1 jalapeno pepper, diced
15-oz. can chili beans
2, 15-oz. cans diced tomatoes
15-oz. can tomato sauce
15-oz. can white hominy
1 tbsp. chili lime hot sauce

In a small bowl, combine all dry spices; set aside. Place light coating of spice mix on beef ribs, reserving remaining mix. Sear all sides of ribs over high heat on a grill. Reduce heat to low; turn heat off under meat. Cook 20 minutes off heat. Remove and let rest 10 minutes; thinly slice meat and set aside. In a 10-quart stockpot cook onion, garlic and olive oil over medium heat until soft. Remove to bowl. Brown ground beef over medium heat in same pot. Add jalapeno and remaining spices; mix well. When all spices are combined into meat, add onions back into chili. Add meat from ribs, chili beans, tomatoes, tomato sauce, white hominy and hot sauce; stir to combine. Simmer 30 minutes; serve.

Ryan Jones, *Polk City*
First Place, 2015 Mother Podolak's Chili

FARMER MEATLOAF

1 lb. ground beef
1/2 lb. ground pork
1 egg
1/4 c. milk
1 tbsp. catsup
1/2 tbsp. prepared mustard

1/2 tsp. thyme
1/2 tsp. sage
1 tsp. garlic powder
1 tbsp. onion powder
1/2 tsp. smoked paprika
1/2 tsp. salt
4 slices dry bread, crumbled

Mix together all ingredients; mix well. Shape into loaf; place in loaf pan. Bake in 350° oven until thermometer registers 150°.

Timothy Farmer, *Nevada*
First Place, 2014 Adventureland Resort Intermediate – Meatloaf

GRANDMA OSTENDORF'S MEATLOAF

For MEATLOAF:

2/3 c. regular rolled oats
1 1/2 lbs. ground beef
1/4 c. chopped onion
1/8 tsp. pepper

1 c. milk
2 beaten eggs
1 tsp. salt
1 tsp. sage

Mix all ingredients and let stand a few minutes to let oats absorb the milk; place in loaf pan and cover with sauce.

For SAUCE:

3 tbsp. brown sugar
1/4 tsp. nutmeg

1/4 c. catsup
1 tsp. dry mustard

Combine all ingredients; spread over loaf. Bake in 350° oven 1 hour.

Lonnie Hartstack, *Clarinda*
First Place, 2014 Nostalgic Comfort Food – Main Dish
Second Place Overall, 2014 Nostalgic Comfort Food

BEEF CURRY IN SWEET PEANUT SAUCE WITH COCONUT RICE

For BEEF CURRY IN SWEET PEANUT SAUCE:

2 1/2 c. coconut milk, divided
3 tbsp. red curry paste
3 tbsp. Thai fish sauce
2 tbsp. palm sugar
2 lemongrass stalks, bruised
1 lb. sirloin steak, cut into thin strips

1/3 c. creamy peanut butter
1 red jalapeno, minced
5 kaffir lime leaves, torn
Salt and freshly ground black pepper
Thai basil leaves, for garnish

Put half the coconut milk into a large pan. Heat gently, stirring constantly, until milk begins to boil and separate. Add red curry paste; cook over medium heat until fragrant. Add fish sauce, palm sugar and lemongrass. Continue to cook until color of the curry deepens. Add remaining coconut milk; bring back to a boil. Add beef and peanut butter; cook 8 to 10 minutes. Add jalapeno and kaffir lime leaves; adjust seasoning. Garnish with Thai basil leaves.

(CONTINUED)

For COCONUT RICE:

1 c. jasmine rice
13-oz. can coconut milk
5 kaffir lime leaves

1 sprig Thai basil, plus more for
garnish

Place all ingredients in a medium pan; bring to boil, stirring occasionally. Cover, reduce heat and cook 15 minutes. Remove from heat, let stand 5 minutes, then fluff with fork. Remove kaffir lime leaves and basil before serving.

Rebecca Howe, *Des Moines*
First Place, 2014 Can You Curry That

HAM LOAF CUPCAKES
WITH SWEET POTATO TOPS

For HAM LOAF:

1/2 lb. ground ham
1/2 lb. ground pork
1 c. bread crumbs

1 egg, well beaten
1 c. milk
1/4 c. barbecue sauce

Mix together meat and bread crumbs; add egg and milk. Spray cupcake tin with cooking spray. Fill 6 cupcake spaces with a level amount of meat. Brush tops with barbecue sauce. Bake in 350° oven 25 minutes. Allow 10 minutes to cool; gently remove from pan.

For SWEET POTATOES:

2 sweet potatoes, peeled
2 tbsp. butter
1/2 tsp. cinnamon

1/4 tsp. nutmeg
3/4 c. half and half
Bacon pieces and chives

Cut potatoes into chunks; place in a medium saucepan in water. Boil until potatoes are tender; drain. Return potatoes to pan; add butter until melted. Add cinnamon and nutmeg and mix. Add half and half; continue to mix until well combined. Fit a piping bag with a large star tip and fill with potatoes. Pipe mashed potatoes onto each ham loaf cupcake like frosting. Garnish with bacon pieces and chives.

Diane Rauh, *Des Moines*
First Place, 2014 My Favorite Meat Loaf

GLAZED SALMON WITH CRISPY TOPPING

1 1/2 lbs. salmon fillet, thawed
2 tsp. sesame oil
Kosher salt
Black pepper
2 tbsp. chili powder
1/4 c. lime juice
1/2 c. peach mango habanero
   jam

Remove any scales still on skin of salmon; remove skin from fillet (in one piece if possible). Rub both sides of skin with sesame oil; sprinkle lightly with salt and pepper. Lay on parchment-lined baking sheet. Bake in 325° oven 30 to 40 minutes until crispy; set aside to cool. Cut salmon fillet cross-wise into 3-inch wide fillets. Combine chili powder and lime juice to make a paste. Rub on all sides of fish; refrigerate 30 minutes. Place fillets on rack over baking sheet. Bake in 400° oven 4 minutes. While baking, heat peach mango habanero jam to a semi-liquid consistency. Remove fillets from oven; brush liberally with jam. Return to oven 4 to 6 minutes more (for medium rare salmon) until glaze is bubbly. When ready to serve, slice crispy skin into thin strips. Garnish as desired and serve with basmati rice.

Cheryl Rogers, *Ankeny*
First Place, 2015 Wildly Wonderful Popsie Salmon

LOBSTER FRA DIAVOLO

2 live lobsters (about 1 lb. each)
1/4 c. extra-virgin olive oil
1 medium onion, chopped
1/2 green bell pepper, chopped
4 cloves garlic, minced
2 tsp. crushed red pepper flakes
2 tbsp. tomato puree
28-oz. can tomatoes, drained
2 tbsp. minced fresh basil
2 tbsp. fresh parsley
1 tsp. minced fresh oregano
1/4 tsp. smoked sweet paprika
1/2 tbsp. brown sugar
1 tbsp. rice wine
2 tbsp. sherry wine
4 oz. cream cheese
1/2 c. heavy cream
Salt
Pepper
1 lb. linguini pasta
1/3 c. shredded white cheddar
   cheese

Bring large pot of water to boil. Add lobsters; boil 2 minutes. Using tongs, transfer lobsters to cutting board. Cut off claws and crack open. Remove meat from tails and cut into bite-size pieces; set aside. Heat oil

(CONTINUED)

in saucepan over medium heat. Add onion, pepper, garlic and pepper flakes. Sauté until vegetables are soft, about 10 minutes. Stir in tomato puree, diced tomatoes, basil, parsley, oregano and paprika; simmer about 10 minutes. Stir; add brown sugar, rice wine and sherry wine. Reduce heat; add cream cheese and cream to tomato mixture. Add half the lobster pieces to mixture. Season with salt and pepper. Cook pasta in pot of boiling salted water to al dente. Drain pasta and return to pot. Stir in cheese; add to lobster-tomato mixture. Divide pasta among plates. Top with tomato-lobster sauce. Divide remaining lobster evenly among plates and place on top of sauce. Garnish with parsley and Parmesan.

Kyle Barton, *West Des Moines*
First Place, 2015 Dei Fratelli Tomato Creations

GARDEN SANDWICHES

For STRAWBERRY SANDWICHES:

1/3 c. cream cheese, softened	**3 slices white bread**
1/2 tsp. lemon juice	**4 to 5 strawberries, sliced thin**
2 tbsp. powdered sugar	

Blend cream cheese with lemon juice and powdered sugar. Spread thin layer on bread. Lay strawberry slices on cream cheese. Refrigerate 1 hour. Trim crust and cut into small squares or circles. If desired, add chopped crystallized ginger to cream cheese.

For VEGETABLE SANDWICHES:

1/3 c. cream cheese, softened	**2 to 3 cherry tomatoes, sliced**
1/2 tsp. lemon juice	**1 medium cucumber, peeled and**
1/2 tsp. chopped chives	**sliced thin**
1/2 tsp. chopped cilantro	**4 small radishes, thinly sliced**
4 slices white bread	

Blend cream cheese with lemon juice, chives and cilantro. Spread thin layer on bread. Top with tomatoes, cucumbers and radishes. Refrigerate sandwiches 1 hour. Trim crust and cut into small squares or circles.

Pat Felderman, *Pleasant Hill*
First Place, 2015 Let's Have Tea – Tea Sandwich (adult)
First Place Overall, 2015 Let's Have Tea

MY FAVORITE CHILI

1 lb. ground beef
1 lb. ground pork
1 onion, chopped
1 red bell pepper, chopped
1/2 c. chopped celery
1 clove garlic, minced
Salt and pepper to taste
3 tbsp. chili powder
1 tbsp. cumin
2 tbsp. brown sugar

14.5-oz. can tomatoes
1 c. salsa
4.5-oz. can green chilies
2, 15-oz. cans chili beans
15-oz. can black beans
15-oz. can beef broth
10-oz. can chicken broth
6-oz. can tomato paste
1 tbsp. masa flour
1/2 c. water

Brown beef and pork; add onion, pepper, celery and garlic. Cook 10 minutes; add salt, pepper and spices. Add brown sugar, tomatoes, salsa, chilies, beans, broths and tomato paste. Cook on low 1 to 2 hours. During last 10 minutes of cooking time, mix masa with water and add to chili.

Anita Van Gundy, *Des Moines*
First Place, 2015 My Favorite Chili

CRANBERRY APPLE SPICY MEATBALLS

For CRANBERRY APPLE SPICY MEATBALLS:

2 c. original flavor bread crumbs
1 medium onion, finely chopped
1 sweet red bell pepper, finely
    chopped
1 medium Granny Smith apple,
    chopped
2 eggs, lightly beaten
1/2 c. canned pumpkin
1/2 c. catsup

2 tsp. garlic powder
1 tsp. salt
1 tsp. pumpkin pie spice
3/4 tsp. pepper
1/2 tsp. crushed red pepper
    flakes
1 lb. medium spicy Iowa
    pork sausage

In a large bowl, combine bread crumbs, onion, pepper, apple, eggs, pumpkin, catsup, garlic powder, salt, pumpkin pie spice, pepper and red pepper flakes. Crumble meat; add to mixture and mix well. Shape into 1-inch balls. Place meatballs on greased racks in shallow baking pans. Bake, uncovered, in 375° oven 15 to 20 minutes or until no longer pink. Drain on paper towels.

(CONTINUED)

For SAUCE:

**14-oz. can wholeberry
    cranberry sauce
1 c. frozen cranberries
12-oz. jar apple jelly**

**3/4 c. catsup
1/2 tsp. crushed red pepper
    flakes
1 tsp. amaretto extract**

In a Dutch oven, combine all ingredients; bring to a boil. Reduce heat; simmer, uncovered, 10 minutes. Gently stir in meatballs; heat through.

Jacqueline Riekena, *West Des Moines*
First Place, 2014 Christmas Favorites

ENCHILADA PIE

For ENCHILADA PIE:

**1 lb. ground meat
1 tbsp. all-purpose seasoning
1/2 c. taco sauce
1 tbsp. taco seasoning (recipe
    below)
16-oz. can enchilada sauce**

**16-oz. can refried beans
Tortilla shells
1 c. cooked Spanish rice
2 c. shredded Mexican cheese
Medium salsa**

Brown meat in skillet; add seasoning. Drain; add taco sauce and taco seasoning. Prepare sauce by mixing enchilada sauce and beans together. In a greased pie pan, spread layer of sauce on bottom of pan. Place tortilla on top of sauce. Layer meat, sauce, rice, cheese and tortilla shell. Repeat layering. Bake in 350° oven about 5 minutes or until cheese is melted and shells start to crisp. Let rest about 10 minutes. Serve with favorite salsa or enchilada sauce.

For TACO SEASONING:

**1/4 c. chili powder
3 tbsp. paprika
3 tbsp. cumin**

**4 1/2 tsp. garlic powder
1 tbsp. salt
Dash of cayenne**

Combine all ingredients in a bowl and mix together. Store in a mason jar for best freshness. One tablespoon seasoning equals one packet of store-bought seasoning.

Mick Wise, *Des Moines*
First Place, 2014 My Best Dish
First Place, 2014 Cooking with Cookies' Sauces and Seasonings

CITRUS GLAZED GRILLED CHICKEN WITH MIXED-GRAIN SALAD

For CITRUS GLAZE:

3/4 c. fresh orange juice
1/4 c. fresh lemon juice
1/4 c. fresh lime juice
1/4 c. chicken stock
1 clove garlic, minced
2 tbsp. orange marmalade

2 tbsp. soy sauce
1 tbsp. rice wine vinegar
1 tbsp. light brown sugar
1 tbsp. butter
Pinch kosher salt
Freshly cracked black pepper

Bring all ingredients to boil in medium-sized saucepan over medium heat, stirring to melt marmalade and keep mixture from burning. Reduce heat to a simmer; let glaze reduce until syrup consistency, about 15 to 20 minutes. Adjust seasonings with salt and pepper to taste.

For GRILLED CHICKEN

4 boneless, skinless chicken
   breasts
Extra-virgin olive oil, for
   brushing

Kosher salt
Freshly cracked black pepper
Mixed greens

Heat grill to medium-high heat. Brush chicken with olive oil just before grilling. Season with salt and pepper to taste. Grill chicken 10 to 12 minutes, turning often, until breasts are done (165° to 170°). Brush with glaze during final few minutes of cooking. Remove from heat; brush chicken with remaining glaze before serving. Top mixed-grain salad with chicken breast.

For MIXED-GRAIN SALAD:

2 tbsp. vegetable oil
1/4 c. chopped shallots
1/2 c. brown rice
1/2 c. wild rice
1/2 c. wheat berries
1 c. water
1 c. chicken stock

1/3 c. dried cranberries
1/4 c. chopped dried apricots
1/4 c. dried currants
1/2 c. coarsely chopped pecans
Salt
Pepper

Heat oil in large saucepan over medium-high heat. Add shallots and sauté until translucent, about 5 minutes. Add brown rice, wild rice and

(CONTINUED)

wheat berries; stir to coat. Add water and stock; bring to boil. Reduce heat to low. Cover and cook until grains are tender and liquid is absorbed, about 40 minutes. Remove from heat; stir cranberries, apricots and currants into grains. Cool to room temperature. Stir pecans into salad; pour dressing over salad and toss. Season with salt and pepper.

For ORANGE-BALSAMIC DRESSING:

1/3 c. orange juice	**1 1/2 tbsp. grated orange zest**
1 1/2 tbsp. white balsamic vinegar	**1 1/2 tsp. ground cumin**
	1/4 c. olive oil

In food processor, blend all ingredients except oil. When well-blended, slowly add oil; process until emulsified.

Rebecca Howe, *Des Moines*
First Place, 2015 Quality Not Quantity

CHICKEN ENCHILADA MAC N' CHEESE

6 oz. enchilada sauce	**6 oz. canned corn**
6 oz. evaporated milk	**12 oz. shredded sharp cheddar cheese**
2 eggs	**6 oz. shredded Monterey Jack cheese**
1 tsp. kosher salt	
1/2 tsp. black pepper	**4-oz. can diced green chilies**
1/2 tsp. chili powder	**2 tbsp. chopped cilantro, plus extra for garnish**
1/2 tsp. cumin	
1/2 lb. chicken breast	**1/2 c. sliced green onions**
1/2 lb. elbow macaroni noodles	**Chopped tomatoes**
4 tbsp. butter	

Whisk enchilada sauce, evaporated milk, eggs and seasonings together until well combined; set aside. Boil chicken breasts in 3 quarts water until center is no longer pink; remove from water and shred. Bring water back to a boil; add macaroni. Cook to al dente. Drain pasta; discard water. Return pot to low heat and add macaroni, butter and corn; stir until butter has melted. Add evaporated milk/egg mixture; slowly add cheeses. Stir until smooth and creamy. Stir in chilies, chicken, cilantro and onion. Once well combined, garnish with tomato and cilantro.

Amy Smith, *Winterset*
First Place, 2015 Adventureland Resort Intermediate – Macaroni & Cheese

STEAK RUB

1 tbsp. black smoked whole
   peppercorns, ground
1 tbsp. hickory smoked sea salt
1 tsp. Worcestershire powder
1 tsp. lemon pepper

2 tsp. roasted garlic powder
2 tsp. granulated onion
1/4 tsp. chipotle chili brown
   powder

Combine all ingredients; apply generously to oiled steaks. Grill to desired doneness.

Matthew Phoenix, *Ankeny*
First Place, 2015 Allspice Rub & Marinade – Steak Rub
First Place Overall, 2015 Allspice Rub & Marinade

PINEAPPLE RUM CHICKEN KABOBS

For PINEAPPLE RUM CHICKEN KABOBS:

20-oz. can crushed pineapple
12-oz. jar pineapple rum sauce,
   divided
1/2 tsp. pepper flakes

2 lbs. chicken breasts, cubed
Fresh pineapple, cubed
Bell peppers, cubed (red, yellow
   green)
Red onion, cubed

Place pineapple, half the pineapple rum sauce and pepper flakes with chicken into a resealable plastic bag. Allow to marinate in refrigerator overnight. Place chunks of chicken on skewer alternating with cubed fresh pineapple, peppers (green, yellow and red) and red onion. Grill or broil 10 minutes. Turn; brush with sauce and grill 5 minutes longer or until juices run clear. Serve with rice.

For SAUCE:

1/2, 12-oz. jar pineapple rum
   sauce
1/4 c. honey

1/2 c. packed brown sugar
Garlic
Salt
Pepper

Combine all ingredients in small saucepan. Cook until brown sugar has dissolved. Brush on kabobs.

(CONTINUED)

For RICE:
2 c. rice
4 c. water

Small pinch saffron

Cook rice in water according to package directions. Add small pinch of saffron for color.

Rose Ridgway, *Johnston*
First Place, 2015 Sauce It Up With Pampered Chef

GRANDPA BOB'S FAVORITE FARM FIELD EGG SALAD SANDWICH

8 oz. cream cheese, softened
2 tbsp. corn
3 green onions, chopped, divided
1/2 tbsp. fresh cilantro
2 tbsp. coarsely chopped celery
2 tbsp. butter, softened
4-oz. can diced green chilies, drained
2 tbsp. heavy cream
6 large hard boiled eggs, sliced
1/2 c. pineapple chunks, sliced and drained on paper towel
1/4 tsp. sea salt
1/8 tsp. cayenne pepper
1/8 tsp. ground black pepper
1 tbsp. prepared mustard
1/4 c. mayonnaise or mayonnaise-style salad dressing
2 dashes hot pepper sauce
1/8 tsp. ground mustard
1/8 tsp. garlic powder
1/8 tsp. white pepper
Fresh spinach leaves
1/4 c. spinach
1/4 c. sliced cucumbers
Tomato slices

Using a food processor, cream together cream cheese, corn, 1 green onion, cilantro, celery, butter, green chilies and heavy cream. After combining, refrigerate at least 2 hours. Combine eggs, remaining green onions, pineapple, sea salt, cayenne pepper, ground black pepper and prepared mustard. Add mayonnaise, hot pepper sauce, ground mustard, garlic powder and white pepper. Combine cream cheese mixture with egg salad mixture and make a sandwich with choice of bread. Add spinach, cucumbers and fresh tomato slices.

Pamela Reynolds, *Norwalk*
First Place, 2015 Nostalgic Comfort Food – Main Dish
First Place Overall, 2015 Nostalgic Comfort Food

CHICKEN RUB

1 1/2 tsp. black smoked whole peppercorns, ground
1 tsp. hickory smoked sea salt
1 tsp. chervil
1 tsp. granulated onion
1 tsp. roasted garlic powder
2 tsp. crushed Aleppo chili
1/2 tsp. rosemary powder
1/2 tsp. ginger powder
1 tsp. annatto powder
1 tsp. smoked sweet paprika

Combine all ingredients. Apply generously to oiled chicken. Smoke or grill to 165° internal temperature.

Matthew Phoenix, *Ankeny*
First Place, 2015 Allspice Rub & Marinade – Chicken Rub

WEEKEND EGGS

1 lb. pork sausage with sage
5 to 6 green onions, sliced
2 to 3 small sweet peppers, diced
1 c. frozen hash brown potatoes
12 eggs, lightly beaten
1 1/2 c. shredded sharp cheddar cheese

Sauté pork sausage, green onions and sweet peppers. Remove from heat and drain. In large bowl, combine all ingredients. Place in two 1 1/2 to 2 quart casserole dishes. Bake in 325° oven 30 minutes.

Mary Tibbetts, *Urbandale*
First Place, 2015 Egg-ceptional Eggs – Quiches, Stratas & Casseroles
Second Place Overall, 2015 Egg-ceptional Eggs

PROVOLONE AND PORK TACOS

For PROVOLONE SHELL:
6 round provolone cheese slices
1/2 tsp. cumin
1/2 tsp. chili powder
1/2 tsp. garlic powder
1/2 tsp. onion powder

Lay cheese on parchment-lined baking sheet. Sprinkle with seasonings. Bake in 350° oven 12 minutes. Immediately place on side of pan so they cool in a taco shell shape.

(CONTINUED)

For PORK FILLING:

1 lb. pork tenderloin
1 large onion, diced
3 c. chopped cilantro
1 bay leaf
1 tbsp. olive oil

4 c. chicken stock
1 jalapeno, minced
1/4 tsp. cumin
2 tbsp. butter, melted

Place all ingredients in slow cooker; cook on high 8 hours. Remove bay leaf; shred pork. Fill shells with pork and top with toppings of choice.

For PICO DE GALLO:

2 tomatoes
1 onion
1 jalapeno

2 tbsp. lime juice
Salt
Pepper

Chop tomato, onion and jalapeno. Toss with lime juice; season with salt and pepper to taste.

Natalie Ridgway, *Johnston*
First Place, 2015 World's Greatest Taco

RICE AND BLACK BEAN BURGERS

6-oz. pkg. roasted red pepper
   flavored brown rice and
   quinoa
1 tbsp. oil
1 medium onion, chopped
1 c. diced zucchini

1/2 c. diced red bell pepper
1 tbsp. minced garlic
15.5-oz. can black beans,
   drained
1 1/2 c. bread crumbs

In a small saucepan, prepare rice according to package directions; set aside to cool. In separate pan combine oil, onion and zucchini. Quickly brown. Add red pepper and garlic. Place beans in food processor; lightly pulse to break up beans. Place beans, rice and vegetables in large bowl; form patties. To help keep patties together, coat with bread crumbs. Fry in large skillet or on grill until brown on both sides. Serve with lettuce and tomatoes. For added spice, serve with hot sauce.

Belinda Myers, *Osceola*
First Place, 2015 Rice Creations – Main Dish
Third Place Overall, 2015 Rice Creations

YUMMY PARTY PIZZA

For DOUGH (makes enough for two 14-inch thin-crust pizzas):

3 c. all-purpose flour
1 pkg. instant yeast
2 tbsp. pizza dough flavor
   powder

1 tsp. kosher salt
1 c. warm water
1 tbsp. olive oil

Place flour, yeast, dough flavoring and salt in bowl of food processor. Pulse to combine. Add water and oil; process until mixture comes together into a ball. Cover with plastic wrap; refrigerate at least 1 hour and up to 24 hours.

For TOPPINGS (for one 14-inch pizza):

2 c. shredded mozzarella cheese
1/4 c. grated Parmesan cheese
2 tbsp. chopped fresh basil
2 tbsp. chopped fresh oregano
2 tsp. dried Italian herb mixture
3 tbsp. sundried tomato pesto
1/4 c. finely diced red bell
   pepper

1/4 c. finely diced green bell
   pepper
1/2 c. thinly sliced yellow onions
8 oz. Italian sausage, browned
   and finely crumbled
1 mushroom slice for every
   square you will cut
1/4 c. toasted pine nuts

In a small bowl, combine mozzarella cheese, Parmesan cheese, basil, oregano and dried herb mixture; set aside. Divide dough into two portions. Reserve one for another use. Each portion should make one 14-inch pizza with a fairly thin crust. Punch down; let rest 10 minutes on a floured board. Roll dough out in a circle. Let rest 5 minutes; re-roll until it holds the desired size and thickness. Transfer crust to parchment; place on pizza stone that has been preheated 15 minutes at 500°. Bake 7 minutes. Remove from oven. Spread sundried tomato pesto thinly over crust. Sprinkle with half of cheese and herb mixture. Next add bell peppers, onions and sausage distributing evenly. Top with remaining cheese mixture. Place one mushroom slice in center of each square you plan to cut. Sprinkle pine nuts over pizza; return to parchment-covered pizza stone and bake 7 to 10 minutes until nicely browned. Let stand 10 minutes before cutting into party squares.

Cheryl Rogers, *Ankeny*
First Place, 2015 Casey's General Stores' Pizza Competition

CALLA LILY SANDWICHES

2 1/2 oz. garlic and herb cream
    cheese
1 1/2 oz. cream cheese, softened
1/8 c. finely chopped toasted
    walnuts
Dash of cayenne pepper

Dash of black pepper
24 slices white bread
Paprika
2 carrots, peeled
Green onions

Combine cream cheeses, walnuts, cayenne pepper and pepper. Beat at medium speed until creamy. Cut circles from bread; roll out to 1/8-inch thickness with rolling pin. Spread 1 teaspoon cream cheese mixture onto each bread round. Sprinkle center with paprika; fold bottom of bread round over, pinching to seal. Cut small pieces of carrot; place in center of each sandwich for a flower stamen. Sprinkle a little paprika around it. Garnish with green onion to form stem.

Joseph Ridgway, *Johnston*
First Place, 2015 Kids Favorite Sandwich (ages 9-12)
First Place Overall, 2015 Kids Favorite Sandwich

QUEEN BEE'S HONEY DO THIS... BBQ SAUCE

1/2 c. turbinado raw sugar
1 1/2 tsp. restaurant black
    pepper
1 tsp. kosher flake salt
1/2 tsp. granulated garlic
1 tsp. American chili powder
2 tsp. smoked paprika
1 tsp. ground cinnamon

1/2 tsp. onion powder
2 tsp. cayenne pepper
1/4 c. apple cider vinegar
2 c. catsup
1/2 c. molasses
1/2 c. honey
2 tsp. liquid smoke

Heat all ingredients in large pan stirring often until it begins to boil. Reduce heat; simmer approximately 20 minutes. Pour into jars; let cool to room temperature before refrigerating. Allow sauce to refrigerate overnight allowing flavors to blend.

Emlin Schnathorst, Jr., *Norwalk*
First Place, 2015 Mine Is The Best BBQ Sauce

TACO SALAD

16 oz. cottage cheese
1/2 c. 1/8 cut cherry tomatoes
1/2, 2.25-oz. can sliced black
   olives (cut each in half)
1/2 c. chopped red onion
2 tbsp. chopped jalapeno
4 cloves garlic, minced
1/2 c. shredded sharp cheddar
   cheese

2 tbsp. finely chopped chives
2 tsp. chili powder
Pinch cumin
2 to 3 large lettuce leaves for
   garnish
1 c. crushed spicy tortilla chips
Green onions or chives
   for garnish
Tortilla chips for garnish

Place cottage cheese in mixing bowl. Place cherry tomatoes on paper towel to dry. Stir olives, tomatoes, onion and jalapeno into cottage cheese; add garlic, cheese and chives. Stir in spices. Let stand in refrigerator 1 hour. Create a lettuce bed for cottage cheese mixture. Sprinkle crushed tortilla chips on top; add green onions or chives for garnish. Serve with tortilla chips around cottage cheese mixture.

Kyle Barton, *West Des Moines*
First Place, 2014 Land O'Lakes Colossal Cottage Cheese Salad

CHEESY ZUCCHINI QUICHE

For CHEESY ZUCCHINI QUICHE:
2 tbsp. extra virgin olive oil
2 to 3 small zucchini, rinsed
   and chopped
1 red onion, chopped
Sea salt

Ground pepper
1 1/2 c. milk
5 eggs, lightly beaten
1/4 tsp. nutmeg
1 c. grated cheddar cheese
Baked 9-inch pie crust

Heat olive oil in large pan over medium-high heat. Cook zucchini until soft, about 8 to 9 minutes. Add onion and cook until translucent and fragrant, about 5 to 7 minutes. Drain off excess oil. Season with salt and pepper; set aside. In a medium bowl, mix milk and beaten eggs; add nutmeg. Spread vegetables evenly in crust; slowly pour in egg mixture. Cover top with cheddar cheese. Bake in 350° oven 35 to 40 minutes or until crust is golden brown and cheese is bubbly. Let cool 10 minutes and serve warm.

(CONTINUED)

For PIE CRUST:

2 1/2 c. all-purpose flour	6 tbsp. shortening, chilled and
1 tsp. salt	cubed
8 tbsp. unsalted butter, chilled	5 to 7 tbsp. ice water
and cubed	1 1/2 tsp. cider vinegar

In a large bowl, stir together flour and salt. With pastry blender or 2 knives, cut in butter and shortening until mixture resembles coarse crumbs with pea-sized pieces. Slowly add 5 tablespoons of water and vinegar, stirring until dough comes together. If dough is dry, sprinkle with additional water. Form into a flat round. Cover and refrigerate at least 1 hour or up to 2 days. Roll out to fit lightly greased 9-inch pie plate. Bake 10 minutes in 450° oven; remove from oven and reduce heat to 350°.

Rhonda Paul, *Des Moines*
First Place, 2015 Quiche Me In The Morning

GLUTEN FREE TACO CASSEROLE

1 lb. pork sausage	1/2 c. sliced olives
3 c. gluten-free penne pasta	2 tbsp. cilantro
3 c. shredded sharp cheddar	1 c. gluten-free tomato-based
cheese, divided	homestyle dressing
1 c. 1/4 cut cherry tomatoes	2 c. gluten-free nacho chips
1 red onion, finely chopped	Green onion, for garnish
1 jalapeno, finely chopped	

Cook sausage until golden brown; drain and set aside. In a stockpot, boil pasta about 10 minutes or until tender. Strain cooked pasta with cold water; add to mixing bowl. Combine with sausage. Add 2 cups cheese, tomatoes, onions, jalapeno, olives, cilantro and dressing. Stir until well combined. Pour into greased casserole. Bake in 350° oven 15 to 20 minutes until cheese is melted and casserole is heated through. Remove from oven; sprinkle with chips. Garnish with green onion.

Kyle Barton, *West Des Moines*
First Place, 2015 Dorothy Lynch Gluten Free Cooking

IOWA SWEET CORN CHILI

1 1/2 lbs. top sirloin seasoned
    with Texas-style barbeque
    rub
1 1/2 lbs. ground beef
1 sweet yellow onion, diced
1 green pepper, diced
3 c. cooked Iowa sweet corn
    kernels
4.5-oz. can green chilies,
    undrained
12-oz. jar jalapeno peppers,
    undrained
12-oz. jar mild pepper rings,
    undrained
15-oz. can chili beans,
    undrained
15-oz. can spicy hot chili
    beans, undrained

15-oz. can dark kidney beans,
    drained
15-oz. can light kidney beans,
    drained
4, 14.5-oz. cans stewed
    tomatoes, undrained
15-oz. can tomato sauce
2, 1.25-oz. pkgs. chili seasoning
1 c. packed brown sugar
1 c. granulated sugar
1 tsp. oregano
2 tsp. sage
1 tsp. cayenne pepper
3 tbsp. Worcestershire sauce
1 tbsp. black pepper
6 to 8-oz. beer of choice

Grill sirloin until cooked medium. In skillet, combine ground beef, onion and green peppers. Brown ground beef. While beef is browning put all remaining ingredients except beer into large kettle on medium heat. Cube cooked sirloin; add to the kettle. When ground beef is browned and onions/peppers are sautéed, drain and add to kettle. Bring to a boil, stirring often; reduce heat to low. Add beer and simmer 30 minutes.

Chris Pike, *Johnston*
First Place, 2014 Coach's Favorite Chili

POTATO-COVERED HAM AND SWISS LOAF SURPRISE

For SAUCE:
10.75-oz. can tomato soup
1/2 c. packed brown sugar
1/2 c. water

1/2 c. cider vinegar
2 tbsp. dry mustard

Mix ingredients in a saucepan; bring to a boil. Reduce heat and simmer 20 minutes until thickened.

(CONTINUED)

For POTATO-COVERED HAM AND SWISS LOAF SURPRISE:

2 lbs. ham loaf meat mixture	2 c. water
2 c. panko bread crumbs	4 tbsp. butter, melted
1 c. milk	2 c. half and half
2 eggs, well beaten	2, 4-oz. four cheese mashed
4 slices Swiss cheese	potato packets

Mix meat mixture, bread crumbs, milk and eggs. Place one-third mixture in bottom of 9x4-inch loaf pan. Top with one-third of sauce. Add another one-third meat on top. Follow with one-third sauce and 4 slices Swiss cheese. Place remaining meat mixture on top. Brush remaining sauce on top of meatloaf. Bake in 350° oven 50 minutes. Bring 2 cups water to a boil. Add half and half and melted butter. Add instant potatoes; mix with fork. Frost the meatloaf to resemble a cake. Top with bacon, chives and cheese sprinkles.

Diane Rauh, *Des Moines*
First Place, 2015 Spud Studs – Best in Mashed

GARDEN GIRL'S PEP
AND VEGGIE SANDWICH

2 slices wheat bread	Green pepper slices
1 tbsp. margarine	Cucumber slices
9 pepperoni slices	Banana pepper slices
1 slice American cheese	Hamburger style pickles
1/4 c. shredded lettuce	Black olive slices
Tomato slices	

Butter two slices of bread on one side each; set aside one slice. Put 9 slices pepperoni on bread. Place cheese slice and shredded lettuce on top. Plate tomatoes, green peppers and cucumbers on sandwich. Add banana peppers, pickles and black olives. Place other slice of bread on top.

Brooklyn Sedlock, *Indianola*
First Place, 2015 Kids Favorite Sandwich Ages 5-8
Second Place Overall, 2015 Kids Favorite Sandwich

SOUR CREAM & ONION TURKEY MEATBALLS

2 lbs. ground turkey
2 c. chopped green onion
1 1/2 c. seasoned croutons,
    crushed

2 eggs, beaten
1/2 c. sour cream
1 1/4 tsp. sea salt
1/2 tsp. black pepper

Combine all ingredients; form into 1 1/2-inch balls. Place on baking sheet. Bake in 350° oven 30 minutes; remove from oven. Eat while hot, or cover lightly with foil for 30 minutes before refrigerating or freezing.

Anita Garrison, *Des Moines*
First Place, 2015 Beginner's Contest – Main Dish
Second Place Overall, 2015 Beginner's Contest

ALFREDO GARLIC THAI PIZZA

For ALFREDO-THAI PIZZA SAUCE:
1/4 c. butter
1/2 onion, finely chopped
4 cloves garlic, minced
1 c. heavy cream
3/4 c. shredded Gruyere cheese
1/2 c. grated Parmesan cheese

1/4 c. parsley
2 tbsp. peanut butter
1/2 c. Thai peanut sauce
1 tsp. teriyaki marinade sauce
1/2 tsp. salt

Melt butter. Sauté onion and garlic just until onion is translucent. Add cream and stir. Add remaining ingredients; stir until cheeses are melted.

For CRUST:
1 c. warm water (105°-115°)
1 tsp. granulated sugar
1 pkg. active dry yeast

2 tbsp. canola oil
1 tsp. salt
2 1/2 c. all-purpose flour

Stir together water, sugar and yeast until dissolved. Add olive oil and salt; stir in flour until dough doesn't stick. Let rise 5 to 10 minutes. Roll dough out onto pan. Bake in 425° oven 10 minutes. Spread Alfredo-Thai pizza sauce over crust; bake 8 minutes more. Reduce oven to 350°.

(CONTINUED)

For PIZZA TOPPINGS:

1 tbsp. grated fresh ginger
1 c. bean sprouts
1 c. (1/4 lb.) shredded grilled
   chicken
1 bell pepper, chopped
2 carrots, shredded
1/4 c. chopped cilantro

1/3 c. coarsely chopped
   pineapple
1/2 c. grated Parmesan cheese
1 c. shredded white sharp
   cheddar cheese
1 tsp. cayenne pepper

Place the ingredients on baked crust in the following order: ginger, bean sprouts, chicken, bell pepper, carrots, cilantro, pineapple, cheeses and cayenne pepper. Bake 15 minutes more or until cheese starts to brown.

Kyle Barton, *West Des Moines*
First Place, 2014 Best Pizza in Iowa – Pizza with White Sauce

---

ITALIAN PITA

2.25-oz. can sliced black olives
2.25-oz. can sliced green olives
1/8 c. finely diced celery
1/8 c. finely diced green pepper
1/8 c. finely diced onion
1/8 c. finely diced red bell
   pepper
Sprinkle of pepper flakes
1/2 tsp. Italian seasoning

Olive oil
Red wine vinegar
4 oz. cream cheese
4 oz. provolone cheese
4 oz. salami
4 oz. pepperoni
4 oz. black forest ham
4 Pita breads

Mix olives, celery, green pepper, onion, red pepper, pepper flakes and Italian seasoning. Add equal amounts olive oil and red wine vinegar to desired consistency. For sandwich pita, spread pita with 1 ounce cream cheese; top with one-fourth of olive spread. Add 1 ounce each of provolone cheese, salami, pepperoni and black forest ham to each pita.

Rose Ridgway, *Johnston*
First Place, 2015 Best Pita Sandwich

BBQ STEAK WRAP

1/4 lb. ostrich steak, cut into
  strips
All-purpose flour
All-purpose seasoning
Olive oil
1/2 c. fresh sweet corn
1/3 c. thinly sliced green onions

1/2 c. barbeque sauce
1/2 c. shredded green cabbage
Flour tortillas
Sour cream
Cherry tomatoes, for garnish
Green onion, for garnish
Sour cream, for garnish

Dredge ostrich strips in flour and seasoning. Fry in olive oil to medium rare. Remove from heat; set aside. In same pan slowly cook fresh sweet corn and thinly sliced green onions with barbecue sauce until corn is done and liquid reduced. Place ostrich, sauce and green cabbage onto tortilla. Dot with sour cream and roll for serving. Garnish with cherry tomatoes, green onion and sour cream.

Helen Wall, *Alden*
First Place, 2015 Ostrich: The Smart Choice

WHITE LASAGNA

3 tbsp. butter
1/3 c. all-purpose flour
1/2 tsp. salt
1/4 tsp. pepper
3 c. fat-free milk
3 oz. reduced-fat cream cheese,
  cubed
3/4 c. grated Parmesan cheese
1 lb. Italian sausage, crumbled
1 medium onion, chopped
4 cloves garlic, minced

7.25-oz. jar roasted red peppers,
  drained and chopped
1/2 c. reduced-sodium chicken
  broth
5 fresh baby spinach leaves,
  roughly chopped
3/4 c. small-cured 2% cottage
  cheese, drained
9 lasagna noodles, cooked
  rinsed and drained
1/2 c. shredded part-skim
  mozzarella cheese

Melt butter in saucepan. Stir in flour, salt and pepper until smooth. Gradually stir in milk. Bring to a boil; cook and stir 1 to 2 minutes until thickened. Stir in cream cheese until melted. Stir in Parmesan cheese just until melted. Remove from heat; set aside. In large skillet coated with

(CONTINUED)

nonstick cooking spray, cook sausage, onion and garlic over medium heat until sausage is no longer pink; drain if necessary. Add roasted peppers and broth. Bring to boil. Reduce heat; simmer uncovered 3 to 5 minutes or until liquid is reduced to 3 tablespoons. Remove from heat; set aside. In small bowl, combine spinach and drained cottage cheese; set aside. Spread 1/2 cup cheese sauce in a 9x13-inch baking dish coated with nonstick cooking spray. Top with 3 noodles, half of sausage mixture, half of spinach mixture and 1 cup sauce; repeat layers. Top with remaining noodles and sauce. Sprinkle with mozzarella cheese. Cover and bake in 375° oven 40 minutes. Uncover, bake 15 to 20 minutes or until heated through and top is lightly browned. Let stand 10 minutes before cutting. Garnish with additional spinach leaves if desired.

Diane Rauh, *Des Moines*
First Place, 2015 Use Your Noodle – Main Dish
First Place, 2015 Barilla Pasta & Sauce – Entrée
Second Place Overall, 2015 Barilla Pasta & Sauce

GROWN-UP GRILLED CHEESE

2 slices sourdough bread
Olive oil
4 tbsp. sundried tomato pesto

1 avocado, mashed with splash
of lemon juice to reduce
browning
4 thick slices brie cheese

Brush outsides of each slice of bread with olive oil. Spread pesto on other side of each slice. Place one slice of bread, olive oil side down, on medium-hot skillet. Spread thick layer of avocado on slice; top with cheese. Top with another slice of bread, olive oil out. Toast until golden brown, turning once.

Sara Harper, *Des Moines*
First Place, 2015 ITSA Panini – Vegetarian

ITALIAN ZUCCHINI PIE
WITH VENISON SALAMI

For PIE CRUST:

1 1/2 c. sifted all-purpose flour
1/2 tsp. salt

1/2 c. cold lard
3 to 4 tbsp. ice cold water

Sift together flour and salt; cut in cold lard. Sprinkle with water, 1 tablespoon at a time, lightly tossing with a fork after each addition until adequately moistened. Gently form into a disc. The less the dough is handled the better. Wrap disc in plastic wrap; chill dough 2 hours. Roll out disc; place in bottom of a 9-inch pie pan.

For ITALIAN ZUCCHINI PIE WITH VENISON SALAMI:

2 tbsp. butter
4 c. thinly sliced zucchini
1 c. chopped onions
1/2 c. hot pepper cheese
** venison salami**
2 tbsp. dried parsley flakes
1/2 tsp. salt
1/2 tsp. pepper

1/4 tsp. garlic powder
1/4 tsp. dried basil leaves
1/4 tsp. dried oregano leaves
2 eggs, well beaten
2 c. Italian blend shredded
** cheese**
2 tsp. stone ground mustard

In 12-inch skillet, melt butter over medium-high heat. Add zucchini and onions; cook 6 to 8 minutes, stirring occasionally, until tender. Stir in salami, parsley flakes, salt, pepper, garlic powder, basil and oregano. In large bowl, mix eggs and cheese. Add cooked vegetable mixture; stir gently to mix. Spread crust with mustard. Pour egg mixture evenly into crust-lined pie plate. Bake in 375° oven 45 to 55 minutes or until knife inserted near center comes out clean. If necessary, cover edge of crust with strips of foil during last 10 minutes of baking to prevent excessive browning. Let stand 10 minutes before serving.

Jennifer Bartles, *Des Moines*
First Place, 2014 Machine Shed Pies – Zucchini
Third Place Overall, 2014 Machine Shed Pies – Cream

MY GRANDMA'S WHOLE HEARTY SPAGHETTI AND MEATBALLS

For MEATBALLS:

1 lb. ground beef
1 lb. Italian sausage
1 1/4 c. bread crumbs
1/2 c. grated Romano cheese
1 tbsp. pizza seasoning

2 eggs
1 tbsp. olive oil
1/2 onion, finely chopped
1 jalapeno, finely chopped
1/4 c. chopped mango

Combine all ingredients in a bowl; mix well. Roll out meatballs into 1 1/2-inch balls. Place on baking sheet; cook in 375° oven 18 to 20 minutes.

For SPAGHETTI:

1 lb. spaghetti
1 tbsp. butter
1/2 c. shredded white sharp
　　cheddar cheese
25-oz. can tomato sauce
6-oz. can tomato paste
1 c. cooked Italian sausage
1/2 onion, finely chopped
1 green bell pepper, finely
　　chopped

1 1/2 c. sliced mushrooms
2 tbsp. chopped basil
1 tsp. ground oregano
4 cloves garlic, minced
2 tbsp. brown sugar
1/2 tsp. salt
Romano cheese, shaved
Parmesan cheese
Parsley

While cooking meatballs, boil pasta in water 8 minutes then drain. Combine butter and cheese in a saucepan on low heat until ingredients have blended; remove from heat. In separate saucepan, combine tomato sauce and paste, sausage, vegetables and spices; bring to a boil. Reduce heat and simmer 15 minutes. Stir cooked meatballs into sauce. Stir cheese sauce into noodles then top noodles with tomato sauce and meatballs. Garnish with cheeses and parsley.

Kyle Barton, *West Des Moines*
First Place, 2014 Sunday Dinner at Mom's (Grandma's) – Main Dish
First Place Overall, 2014 Sunday Dinner at Mom's (Grandma's)

ONION PIE WITH COUNTRY SAUSAGE

For PIE CRUST:
2 c. all-purpose flour
1 tsp. salt
1 c. cold butter

1 tbsp. cider vinegar
1/2 c. cold milk

In large bowl, combine flour and salt; cut in butter until crumbly. Sprinkle with vinegar. Gradually add milk, tossing with fork until dough forms a ball. Cover and refrigerate 20 minutes or until easy to handle. Roll to fit a 9-inch pie pan; place dough in pan. Crimp edges; poke sides and bottom with fork. Bake in 425° oven 12 minutes.

For ONION PIE WITH COUNTRY SAUSAGE:
1 lb. country sausage
4 yellow onions, thinly sliced
2 eggs
1 c. half and half
2 tbsp. all-purpose flour
1 tsp. salt

1/8 tsp. pepper
Pinch nutmeg
2 oz. grated Swiss cheese
1 to 2 tbsp. parsley flakes
Baked 9-inch pie crust
Parsley for garnish

Brown sausage; remove with slotted spoon and set aside. Sauté onions in sausage grease over low heat until golden brown. Drain and set aside. Beat eggs, half and half, flour, salt, pepper and nutmeg. Add onions, sausage and half the cheese. Pour into crust. Sprinkle remaining cheese on top. Bake in 375° oven 25 to 30 minutes or until golden brown.

Diane Rauh, *Des Moines*
First Place, 2015 Purnell Old Folks' Sausage Cook Off – Casserole

---

SAUSAGE GRAVY BISCUIT

For COUNTRY SAUSAGE GRAVY:
1 lb. country sausage
3 tbsp. all-purpose flour

Salt and pepper to taste
2 c. 2% milk

In large skillet over medium heat, brown sausage. Add flour, salt and pepper. Stirring quickly, add milk. Cook until mixture thickens. Pour into parchment-lined 8x8-inch pan. Place in freezer; let set until almost frozen. Remove from freezer. Using a 2 1/2-inch biscuit cutter, cut 9 circles and return to freezer.

(CONTINUED)

For BISCUITS:

2 c. all-purpose flour	**1/2 tsp. salt**
4 tsp. baking powder	**1/4 c. cold butter**
1/2 tsp. cream of tartar	**1/4 c. shortening**
1 tbsp. granulated sugar	**2/3 c. 2% milk**

Combine flour, baking powder, cream of tartar, sugar and salt in large mixing bowl; stir thoroughly. Cut in butter and shortening until mixture resembles coarse crumbs. Make a well in center; add milk all at once. Stir just until dough clings together. Turn out onto lightly floured surface; knead 10 to 12 strokes. Roll out to 1/4-inch thickness. Using a 3-inch biscuit cutter, cut 18 circles. Cover a baking sheet with parchment paper; place in freezer 15 minutes. Remove both gravy and biscuits from freezer. Place 1 gravy circle on biscuit, top with another biscuit and pinch edges together. Repeat with remaining gravy and biscuits. Place in 9x9-inch greased cake pan. Bake in 425° oven 15 minutes. Remove from oven; place on cooling rack and brush with melted butter.

Connie Schaffer-Sherman, *Pleasant Hill*
First Place, 2015 Purnell Old Folks' Sausage Cook Off – Breakfast
First Place Overall, 2015 Purnell Old Folks' Sausage Cook Off

PORK RUB

2 tbsp. chervil	**1 tbsp. ground thyme**
4 tsp. black smoked whole peppercorns, ground	**1 tbsp. turbinado sugar**
	1/4 tsp. chipotle chili brown
1 1/2 tsp. lemon pepper	**powder**
1/2 tsp. crushed Aleppo chili	**1 tbsp. hickory smoked sea salt**
1 1/2 tsp. ground allspice	

Combine all ingredients. Apply generously to oiled pork chops. Grill to an internal temperature of at least 145°.

Matthew Phoenix, *Ankeny*
First Place, 2015 Allspice Rub & Marinade – Pork Rub

MOROCCAN MERGUEZ MEATBALLS WITH SPICED YOGURT SAUCE

For MOROCCAN MERGUEZ MEATBALLS:

1 egg
3 to 4 tbsp. milk
2/3 c. fresh bread crumbs
2 cloves garlic, minced
2 tsp. paprika
3/4 tsp. ground cumin
3/4 tsp. harissa paste
1/4 tsp. ground cloves
1/4 tsp. ground cinnamon
1/8 tsp. ground nutmeg
1/8 tsp. ground allspice
1/8 tsp. ground turmeric
1 tsp. kosher salt
1/2 tsp. freshly ground black pepper
1/2 lb. ground chuck
1/2 lb. ground pork
2 tbsp. chopped cilantro

In a food processor, blend egg, milk, bread crumbs and spices. Place ground beef, ground pork and cilantro in a large bowl. Add egg and spice mixture; mix gently with your hands. Shape into 1-inch balls. Cook meatballs in a large skillet over medium heat, turning often, until nicely browned and cooked through. Drain on paper towel-lined plate. Serve with spiced yogurt sauce.

For SPICED YOGURT SAUCE:

1 c. plain Greek yogurt
1/2 c. diced English cucumber, drained well
1 medium clove garlic, minced
2 tsp. fresh lemon juice
2 tsp. extra virgin olive oil
1 tsp. ground turmeric
1 tsp. ground cumin
1/8 tsp. cayenne pepper
Salt and freshly ground pepper
1 tbsp. minced cilantro

Line a strainer with cheesecloth. Place over a bowl; spoon yogurt into strainer. Allow yogurt to drain in refrigerator 3 hours. Transfer drained yogurt from cheesecloth to another bowl. Blend in cucumber, garlic, lemon juice, oil, turmeric, cumin and cayenne. Season to taste with salt and black pepper; stir in cilantro.

Rebecca Howe, *Des Moines*
First Place, 2015 Favorite Tone's Recipe for Casual Appetizers

WILD GAME POT PIE

For FILLING:

1 lb. venison, diced into bite-sized pieces	2 c. diced, peeled potatoes
Olive oil	1/2 c. chopped celery
2 tbsp. chopped onion	1 c. fresh sweet corn
1 clove garlic, minced	1 c. sweet peas
1 tsp. thyme	2 tbsp. all-purpose flour
1 c. beef broth	1/2 c. heavy cream

Brown venison in olive oil. Add onion, garlic and thyme. Stir in beef broth; simmer 60 minutes. In separate pot, combine potatoes, celery, corn and peas. Cover with water and cook until tender; drain. Add flour to meat; mix in cream and drained cooked vegetables.

For PASTRY:

2 1/2 c. all-purpose flour	3/4 c. shortening
1/2 tsp. salt	2 tbsp. butter
1/2 tsp. paprika	1 egg
1/2 tsp. thyme	Approx. 1/2 c. water
	1 tsp. vinegar

Mix flour and seasonings; cut in shortening and butter. Mix together egg, water and vinegar. Add enough liquid to flour to make dough come together. Divide dough in half; roll each half out on a lightly floured surface. Fit one pastry into pie pan. Fill with venison mixture; top with second pastry. Flute and seal edges; cut slits in top. Bake in 350° oven 50 to 55 minutes.

Cinnamon Weinman, *Pleasant Hill*
First Place, 2014 Wild Game Cook Off – Meats

RICOTTA MEATBALLS
WITH CHIANTI SAUCE

For CHIANTI SAUCE:

1/2 c. finely minced onion
1/4 c. extra-virgin olive oil
3 cloves garlic, peeled and minced

2 oz. prosciutto, finely diced
1/2 c. dry red wine
28-oz. can crushed tomatoes
1 c. beef broth

In bottom of 12-inch Dutch oven which has been sprayed with nonstick coating, sauté minced onions in olive oil 5 minutes. Add garlic and prosciutto; continue to sauté 1 minute. Add wine; cook 1 additional minute. Add crushed tomatoes and beef broth; simmer 30 minutes. Start out with 16 coals on bottom and 8 on top. When starting to simmer, switch to 16 on top and 8 on bottom to reach 350°.

For MEATBALLS:

1 lb. lean ground beef
1 lb. ground pork
1 c. fresh bread crumbs
1/2 c. chopped fresh parsley
2/3 c. ricotta cheese
2 large eggs, beaten

2 tsp. fennel seeds
1 tsp. cumin
1 tsp. dried chili flakes
1 tsp. kosher salt
1 tsp. freshly ground pepper

Preheat Dutch oven with 23 coals on top, 11 coals on bottom to 450°. Spray Dutch oven with nonstick coating. Place all ingredients in large bowl; mix together by hand. Roll into 2 inch balls. Place into preheated Dutch oven; bake 10 minutes. Remove meatballs from Dutch oven; transfer to Dutch oven with Chianti Sauce. Simmer 15 minutes or until cooked through.

Marllyn Hoksbergen, *Pella*
First Place, 2015 Dutch Oven Cooking – Main Dish/Side Dish
Second Place Overall, 2015 Dutch Oven Cooking

SEAFOOD ALFREDO LASAGNA

2 tbsp. vegetable oil
2 tbsp. plus 1/2 c. butter, divided
1 green onion, chopped
1/2 c. chicken broth
8-oz. bottle clam juice
8 oz. scallops, chopped
12 oz. small cooked shrimp, tails removed
8-oz. pkg. imitation crabmeat, chopped
1/4 tsp. black pepper, divided
1/2 c. all-purpose flour
1 1/2 c. milk
1/2 tsp. salt
1 c. heavy cream
1/2 c. grated Parmesan cheese, divided
3/4 c. dried bread crumbs or cubes
12 lasagna noodles, cooked and drained

Heat oil and 2 tablespoons butter in large skillet over medium heat. Sauté green onion until tender. Stir in broth and clam juice; bring to a boil. Add scallops, shrimp, crabmeat and 1/8 teaspoon pepper. Return to boiling; simmer uncovered 4 to 5 minutes. Drain seafood mixture, reserving liquid. Melt remaining butter in a saucepan over medium heat. Stir in flour until smooth. Combine milk and reserved cooking liquid; add to saucepan. Add salt and remaining 1/8 teaspoon pepper. Bring to a boil and cook 2 minutes, stirring until thickened. Remove white sauce from heat. Stir in heavy cream and 1/4 cup Parmesan cheese. Stir 3/4 cup sauce into seafood mixture. Spread 1/2 cup white sauce in greased 9x13-inch dish. Top with 4 lasagna noodles. Spread half the seafood mixture over noodles. Top with 1 1/4 cups white sauce. Layer 3 more noodles, remaining seafood mixture, and another 1 1/4 cups white sauce. Top with remaining 3 noodles, remaining white sauce, bread crumbs, and remaining Parmesan cheese. Bake, uncovered, in 350° oven until golden brown, 35 to 40 minutes. Let stand 15 minutes before cutting.

Ann Carter, *Carlisle*
First Place, 2015 My Best Dreamfield's Pasta Dish

GLUTEN FREE FRENCH ONION SALISBURY STEAK

For FRENCH ONION SALISBURY STEAK:

1 1/4 lbs. ground chuck	1 tbsp. canola oil
1/4 c. minced fresh parsley	2 1/2 c. sliced onions
3 tbsp. minced onion	1 tbsp. granulated sugar
3 tsp. salt, divided	2 tbsp. tomato paste
1 tsp. pepper	2 c. gluten free beef broth
2 tbsp. white rice flour	

Mix ground chuck, parsley, minced onion, 2 teaspoons salt and pepper; form into 5 patties. Dredge each patty in rice flour; reserve leftover flour. Heat oil in skillet and sauté each patty until browned; remove from pan. Sauté onions with sugar 5 minutes. Stir in tomato paste; sauté 1 minute. Add leftover flour; cook 1 minute. Add beef broth and remaining salt. Return meat to pan; bring to a boil. Simmer 20 minutes; serve with mashed potatoes.

For MASHED POTATOES:

5 large Idaho russet potatoes, diced	1/4 c. butter
2 cloves garlic, minced	1/4 c. heavy cream
	1 tbsp. salt

Boil potatoes until tender and drain. Sauté garlic in butter 1 minute. Add butter mixture, heavy cream and salt to the potatoes and mash. Serve immediately.

Meredith Hodges, *Des Moines*
First Place, 2014 Gracefully Gluten Free – Entrees & Appetizers

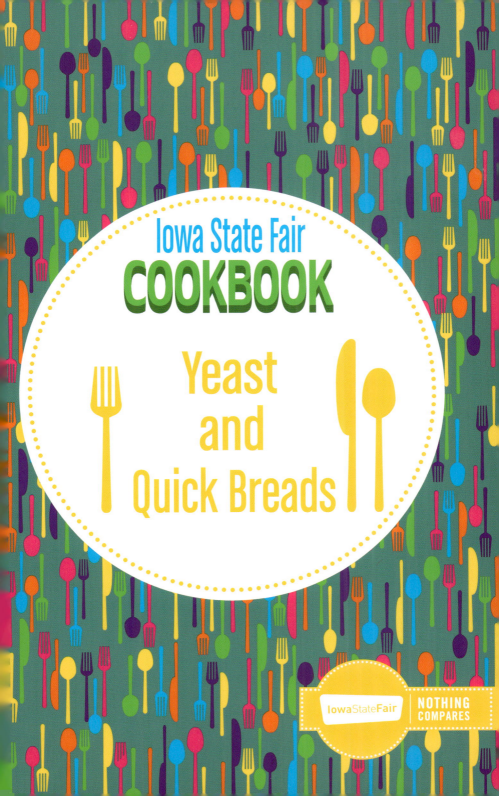

Iowa State Fair
COOKBOOK

ANADAMA BREAD

3/4 c. yellow cornmeal
1 1/4 tsp. salt
3 tbsp. butter
1/4 c. dark molasses
1 c. boiling water

1/4 c. nonfat dry milk
2 c. unbleached all-purpose
  flour
1 c. white whole wheat flour
2 1/2 tsp. instant yeast

Whisk together cornmeal and salt; add butter and molasses. Pour in boiling water, stirring until butter has melted and mixture is smooth. Let cool approximately 15 minutes. Mix in dry milk, flours and yeast. Let dough rest 20 minutes. Knead dough 7 minutes at medium speed. Cover and let dough rise until doubled (approximately 1 hour). Gently deflate dough; shape into 8-inch log. Place in 8 1/2 x 4 1/2-inch loaf pan; cover and let dough rise 90 minutes. Bake in 350° oven 35 to 40 minutes.

Valerie Singer, *Altoona*
First Place, 2014 King Arthur Flour Bread – Anadama Bread

RASPBERRY KOLACHES

1/2 c. milk
2 pkgs. active dry yeast
1 c. warm water (105°-115°)
3/4 c. butter
1/2 c. honey

1 tsp. salt
3 eggs
4 c. all-purpose flour, sifted
Raspberry preserves

Scald milk; cool. Sprinkle yeast over warm water; let stand to dissolve. Beat butter, honey, salt and eggs. Add yeast mixture and milk. Add flour; mix until smooth. Turn out onto lightly floured surface; knead until smooth and elastic. Place in a warm greased bowl, turning to grease surface. Cover; let rise until doubled. Punch dough down and let rise 2 more times, punching down each time. Divide dough into 18 pieces. Form each piece into a circle; flatten slightly. Let rise 15 minutes. Using shot glass make indentation in center of kolache. Fill with jam; let rise about 30 minutes. Bake in 350° oven about 18 minutes, until golden. Let cool. If desired, drizzle with powdered sugar glaze.

Joyce Larson, *New Market*
First Place, 2014 King Arthur Flour Yeast Rolls – Kolaches

YEAST BREADS AND QUICK BREADS

ENGLISH MUFFIN BREAD

2 1/4 c. all-purpose flour
1/2 tbsp. granulated sugar
3/4 tsp. salt

1 1/4 tsp. instant yeast
1 tbsp. lard
1 c. buttermilk, divided
White cornmeal for dusting

In large mixing bowl, combine flour, sugar, salt and yeast. Stir in lard and 3/4 cup buttermilk until ingredients form a ball. Dough should be soft and pliable, not stiff. Turn dough out onto lightly floured surface. Knead about 7 minutes, until dough is smooth. Add additional flour as needed. Transfer dough to lightly greased bowl, turning to grease surface. Cover with plastic wrap; let rise until doubled, 60 to 90 minutes. Divide dough in half; shape each half into a loaf. Sprinkle each loaf with white cornmeal. Place loaves in 2 greased 9x5-inch bread pans. Cover with plastic wrap; let rise until 1 to 1 1/2-inch above pan rim. Bake in 350° oven 35 to 45 minutes. Let cool before removing from pans.

Karen Steggerda, *Urbandale*
First Place, 2014 King Arthur Flour Bread – English Muffin Bread

---

WHOLE WHEAT BREAD

2 tbsp. butter
2 tbsp. honey
3 tbsp. dry milk
1 tsp. salt
1 tbsp. instant yeast
1 egg

1 c. warm water (105°-115°)
2 tsp. grated orange zest
2 tsp. grated lemon zest
1 1/2 c. white whole wheat
    flour
1 1/2 c. unbleached all-
    purpose flour

Combine all ingredients in large bowl. Turn out onto lightly floured surface; knead 12 to 15 minutes. Place in greased bowl, turning to grease surface. Cover; let rise until doubled. Punch dough down; divide into 3 equal parts. Form each piece into a rope and braid pieces together. Place braid in greased 9x5-inch loaf pan; let rise until doubled. Bake in 350° oven 35 minutes. Remove from pan; cool on rack. Brush top with butter.

Marianne Carlson, *Jefferson*
First Place, 2015 King Arthur Flour Bread – Whole Wheat Bread
Third Place Overall, 2015 King Arthur Flour Bread

BREWER'S RYE BREAD

5 to 6 c. white bread flour
4 c. rye flour
2 c. milk
1 tbsp. salt
1/3 c. molasses
1/4 c. butter

1 1/4 c. warm beer (105°-115°)
2 pkgs. active dry yeast
1 tsp. fennel seed
1 egg white beaten with
   1 tbsp. water
Fennel seed for garnish

Combine flours and set aside. Scald milk; stir in salt, molasses and butter. Cool to lukewarm. Add warm beer to large warm bowl. Sprinkle in yeast; stir until dissolved. Stir in lukewarm milk mixture, fennel seed and 4 cups flour mixture; beat until smooth. Cover and let batter rise in warm place, until doubled, about 30 minutes. Stir batter down; stir in enough additional flour mixture to make dough stiff. Turn out onto lightly floured surface; knead until smooth and elastic, about 12 minutes. Place in greased bowl, turning to grease surface. Let rise in warm place until doubled, about 45 minutes. Punch dough down; divide in half. Shape into 2 loaves; place in 2 greased 9x5-inch loaf pans. Let rise in warm place until doubled, about 50 minutes. Brush tops with egg mixture; sprinkle with fennel seeds. Bake in 375° oven 45 minutes.

Emma Whitlock, *Indianola*
First Place, 2014 & 2015 Keith's Beer Breads – Yeast Beer Bread
First Overall, 2014 & 2015 Keith's Beer Breads Contest

BEER BREAD

1 pkg. active dry yeast
12-oz. can light beer, warm
2 tbsp. granulated sugar
1 tsp. bread salt

4 tbsp. butter, room
   temperature
1 1/2 c. all-purpose flour
2 1/2 c. whole wheat flour

Place yeast in mixing bowl; pour in beer and let stand until bubbly. Add sugar, salt, butter and all-purpose flour; blend well. Add whole wheat flour gradually. Mix 5 minutes; place in greased bowl, turning to grease surface. Let rise until doubled. Punch dough down; knead until smooth. Shape into loaf; place in greased bread pan. Let rise until doubled. Bake in 375° oven 35 to 40 minutes. Cool on wire rack.

Hester Derscheid, *Ellston*
First Place, 2015 King Arthur Flour Bread – Beer Bread

HONEY WHEAT BREAD

2 1/2 c. warm water (105°-115°), divided
4 1/2 tsp. (2 packets) instant yeast or active dry yeast
1/3 c. plus 1 tsp. honey, divided
3 c. all-purpose flour
3 c. white whole wheat flour
2 tsp. salt
1/2 c. nonfat dry milk
1/4 c. vegetable oil
1 tbsp. cider vinegar
1 egg beaten with 1 tbsp. water

Combine 1/2 cup warm water, yeast and 1 teaspoon honey in small bowl; set aside to proof yeast until foamy (5 minutes). Combine flours, salt and dry milk in large mixing bowl. Whisk well; set aside. In small bowl, combine remaining warm water, oil, remaining honey, vinegar and yeast mixture. Stir well; add to flour mixture. Stir 1 minute until a shaggy mass forms. Turn out onto lightly floured surface; knead 30 seconds. Cover with a cloth; let stand 5 minutes so flours can absorb liquids. Uncover and knead by hand 10 minutes. Place in clean oiled mixing bowl, turning to grease surface. Cover with plastic wrap; let rise until doubled. Punch dough down; shape into 2 loaves. Place into well-oiled 9x5-inch or 8x4-inch loaf pans. Cover; let rise until doubled. Brush risen loaves with egg wash. Bake in 350° oven 45 minutes. Tent with foil during last few minutes of baking so bread does not overbrown. Remove from oven; turn out onto cooling racks and let rest 1 hour.

Cristen C. Clark, *Runnells*
First Place, 2014 Foods Made with Honey – Honey Wheat Bread

BLACK OLIVE PESTO BREAD

For BLACK OLIVE PESTO:
6-oz. can black olives, drained
2 tbsp. lemon juice
2/3 c. packed fresh basil leaves
2 tbsp. parsley
2 tsp. thyme
1/4 c. olive oil
2 tbsp. red wine vinegar
2 tbsp. cilantro
2 tbsp. chives
1/2 tsp. salt

Place olives in food processor; process until finely chopped. Transfer olives to bowl; set aside. Place remainder of ingredients into processor; process until finely chopped. Add to olives; mix well. Makes enough pesto for 2 loaves of bread.

(CONTINUED)

For DOUGH:

1 tbsp. or pkg. active dry yeast	2 tbsp. extra virgin olive oil
1 c. warm water (105°-115°)	1 tsp. salt
3 3/4 c. unbleached all-purpose flour	1/2 c. olive pesto (recipe above)

In small bowl, combine yeast and warm water; set aside until bubbly. Transfer to mixing bowl; add 1 cup flour and remainder of ingredients. Mix with dough hook until well blended; add remainder of flour. Turn into greased bowl, turning to grease surface. Let rise until doubled; punch dough down. Turn out onto lightly floured surface; knead until smooth and shape dough into a loaf. Placed in greased bread pan. Let rise until almost doubled. Bake in 375° oven 35 to 40 minutes. Place on wire rack to cool.

Hester Derscheid, *Ellston*
First Place, 2015 King Arthur Flour Bread – Black Olive Pesto Bread

OATMEAL BREAD

2 pkgs. active dry yeast	1/3 c. butter
1/2 c. warm water (105°-115°)	2 tsp. salt
1 1/8 c. water	2 c. regular rolled oats
1 1/8 c. evaporated milk	1/4 c. oat bran
1/4 c. steel cut oats	6 c. bread flour
1/3 c. honey	

Dissolve yeast in warm water. Heat remaining water and evaporated milk until bubbles begin to form around edge of pan. Add steel cut oats, honey, butter and salt; stir until smooth. Remove from heat. When mixture cools to lukewarm, add dissolved yeast. Gradually add regular oats, oat bran and bread flour. Mix until dough is stiff. Turn out onto lightly floured surface; knead until smooth and elastic. Place dough in greased bowl, turning to grease surface. Cover; let rise in warm place until doubled in size. Punch down; cover and let rest 15 minutes. Shape into 2 loaves. Place in 2 greased 9x5-inch bread pans. Allow to rise until barely rounded above tops of pans. Bake in 350° oven 45 minutes.

Emma Whitlock, *Indianola*
First Place, 2014 King Arthur Flour Bread – Oatmeal Bread

BEER BREAD

1 1/2 tsp. active dry yeast	1/2 c. chopped chives
4 1/2 c. all-purpose flour, divided	1/2 c. shredded cheddar cheese
1/2 c. warm water (100°)	1/2 c. mashed potatoes
12-oz. bottle of beer	1 tsp. garlic bread sprinkle
1 1/2 tsp. fine salt	All-purpose flour for dusting

In a large bowl, stir together yeast, 1/2 cup flour and warm water. Cover and let sit in warm spot about 30 minutes. Stir in beer, remaining flour, salt, chives, cheddar cheese, mashed potatoes and garlic bread sprinkle. Mix until all flour is incorporated and forms thick sticky dough that pulls away from sides of bowl. Cover; let rise in a warm place until doubled, about 2 hours. Scrape all dough from bowl with rubber spatula. Place on well-floured surface. Generously flour top of dough; form into loaf shape. Transfer loaf to cloche pan or round baking dish; sprinkle top with flour. Cover loosely with towel and let rise 30 to 40 minutes. Place small loaf pan of warm water on lower rack in 425° oven. Place bread in oven on rack above water; bake 35 minutes or until loaf is golden brown. Transfer to a cooling rack and let cool completely.

Joe Behounek, *Chelsea*
First Place, 2014 King Arthur Bread Flour – Beer Bread

KOLACHES

For KOLACHES:

15-oz. can evaporated milk	4 eggs
1/2 c. water	3/4 c. oil
1/4 c. instant potatoes	1/2 c. granulated sugar
2 pkgs. active dry yeast	1 tsp. salt
1/4 c. warm water (105°-115°)	4 1/2 c. all-purpose flour

Warm milk; add 1/2 cup water and pour over instant potatoes. Dissolve yeast in warm water. Add eggs, oil, sugar, salt and flour to potato mixture. Turn out onto lightly floured surface; knead 2 minutes. Place in large greased bowl, turning to grease surface. Cover; let dough rise until doubled. Form into 1-inch balls. Place on 11x17-inch jelly roll pan; let double. Make indentation in center; add cherry filling. Let dough rise 30 minutes. Bake in 425° oven 8 minutes.

(CONTINUED)

For FILLING:

6 oz. pkg. cherries	1 c. granulated sugar
1/2 tsp. vanilla	1/2 tsp. almond extract
2 tbsp. all-purpose flour	

In saucepan, combine all ingredients. Heat until boiling and thick. Remove from heat.

Cindy Paulsen, *Cedar Rapids*
First Place, 2015 King Arthur Flour Yeast Rolls – Kolaches

PINWHEEL BREAD

2 pkgs. active dry yeast	2 tbsp. salt
2 c. warm water (105°-115°)	8 1/2 c. unbleached all-purpose
2 c. milk	flour
1/2 c. granulated sugar	1/4 c. molasses
1/2 c. vegetable shortening	4 1/2 c. whole wheat flour

In large mixing bowl, dissolve yeast in warm water. In saucepan, add milk, sugar, shortening and salt; heat to 110°-115°. Add milk mixture to yeast mixture. Stir in 4 cups all-purpose flour; beat until smooth. Cover and let rest 1 hour. Stir batter down; divide into 2 equal portions. To one half, stir in enough of the remaining all-purpose flour to make stiff dough. Turn out onto a floured surface; knead 6 to 8 minutes. Place in a greased bowl, turning to grease surface. Cover and let rise until doubled. To other half, beat in molasses; add as much whole wheat flour as needed to make stiff dough. Turn out onto floured surface; knead 6 to 8 minutes. Place in greased bowl, turning to grease surface. Cover and let rise until doubled. Punch down both doughs; divide each into 3 equal portions. Roll each out to a 12x8-inch rectangle. Place 1 dark portion on top of each white portion. Roll up tightly (from 8 inch end). Lightly grease three 9x5-inch loaf pans. Place 1 loaf seam-side down in each loaf pan. Cover loosely; let rise 45 to 60 minutes. Bake in 375° oven 30 to 35 minutes. Cover with foil after 20 minutes to prevent overbrowning.

Cheryl Rogers, *Ankeny*
First Place, 2014 King Arthur Flour Bread – Yeast Bread Other Than Named
Second Place Overall, 2014 King Arthur Flour Bread
First Place, 2014 Baking the Wheat Montana Way

TOMATO, BASIL & GARLIC FILLED PANE BIANCO

1/2 c. warm water (105°-115°)
1/4 c. granulated sugar
4 tsp. instant yeast
1 c. warm low-fat milk
1/3 c. extra virgin olive oil
2 large eggs
2 tsp. salt

6 c. unbleached bread flour
8.5-oz. jar oil-packed
   sundried tomatoes
3/4 tsp. granulated garlic or
   garlic powder
1 1/2 c. shredded Italian
   blend cheese, divided
2/3 c. chopped fresh basil

Combine water, sugar, yeast, milk, olive oil, eggs, salt and flour; mix and knead by hand to make soft dough. Place dough in greased bowl, turning to grease surface. Cover; let rise in warm place until doubled, about 45 minutes. Thoroughly drain sundried tomatoes; lay on paper towel to absorb any excess oil. Finely chop tomatoes. Line 2 baking sheets with parchment. Gently deflate dough; divide in half. Roll 1 piece into 22 x 8 1/2-inch rectangle. Sprinkle half the garlic, cheese, basil and tomatoes onto dough. Starting with long edge, roll dough into a log. Pinch edges to seal. Place log seam-side down on baking sheet. Using kitchen shears or sharp knife, start 1/2-inch from one end and make a continuous cut about 1-inch deep down the center top, stopping about 1/2-inch from end. Keeping cut side up, form an "S" shape. Tuck both ends under center of "S" to form a "figure 8". Pinch ends together to seal. Cover; let rise in warm place until doubled, 45 to 60 minutes. Repeat with remaining dough. Bake in 350° oven 35 to 40 minutes. Tent loaf with foil after 15 to 20 minutes to prevent overbrowning. Remove from pans; cool on racks.

Jennifer Bartles, *Des Moines*
First Place, 2015 King Arthur Flour Bread – Herb Bread

SPELT SOURDOUGH

For LEAVEN:
1/4 c. whole wheat flour
1/4 c. unbleached bread flour

1/4 c. water (70°)
1 tbsp. sourdough starter

Combine all ingredients; mix well. Cover and let stand at room temperature 10 hours.

(CONTINUED)

For DOUGH:

1 c. organic spelt flour	2 tsp. salt
3 1/2 c. unbleached bread flour	2 tbsp. water (80°)
1 1/2 c. minus 2 tbsp. water (80°)	Rice flour

Combine leaven, flours and scant 1 1/2 cups water; mix well. Cover; let rest 30 minutes at room temperature. Add salt and remaining water to mixture; mix well 5 to 10 minutes. Cover; let rest 5 minutes. Mix well for 5 minutes. Place dough in oiled container. Cover; let rest 30 minutes. Stretch and fold dough; let rest 30 minutes. Repeat 4 times. Pour dough onto floured surface and divide into 2 parts. Loosely shape loaves. Cover; let rest 30 minutes. Shape loaves and place in cloth-lined bowls dusted with rice flour. Cover and refrigerate 7 to 8 hours. Preheat oven and cast iron Dutch ovens at 460°. Bake loaves in covered Dutch ovens 16 minutes. Remove lids; continue baking 16 minutes more. Cool loaves on a wire rack.

Nicholas Koszewski, *Ames*
First Place, 2015 King Arthur Flour Bread – Sourdough Bread

POTATO BUNS

3 1/2 c. whole milk	2 pkgs. active dry yeast
2/3 c. lard	1/2 c. warm water (105°-115°)
1/3 c. honey	2 beaten eggs
1 tbsp. salt	10 c. bread flour
1/2 c. instant dry potatoes	

Warm milk; do not boil. Stir in lard, honey and salt; mix well. Add instant potatoes; cool to lukewarm. In large bowl combine yeast and warm water; let sit until foamy. Add eggs. Stir in milk mixture. Add just enough flour to make soft dough. Turn out onto lightly floured surface; knead until soft. Place in a warm buttered bowl, turning to grease surface. Cover; let rise until doubled. Punch dough down. Repeat 2 more times. Form into 36 rolls. Let rise until light. Bake in 350° oven 20 minutes.

Joyce Larson, *New Market*
First Place, 2014 Spotlighting Spuds – Convenience Potatoes
First Place Overall, 2014 Spotlighting Spuds

SESAME CHEDDAR BREAD

1/4 c. granulated sugar
2 tbsp. (2 pkgs.) active dry
    yeast
2 c. warm water (105°-115°)
5 c. bread flour
2 tsp. salt

2 eggs, slightly beaten
2 tbsp. butter, room
    temperature
1/2 c. sesame seeds, toasted
3 c. shredded sharp cheddar
    cheese, divided

In large bowl, combine sugar, yeast and warm water; let stand until foamy. Beat in 2 cups flour. Beat in salt, eggs, butter, sesame seeds and 2 cups cheese. Gradually beat in remainder of flour. Beat to make stiff dough. Turn out onto lightly floured surface; knead until smooth and elastic. Place in large greased bowl, turning to grease surface. Cover; let rise until doubled. Punch dough down. Turn out onto lightly floured surface. Flatten bread with heels of hands to form 15-inch square. Sprinkle on remainder of cheese. Roll dough up; knead so cheese is marbled throughout. Divide dough into thirds; shape each into loaf. Place into greased 8 1/2 x 4 1/2-inch loaf pans. Cover; let rise until almost doubled. Bake in 350° oven approximately 45 minutes.

Louise Piper, *Garner*
First Place, 2015 King Arthur Flour Yeast Bread – Sesame Cheddar Bread

---

MAGIC CHRISTMAS WREATH

For DOUGH:
1 c. evaporated milk
1 c. water
3 to 4 tbsp. shortening,
    margarine or butter
2 pkgs. active dry yeast
1/2 c. warm water (105°-115°)

1/2 c. granulated sugar
1 tsp. salt
2 eggs, room temperature
    and beaten
8 c. all-purpose flour

Scald together evaporated milk and water. Add shortening and cool to lukewarm. In separate bowl, dissolve yeast in warm water. Once milk mixture has cooled, add sugar, salt and eggs. Add yeast and flour. Turn out onto lightly greased surface; knead well. Place in greased bowl, turning to grease surface. Cover; let rise until doubled. Punch dough down; divide into 2 parts. Roll each into rectangles.

(CONTINUED)

For FILLING:

7-oz. can almond paste	1/2 tsp. almond extract
1/4 tsp. salt	1/4 c. granulated sugar
2 tbsp. butter, softened	1 tsp. cinnamon
2 egg whites, beaten until fluffy	

Mix all ingredients and spread on rectangles. Roll up starting on long side, pinching to seal. Form into ring on parchment-lined baking sheet. Using scissors or knife, cut about three-fourths of the way through the ring at 1-inch intervals around the ring. Turn each section slightly sideways. Repeat with remaining dough and filling. Cover loosely and let rise until doubled. Bake in 350° oven 20 to 25 minutes or until lightly browned.

For FROSTING:

1/4 c. butter, softened	Cream or milk to thin
2 c. powdered sugar	1 tsp. almond extract

Mix ingredients and frost bread rings. Decorate with candied fruit and pecans if desired. In some traditions, a coin is inserted into one of the rolls before frosting.

Starr Hinrichs, *Johnston*
First Place, 2014 Herring Holiday Heritage Bread

ARTISAN ITALIAN BREAD

2 c. warm water (105°-115°)	1 tbsp. brown sugar
2 pkgs. active dry yeast	2 tbsp. olive oil
6 c. bread flour	1 tbsp. salt

Combine warm water and yeast; set aside 5 minutes until foamy. Using mixer, combine yeast mixture, flour and sugar on low. Drizzle olive oil and salt into dough; beat on medium speed 8 to 10 minutes. Transfer dough to oiled bowl, turning to grease surface. Wrap bowl in plastic wrap; let rise in warm area at least 2 hours. Remove plastic wrap; punch dough down and form a single loaf with rounded corners. Let dough rest 1 hour. Score top of dough 3 times. Spray loaf with water to ensure crispy crust. Bake in 425° oven 30 to 35 minutes.

Jenna Brady, *Runnells*
First Place, 2015 King Arthur Flour Bread – Artisan Bread

WHOLE WHEAT HARVEST GRAIN ROLLS

2 pkgs. active dry yeast
1/2 c. warm potato water
2 c. milk
2 eggs
1/2 c. granulated sugar
1 tbsp. salt
2 tbsp. butter
1 potato, cooked and mashed

2/3 c. harvest grains blend
   for bread
1/3 c. dried sweetened
   cranberries
1/3 c. toasted walnuts
4 c. whole wheat flour
2 3/4 to 3 c. all-purpose flour
Kosher salt for garnish

Dissolve yeast in water. Warm milk. In large bowl, combine eggs, sugar, salt, butter, potato and warm milk. Add yeast, harvest blend, cranberries and walnuts; mix well. Add whole wheat flour and gradually add all-purpose flour until soft dough develops. Turn out onto lightly floured surface; knead 5 to 7 minutes. Let rise until doubled, about 1 hour. Punch down dough. Form rolls and place 9 in a greased 9-inch pan. Let rise again 40 to 50 minutes. Bake in 350° oven 12 to 18 minutes. Remove from pan; brush with butter. Sprinkle with salt and let cool.

Lana Ross, *Indianola*
First Place, 2014 Superior Whole Grain Breads with Red Star Platinum Yeast

WHITE FRENCH BREAD

1 pkg. active dry yeast
1 1/3 c. warm water
   (105°-115°)
2 tbsp. granulated sugar

1 1/2 tsp. salt
1 1/2 tbsp. butter
4 to 5 c. all-purpose flour

In large bowl, dissolve yeast in water. Add sugar, salt and butter; mix well. Mix in flour, 1 cup at a time, until dough is easy to handle. Turn out onto lightly floured surface; knead until smooth and elastic. Place into greased bowl, turning to grease surface. Let rise until doubled. When risen, punch dough down. Divide into 2 portions; shape into 2 long, thin loaves. Let rise again. Bake in 350° oven 20 to 25 minutes or until golden brown.

Deborah Harbison, *Ames*
First Place, 2015 King Arthur Flour Bread – French Bread

NEW YORK DELI RYE BREAD

For SPONGE:
3/4 c. bread flour
3/4 c. rye flour
1/2 tsp. instant yeast

2 tbsp. granulated sugar
1 1/2 c. water, room
temperature

Combine all ingredients in large mixing bowl. Whisk until very smooth to incorporate air; set aside.

For FLOUR MIXTURE:
2 1/4 c. bread flour
1/2 tsp. plus 1/8 tsp. instant
yeast
2 tbsp. caraway seeds

1/2 tbsp. coarse salt
1/2 tbsp. vegetable oil
2 tsp. cornmeal

In large bowl, whisk together flour, yeast, caraway seeds and salt; gently scoop over sponge to cover completely. Cover bowl tightly with plastic wrap. Allow mixture to ferment 1 to 4 hours at room temperature. Add oil. Using dough whisk, stir until flour is moistened. Knead dough in bowl until it comes together; scrape onto lightly floured surface. Knead dough 5 minutes. Cover with inverted bowl; allow dough to rest 20 minutes. Knead dough another 5 to 10 minutes or until dough is very smooth and elastic. Place dough in large lightly oiled bowl. Oil top of dough; allow to rise until doubled, 1 1/2 to 2 hours. Flip bowl over; let dough fall out onto lightly floured surface. Press dough down gently; fold or form into ball. Allow dough to rise a second time in bowl covered with plastic wrap for about 45 minutes. Shape dough into ball; let rise. Turn dough out onto lightly floured surface; gently press down again. Shape dough into round loaf. Sprinkle baking sheet with cornmeal; set loaf on baking sheet. Cover with oiled plastic wrap; let rise until almost doubled, 1 to 1 1/4 hours. On rack at lowest level, place separate baking sheet or bread stone in 450° oven to heat. With sharp knife make 1/4 to 1/2-inch deep slashes in top of dough. Mist dough with water. Quickly, but gently set baking sheet on hot stone or hot baking sheet. Bake 15 minutes; reduce temperature to 400°. Continue baking 30 to 40 minutes or until bread is golden brown and a skewer inserted into middle comes out clean. Cool on wire rack.

Joe Behounek, *Chelsea*
First Place, 2015 King Arthur Flour Bread – Caraway Rye Bread
Second Place Overall, 2015 King Arthur Flour Bread

OAT SUNFLOWER MILLET BREAD

1 1/8 c. water
1/4 c. canola oil
1/4 c. honey
1/4 c. granulated sugar
3/4 tsp. salt
3 tbsp. millet
1 1/2 tbsp. sunflower kernels
3 tbsp. chopped walnuts
3/4 c. white whole wheat
   flour
1/4 c. regular rolled oats
2 1/3 c. unbleached flour
1 1/2 tbsp. dry milk
1 pkg. instant yeast

Place ingredients in bread machine according to manufacturer's directions. Set machine for dough cycle; press start. When dough cycle is completed, remove dough from machine. Punch dough down; form into a loaf. Place seam side down into greased 9x5-inch bread pan. Cover with damp cloth; let rise until doubled, about 45 minutes. Place pan on rack in center of 375° oven. Bake 40 to 45 minutes or until browned and loaf sounds hollow when tapped. Remove from pan. Brush top with melted butter.

Rebecca Howe, *Des Moines*
First Place, 2015 Baking the Wheat Montana Way

HONEY BUTTER ROLLS

1/3 c. butter
1 c. milk
2 tbsp. instant yeast
1/3 c. honey
1/2 tsp. salt
1 large egg
4 c. all-purpose flour
2 tbsp. butter, melted

In small saucepan, melt 1/3 cup butter. When melted, stir in milk; heat to 100°. In separate bowl, combine yeast and honey. When milk is at temp, remove from heat. Add yeast mixture and stir. Add salt and egg; stir. Stir in 2 cups flour. Add remaining flour, half cup at a time, until dough clings together and pulls from sides of bowl. Dough will still be a little sticky. Flour hands and shape dough into 12 rolls. Place on baking sheet. Cover; let rise 10 minutes. Bake in 400° oven 10 to 12 minutes or until lightly golden. Remove from oven; brush with melted butter.

Brooklynn Sedlock, *Indianola*
First Place, 2015 Foods Made with Honey – Youth Entries

CRUSTY ITALIANO BREAD

1 c. plus 2 tbsp. water
2 tbsp. margarine
3 c. bread flour
2 tbsp. dry milk

0.7-oz. pkg. dry Italian dressing
mix
3 tbsp. granulated sugar
1 1/4 tsp. salt
2 1/4 tsp. active dry yeast

Place all ingredients in bread machine in order suggested by manufacturer. Bake according to manufacturer's instructions.

Colette Wortman, *Urbandale*
First Place, 2015 King Arthur Flour Bread – Bread Machine Bread

CHEESY POTATO BREAD

2 medium potatoes
3/4 c. lukewarm potato water
(110°)
1 pkg. active dry yeast
4 tbsp. granulated sugar,
divided
3/8 c butter, softened
3/4 tbsp. salt

1 egg
1 tsp. grated onion
1 tsp. dill weed
1 c. grated cheddar cheese
3 c. unbleached bread flour
1 tbsp. melted butter
1 tbsp. grated Parmesan cheese

Boil potatoes in water until tender. Drain, reserving 3/4 cup water. Cool to lukewarm. Mash potatoes; set aside 1 cup. Dissolve yeast and 1 tablespoon sugar in lukewarm potato water. Pour into large bowl; beat in butter, remaining sugar, salt, egg and potatoes. Beat in onion, dill weed, cheddar cheese and enough flour to make soft dough. Turn out onto lightly floured surface; knead until smooth and elastic, about 10 minutes. Place in greased bowl, turning to grease surface. Cover with towel. Let rise until doubled. Punch dough down. Shape into a loaf; place in greased 9x5-inch loaf pan. Cover; let rise until doubled, about 1 hour. Brush loaf with melted butter. Sprinkle with Parmesan cheese. Bake in 375° oven 35 to 45 minutes, or until instant read thermometer registers 190°. Remove from pan onto wire rack to cool.

Sonny Melchers, *Fairfield*
First Place, 2015 King Arthur Flour Bread – Cheesy Potato Bread

CINNAMON BREAD

4 1/2 to 5 1/2 c. all-purpose flour, divided
1/4 c. plus 1/3 c. granulated sugar, divided
1 tsp. salt

1 pkg. active dry yeast
1 1/4 c. milk
1/4 c. butter
2 eggs, room temperature
Melted butter
1 1/2 tsp. cinnamon

In large bowl, combine 1 3/4 cups flour, 1/4 cup sugar, salt and yeast. In saucepan, combine milk and 1/4 cup butter; heat over low heat until milk is warm and butter is melted. Gradually add to dry ingredients. Beat at medium speed 2 minutes. Add eggs and 1/4 cup flour or enough flour to make a thick batter. Beat at high speed 2 minutes. Stir in enough additional flour to make soft dough. Turn onto a lightly floured surface; knead until smooth and elastic, 8 to 10 minutes. Place in greased bowl, turning to grease surface. Cover and let rise until doubled. Punch dough down; turn out on lightly floured surface. Divide dough into 2 equal parts; roll each part into 12x8-inch rectangle. Brush lightly with melted butter. Combine cinnamon and remaining sugar; sprinkle over each rectangle. Roll tightly from 8-in side as for jellyroll. Seal edges and ends firmly. Fold ends firmly underneath. Place loaf seam side down in greased loaf pans; let rise in a warm place until 1 to 1 1/2 inches above rim of pan. Bake in 350° oven about 30 minutes or until loaf sounds hollow when tapped.

Phyllis Olson, *Newton*
First Place, 2014 King Arthur Flour Bread – Cinnamon Bread

CHERRY RHUBARB CREAM CHEESE BRAID

For BREAD:
1 tbsp. active dry yeast
1/2 c. warm water (105°-115°)
4 to 4 1/4 c. all-purpose flour, divided
3/4 c. sour cream

3/4 c. mashed potatoes
6 egg yolks
1/3 c. granulated sugar
1 1/2 tsp. salt
1/3 c. lard, softened

In large bowl, dissolve yeast in water. Add 1 cup flour; mix well. Stir in sour cream, potatoes, egg yolks, sugar and salt. Let stand 5 minutes. Add

(CONTINUED)

3 cups flour; knead in lard to form soft dough. Add additional flour if needed. Turn out onto lightly floured surface; knead 20 times or until smooth. Place in greased bowl, turning to grease surface. Cover; let rise in warm place until doubled, about 1 1/4 hours. Punch dough down. Turn out onto lightly floured surface; roll out into 12x9-inch rectangle. Spread cream cheese filling 2-inches wide down center of rectangle. Top with cherry/rhubarb filling. Cut with sharp knife or pizza cutter 3 inches in from edges on both sides, about 1 inch apart. Starting at one end, fold first strip over filling. Fold strip on opposite side over filling, until filling is enclosed. Pinch ends together. Place loaf on greased baking sheet. Cover; let rise until doubled, about 30 minutes. Bake in 375° oven 15 to 20 minutes or until golden brown. Remove from pan to wire rack. Drizzle with glaze.

For CREAM CHEESE FILLING:

4 oz. cream cheese　　　　　**2 tbsp. granulated sugar**
1 egg　　　　　　　　　　　　**1/2 tsp. vanilla**

In small mixing bowl, beat cream cheese, egg, sugar and vanilla until smooth; set aside.

For RHUBARB-SOUR CHERRY FILLING:

3 1/2 c. pitted sour cherries　　**2 tsp. vanilla**
3 1/2 c. sliced rhubarb　　　　**1 1/2 tsp. cinnamon**
1 c. packed brown sugar　　　**5 tbsp. instant cornstarch**
　　　　　　　　　　　　　　　　　thickener

Combine cherries and rhubarb. Place 5 cups in heavy saucepan. Add brown sugar, vanilla, cinnamon and thickener. Simmer over medium-low heat 10 to 15 minutes or until rhubarb breaks down. Transfer to bowl, stir in remaining rhubarb-cherry mixture; cool. Refrigerate until ready to use.

For GLAZE:

1 1/4 c. powdered sugar　　　**2 tbsp. milk**
1 tsp. vanilla

Combine all ingredients; mix well.

Joe Behounek, *Chelsea*
First Place, 2015 King Arthur Flour Bread – Braided Bread
First Place Overall, 2015 King Arthur Flour Bread

SANDWICH BREAD

3 c. gluten-free multi-purpose
    flour
3 tbsp. granulated sugar
1 1/4 tsp. salt
2 tsp. instant yeast

1 1/4 tsp. xanthan gum
1 c. warm milk
1/4 c. butter, softened
3 large eggs

Combine flour, sugar, salt, yeast and xanthan gum in mixing bowl. Beat in milk slowly. Add butter; beat until thoroughly blended. Beat eggs, adding one at a time. Beat on high 3 minutes to make very smooth thick batter. Cover bowl; let batter rise 1 hour. Scrape down sides of bowl, gently deflating dough. Scoop dough into greased 9x4-inch gluten-free bread pan. Press dough level using spatula or wet fingers. Cover with greased plastic wrap; set in warm place to rise until dough comes to top of pan, 45 to 60 minutes. Bake in 350° oven 38 to 42 minutes, until golden brown. Turn out of pan on wire rack to cool.

Hester Derscheid, *Ellston*
First Place, 2015 King Arthur Flour Bread – Gluten Free Bread

SUMMER SQUASH SEVEN GRAIN ROLLS

2 pkgs. active dry yeast
1/2 c. warm water (105°-115°)
1 c. milk
2 eggs
1/3 c. granulated sugar
2 tsp. salt

1/2 c. butter
2 c. cooked and mashed
    summer squash
2 c. seven grain flour
2 3/4 to 3 c. all-purpose flour

Dissolve yeast in water. Warm milk; add to eggs, sugar, salt, butter and squash. Add yeast; mix well. Add seven grain flour; gradually add all-purpose flour until soft dough forms. Turn out onto lightly floured surface; knead dough 5 to 7 minutes. Place in greased bowl, turning to grease surface. Let rise until doubled, about 1 hour. Punch dough down; shape into rolls. Place on baking sheets; let rise 1 hour. Bake in 350° oven 15 to 18 minutes. Brush with butter.

Lana Shope, *Indianola*
First Place, 2015 King Arthur Flour Yeast Rolls – Non-Sweet Yeast Rolls Other Than Named
Second Place Overall, 2015 King Arthur Yeast Rolls

HONEY WHEAT BREAD

2 pkgs. active dry yeast
2 1/4 c. warm water
   (105°-115°), divided
1/3 c. plus 1 tbsp. honey

1/4 c. vegetable shortening
2 3/4 tsp. salt
3 c. whole wheat flour
2 to 3 c. white bread flour

Combine yeast and 1/2 cup warm water in mixing bowl; let stand 5 minutes. Add honey, shortening, salt, remaining water and whole wheat flour. Beat on low speed until combined then medium speed, 3 minutes. Gradually beat in bread flour to make stiff dough. Turn out onto lightly floured surface. Knead until smooth and elastic. Place into large bowl; cover and let rise in warm place until doubled. Punch dough down. Turn out onto lightly floured surface. Divide into 2 equal portions; shape into loaves. Place into greased loaf pans. Let rise until almost doubled. Bake in 350° oven 40 to 45 minutes. Remove from pans; cool on racks.

Louise Piper, *Garner*
First Place, 2015 Foods Made with Honey – Honey Wheat Bread
First Place Overall, 2015 Foods Made with Honey – Breads & Rolls

BUTTERHORNS

2 1/2 c. all-purpose flour
1 1/2 tbsp. plus 2 tsp. granulated
   sugar, divided
1/2 tsp. salt
1/2 c. butter

1 tbsp. active dry yeast
1/4 c. warm water (105°-115°)
1/2 c. whole milk, room
   temperature
1 egg, room temperature
Melted butter

Combine flour, 1 1/2 tablespoons sugar and salt in a bowl. Cut butter into flour mixture until butter pieces are pea size; set aside. In large bowl, mix remaining sugar, yeast and water; cover and let stand 6 minutes. Add milk and egg; stir in flour mixture using mixer. Cover with plastic wrap; refrigerate overnight. Roll out dough into large circle about 1/2-inch thick. Cut into wedges; roll up from wide section to point; curve edges. Brush wedges with melted butter prior to rolling up. Place on parchment-lined baking sheet. Cover; let rise until doubled, about 1 hour. Bake in 400° oven 12 to 15 minutes. Brush with melted butter.

Luann Sutter, *Ankeny*
First Place, 2014 King Arthur Flour Rolls – Butterhorn Rolls

YEAST BREADS AND QUICK BREADS

CHERRY RASPBERRY ALMOND DANISH

For DOUGH:

1/2 c. warm water (105°-115°)
4 1/2 tsp. active dry yeast
1/3 c. plus 1 tsp. granulated
   sugar, divided
1 1/4 c. buttermilk
3/4 c. fluffy mashed potatoes

2 eggs
1 1/2 tsp. salt
1 c. butter, room temperature
5 c. all-purpose flour
1 egg beaten with 1 tbsp. water

Mix warm water, yeast, and 1 teaspoon sugar together in a small bowl. Set aside until foamy. Add buttermilk, mashed potatoes, eggs, salt, remaining sugar and butter; whisk well. Add flour; mix in until soft dough forms and butter is thoroughly incorporated. Turn out onto lightly floured surface; knead dough by hand 8 minutes until smooth and elastic. Place dough in a greased bowl, turning to grease surface. Cover with plastic wrap; let rise at room temperature until doubled, 1 to 1 1/2 hours. Deflate dough; cover bowl again. Refrigerate overnight or at least 5 to 6 hours until well chilled. Before shaping Danish, make fillings. Once filling has cooled, take dough out of refrigerator and gently deflate. Divide into 18 pieces. Roll each piece into a 9-inch rope. Using a rolling pin, roll rope flat to 1/4-inch thickness (9x3 rectangles, 1/4-inch thick). Cut small rectangle in half lengthwise. Take 2 dough strips and twist around each other and into a circle, securing ends. Place on silicone mat-lined baking sheets 3-inches apart. Spray with nonstick spray, cover with plastic wrap and let rise in a warm place until doubled. When fully risen, brush with egg mixture. Place 1/2 tablespoon cream cheese filling in bottom center of Danish. Add a scant tablespoon of cherry red raspberry filling on top of cream cheese. Bake on center rack of 350° oven approximately 15 to 18 minutes, rotating once after 20 minutes to bake evenly. Remove from oven; allow pastries to cool slightly. Drizzle with icing. Serve warm.

For CHERRY RED RASPBERRY FILLING:

2 tsp. grated lemon zest
1/2 c. granulated sugar
1/4 c. cornstarch
3 c. pitted frozen sour cherries,
   thawed, juice reserved

1/2 c. cherry juice from thawed
   sour cherries
2 c. red raspberries
1 tsp. almond extract

(CONTINUED)

Combine all ingredients in a small saucepan. Bring to boil over medium heat while stirring constantly. Reduce heat; simmer 5 minutes. Remove from heat and cool.

For CREAM CHEESE FILLING:

12 oz. cream cheese
2 tbsp. granulated sugar

1/2 vanilla bean, seeds scraped

Combine cream cheese, sugar and vanilla bean seeds; mix well.

For ICING:

2 c. powdered sugar
2 tbsp. milk

1/2 vanilla bean, seeds scraped
1 tsp. almond extract

Combine powdered sugar, milk, vanilla bean seeds and almond extract; beat until smooth icing forms.

Cristen C. Clark, *Runnells*
First Place, 2014 My Favorite Tone's Recipe – That I Love to Bake

SWEDISH RYE BREAD

2 c. milk
1/2 c. shortening
3/4 c. sorghum
1/2 c. plus 1 tsp. granulated
    sugar, divided

2 pkgs. active dry yeast
1/4 c. warm water (105°-115°)
2 c. rye flour
4 c. all-purpose flour

In saucepan, bring milk to boil. Add shortening, sorghum and 1/2 cup sugar; set aside until warm (110°). Dissolve yeast in warm water. Add 1 teaspoon sugar; let stand until foamy. In large bowl, combine milk mixture and yeast mixture. Add rye flour to liquid; mix until batter is smooth. Gradually add all-purpose flour. Mix until stiff dough forms. Finish mixing with hands. If necessary, add additional flour until no longer sticky. Knead lightly on floured surface. Form dough into ball. Place in greased bowl, turning to grease surface. Cover; let rise until doubled. Punch dough down; divide into 3 sections. Shape into loaves; place in greased pans. Let rise until doubled. Bake in 350° oven 30 to 35 minutes or until loaf sounds hollow when tapped.

Phyllis Olson, *Newton*
First Place, 2015 Cooking with Sorghum – Breads

FROSTED CINNAMON ROLLS

For DOUGH:
4 tsp. active dry yeast
1/2 c. warm water (105°-115°)
3/4 c. warm milk (105°-115°)
6 tbsp. unsalted butter, cut
    into pieces
1/2 c. granulated sugar

5 to 5 1/2 c. unbleached all-
    purpose flour, divided
1/2 c. fresh orange juice (1 to 2
    oranges)
1 to 1 1/2 tsp. grated orange zest
2 eggs, slightly beaten
1 1/2 tsp. salt

In a small bowl dissolve yeast in warm water; let stand 15 minutes. In large bowl, pour warm scalded milk over butter pieces. Let warm milk melt butter; add sugar and stir until all is combined. Let cool to lukewarm. Pour dissolved yeast and 2 cups flour into milk mixture. Stir well until combined. Cover with plastic wrap; let stand 20 minutes. Mix orange juice, orange zest, eggs and salt into yeast mixture until well incorporated. Add remaining flour, 1 cup at a time until shaggy dough forms. Turn out onto lightly floured surface; knead until smooth and satiny, about 2 minutes, adding only 1 tablespoon flour at a time as necessary to prevent sticking. Place in well-greased bowl, turn to coat surface. Cover with plastic wrap. Let rise at room temperature until doubled, 1 to 1 1/2 hours. Meanwhile, prepare filling. Gently punch down dough; cut in half. Let dough rest 20 minutes. Keep other half of dough covered while working with first half. Taking one half at a time, roll out to 10x18-inch rectangle (about 1/4-inch thick). Spread half of filling over, roll jellyroll style, and cut into 12 pieces. Place each piece in greased baking pans. Repeat with remainder of dough. Cover shaped rolls loosely with plastic wrap; let rise at room temperature until puffy, about 40 to 50 minutes. Bake in 350° oven 30 to 40 minutes. Let rolls cool slightly; frost while still warm.

For FILLING:
5 tbsp. unsalted butter, room
    temperature

1/2 c. granulated sugar
1 1/2 tsp. cinnamon

Mix butter, sugar and cinnamon by hand to make a paste. Set aside.

(CONTINUED)

For CREAM CHEESE FROSTING:

8 oz. cream cheese, room temperature
1/2 c. unsalted butter, cut into pieces and room temperature

1 c. powdered sugar
1 tsp. vanilla

Place cream cheese in a medium mixing bowl. Using rubber spatula, soften cream cheese. Gradually add butter; continue beating until smooth and well blended. Sift in powdered sugar; continue beating until smooth. Add vanilla and stir to combine.

Joe Behounek, *Chelsea*
First Place, 2014 King Arthur Flour – Cinnamon Rolls (frosted)

BRAIDED EGG BREAD

1 3/4 c. warm water (105°-115°), divided
2 tbsp. active dry yeast
1/3 c. granulated sugar, divided
7 to 8 c. all-purpose flour, divided

Pinch of ground cinnamon
3 eggs
2 3/4 tsp. salt
1/2 c. vegetable oil
1 egg beaten with 1 tbsp. water
Sesame seeds

In mixing bowl, combine 1 cup water, yeast, 1 tablespoon sugar, 1 cup flour and cinnamon. Stir briefly; let yeast mixture sit until foamy. Briskly stir in remaining water and sugar. Add eggs, salt and oil. Fold in remaining flour. Knead 10 minutes by hand or dough hook, adding enough flour to make soft, elastic dough. Divide dough in half. Shape each into a ball; place in lightly greased bowls. Cover; let rise until doubled. Gently deflate dough. Line 2 baking sheets with parchment paper; set aside. Working with 1 dough ball at a time, divide each into 6 pieces and form into ropes about 18-inches in length. Using 3 ropes, braid together and pinch ends to seal. Place shaped loaves on lined baking sheets. Cover with a tea towel and let rest until loaves have almost doubled in size, about 45 to 60 minutes. Just before placing loaves in oven, brush each loaf with egg mixture and sprinkle with sesame seeds. Place baking sheets on center rack of oven. Bake in 350° oven approximately 30 minutes or until golden brown. Remove from oven; let loaves cool on rack 1 hour before slicing.

David Coziahr, *Council Bluffs*
First Place, 2015 King Arthur Flour Bread – Egg Bread

CHRISTMAS STÖLLEN

For FRUIT AND SPONGE:

1 c. diced candied fruit
1 c. raisins
3 tbsp. rum
1 scant tbsp. active dry yeast

1/4 c. warm water (105°-115°)
2/3 c. milk
1 tsp. honey
1 c. all-purpose flour

Combine fruit, raisins and rum; cover and set aside. Shake or stir mixture occasionally to coat fruit with rum (can be prepared the day before). In large bowl, sprinkle yeast in water to soften. Heat milk to 110°; add to yeast along with honey and flour. Cover sponge with plastic wrap; let rise until light and full of bubbles, about 30 minutes.

For DOUGH:

1/3 c. honey
1 large egg, beaten
1/2 c. unsalted butter,
     softened
1 tbsp. grated lemon zest

1 tsp. salt
1/2 tsp. ground mace
1/2 c. toasted and chopped
     almonds
3 to 4 c. all-purpose flour

Add fruit mixture, honey, egg, butter, lemon zest, salt, mace, almonds and 2 cups flour to sponge. Beat 2 minutes. Gradually add remaining flour, 1/4 cup at a time, until dough begins to pull away from sides of bowl. Turn dough out onto lightly floured surface. Knead, adding flour a little at a time, until dough is smooth and elastic. Place dough in greased bowl, turning to grease surface. Cover with tightly woven towel; let rise until doubled, about 1 hour. Turn out dough onto lightly oiled surface. Divide dough in half. Roll each half into 7x9-inch oval.

For FILLING AND TOPPING:

4 tbsp. unsalted butter,
     softened
1/4 c. ground Vietnamese
     cinnamon
1/3 c. fine granulated sugar

1/4 c. butter, melted
1/2 c. powdered sugar
Red and green candied
     cherries
Toasted almonds

Brush softened butter over ovals. Combine cinnamon and sugar. Add melted butter to form a paste. Spread over one half of oval lengthwise.

(CONTINUED)

Fold dough in half lengthwise. Carefully lift loaves onto baking sheet lined with parchment paper. Press lightly on folded side to help loaf keep its shape during rising and baking. Cover with tightly woven towel; let rise 45 minutes. Bake in 375° oven 25 minutes until internal temperature reaches 190°. Immediately remove from baking sheet; place on rack to cool. Sprinkle heavily with powdered sugar; garnish with candied cherries and almonds.

Andrea Spencer, *Stanton*
First Place, 2015 Herring Heritage Bread

GLAZED RAISIN BREAD

1/2 c. seedless raisins	4 c. all-purpose flour
1/2 c. seedless golden raisins	2 large eggs, room
1/4 c. unsalted butter	temperature, slightly
1/4 c. granulated sugar	beaten
1 1/2 tsp. salt	1 c. powdered sugar
2 1/4 tsp. active dry yeast	1 1/2 tbsp. orange juice
3/4 c. buttermilk, room	
temperature	

In large bowl, combine raisins, butter, granulated sugar, salt, yeast and buttermilk. Add 1 1/2 cups flour; beat well, 75 strokes by hand or 1 minute with mixer. Pour in eggs; blend thoroughly. Gradually add remaining flour, 1/2 cup at a time, until dough is soft and has separated from sides of bowl. If dough continues to be sticky, add sprinkles of flour. Turn out onto lightly floured surface; knead vigorously by hand or in mixer bowl. Dough will become smooth and elastic, about 8 minutes. Place dough in greased bowl; pat with greased fingers. Cover bowl with plastic wrap. Let rise until doubled, 1 1/2 hours. Remove plastic wrap; punch down dough. Turn out onto work surface; let rest 10 minutes. Shape dough into loaf; place in greased loaf pan. Cover with wax or parchment paper. Allow to double, about 50 minutes. Bake in 375° oven until loaf is well browned and loose in the pan, about 40 minutes. Turn out loaf and tap bottom crust with finger. A hard hollow sound means bread is done. If it is soft, return to oven 5 to 10 minutes more. Remove from oven; place on wire rack to cool. Combine powdered sugar and orange juice. Drizzle over cooled loaf.

Michelle Jackson, *Van Meter*
First Place, 2015 King Arthur Flour Bread – Raisin Bread

CINNAMON BEAR CLAWS WITH MILK AND HONEY GLAZE

For DOUGH:
1 1/4 c. unsalted butter, very cold	1/2 tsp. salt
3 1/2 c. all-purpose flour	2 eggs, room temperature
2 pkgs. active dry yeast	1/4 c. honey
1/2 c. warm water (105°-115°)	1 egg, beaten
1/2 c. heavy cream	Sliced almonds
	Large crystal sugar
	All-purpose flour for dusting

In small bowl, cut butter into 1/4-inch slices. Add to flour. Process mixture until butter is about size of kidney beans. In large bowl, dissolve yeast in warm water; let stand 5 minutes. Stir in cream, salt, 2 eggs and honey. Add flour-butter mixture to liquid ingredients; mix until dry ingredients are moistened. Cover with plastic wrap; refrigerate 4 hours, overnight or up to 4 days. Turn out onto lightly floured surface. Dust with flour; flatten dough with rolling pin. Roll out to make 16x20-inch rectangle. Fold into thirds making 3 layers. Turn dough; roll out again. Fold into thirds. Place in refrigerator 30 minutes. On lightly floured surface, roll chilled dough out to make a 16x18-inch rectangle. Cut lengthwise into 4 strips. Remove filling from refrigerator; spread 2 tablespoons filling down center of each strip. Roll each strip from long side, jelly-roll style and place seam-side down on work surface. Roll lightly to flatten and seal edges. Cut each strip into 4 to 6-inch pieces. Cut 3 to 5 slits for claws. Place pieces on parchment-lined baking sheets, curving slightly. Allow to rise in warm place 20 minutes or until puffy. Brush with beaten egg; place a sliced almond on each bear claw. Sprinkle with crystal sugar. Bake in 400° oven 5 to 8 minutes for small pastries, 10 to 12 minutes for larger pastries. Let cool slightly on wire racks. Drizzle glaze on top.

For FILLING:
1 egg white	3/4 c. honey
2/3 c. almond paste	1 tsp. cinnamon

In small bowl, beat all ingredients with mixer until very smooth. Refrigerate until ready to use.

(CONTINUED)

For GLAZE:

1 c. powdered sugar	1 to 2 tbsp. whole milk
2 tbsp. honey	1/2 tsp. vanilla

Stir together all ingredients; whisk until smooth. Add additional powdered sugar if too thin or more milk if too thick. Drizzle over warm pastries.

Joe Behounek, *Chelsea*
First Place, 2015 King Arthur Flour Yeast Rolls – Sweet Rolls Other Than Named
First Place Overall, 2015 King Arthur Flour Yeast Rolls

OLD ORDER AMISH BREAD

5 to 6 c. bread flour	1 1/2 c. hot water (120°-130°)
1 pkg. active dry yeast	1/3 c. vegetable oil
1/3 c. granulated sugar	1 tbsp. butter, softened
2 tsp. salt	

In large mixing bowl, add 2 cups flour, yeast, sugar, salt, water and oil. Stir with wooden spoon until well blended. Add additional flour, 1/2 cup at a time, working together first with spoon and then with hands until rough mass has formed and dough has cleaned sides of bowl. Dough will be elastic but not sticky. Turn dough out onto a generously floured surface; knead about 8 minutes. If dough seems slack and doesn't hold its shape, add additional flour and work in. Place dough in greased bowl; turning to grease surface. Cover tightly with plastic wrap. Leave bowl at room temperature until dough has doubled, about 1 hour. Punch down dough. Replace plastic wrap and let dough rise again, about 45 minutes. Turn dough onto work surface, punch down and knead briefly to work out bubbles. Divide into 2 pieces. Form loaves; place in greased 8 1/2 x 4 1/2-inch pans. Cover loaves with wax paper; let stand at room temperature 40 minutes or until dough has risen about 1-inch above edge of pans. Bake loaves in 400° oven 10 minutes; reduce heat to 350°. Bake 30 minutes until loaves are golden brown. Remove from oven; turn out from pans immediately. Brush softened butter on top of loaves shortly after removing from oven. Cool on metal rack.

Michelle Jackson, *Van Meter*
First Place, 2014 King Arthur Flour Bread – White Bread

CINNAMON RAISIN BREAD

1 1/2 c. milk
1/4 c. butter
1 heaping c. raisins
1 c. rolled oats
1/2 c. plus 1 tbsp. brown sugar, divided
2 tsp. salt
2 tbsp. ground cinnamon
5 1/2 to 6 c. unbleached all-purpose flour
2 1/2 tsp. instant yeast
1/2 c. lukewarm water (110°)
1 egg white beaten with 1 tbsp. water

Heat milk and butter until just hot to the touch (about 120°). Transfer to bowl; add raisins, oats, 1/2 cup brown sugar, salt and cinnamon. Stir well; set aside. In medium bowl, mix 3 cups flour with instant yeast and water. When milk mixture has cooled to lukewarm, add yeast/flour mixture; mix on low speed. Add remaining 2 1/2 to 3 cups flour, 1/2 cup at a time, until dough pulls away from sides of bowl. Knead on medium speed about 5 minutes. Place dough in lightly oiled bowl, turn to coat dough on all sides. Cover with plastic wrap; let rise in warm place until doubled, 1 1/2 to 2 hours. Punch dough down; knead briefly on lightly floured surface. Divide dough in half. Shape into loaves and place into 2 lightly greased 8 1/2 x 4 1/2-inch loaf pans. Cover with plastic wrap; let rise until doubled, about 1 hour. Brush tops of loaves with egg mixture. Bake in 375° oven 30 to 35 minutes, until nicely browned and internal temperature reaches 185 to 190°. If loaves are browning too quickly, cover with aluminum foil, shiny-side up. Turn out onto wire rack to cool.

Kelly McCulley, *Des Moines*
First Place, 2014 King Arthur Flour Bread, Raisin – Cinnamon Bread

---

HONEY BANANA NUT BREAD

3 medium ripe bananas, mashed
3/4 c. honey
1 egg
1 1/2 c. all-purpose flour
1/4 c. vegetable oil
1 tsp. vanilla
1 tsp. salt
1 tsp. baking soda
3/4 c. chopped walnuts

Combine all ingredients except nuts; mix well. Add nuts; pour into greased 8x4-inch bread pan. Bake in 350° oven 1 hour.

Molly Thomas, *Centerville*
Second Place, 2014 Foods Made With Honey – Honey Banana Nut Bread

HONEY-MUSTARD OATMEAL BREAD

3 to 3 1/2 c. bread flour, divided
1/2 c. quick-cooking rolled oats
1 tsp. salt
1/3 c. pure honey
2 tbsp. Dijon mustard
2 tbsp. butter, softened

1 pkg. active dry yeast
1 c. very warm water (120°-125°)
1 large egg
1 egg white, slightly beaten
1 tbsp. water
Quick-cooking oats

Mix 1 1/2 cups flour, oats, salt, honey, mustard, butter and yeast in large bowl. Add 1 cup warm water. Beat on low speed 1 minute, scraping bowl frequently. Beat 1 minute more on medium speed, scraping bowl frequently. Beat in egg. Stir in enough remaining flour, 1/2 cup at a time, to make dough easy to handle. Turn dough onto lightly floured surface. Knead 10 minutes or until smooth and elastic. Place in greased bowl and turn greased side up. Cover and let rise until doubled. Grease bottom and side of pie plate with shortening. Punch dough down; shape into ball. Place in pie plate; flatten slightly. Mix egg white and 1 tablespoon water; brush on loaf. Sprinkle with oats. Cover and let rise until doubled. Bake in 375° oven 35 minutes or until loaf sounds hollow when tapped and is a deep golden brown. Remove from plate to wire rack and cool.

Phyllis Olson, *Newton*
First Place, 2014 Foods Made with Honey – Honey Oatmeal Bread
First Place Overall, 2014 Foods Made with Honey – Breads and Rolls

SAVORY CHEDDAR BREAD

2 c. all-purpose flour
4 tsp. baking powder
1 tbsp. granulated sugar
1/2 tsp. onion salt
1/2 tsp. leaf oregano
1/4 tsp. dry mustard

1 egg, well beaten
1 c. milk
1 tbsp. butter, melted
1 1/4 c. shredded sharp cheddar
   cheese

Combine flour, baking powder, sugar, onion salt, leaf oregano and dry mustard. In separate bowl, combine egg, milk, butter and cheese. Add to dry ingredients, stirring until moistened. Spread batter in greased 9x5-inch loaf pan. Bake in 350° oven 45 minutes.

Barb Miller, *Prairie City*
First Place, 2014 Iowa Bed & Breakfast Quick Breads – Cheese Bread

FOCCACIA

3 c. unbleached all-purpose
    flour
1 2/3 c. water, room temperature
1 1/4 tsp. salt
1 1/2 tsp. instant yeast

1 1/4 tsp. granulated sugar
5 tbsp. extra virgin olive oil,
    divided
1 tsp. coarse salt
2 tbsp. coarsely chopped
    rosemary

Mix flour, water and salt on low speed until no patches of dry flour remain, 3 to 4 minutes. Let dough rest 20 minutes. Sprinkle yeast and sugar over dough. Knead on low speed 1 to 2 minutes. Increase mixer speed to high; knead until dough is glossy and smooth, 6 to 10 minutes. Coat large bowl with 1 tablespoon olive oil. Transfer dough to greased bowl and pour 1 tablespoon oil over top. Flip dough over so it is coated with oil. Cover tightly with plastic wrap. Let dough rise until tripled, 2 to 2 1/2 hours. Coat rimmed baking sheet with 2 tablespoons oil. Turn dough out on baking sheet and press to sides of pan. Let dough rest 5 to 10 minutes. Poke surface with fork 30 to 40 times. Sprinkle with coarse salt. Bake in 450° oven 20 to 30 minutes, sprinkling rosemary over top halfway through baking. Brush dough with remaining olive oil.

Valerie Singer, *Altoona*
First Place, 2014 King Arthur Flour Bread – Focaccia

BUTTER PECAN BREAD

1/2 c. butter, softened
3.4-oz. pkg. instant
    butterscotch pudding mix
4 eggs
1/4 c. applesauce
3/4 c. water

15.25-oz. pkg. butter pecan
    cake mix
1 c. chopped and toasted
    pecans
1/4 c. chopped pecans for
    topping

Beat butter until soft; mix in pudding mix. Add eggs, one at a time, beating well after each addition. Add applesauce, water and cake mix; beat well. Stir in 1 cup pecans. Pour into 2 greased 8x4-inch loaf pans. Sprinkle remaining pecans over top. Bake in 350° oven 35 to 45 minutes.

Emma Whitlock, *Indianola*
First Place, 2015 Iowa Bed & Breakfast Quick Breads – Cake Mix Bread

BRAIDED COFFEE CAKE

For SPONGE:

1/3 c. warm water (105°-115°)	1 1/2 tsp. instant yeast
1 tsp. granulated sugar	1/4 c. bread flour

In a small bowl, combine all ingredients. Stir well to combine; cover loosely with plastic wrap. Set aside 10 to 15 minutes until foamy.

For DOUGH:

1/2 c. plain yogurt	1 tsp. buttery sweet dough
1/4 c. unsalted butter, softened	flavor or vanilla
1 large egg, beaten	2 1/2 c. bread flour
1/4 c. granulated sugar	1/2 c. jam
1 tsp. salt	1 egg beaten with 1 tbsp. water
	Sparkling white sugar

Combine sponge, yogurt, butter, egg, sugar, salt and flavoring. Add flour and knead 5 to 7 minutes. Place dough in greased bowl, turning to grease surface. Cover with plastic wrap and let rise until doubled, about 60 to 90 minutes. Gently deflate dough. On parchment paper, roll out dough into rectangle, about 10x15-inches. With a bench knife, lightly press two lines down dough lengthwise, dividing into 3 equal sections. Spread jam down center of dough, leaving 1 inch free on each side. Fold over 1 inch of top and bottom edges of dough, covering jam. These flaps will seal in the ends. To form mock braid, cut 1-inch crosswise strips down length of outside sections, making sure to have same number of strips down each side. Beginning on the left, lift top dough strip and gently bring it across filling diagonally. Repeat on other side with top dough strip, so that the 2 strips crisscross each other. Continue down entire braid, alternating strips to form the loaf. Tuck the edges underneath the bottom of the braid. Cover with plastic wrap; allow to rise until quite puffy, about 45 to 60 minutes. Transfer braid to a baking sheet. Brush with egg mixture and sprinkle with sparkling sugar. Bake in upper third of 375° oven 20 to 25 minutes, turning sheet around halfway through baking time. Cool before slicing.

Deirdre Scott, *Grimes*
First Place, 2014 King Arthur Flour Yeast Rolls – Coffee Cake

HALLE'S HONEY CRESCENT ROLLS

1 c. lukewarm buttermilk
1 tbsp. instant yeast
1/4 c. plus 2 tbsp. honey, divided
1/4 c. nonfat dry milk
1 3/4 tsp. salt

3 eggs, lightly beaten
1/2 c. creamy mashed potatoes
1 c. butter, softened
4 to 5 c. all-purpose flour
2 tbsp. butter

Combine buttermilk, yeast, and 1/4 cup honey in a medium mixing bowl. Let stand until foamy, 5 minutes. Add dry milk, salt, eggs, mashed potatoes, softened butter and flour. Stir until soft dough forms. Turn out onto lightly floured surface; knead 6 to 8 minutes. Place in well-oiled bowl, turning to grease surface. Cover and let rise until doubled. Punch dough down. Lightly oil top of dough again; cover and refrigerate 6 to 10 hours. When ready to bake, divide dough into 3 portions. Roll into circle 1/4-inch thick. Cut into 12 wedges. Roll up from long side of triangle to short. Cover; let rise 1 1/2 to 2 hours until doubled. Bake in 400° oven 9 minutes or until internal temperature registers 190° on an instant read thermometer. Cool 5 minutes. Combine 2 tablespoons butter and 2 tablespoons honey; brush on rolls. Serve warm.

Halle Tanna Clark, *Runnells*
First Place, 2014 Foods Made with Honey – Youth Entries

SWEET POTATO CORN BREAD

3/4 c. yellow cornmeal
3/4 c. all-purpose flour
1 tbsp. baking powder
1/2 tsp. cinnamon
1/2 tsp. salt
1/2 c. butter, room temperature

2 eggs
1/2 c. honey
1 c. mashed baked sweet potato
1/2 c. half and half
1/2 c. white shoepeg corn

Combine cornmeal, flour, baking powder, cinnamon and salt. In separate bowl, cream together butter and eggs. Add honey, sweet potato and half and half. Mix until smooth. Add dry ingredients; mix well. Fold in corn. Pour into greased 9-inch pan. Bake in 350° oven until firm, about 30 minutes. Serve with honey butter.

Pamela Cooper, *Mount Ayr*
First Place, 2014 Foods Made With Honey – Honey Corn Bread

POTATO BREAD

1 medium potato	2 tbsp. granulated sugar
Water	1 tbsp. salt
Hot tap water	1 c. warm milk (105°-115°)
2 pkgs. active dry yeast	6 1/2 to 7 1/2 c. all-purpose flour
2 tbsp. butter	

Pare and dice potato; boil in water until tender. Drain, reserving liquid. Add enough hot water to potato liquid to make 1 cup. Cool to 105°–115°. Mash potato; set aside. Pour potato water into bowl; add yeast. Stir until dissolved. Add butter, sugar and salt. Stir in potato, warm milk and 3 cups flour; beat until smooth. Stir in enough additional flour to make stiff dough. Turn out onto lightly floured surface; knead 8 to 10 minutes or until smooth and elastic. Place in greased bowl, turning once to grease surface. Cover; let rise until doubled, about 35 minutes. Punch dough down; turn over. Let rise 20 minutes more. Punch down; turn out onto board, divide in half. Roll to 14x9-inch rectangle. Shape into loaves. Place in 2 greased 9x5-inch loaf pans. Cover; let rise until doubled, about 50 minutes. Bake in 375° oven 35 to 40 minutes, or until it reaches 190° on thermometer. Remove immediately and cool on racks.

Sonny Melchers, *Fairfield*
First Place, 2015 King Arthur Flour Bread – Potato Bread

GRANDMOTHER'S BUTTERMILK CORNBREAD

1/2 c. melted butter	1/2 tsp. baking soda
1/4 c. honey	3/4 tsp. salt
2 eggs	1 c. cornmeal
1 c. buttermilk	1/4 tsp. dried red pepper
1 c. all-purpose flour	flakes
1 1/2 tsp. baking powder	

In large bowl, stir together butter and honey. Add eggs; beat until well blended. Mix in buttermilk, flour, baking powder, baking soda, salt, cornmeal and red pepper flakes. Pour into greased 8-inch pan. Bake in 375° oven 35 to 40 minutes.

Marjorie Rodgers, *Indianola*
First Place, 2015 Foods Made with Honey – Honey Corn Bread

FLUFFY HONEY DINNER ROLLS

1 tbsp. instant yeast
1/4 c. warm water (105°-115°)
1/4 c. plus 2 tsp. honey, divided
3/4 c. fluffy mashed potatoes,
   seasoned with butter and salt
1/4 c. dry milk
2 tsp. salt
1 1/4 c. lukewarm buttermilk

4 tbsp. unsalted
   butter, softened
5 c. unbleached all-purpose
   flour
2 tbsp. butter
2 tbsp. honey
Pinch of salt
1 egg beaten with 1 tsp. water

Dissolve yeast in warm water with 2 teaspoons honey; let stand until foamy. Add mashed potatoes, dry milk, 1/4 cup honey, salt, buttermilk and softened butter; whisk well. Add flour; stir to combine until ball of dough is formed. Turn out onto lightly floured surface; knead 8 minutes. Place dough in a greased bowl, turning to grease surface. Cover with greased plastic wrap; set in warm, draft free area until doubled. Gently deflate dough; transfer to lightly greased work surface. Divide into 18 pieces. Roll into balls in circular motion. Lightly butter two 8-inch square or round cake pans. Place 9 rolls in each pan. Cover pans; let rise until doubled. To make glaze, melt 2 tablespoons butter in saucepan over medium heat; skim white solids off top of melted butter, discard solids. Add 2 tablespoons honey and pinch of salt; stir well. Set aside until rolls are out of oven. Brush with egg wash and bake in 350° oven 22 to 24 minutes, until golden and 190° internal temperature. Remove rolls from oven; brush with honey butter glaze. Turn out of pans onto cooling racks.

Cristen C. Clark, *Runnells*
First Place, 2014 Foods Made with Honey – Honey Dinner Rolls

MULTIGRAIN SUNFLOWER BREAD

For PATE FERMENTEE and SOAKER:
1/8 tsp. active dry yeast
1 1/2 c. room temperature water,
   divided

1 c. bread flour
1/2 tsp. salt
1 1/2 c. 10-grain hot cereal mix

(CONTINUED)

For fermentee, mix yeast with 1/4 cup water. Add flour and salt; mix until smooth. Cover with plastic wrap; let stand overnight. For soaker, mix cereal mix and remaining water until combined. Cover with plastic wrap; let stand overnight.

For DOUGH:

2 1/2 c. bread flour	**2 tbsp. vegetable oil**
1/2 c. water	**2 tbsp. barley malt syrup**
1 1/2 tbsp. salt	**6 tbsp. roasted, salted sunflower**
4 tsp. vital wheat gluten	**seeds**
1 tsp. active dry yeast	

In bowl, combine flour, water, salt, vital wheat gluten, yeast, oil, syrup, sunflower seeds and soaker. Mix on low 3 minutes. As dough is coming together, add pate fermentee in small portions. Turn mixer to medium speed and mix an additional 3 minutes. Turn out onto lightly floured surface; lightly knead and shape. Place in lightly oiled container. Lightly oil top of dough; cover container with plastic wrap. Allow to rise 1 hour. Turn dough out onto lightly floured surface; press into rectangle with palms of hands. Fold left side to the middle, fold right side to the middle, fold bottom to the middle and fold top to the middle. Re-oil the container and place dough in container. Lightly oil top of dough. Cover with plastic wrap; let rise 1 hour. Turn dough out onto lightly floured surface. Flatten dough with palm of your hand and pull together into a loose round form. Cover and allow to rest 10 minutes. Flatten dough again and more carefully shape into round loaf. Place loaf on a baking sheet covered with parchment paper. Cover with a towel; allow to rise 1 hour at room temperature. While dough is rising, place a baking stone in oven. On lowest rack, place a rimmed baking sheet. Measure 1 cup of water and have next to oven. Preheat oven to 425°. When dough has risen, slash the loaf and quickly move loaf onto baking sheet and place sheet on the baking stone. Pour water into rimmed baking sheet under baking stone. Bake until middle is 200°. Remove from oven and place on cooling rack until cool.

Michelle Melchers, *Cedar Rapids*
First Place, 2015 King Arthur Flour Bread – Mixed Grain Bread

YEAST BREADS AND QUICK BREADS

HONEY DINNER YEAST ROLLS

1/2 c. cornmeal
1/3 c. honey
1 tbsp. salt
2 c. boiling water
1/2 c. vegetable oil
2 pkgs. active dry yeast

1/2 c. warm water (105°-115°)
1 c. whole wheat flour
3/4 c. rye flour
3 to 4 c. unbleached all-
   purpose flour

In large mixing bowl, combine cornmeal, honey and salt. Pour in boiling water; mix well. Add vegetable oil; beat well. Allow to cool to lukewarm. In small bowl, mix together yeast and warm water. Let stand 5 minutes. Add to cornmeal mixture. Stir in whole wheat flour and rye flour; beat well. Gradually beat in all-purpose flour to make stiff dough. Turn out onto lightly floured surface. Knead thoroughly until smooth and elastic. Place dough into large bowl. Cover; let rise until doubled. Punch dough down. Turn out onto lightly floured surface. Shape pieces of dough into small balls; place into well-greased muffin tin or side-by-side in greased baking pan. Let rise until almost doubled. Bake in 350° oven 20 to 25 minutes. Remove from pans; cool on wire rack.

Louise Piper, *Garner*
First Place, 2015 Foods Made with Honey – Honey Dinner Rolls

TACO CHEESE BREAD

2 c. all-purpose flour
2 tbsp. granulated sugar
1 tbsp. baking powder
1 tsp. salt
1 tsp. cumin
1/2 tsp. finely chopped
   cilantro

1/4 tsp. red pepper flakes
1 1/2 c. taco seasoned
   shredded cheddar and
   Monterey Jack cheese
1 egg, beaten
3/4 c. plus 2 tbsp. milk
3 tbsp. vegetable oil

Sift together flour, sugar, baking powder, salt, cumin, cilantro and red pepper flakes; add cheese. Combine egg, milk and oil; add to dry ingredients. Mix until moistened. Pour into greased 8x4-inch loaf pan. Bake in 350° oven 55 to 60 minutes.

Emma Whitlock, *Indianola*
First Place, 2015 Iowa Bed & Breakfast Quick Breads – Cheese Bread

CROISSANTS

1 1/2 c. butter	1 tsp. salt
1/3 c. all-purpose flour	1 egg
2 pkgs. active dry yeast	3 3/4 to 4 1/4 c. all-purpose
1/2 c. warm water (105°-115°)	flour
3/4 c. milk	1 egg yolk
1/4 c. granulated sugar	1 tbsp. milk

Cream together butter with 1/3 cup flour. Roll between wax paper into 12x6-inch rectangle. Chill at least 1 hour. Soften yeast in warm water. In saucepan, heat milk, sugar and salt until dissolved. Remove from heat. Transfer to large bowl. Add yeast mixture and egg; beat well. Add 2 cups flour; mix well. Gradually add enough flour to make moderately stiff dough. Roll into a 14x14-inch square. Place chilled butter on one half and fold over other half. Seal edges; cover with plastic wrap and chill at least 2 hours. Remove from refrigerator; fold into thirds. Roll dough into 21x12-inch rectangle. Fold into thirds; cover and chill. Roll and fold 2 more times, chilling after each time. After third time, cut dough into fourths; fold each section into 22x7-inch rectangle. Cut into 6 triangle pieces; loosely roll from large end to point. Place on ungreased baking sheet. Let rise until doubled, about 1 hour. Mix egg yolk and milk; brush each croissant with mixture. Bake in 375° oven 12 to 15 minutes.

Lana Shope, *Indianola*
First Place, 2015 King Arthur Flour Yeast Rolls – Refrigerated Rolls

COCONUT MUFFINS

For COCONUT MUFFINS:

2 c. all-purpose flour	1/2 c. honey
3 tsp. baking powder	1/3 c. vegetable oil
1/4 tsp. salt	1/2 tsp. coconut extract
1 egg	1/2 c. flake coconut
2/3 c. milk	

In a large bowl, combine flour, baking powder and salt. In separate bowl, combine egg, milk, honey, oil and extract; mix well. Stir in dry ingredients until combined. Stir in flake coconut. Fill greased or paper-lined muffin cups two-thirds full.

(CONTINUED)

For TOPPING:

1/4 c. flake coconut	1/2 tsp. cinnamon
1 tbsp. butter	

Combine all ingredients; sprinkle over batter. Bake in 375° oven 18 to 20 minutes or until toothpick inserted in center comes out clean. Cool 5 minutes before removing to wire rack.

Marjorie Rodgers, *Indianola*
First Place, 2014 Foods Made With Honey – Honey Muffins

BUTTERSCOTCH ROLLS

1 pkg. active dry yeast	1/3 c. lard, melted
1 c. warm water (105°-115°)	2 tsp. salt
Pinch of ginger	2 tbsp. butter, softened
3/4 c. plus 1 tbsp. granulated sugar, divided	2 tsp. cinnamon
	1/3 c. butter, melted
1 c milk, warmed	1 tbsp. light corn syrup
7 c. all-purpose flour	1/2 c. packed brown sugar
2 large eggs, beaten	1/2 c. chopped pecans

Combine yeast, warm water, ginger and 1 tablespoon sugar; let stand a few minutes. Add milk and 3 cups flour. Cover, let stand 30 minutes. Add eggs, lard, 1/4 cup sugar, salt and remaining flour. Turn out onto lightly floured surface; knead dough until smooth. Place in greased bowl, turning to grease surface. Cover; let rise until doubled. Roll dough into 15x9-inch rectangle. Spread dough with 2 tablespoons butter; sprinkle with remaining sugar and cinnamon. Roll up tightly; cut into 1-inch slices. In saucepan, melt remaining butter, corn syrup, brown sugar and pecans. Spread in bottom of baking pan. Place dough slices on top of butter mixture. Cover; let rise until doubled. Bake in 350° oven 25 to 30 minutes. Immediately invert on large tray.

Nancy Tuttle, *Winterset*
First Place, 2015 King Arthur Flour Yeast Rolls – Cinnamon Rolls (with nuts)

CINNAMON RAISIN BREAD

2 pkgs. active dry yeast
1 c. warm water (105°-115°)
1 1/2 c. plus 2 tbsp. milk,
    divided
3 eggs
1/2 c. butter, softened

1 1/2 c. granulated sugar,
    divided
1 tsp. salt
1 c. raisins
8 c. bread flour
3 tbsp. cinnamon

Dissolve yeast in water; let stand until foamy, about 5 minutes. Heat 1 1/2 cups milk in saucepan on low until bubbles form. Remove from heat; cool to lukewarm and add to yeast mixture. Stir in eggs, butter, 1/2 cup sugar, salt and raisins. Gradually add flour to form stiff dough. Turn out onto lightly floured surface; knead dough until smooth. Place dough in greased bowl, turning to grease surface. Wrap bowl in plastic wrap. Let dough rise in warm area at least 2 hours. Remove plastic wrap. Roll out dough on floured surface until 1/2-inch thick. Spread remaining milk on top of dough. Mix together remaining sugar and cinnamon. Sprinkle evenly across dough. Roll and pinch edges. Cut in thirds and place in 3 greased 8x3-inch loaf pans. Let rise 1 hour. Bake in 350° oven 35 minutes.

Jenna Brady, *Runnells*
First Place, 2015 King Arthur Flour Bread – Raisin Cinnamon Bread

---

CHIPOTLE CHEDDAR CORN BREAD

1 c. cornmeal
1 c. all-purpose flour
3 tsp. baking powder
1 tsp. salt
3 oz. fresh corn (approx. 1 ear)
1 c. buttermilk

1/2 c. granulated sugar
1 chipotle chili, chopped
2 eggs
4 tbsp. butter, melted and
    cooled
4 oz. shredded sharp cheddar
    cheese

Whisk together cornmeal, flour, baking powder and salt. In food processor, blend corn, buttermilk, sugar and chipotle for 5 seconds. Add eggs; process 5 seconds more. Fold wet ingredients, butter and cheddar cheese into dry ingredients. Preheat 10-inch cast iron skillet in 350° oven. Pour batter into skillet; bake 25 to 30 minutes.

Matthew Phoenix, *Ankeny*
First Place, 2014 Iowa Bed & Breakfast Quick Breads – Corn Bread

BEST EVER BANANA BREAD

1 3/4 c. all-purpose flour
1 1/2 c. granulated sugar
1/8 tsp. ground cinnamon
1 tsp. baking soda
1/2 tsp. salt
2 eggs

1 c. mashed bananas (approx.
   2 medium ripe bananas)
1/2 c. vegetable oil
1/4 c. plus 1 tbsp. buttermilk
1 tsp. vanilla
1 tsp. rum extract
1 c. banana chips for garnish

In large bowl, combine flour, sugar, cinnamon, baking soda and salt. In separate bowl, combine eggs, bananas, oil, buttermilk, vanilla and rum extract; add to flour mixture, stirring until combined. Pour into greased 9x5-inch baking pan. Add banana chips to top of bread (optional). Bake in 325° oven 1 hour and 20 minutes or until toothpick inserted near the center comes out clean. Cool on wire rack.

Jacqueline Riekena, *West Des Moines*
First Place, 2014 Chiquita Ultimate Banana Bread – No Nuts
First Place Overall, 2014 Chiquita Ultimate Banana Bread

CRANBERRY WHOLE WHEAT BREAD

1/4 c. hot water
1 c. diced dried cranberries
2 c. all-purpose flour
1 c. whole wheat flour
1 tsp. baking powder
1 tsp. baking soda

1/2 tsp. salt
1/4 c. butter
3/4 c. granulated sugar
1 large egg
1 1/2 c. buttermilk

Thirty minutes before baking, combine hot water and cranberries in small bowl. Cover; set aside in warm place. In large bowl, blend together flours, baking powder, baking soda and salt. In medium bowl, beat butter and sugar together until light and fluffy; beat in egg. Add alternately dry ingredients and buttermilk. Blend until well moistened. Beat in cranberry mixture. Scrape batter into 2 greased 7x3-inch loaf pans. Bake in 350° oven 45 to 50 minutes. Remove from pans; cool on wire rack.

Marjorie Rodgers, *Indianola*
First Place, 2015 Iowa Bed & Breakfast Quick Breads – Cranberry Bread

ONION HERB BISCUITS

2 c. all-purpose flour
1 tbsp. baking powder
1 tsp. dried thyme
1 tsp. dried savory
1/2 tsp. salt

1/4 tsp. baking soda
1/4 tsp. pepper
1 1/2 c. sour cream
2 tbsp. olive oil
1/4 c. thinly sliced green
onions

Combine flour, baking powder, thyme, savory, salt, baking soda and pepper. In separate bowl, combine sour cream and oil; stir into dry ingredients until blended. Stir in green onions. Turn out onto lightly floured surface; gently knead 3 or 4 times. Roll dough to 3/4-inch thickness; cut with biscuit cutter. Place 1 inch apart on ungreased baking sheet. Bake in 400° oven 14 to 18 minutes or until lightly browned.

Colette Wortman, *Urbandale*
First Place, 2015 Iowa Bed & Breakfast Quick Breads – Flavored Biscuits
Second Place Overall, 2015 Iowa Bed & Breakfast Quick Breads

BUTTERMILK BISCUITS

2 c. unbleached all-purpose
flour
2 tbsp. baking powder
2 tsp. granulated sugar
1 tsp. salt

5 tbsp. European style
unsalted butter,
chilled and diced
1 c. buttermilk
1 egg beaten with 1 tbsp.
water

In medium bowl, mix flour, baking powder, sugar and salt. Cut in butter until pieces are no larger than small peas. Add buttermilk while tossing with fork until dough holds together. Turn dough out onto floured work surface. Fold over a few times until it becomes cohesive; cover with clean kitchen towel. Let rest 30 minutes. Roll dough to 3/4 to 1-inch thickness; be careful not to overwork dough. Using a 2 1/2 to 3-inch diameter floured biscuit cutter, cut dough into biscuits. Place on parchment-lined baking sheets. Brush tops with egg mixture. Bake in 425° oven 10 to 14 minutes, until tops are golden brown. Serve warm.

Jeffrey King, *Newton*
First Place, 2015 Iowa Bed & Breakfast Quick Breads – Biscuits

BANANA BREAD

1 1/2 c. granulated sugar
1/2 c. canola oil
2 eggs, beaten
1 tsp. vanilla
1 1/4 c. mashed bananas
1 3/4 c. all-purpose flour

1 tbsp. plus 1 tsp. powdered
buttermilk
1 tsp. baking soda
1/8 tsp. salt
1/4 c. plus 1 tbsp. water

Combine sugar and oil with mixer. Add eggs, vanilla and bananas. Sift together flour, powdered buttermilk, baking soda and salt; add to banana mixture alternately with water. Beat until blended. Pour into 3 greased 7 1/2 x 3 1/2-inch loaf pans. Bake in 325° oven 45 minutes. Cool 10 minutes in pans; remove and cool thoroughly on wire rack. Wrap and store overnight before slicing.

Carol Shafer, *Norwalk*
First Place, 2015 Ultimate Banana Bread – Banana Bread (no nuts)
First Place Overall, 2015 Ultimate Banana Bread

STRAWBERRY BANANA WALNUT BREAD

3 c. all-purpose flour
1 1/2 tsp. cinnamon
1 tsp. baking soda
1 tsp. cardamom
1/2 tsp. salt
1/4 tsp. nutmeg
4 eggs, beaten
2 c. granulated sugar

1 1/2 c. mashed strawberries
1 c. vegetable oil
1 c. mashed bananas
1 tbsp. finely shredded
orange zest
2 c. finely chopped and
toasted walnuts, divided

In large mixing bowl, stir together flour, cinnamon, baking soda, cardamom, salt and nutmeg. In separate bowl, stir together eggs, sugar, strawberries, oil, banana and orange zest. Add to dry ingredients, stirring until moistened. Carefully stir in 1 cup nuts. Sprinkle remaining nuts in bottoms of 2 greased and floured 8x4-inch loaf pans. Transfer batter to pans. Bake in 350° oven 1 hour.

Emma Whitlock, *Indianola*
First Place, 2015 Iowa Bed & Breakfast Quick Breads – Fresh Fruit

BANANA NUT AND GINGER BREAD

1 c. packed brown sugar
1/2 c. mashed bananas
1 egg
1/2 tsp. vanilla
1 tbsp. melted butter
1 1/2 c. all-purpose flour
1 tsp. baking soda
1/2 tsp. salt
3/4 tsp. ground cinnamon

1/4 tsp. ground allspice
1 tsp. ground cardamom
1/4 tsp. ground cloves
1 c. vanilla porter beer
3/4 c. chopped walnuts
1 tbsp. all-purpose flour
1 c. pitted and chopped dates
1 tbsp. minced fresh ginger root

In large bowl, cream brown sugar, banana, egg, vanilla and butter. In separate bowl, sift together flour, baking soda, salt, cinnamon, allspice, cardamom and cloves. Alternately blend flour mixture and beer into creamed mixture. Toss walnuts with remaining flour. Add to batter. Stir in dates and ginger; blend well. Pour into greased 9x5-inch loaf pan. Bake in 350° oven 1 hour or until toothpick inserted near center comes out dry and clean.

Rebecca Howe, *Des Moines*
First Place, 2014 Keith's Beer Breads – Non-Yeast Beer Bread
Second Place Overall, 2014 Keith's Beer Breads

CHOCOLATE CHIP AND COCONUT BANANA BREAD

3 overly ripe bananas, mashed
2 eggs
1/2 c. margarine
1 1/2 tbsp. vanilla
1 tsp. baking soda

1 tsp. salt
1 c. granulated sugar
2 c. all-purpose flour
2/3 c. coconut
3/4 c. miniature chocolate chips

In large bowl, mix bananas, eggs and margarine. Mix in vanilla, baking soda, salt and sugar. Slowly add flour. Mix in coconut and chocolate chips by hand. Pour into greased 9x5-inch loaf pan. Bake in 350° oven 1 hour or until golden brown.

Heather Nelson, *Des Moines*
First Place, 2014 Beginner's Contest – Bread
Second Place Overall, 2014 Beginner's Contest

YEAST BREADS AND QUICK BREADS

CARAMEL APPLE BUTTERMILK MUFFINS

2 1/2 c. all-purpose flour
1/4 tsp. salt
2 1/2 tsp. baking powder
1/2 tsp. baking soda
1/2 c. vegetable oil
1 1/3 c. packed light brown
    sugar

1 egg
1 c. buttermilk
2 tsp. vanilla
1 3/4 c. coarsely chopped
    peeled Granny Smith
    apples

Combine flour, salt, baking powder and baking soda; set aside. In separate bowl, combine oil, brown sugar and egg. Stir in buttermilk and vanilla. Add wet ingredients to dry ingredients; mix well. Gently mix in apple. If batter seems too thin, add a tiny bit more flour. Batter should be fairly stiff. Spoon batter into 18 paper-lined muffin tins. Fill tins approximately three-fourths full. Divide streusel topping equally among muffins. Bake in 400° oven 5 minutes. Reduce heat to 350°; bake 15 minutes or until toothpick inserted in center comes out clean. Let muffins cool in pan 10 minutes; remove and let cool 15 to 20 minutes on wire rack. Drizzle with caramel icing.

For STREUSEL TOPPING:
1 tbsp. cold butter
1/3 c. firmly packed brown
    sugar

1/2 tsp. ground cinnamon
1/2 c. finely chopped
    walnuts, toasted

Combine all ingredients with fingers until mixture is crumbly.

For CARAMEL ICING:
2 tbsp. butter
1/4 c. packed light brown
    sugar

2 tbsp. milk
1 tsp. vanilla
1 c. powdered sugar

Combine butter, brown sugar and milk in medium microwave-safe bowl. Microwave on high 30 seconds; add vanilla, stir well. Return to microwave 15 seconds. Add powdered sugar; mix vigorously until smooth and creamy. Mixture should not be runny. Add additional milk or powdered sugar to adjust thickness.

Daphane Trevillyan, *Kelley*
First Place, 2015 Iowa Bed & Breakfast Quick Breads – Fruit Muffins

CHOCOLATE ZUCCHINI BREAD

3 eggs
1 c. oil
2 c. granulated sugar
1 tsp. vanilla
2 c. finely shredded zucchini
3 c. all-purpose flour

1/2 c. unsweetened cocoa
powder
1/2 tsp. salt
1 tsp. baking soda
1 tsp. cinnamon
1/4 tsp. baking powder
1/2 c. chopped nuts

In bowl, beat together eggs, oil, sugar and vanilla. Stir in zucchini. In large bowl, combine flour, cocoa, salt, baking soda, cinnamon and baking powder; stir to mix. Add flour mixture to zucchini mixture; stir until moistened. Stir in nuts. Spoon into 3 greased 7x3-inch loaf pans. Bake in 350 degree oven 1 hour or until toothpick inserted in center comes out clean. Cool in pans 10 minutes. Remove from pans; cool completely on wire racks.

Marjorie Rodgers, *Indianola*
First Place, 2015 Iowa Bed & Breakfast Quick Breads – Zucchini Bread

HONEY-BLUEBERRY MUFFINS

2 1/4 c. all-purpose flour
1/2 tsp. salt
3 tsp. baking powder
1 c. buttermilk
1/2 c. honey

1 egg, beaten
1/2 c. butter, melted
3/4 c. blueberries
1/2 c. sliced almonds
Honey for drizzle

Stir together flour, salt and baking powder. In separate bowl, combine buttermilk, honey, egg and butter. Add to dry ingredients; stir to moisten. Add blueberries. Fill greased muffin tins; top with sliced almonds. Bake in 375° oven 20 minutes. Drizzle with honey.

Anita Van Gundy, *Des Moines*
First Place, 2015 Taste of Honey Challenge – Breads
First Place Overall, 2015 Taste of Honey Challenge

HONEY GINGERBREAD

1/3 c. lard
1/3 c. granulated sugar
1/2 c. molasses
1/2 c. honey
1 egg
2 1/2 c. all-purpose flour

1/2 tsp. salt
1 tsp. baking soda
1/2 tsp. baking powder
1 tsp. cinnamon
2 tsp. ginger
1 c. buttermilk

In large bowl, cream together lard and sugar. Add molasses and honey; cream until light. Add egg; beat well. In separate bowl, sift together flour, salt, baking soda, baking powder, cinnamon and ginger. Add dry ingredients alternately with buttermilk to creamed mixture. Beat until smooth. Pour into greased and wax paper-lined 9-inch round or square baking pan. Bake in 350° oven 45 minutes. Turn out onto wire rack to cool.

Marjorie Rodgers, *Indianola*
First Place, 2015 Make It with Lard – Gingerbread
First Place Overall, 2015 Make It with Lard – Desserts

ALMOND CINNAMON NUT BREAD

1/4 c. butter
1 1/2 c. packed brown sugar
2 eggs
2 1/2 c. all-purpose flour
1 1/2 tsp. cinnamon
1 1/2 tsp. baking soda
3/4 tsp. baking powder

1/2 tsp. salt
1 1/2 c. sour cream
1 tsp. almond flavoring
1 c. chopped and toasted
   slivered almonds
1/2 c. chopped almonds
   for topping

Cream butter; gradually add brown sugar and beat until light and fluffy. Beat in eggs, one at a time. Sift together flour, cinnamon, baking soda, baking powder and salt. Add to creamed mixture alternately with sour cream, beginning and ending with dry ingredients. Add almond flavoring. Stir in slivered almonds. Pour into 2 greased 8x4-inch loaf pans. Sprinkle loaves with chopped almonds. Bake in 350° oven 60 minutes.

Emma Whitlock, *Indianola*
First Place, 2014 Iowa Bed & Breakfast Quick Breads – Nut

STAR-SPANGLED HONEY SCONES

1 c. all-purpose flour
1 1/2 tsp. baking powder
1/8 tsp. salt
1/4 c. cold butter
2 tbsp. 2% milk
1 egg, beaten

1/8 c. plus 2 tbsp. honey
1/4 c. dried fruit
   (cranberries/blueberries)
1 tbsp. honey mixed with
   1 tbsp. melted butter

In small bowl, combine flour, baking powder and salt. Cut in butter until mixture resembles coarse crumbs. In separate bowl, combine milk and 2 tablespoons egg. Add milk mixture and honey to flour mixture until moistened. Add dried fruit. Turn out onto floured surface; knead gently 6 to 8 times. Pat into 6-inch circle; cut into star shapes. Place on parchment-lined baking sheet. Bake in 425° oven 9 to 12 minutes or until golden brown. Remove from oven; brush tops with honey butter mixture.

Diane Rauh, *Des Moines*
First Place, 2014 Foods Made with Honey – Honey Scones

DATE-NUT LOAF

1/2 c. boiling water
8.5-oz. pkg. pitted dates,
   finely chopped
3 tbsp. shortening
1 tbsp. grated orange zest
1/3 c. honey
1/2 c. orange juice

1 egg, beaten
2 c. all-purpose flour
1 tsp. baking powder
1 tsp. baking soda
1/2 tsp. salt
1/2 c. chopped pecans

Pour boiling water over dates and shortening; cool to room temperature. Add orange zest, honey and orange juice; stir in egg. Sift together flour, baking powder, baking soda and salt. Add to date mixture, stirring just until mixed. Stir in pecans. Pour into 2 greased 7x3-inch loaf pans. Bake in 325° oven 50 minutes. Cool 10 minutes in pans; turn out of pans to wire cooling racks.

Marjorie Rodgers, *Indianola*
First Place, 2014 Foods Made with Honey – Honey Fruit Bread

LEMON GINGER SCONES

3 c. all-purpose flour
3 tbsp. granulated sugar
4 tsp. baking powder
1/2 tsp. salt
2 tsp. ground ginger
2 tbsp. finely grated lemon
    zest

3/4 c. unsalted butter
1/2 c. diced crystallized
    ginger
3/4 c. cold buttermilk
1 large egg
1 tsp. lemon flavoring
Milk
Granulated sugar

In large bowl, whisk together flour, sugar, baking powder, salt and ground ginger. Stir in lemon zest. Cut or rub butter into flour mixture. Butter should be roughly pea size pieces. Stir in ginger pieces. Pour buttermilk into separate bowl; whisk in egg until blended. Mix in lemon flavoring. Make a well in center of dry ingredients; pour in buttermilk. Mix with fork until dough clings together. Transfer to floured surface and lightly knead together. Pat dough into 2 discs. Slice each into 8 wedges; place on 2 parchment-lined baking sheets. Brush with milk; sprinkle with sugar. Bake in 425° oven 12 to 15 minutes.

Sara Woolery, *Grinnell*
First Place, 2014 Scones with a Twist

LEMON-CHAI CRANBERRY ORANGE SCONES

2 c. all-purpose flour
4 tsp. baking powder
3/4 tsp. salt
6 tbsp. butter
1/3 c. honey
1 egg

3/4 c. heavy cream
1/4 c. dried cranberries
1/4 tsp. grated orange zest
1/4 tsp. grated lemon zest
2 tbsp. chai seeds

Combine flour, baking powder and salt; cut in butter. Stir in honey; add egg and cream, mixing well. Stir in fruit, zests and seeds. Roll out to 1/2-inch thick and cut into rounds. Bake in 375° oven 15 minutes or until browned; cool. If desired, top with additional honey and zest. Serve with cream and compote.

(CONTINUED)

For CREAM:

1 c. heavy cream	1 tsp. vanilla bean paste
1/3 c. honey	

Combine all ingredients; mix well. Beat until stiff peaks form. Keep chilled.

For RHUBARB BERRY COMPOTE:

1 c. chopped rhubarb	1 c. blackberries
1/3 c. honey	1 c. raspberries
1 tsp. grated orange zest	1 c. blueberries

In saucepan, combine all ingredients. Simmer until reduced and thick.

Angela Lawler, *West Des Moines*
First Place, 2015 Foods Made with Honey – Honey Scones
First Place Overall, 2015 Foods Made with Honey – Quick Breads

SALSA CORN MUFFINS

For TOPPING:

2 tbsp. all-purpose flour	2 tbsp. butter
2 tbsp. cornmeal	2 tsp. granulated sugar

Combine all ingredients; mix until crumbly; set aside.

For BATTER:

1 1/4 c. cornmeal	1 c. milk
1 c. all-purpose flour	2 tbsp. oil
1/4 c. granulated sugar	1/4 c. finely sliced green
4 tsp. baking powder	onions
1/2 tsp. salt	1/4 c. chunky salsa
2 eggs	2 tbsp. chopped cilantro

In medium bowl, combine cornmeal, flour, sugar, baking powder and salt. In separate bowl, mix together eggs, milk, oil, onions, salsa and cilantro. Add to dry ingredients; mix until blended. Spoon into 12 greased muffin tins. Sprinkle with topping. Bake in 425° oven 12 to 15 minutes.

Emma Whitlock, *Indianola*
First Place, 2015 Iowa Bed & Breakfast Quick Breads – Cornmeal Muffins

YEAST BREADS AND QUICK BREADS

HOLIDAY FRUIT BREAD

3 medium ripe bananas,
  mashed
1 c. granulated sugar
1 egg
1 1/2 c. all-purpose flour
1/4 c. melted lard
1 tsp. vanilla
1/4 c. orange marmalade
1 tsp. salt

1 tsp. baking soda
1/3 c. coarsely chopped
  candied pineapple
1/3 c. coarsely chopped
  candied red cherries
1/3 c. coarsely chopped
  candied green cherries
1/2 c. chopped toasted
  pecans

Combine bananas, sugar, egg, flour, lard, vanilla, marmalade, salt and baking soda; mix well. Gently fold in candied fruits and pecans. Pour into greased 8 1/2 x 4 1/2-inch baking pan. Bake in 350° oven 1 hour.

Molly Thomas, *Centerville*
First Place, 2015 Make It with Lard – Fruit Bread
First Place Overall, 2015 Make It with Lard – Quick Breads

APRICOT NUT BREAD

1 c. boiling water
1 1/4 c. chopped dried
  apricots
2 c. all-purpose flour
2/3 c. granulated sugar
1 1/2 tsp. baking powder
1 tsp. salt
1/4 tsp. baking soda

1 egg
3/4 c. apricot nectar
2 tbsp. butter, melted
1/2 c. chopped and toasted
  pecans
1 tbsp. grated orange zest
1/4 c. chopped pecans for
  topping

In small bowl, pour boiling water over apricots; set aside. In large bowl, combine flour, sugar, baking powder, salt and baking soda. In separate bowl, whisk together egg, apricot nectar and butter; stir into dry ingredients until moistened. Drain apricots; fold into batter with 1/2 cup pecans and orange zest. Pour into greased 8x4-inch loaf pan. Sprinkle top with remaining pecans. Bake in 350° oven 55 to 65 minutes.

Emma Whitlock, *Indianola*
First Place, 2015 Iowa Bed & Breakfast Quick Breads – Apricot Bread

PIÑA COLADA ZUCCHINI BREAD

4 c. all-purpose flour
3 c. granulated sugar
2 tsp. baking powder
1 1/2 tsp. salt
1 tsp. baking soda
4 eggs
1 1/2 c. canola oil
1 tsp. coconut extract

1 tsp. rum extract
1 tsp. vanilla
3 c. shredded zucchini
1 c. canned crushed
   pineapple, drained
1/2 c. chopped and toasted
   pecans

In large bowl, combine flour, sugar, baking powder, salt and baking soda. In separate bowl, whisk eggs, oil and extracts. Stir into dry ingredients until moistened. Fold in zucchini, pineapple and pecans. Line bottom of 3 greased and floured 8x4-inch pans with wax paper then grease wax paper. Transfer batter to pans. Bake in 350° oven 60 minutes or until toothpick inserted near center comes out clean. Cool 10 minutes before removing from pans to wire racks. Gently remove wax paper.

Emma Whitlock, *Indianola*
First Place, 2015 Iowa Bed & Breakfast Quick Breads – Vegetable

---

APRICOT BREAD

2 c. granulated sugar
1 c. margarine
4 eggs
4 c. all-purpose flour
2 tsp. baking soda
1 tsp. salt

1/2 tsp. baking powder
2, 6-oz. jars apricot sauce
   baby food
4 tbsp. water, divided
6 tbsp. sour cream
15 oz. dried apricots, diced

Cream together sugar and margarine; add eggs. In separate bowl, mix flour, baking soda, salt and baking powder; add to creamed mixture. Add baby food; rinse each jar with 2 tablespoons water and add to mixture. Fold in sour cream and apricots. Grease three 8x4-inch loaf pans. Fill each pan half full. Bake in 350° oven 35 to 40 minutes. Cool in pans 10 minutes. Remove from pans; cool on wire racks.

Cynthia Murphy, *Des Moines*
First Place, 2014 Iowa Bed & Breakfast Quick Breads – Apricot Bread

CREAM CHEESE BANANA NUT BREAD

For CREAM CHEESE BANANA NUT BREAD:

3/4 c. butter, softened
8 oz. cream cheese, softened
2 c. granulated sugar
2 large eggs
3 c. all-purpose flour
1/2 tsp. baking powder
1/2 tsp. baking soda
1/2 tsp. salt
1 1/2 c. mashed bananas
   (approx. 4 bananas)
1 c. toasted chopped pecans
   or walnuts
1/2 tsp. vanilla

Beat together butter and cream cheese at medium speed until creamy. Gradually add sugar, beating until light and fluffy. Add eggs, one at a time, until blended after each. Combine flour, baking powder, baking soda and salt. Gradually add to butter mixture. Stir in bananas, nuts and vanilla. Spoon into 2 greased and floured 8x4-inch pans. Top with cinnamon topping. Bake in 350° oven 1 hour, or until toothpick inserted near center comes out clean. Cool in pans 10 minutes. Remove and cool on wire racks.

For CINNAMON TOPPING:

1/2 c. packed brown sugar
1/2 c. chopped toasted pecans
1 tbsp. all-purpose flour
1 tbsp. melted butter
1/8 tsp. cinnamon

Combine all ingredients; sprinkle over batter before baking.

Clarissa Ridgway, *Johnston*
First Place, 2014 Adventureland Resort Intermediate – Banana Nut Bread

---

ALMOND POPPY SEED BREAD

3 c. all-purpose flour
1 1/2 tsp. salt
1 1/2 tsp. baking powder
2 1/2 c. granulated sugar
1 1/2 tsp. vanilla
1 1/2 c. milk
1 1/3 c. oil
1 1/2 tbsp. poppy seeds
3 eggs
1 1/2 tsp. almond extract

Mix together all ingredients; beat 2 minutes. Pour batter into 2 large or 6 small greased bread pans. Bake in 350° oven 1 hour 15 minutes. Adjust baking time if making smaller loaves. Glaze loaves.

(CONTINUED)

For GLAZE:
3/4 c. granulated sugar
1/4 c. orange juice
1/2 tsp. vanilla

1/2 tsp. almond extract
2 tsp. melted butter

Mix together all ingredients until well combined.

Natalie Ridgway, *Johnston*
First Place, 2015 Iowa Bed & Breakfast Quick Breads – Quick Bread
Other Than Named

RUSTIC PUMPKIN BREAD

For RUSTIC PUMPKIN BREAD:
3 c. granulated sugar
15-oz. can pumpkin puree
1 c. canola oil
4 eggs
2/3 c. water
3 1/2 c. all-purpose flour
2 tsp. baking soda

1 tsp. salt
1 tsp. cinnamon
1 tsp. nutmeg
1/2 tsp. cloves
1/2 c. toasted and chopped
    pecans

In large bowl, beat sugar, pumpkin, oil, eggs and water until blended. In separate bowl, combine flour, baking soda, salt, cinnamon, nutmeg and cloves; gradually beat into pumpkin mixture until blended. Stir in pecans. Pour into 2 greased 9x5-inch loaf pans.

For TOPPING:
1/3 c. all-purpose flour
1/4 c. packed brown sugar
1/2 tsp. cinnamon

2 tbsp. cold butter
1/4 c. chopped pecans

In small bowl, combine flour, brown sugar and cinnamon; cut in butter until mixture resembles coarse crumbs. Stir in pecans. Sprinkle over batter. Bake in 350° oven 60 to 65 minutes or until a toothpick inserted near center comes out clean. Cool loaves 10 minutes before removing from pans to wire racks.

Emma Whitlock, *Indianola*
First Place, 2014 Bake Your Best Pumpkin Bread

HONEYCOMB COFFEE CAKE

1 3/4 c. all-purpose flour
2/3 c. honey, divided
1 c. unsalted butter, divided
1/3 c. plus 1 tbsp. milk,
    divided
2 eggs

2 tsp. baking powder
1/2 tsp. almond extract
1 tsp. orange extract, divided
1/2 c. chopped pecans
1/2 tsp. ground nutmeg

Combine flour, 1/3 cup honey, 1/2 cup butter, 1/3 cup milk, eggs, baking powder, almond extract and 1/2 teaspoon orange extract; mix well. Spread batter into greased and floured 9-inch square baking pan. In heavy saucepan, combine remaining butter, pecans, honey, nutmeg, milk and orange extract. Cook over medium heat, stirring occasionally until mixture comes to full boil. Continue cooking, stirring occasionally, 2 to 3 minutes. Pour mixture evenly over batter. Bake in 350° oven 22 to 27 minutes or until toothpick inserted in center comes out clean.

Amy Smith, *Winterset*
First Place, 2014 Foods Made with Honey – Youth Entries
First Place Overall, 2014 Foods Made with Honey – Youth & Quick Breads

MAPLE-DRIZZLE APPLE MUFFINS

For APPLE MUFFINS:
1 1/3 c. all-purpose flour
1 c. quick-cooking rolled oats
2/3 c. granulated sugar
1 tbsp. baking powder
1 1/2 tsp. ground cinnamon
1/2 c. milk

1/3 c. butter, melted
1/4 c. maple syrup
1 egg, lightly beaten
2 c. chopped, peeled apples
12 pecan halves

In large bowl, combine flour, oats, sugar, baking powder and cinnamon. In small bowl, mix milk, butter, syrup and egg. Stir into dry ingredients until moistened. Fold in apples. Fill greased or paper-lined muffin cups three-quarters full. Top each with a pecan half. Bake in 400° oven 18 to 20 minutes or until toothpick inserted in center comes out clean. Cool in pan 10 minutes before moving to wire rack.

(CONTINUED)

For GLAZE:
1/3 c. powdered sugar   **2 tbsp. maple syrup**

Mix sugar and syrup; drizzle over muffins.

Rhonda Paul, *Des Moines*
First Place, 2014 Iowa Bed & Breakfast Quick Breads – Fruit Muffins
First Place Overall, 2014 Iowa Bed & Breakfast Quick Breads Contest

CHOCOLANUTTY BANANA COFFEE CAKE

3/4 c. butter
3/4 c. buttermilk
3 eggs
1/3 c. regular rolled oats
1/3 c. packed brown sugar
1/4 c. butter, chilled
1 c. chopped pecans,
**   lightly toasted**
2 1/4 c. granulated sugar
1/2 tsp. salt

1 tsp. baking soda
1 tsp. baking powder
2 1/4 c. ripe mashed bananas
1 tbsp. grated orange zest
2 tsp. vanilla
3 c. all-purpose flour
3/4 c. chocolate baking
**   pieces**
2 tbsp. butter, melted
1 c. powdered sugar
3 to 4 tsp. orange juice

Allow 3/4 cup butter, buttermilk and eggs to stand at room temperature 30 minutes. In medium bowl, combine oats and brown sugar; cut in 1/4 cup chilled butter until mixture resembles coarse crumbs. Stir in pecans; set aside. In large mixing bowl, beat 3/4 cup butter on medium speed 30 seconds. Gradually add sugar, beating until light and fluffy. Beat in salt, baking soda and baking powder. Add eggs, one at a time, beating after each addition. Beat in bananas, orange zest and vanilla. Alternately add flour and buttermilk, beating on low to medium speed. Pour half the batter into a greased and floured 10-inch Bundt pan, spreading evenly. Sprinkle with half the pecan mixture and all of the chocolate pieces. Spread remaining batter in pan. Sprinkle with remaining pecan mixture. Bake in 325° oven 70 minutes. Cool in pan on wire rack 15 minutes. Remove from pan; cool completely. In small bowl, whisk together melted butter, powdered sugar and enough orange juice to reach drizzle consistency. Drizzle on cake.

Marjorie Rodgers, *Indianola*
First Place, 2015 Iowa Bed & Breakfast Quick Breads – Coffee Cake

YEAST BREADS AND QUICK BREADS

"CORN"UCOPIA MUFFINS

2 c. all-purpose flour
2 tsp. salt
7 tsp. baking powder
5 tbsp. granulated sugar
2 c. coarse cornmeal
2 eggs, beaten
2 c. whole milk

2/3 c. vegetable oil
1/4 c. diced yellow onion
1/4 c. diced red bell pepper
1/4 c. diced green bell pepper
1/4 c. diced dried beef
15-oz. can whole kernel corn,
    drained

In large bowl, sift together flour, salt, baking powder, sugar and cornmeal. In separate bowl, combine eggs, milk and oil until blended. Place onion, red peppers and green peppers on microwaveable plate. Microwave on high 2 minutes or until softened. Add egg mixture to dry ingredients; mix gently just until blended. Do not over mix. Fold in onion, peppers, dried beef and corn. Spoon batter into greased, extra-large muffin tins until each well is filled two-thirds full. Place tins on middle rack in oven and bake in 325° oven 30 minutes or until lightly golden. Cool 15 minutes; remove from tins.

Jeanne Stall, *Huxley*
First Place, 2014 Butter Kernel Corn Creation

SOUR CREAM PUMPKIN COFFEE CAKE

For CAKE:
1/2 c. butter
3/4 c. granulated sugar
1 tbsp. vanilla
1 tsp. cinnamon
1/2 tsp. nutmeg
1/2 tsp. allspice
1/8 tsp. cloves

1/4 tsp. ginger
3 eggs
2 c. all-purpose flour
1 tsp. baking powder
1 tsp. baking soda
1 c. sour cream

Cream together butter, sugar, vanilla and spices; add eggs. In separate bowl, combine flour, baking powder and baking soda; add to butter mixture alternately with sour cream. Spoon half the cake batter into greased 9x13-inch pan and spread to edges. Sprinkle half the streusel over batter. Spread pumpkin filling over streusel. Carefully spread remaining batter over pumpkin filling; sprinkle remaining streusel over top. Bake in 325° oven 50 to 60 minutes.

(CONTINUED)

For PUMPKIN FILLING:
1 3/4 c. pumpkin puree
1 egg, slightly beaten

1/3 c. granulated sugar
1 tsp. pumpkin pie spice

Combine all ingredients; mix well.

For STREUSEL:
1 c. packed brown sugar
1/3 c. butter

2 tsp. cinnamon
1 c. chopped nuts

Combine all ingredients; mix well.

Lana Ross, *Indianola*
First Place, 2014 Cooking with Pumpkin – Cooking with Pumpkin

HONEY GLAZED BUTTERMILK COFFEE CAKE

**1 c. plus 2 tbsp. honey,
    divided**
**1/3 c. plus 1/4 c. melted
    butter, divided**
2 tsp. grated lemon zest
4 tsp. lemon juice
1 c. chopped pecans, divided

1 1/2 c. regular rolled oats
1 c. all-purpose flour
1 tsp. baking powder
3/4 tsp. baking soda
1/2 tsp. salt
2 eggs, lightly beaten
2/3 c. buttermilk
1 1/2 tsp. vanilla

In small bowl, combine honey, 1/3 cup melted butter, lemon zest and lemon juice. Stir in 1/2 cup pecans. Pour into generously greased 9-inch round cake pan. Spread evenly; set aside. Place oats in blender or food processor. Process until finely ground. Transfer to large bowl. Stir in flour, remaining pecans, baking powder, baking soda and salt. Make a well in center of flour mixture. In medium bowl, combine eggs, buttermilk, remaining honey, remaining melted butter and vanilla. Add egg mixture to well in flour mixture. Stir until moistened; batter should be lumpy. Pour batter over honey mixture in pan, spreading evenly. Bake in 350° oven 25 minutes. Immediately invert cake onto serving plate. Spoon any honey mixture remaining in pan onto cake.

Marjorie Rodgers, *Indianola*
First Place, 2014 Foods Made with Honey – Honey Coffee Cake

APPLE-NUT COFFEE CAKE

1 c. all-purpose flour
1/2 tsp. baking powder
1/2 tsp. baking soda
1/8 tsp. salt
1/2 c. granulated sugar
1/4 c. shortening
1 egg
1/2 tsp. vanilla

1/2 c. sour cream
1 medium apple, peeled and
  chopped
1/4 c. chopped walnuts
1/4 c. packed brown sugar
1 tbsp. butter
1/2 tsp. cinnamon

In medium bowl, stir together flour, baking powder, baking soda and salt. In large bowl, beat together sugar and shortening until fluffy. Beat in egg and vanilla. Stir half the flour mixture into sugar mixture. Stir in sour cream, remainder of flour mixture and apple. Spread evenly into greased and floured 8-inch round cake pan. Place nuts, brown sugar, butter and cinnamon into small bowl and mix until crumbly. Sprinkle over batter. Bake in 350° oven 30 minutes. Serve warm.

Emma Whitlock, *Indianola*
First Place, 2014 Iowa Bed & Breakfast Quick Breads – Coffee Cake

---

ORANGE PECAN TEA BREAD

For BREAD:
1 3/4 c. all-purpose flour
1 tsp. baking powder
1/2 tsp. baking soda
1/4 tsp. salt
1/4 tsp. ground nutmeg
1/4 tsp. ground allspice
1/2 c. granulated sugar

1/2 c. low-fat buttermilk
1/4 c. chopped pecans
3 tbsp. 1% low-fat milk
3 tbsp. vegetable oil
3 tbsp. orange marmalade
2 tsp. grated orange zest
2 large eggs

Combine flour, baking powder, baking soda, salt, nutmeg and allspice in large bowl. Stirring with a whisk, make a well in center of mixture. In separate bowl, combine remaining ingredients. Add to flour mixture, stirring until moist. Spoon into greased 8x4-inch loaf pan. Bake in 350° oven 45 minutes or until toothpick inserted in center comes out clean. Cool 10 minutes in pan on wire rack; remove from pan. Cool completely on wire rack.

(CONTINUED)

For GLAZE:

1/2 c. powdered sugar	**1 1/2 tsp. chopped pecans**
2 tsp. fresh orange juice	

Combine powdered sugar and orange juice, stirring until smooth. Drizzle over bread; sprinkle with pecans.

Pat Becker, *Cumberland*
First Place, 2014 Iowa Bed & Breakfast Quick Breads – Quick Bread Other Than Named

---

HONEY OATMEAL COFFEE CAKE

1 1/4 c. boiling water	**1 tsp. baking soda**
1 c. quick-cooking rolled oats	**3/4 tsp. salt**
1/2 c. raisins	**1/4 tsp. freshly ground**
1/2 c. butter	**nutmeg**
1 1/2 c. honey	**1 tsp. ground cinnamon**
2 eggs	**1/4 tsp. ground ginger**
1 tsp. vanilla	**1/2 c. chopped walnuts**
1 3/4 c. whole wheat flour	

Pour boiling water over oats, raisins and butter; set aside 20 minutes. Mix together honey, eggs and vanilla; add to oat mixture. Combine flour, baking soda, salt and spices; add to other ingredients and mix well. Fold in walnuts. Pour into 2 greased 9x9-inch pans. Bake in 350° oven 30 minutes until toothpick inserted near center comes out clean. Cool completely in pan. Top with honey sweetened whipped cream.

For HONEY SWEETENED WHIPPED CREAM:

1 c. heavy cream, very cold	**2 tbsp. honey**
1 tsp. vanilla	

Whip cream using cold beaters and cold bowl; beat until frothy. Gradually add vanilla and honey; beat until soft peaks form.

Cassandra Hyatt, *Ankeny*
First Place, 2014 Foods Made with Honey – Honey Oatmeal Cake

RASPBERRY CORN MUFFINS

3 c. all-purpose flour
1 c. granulated sugar
1 c. stone ground cornmeal
2 tbsp. baking powder
1 1/2 tsp. salt

1 1/2 c. whole milk
2 large eggs
8 tbsp. unsalted butter, melted
   and cooled
3/4 c. raspberry preserves

In large bowl, combine flour, sugar, cornmeal, baking powder and salt; whisk to combine. In separate bowl, combine milk, eggs and butter. Combine wet ingredients with dry ingredients; mix until combined. Add paper liners to muffin tin. Fill papers equally with batter. Bake in 350° oven 25 to 30 minutes until muffin tops are golden and firm, rotating muffin tin front to back halfway through baking time. Cool on wire rack. Using grapefruit spoon or similar utensil, hollow out 1/2-inch cylinder about three-fourths of the way through middle of each muffin. Fill pastry bag fitted with round tip with raspberry preserves. Fill each muffin, mounding preserves slightly over top.

Jeffrey King, *Newton*
First Place, 2014 Iowa Bed & Breakfast Quick Breads – Corn Meal Muffins

---

CHEDDAR CHEESE CORNBREAD

1 1/3 c. yellow cornmeal
2/3 c. all-purpose flour
1 tbsp. baking powder
1 tsp. salt
1/4 tsp. dried red pepper
   flakes
1 tsp. ground coriander

1 c. sour cream
1/3 c. half and half
2 eggs, well beaten
1/4 c. butter, melted
1 1/2 c. grated sharp
   cheddar cheese

Sift together cornmeal, flour, baking powder and salt. Mix in red pepper flakes and coriander. In large mixing bowl, whisk together sour cream and half and half. Add beaten eggs; whisk thoroughly. Whisk in melted butter; stir in cheese. Add cornmeal mixture; blend well. Pour into greased 9-inch round baking pan. Bake in 425° oven 20 to 30 minutes until edges begin to brown. Serve hot.

Emma Whitlock, *Indianola*
First Place, 2015 Iowa Bed & Breakfast Quick Breads – Corn Bread

BAKING POWDER BISCUITS

2 c. all-purpose flour
4 tsp. baking powder
2 tbsp. granulated sugar
1/2 tsp. baking soda
3/4 tsp. kosher salt
2 tbsp. unsalted butter, chilled

1/4 c. vegetable shortening,
   chilled
1 c. low-fat buttermilk
1 tsp. butter flavoring
Softened butter for brushing
   tops

In large bowl, whisk together flour, baking powder, sugar, baking soda and salt. Using fingertips, rub butter and shortening into dry ingredients until mixture resembles coarse crumbs. Make a well in middle of flour mixture; pour in buttermilk and butter flavoring. Stir until dough comes together. Knead until flour has been incorporated. Turn dough out onto lightly floured surface; fold dough over on itself, gently kneading 30 seconds or until dough is soft and smooth. Press dough into 3/4-inch thick round. Using 2-inch biscuit cutter, cut biscuits. Place biscuits on baking sheet barely touching. Reroll scraps; punch out as many biscuits as possible. Using thumb, create a shallow dimple in top center of each biscuit. Bake in 400° oven 15 to 20 minutes. Brush tops with butter.

Diane Rauh, *Des Moines*
First Place, 2014 Iowa Bed & Breakfast Quick Breads – Biscuits

BLUEBERRY-LEMON MUFFINS

1/2 c. butter
3/4 c. honey
2 eggs
1/2 c. buttermilk
1 tsp. vanilla
2 tsp. grated lemon zest

2 c. all-purpose flour
2 tsp. baking powder
1/4 tsp. salt
1/2 tsp. cinnamon
2 c. fresh or frozen
   blueberries, unthawed

Cream together butter and honey until light. Add eggs, one at a time, beating well after each addition. Beat in buttermilk, vanilla and lemon zest. In separate bowl, whisk flour, baking powder, salt and cinnamon. Add dry mixture to creamed mixture; stir until moistened. Fold in blueberries. Fill greased muffin cups two-thirds full. Bake in 375° oven 15 to 20 minutes or until toothpick inserted near center comes out clean.

Marjorie Rodgers, *Indianola*
First Place, 2015 Foods Made with Honey – Honey Fruit Muffins

APRICOT MANGO SCONES

2 c. all-purpose flour
2 tsp. baking powder
1/2 tsp. baking soda
1/4 c. granulated sugar
1/4 tsp. salt
1/2 c. butter, cold
1 c. heavy cream
1 egg
1 tsp. vanilla
2 tsp. lemon juice
1/2 tsp. grated lemon zest
1/3 c. chopped dried mango
1/3 c. chopped dried apricot
1/4 c. chopped pecans
2 tbsp. chopped crystallized
  ginger
Cream
Sparkling sugar
Crystallized ginger

Sift together flour, baking powder, baking soda, sugar and salt. Cut in butter. Gently add cream, egg, vanilla, lemon juice and lemon zest. Add fruits, pecans and ginger. Roll out to 1/2-inch thick. Cut in 3 to 4-inch squares. Place on parchment-lined baking sheets. Brush tops with light coat of cream; sprinkle sparkling sugar and crystallized ginger on top. Bake in 375° oven 20 to 25 minutes.

Pat Felderman, *Pleasant Hill*
First Place, 2015 Scones with a Twist

PUMPKIN NUT BREAD

2 1/2 c. all-purpose flour
2 tsp. baking soda
1/2 tsp. salt
1 tsp. cinnamon
1 tsp. nutmeg
3 c. granulated sugar
1 c. vegetable oil
4 eggs, beaten
3/4 c. buttermilk
1 tsp. vanilla
1 tsp. butter flavoring
15-oz. can pumpkin puree
1 c. chopped pecans

In large bowl, sift together flour, baking soda, salt, cinnamon and nutmeg. Add sugar, oil, eggs and buttermilk; mix well. Stir in vanilla, butter flavoring, pumpkin and pecans. Pour into 2 greased 7x3-inch loaf pans. Bake in 350° oven 60 to 65 minutes. Let stand 10 minutes before removing from pans; cool on wire rack.

Marjorie Rodgers, *Indianola*
First Place, 2015 Iowa Bed & Breakfast Quick Breads – Pumpkin (with nuts)

LAVENDER WALNUT SCONES

For SCONES:

1/2 c. chopped walnuts	1 tbsp. dried edible lavender
3 c. all-purpose flour	12 tbsp. unsalted butter, cold
1/4 c. plus 3 tbsp. granulated sugar, divided	1 large egg
	3/4 c. buttermilk
4 tsp. baking powder	1/4 c. heavy cream
3/4 tsp. salt	

Spread walnuts on parchment-lined baking sheet. Toast in 425° oven 2 to 3 minutes, until fragrant. In large bowl, mix flour, 3 tablespoons sugar, baking powder and salt. Crush lavender using a mortar and pestle; add lavender to flour mixture. Cut or rub butter into flour. Mixture should be crumbly; butter pieces should be pea sized. Add walnuts. In separate bowl, whisk together egg and buttermilk. Make a well in center of flour; add buttermilk all at once. Mix with fork until dough clings together. Turn dough out onto lightly floured surface; gently knead together. Separate dough into 2 equal parts. Flatten into a disc. Cut disc into 6 to 8 triangle wedges. Repeat with second half. Place on parchment-lined baking sheets. Brush cream on each; sprinkle with remaining sugar. Bake in 425° oven 12 to 15 minutes. Scones should be lightly browned. Remove from oven to wire racks to cool.

For GLAZE:

1 tbsp. heavy cream	4 tbsp. powdered sugar
2 tbsp. honey	

Beat all ingredients until smooth, adjusting cream and sugar depending on consistency desired. Drizzle over cooled scones. If desired, garnish with lavender.

Sara Woolery, *Grinnell*
First Place, 2015 Iowa Bed & Breakfast Quick Breads – Scones

NUTTY BANANA BREAD

For BREAD:
1 c. granulated sugar
1/2 c. butter
2 eggs
1 c. mashed overly ripe
    bananas

2 c. all-purpose flour
1/2 tsp. salt
1/2 tsp. baking soda
4 tbsp. milk
1 c. toasted pecans

Cream together sugar and butter; beat in eggs and then bananas. In separate bowl, combine flour, salt and baking soda. Add to banana mixture alternately with milk. Fold in pecans. Pour into greased 9x4-inch loaf pan. Sprinkle topping over bread. Bake in 350° oven 1 hour.

For PECAN TOPPING:
1/2 c. packed brown sugar
1 tbsp. all-purpose flour
1/8 tsp. cinnamon

1/2 c. chopped toasted
    pecans
1 tbsp. melted butter

Combine all ingredients; mix well.

Natalie Ridgway, *Johnston*
First Place, 2015 Iowa Bed & Breakfast Quick Breads – Banana Bread

Iowa State Fair
COOKBOOK

HONEY PIE

For HONEY PIE FILLING:

3 eggs, slightly beaten
1 c. honey
3 tbsp. butter
1/4 tsp. salt

1 c. chopped pecans
Dash of nutmeg
Baked 9-inch pie crust

In medium saucepan over medium heat, whisk eggs and honey until well blended. Add butter and salt. Cook over medium heat, stirring constantly, until mixture is thick, bubbly and coats back of metal spoon. Remove from heat; stir in pecans and nutmeg. Pour into pie shell. Bake in 325° oven 25 minutes or until set; let pie cool. Garnish with honey whipped cream.

For HONEY WHIPPED CREAM:

3/4 c. heavy cream

1 tbsp. honey

Combine heavy cream and honey in chilled bowl. Beat until soft peaks form.

Keri Crowley, *Indianola*
First Place, 2015 Taste of Honey Challenge – Desserts (adult)

OATMEAL PECAN RAISIN PIE

3 large eggs
1/2 c. dark corn syrup
1/2 c. light corn syrup
1/2 c. packed brown sugar
1/2 c. whole milk

6 tbsp. melted butter
1 tsp. vanilla
3/4 c. regular rolled oats
1/2 c. toasted walnuts
1/2 c. raisins
Pastry for single-crust
**   8-inch pie**

In mixing bowl, combine eggs, syrups and brown sugar; mix well. Add milk, butter and vanilla; continue mixing until well blended. Stir in remaining ingredients. Pour into pie shell. Bake in 350° oven 40 to 45 minutes.

Lana Ross, *Indianola*
First Place, 2014 Machine Shed Pies – Oatmeal Pecan

PIES, CAKES AND DESSERTS

DOUBLE STRAWBERRY PIE

5 c. whole fresh stemmed
   strawberries, divided
6 oz. white chocolate
1 3/4 tsp. unflavored gelatin
2 tbsp. cold water
8 oz. cream cheese, room
   temperature

1 tsp. vanilla
1 1/2 c. plus 3 tbsp.
   powdered sugar, divided
3 1/2 c. heavy cream, divided
Baked 8-inch pie crust

Slice 2 1/2 cups strawberries. Using food processor, puree; set aside. In large bowl, melt chocolate in microwave, being careful not to burn; set aside. In separate small bowl, combine gelatin and cold water. Stir and let stand 5 minutes. Microwave 15 seconds or until gelatin is completely dissolved. In separate large bowl, cream together cream cheese and vanilla. Add gelatin mixture and melted chocolate; mix completely. Beat in 1 1/2 cup powdered sugar until smooth; add strawberry puree and mix well. Beat 2 cups heavy cream until stiff peaks form. Fold into strawberry puree mixture. Arrange remaining strawberries in bottom of baked pie crust. Pour strawberry mixture over crust; chill until set. Whip remaining heavy cream in large bowl with remaining powdered sugar until stiff peaks form. Spread whipped cream over pie; garnish as desired.

Christine Montalvo, *Windsor Heights*
First Place, 2014 North "40" Pie Contest

APRICOT PIE

For CRUST:
2/3 c. solid vegetable
   shortening
2 c. all-purpose flour

1 tsp. salt
1 tsp. almond extract
2 1/2 tbsp. ice water

Using pastry cutter, combine shortening, flour and salt in medium bowl until mixture is crumbly. Add almond extract and water; mix with fork until mixture starts to stick together. Depending on humidity, you may need to add more water. Add water, 1 teaspoon at a time, until mixture can be worked into a ball of dough. Roll dough out to fit pie pan; place in pan. Set crust aside; repeat for top crust.

(CONTINUED)

For APRICOT PIE FILLING:

1 qt. fresh apricots	1 tsp. freshly squeezed
1 c. granulated sugar	lemon juice
2 1/2 tbsp. cornstarch	3 tsp. unsalted butter
1/4 tsp. salt	1 tbsp. milk
1/2 tsp. grated lemon zest	Sliced almonds

Slice apricots into bite-size pieces. Place apricots in medium size bowl. Add sugar, cornstarch, salt, lemon zest and lemon juice; mix well. Pour into unbaked pie crust; dot with butter. Cut top crust into strips; weave across apricots. Press sides of crust around pan to create a ridge. Brush with milk; sprinkle with sugar and top with sliced almonds. Bake in 375° oven 30 minutes or until crust is golden brown.

Keri Crowley, *Indianola*
First Place, 2015 Machine Shed and Gold Medal Flour Pies – Apricot
Second Place Overall, 2015 Machine Shed and Gold Medal Flour Pies – Fruit

GERMAN CHOCOLATE PIE

For FILLING:

2 c. milk	2 oz. dark chocolate
2/3 c. granulated sugar	2 tsp. vanilla
1/3 c. all-purpose flour	1 c. toasted coconut
3 eggs	1/2 c. toasted pecans
4 oz. German chocolate	Baked 9-inch pie crust

In saucepan, combine milk, sugar, flour and eggs. Cook until mixture begins to thicken; add chocolates and vanilla. Pour half the filling in prepared crust. Sprinkle with half the toasted coconut and pecans. Pour remaining filling over top; top with remaining coconut and pecans; cool.

For TOPPING:

1 c. heavy cream	1 tsp. vanilla
4 tbsp. granulated sugar	

Combine all ingredients; whip until soft peaks form. Spread over top of pie. Cool.

Lana Ross, *Indianola*
First Place, 2014 Machine Shed Pies – Pies Other Than Named

ORANGE AND SPICE MINCEMEAT PIE

1 c. shredded cooked roast beef
1/2 c. orange juice
1/2 c. water
2 c. shredded apple
1 1/2 c. dark raisins
1 c. packed light brown sugar
1 tsp. grated orange zest
1 tsp. salt
1/2 tsp. cinnamon
1/2 tsp. allspice
1/2 tsp. cloves
1/2 tsp. coriander
1/2 tsp. mace
1/2 tsp. nutmeg
2 tbsp. gold rum
1 tbsp. all-purpose flour
1/4 tsp. cornstarch
1 tsp. milk
1/2 tbsp. granulated sugar
Pastry for double-crust 7-inch pie

Combine all ingredients except rum, flour, cornstarch, milk and granulated sugar in large saucepan. Bring to boil; reduce heat and simmer 5 minutes, stirring occasionally. Cool to room temperature; stir in rum. Place mincemeat in strainer; allow liquid to drain, reserving 1 cup. Place 1 cup liquid in medium saucepan. Combine flour and cornstarch; whisk into liquid. Cook over medium heat until mixture starts to bubble. Continue to cook 1 minute. Remove from heat; allow to cool, stirring occasionally. When thickened liquid is cool, stir in meat mixture. Spoon into pastry shell. Place top crust over meat mixture; flute and seal edges. Cut slits in top crust. Brush with milk; sprinkle with sugar. Bake in 375° oven 45 minutes or until crust is golden brown.

Marcia G. Miller, *Urbandale*
First Place, 2014 Machine Shed Pies – Mincemeat
Second Place Overall, 2014 Machine Shed Pies – Fruit Pies

PEANUT BUTTER PIE

For CRUST:
1/2 c. butter
16 graham crackers, crushed
3 tbsp. granulated sugar

Melt butter in large saucepan. Add crackers and sugar and stir. Press mixture into 9-inch pie pan. Bake in 375° oven 8 minutes or until lightly brown.

(CONTINUED)

For PEANUT BUTTER PIE FILLING:

1 c. creamy peanut butter
8 oz. cream cheese
1 c. powdered sugar
1 1/2 c. whipped cream
   (recipe below)

1 snack-size chocolate
   covered crispy peanut
   butter candy bar

Cream together peanut butter, cream cheese and powdered sugar until smooth and creamy. Fold in whipped cream. Place mixture in crust; refrigerate 4 hours or until set. Top with remaining whipped cream and crumbled candy bar.

For WHIPPED CREAM:

1 1/2 c. heavy cream
3/4 tsp. vanilla

6 tbsp. granulated sugar

Beat heavy cream, vanilla and sugar until soft peaks form.

Tanya K. Hardy, *Osceola*
First Place, 2014 Machine Shed Pies – Peanut Butter
Second Place Overall, 2014 Machine Shed Pies – Cream Pie

RHUBARB CUSTARD PIE

2 eggs
1 tsp. vanilla
1/4 tsp. lemon extract
1/8 tsp. almond extract
1 1/2 c. granulated sugar
1/3 c. all-purpose flour

4 c. washed and diced
   fresh rhubarb
Milk
Granulated sugar
Pastry for double-crust
   9-inch pie

Beat eggs and extracts until light and foamy. While still beating, slowly add sugar. Gently fold in flour then rhubarb. Pour into prepared pie shell. Cover with top crust; seal and flute edges. Brush top crust with milk; sprinkle with sugar. Bake in 325° oven 55 to 60 minutes. Cover lightly with foil during later stage of baking if crust is getting too brown. Cool completely on wire rack; store in refrigerator.

Jennifer Bartles, *Des Moines*
First Place, 2015 Machine Shed and Gold Medal Flour Pies – Rhubarb Custard

PIES, CAKES AND DESSERTS

STRAWBERRY RHUBARB PIE

2 c. frozen strawberries,
thawed, drained and
juice reserved
1 c. granulated sugar
2 tbsp. cornstarch
3 c. chopped frozen rhubarb,
partially thawed

2 tbsp. cold butter, cut into
small pieces
1 egg yolk beaten with
1 to 3 tsp. water
3 tbsp. coarse sugar
Pastry for double-crust
9-inch pie

Place reserved strawberry juice in large bowl; set aside. In small bowl, mix sugar and cornstarch; whisk into reserved strawberry juice. Stir in rhubarb and strawberries; spoon into crust-lined pie plate. Dot with butter. To make lattice top, cut second crust into 1/2-inch wide strips. Place half the strips across filling in pie plate. Weave remaining strips with first strips to form lattice. Trim edges of strips even with edge of bottom crust. Fold trimmed edge of bottom crust over ends of strips forming high stand-up rim. Seal and flute edges. Brush lattice strips with egg yolk mixture; sprinkle with sugar. Bake in 400° oven 20 minutes; cover edge of crust with strips of foil to prevent excessing browning. Bake 20 to 30 minutes more or until golden brown. Cool at least 2 hours before serving.

Susan Schultz, *Haverhill*
First Place, 2015 Old Threshers Family Reunion

BUTTERNUT SQUASH PIE

For FILLING:
1 3/4 c. pureed cooked
butternut squash
3/4 c. granulated sugar
1/2 tsp. salt
1/2 tsp. cinnamon
1/8 tsp. allspice

1/8 tsp. cloves
1/8 tsp. ginger
2 eggs
3/4 c. half and half
Pastry for single-crust
8-inch pie

In large bowl, combine squash puree, sugar, salt and spices; mix in eggs. Add half and half; mix just until combined. Pour into prepared pie crust. Bake in 350° oven 60 minutes or until center is set. Cool on wire rack to room temperature. When cool, garnish with whipped cream and brittle.

(CONTINUED)

For BUTTERNUT SQUASH SEED BRITTLE:

4 tbsp. butter
1/4 c. granulated sugar

1/2 tbsp. light corn syrup
1/4 c. butternut squash seeds

In small saucepan, melt butter. Stir in sugar and corn syrup. Bring to boil over medium-high heat, stirring constantly. Cook until mixture is golden brown. Stir in squash seeds. Pour mixture onto jelly roll pan lined with parchment paper or aluminum foil. When brittle is cool, break into pieces.

Marcia G. Miller, *Urbandale*
First Place, 2015 Cooking with Pumpkin or Winter Squash

NOTHING COMPARES
IOWA STATE FAIR CORN PIE

For FILLING:

1 1/2 c. cooked fresh corn kernels
2/3 c. half and half
3/4 c. granulated sugar
1 c. heavy cream

Pinch of salt
Pinch of nutmeg
4 eggs
2 egg whites
Pastry for single-crust 8 or 9-inch pie

Place half the corn, half and half and sugar in a blender; process until corn is chopped. In large bowl, combine remaining corn, cream, salt, nutmeg and eggs; mix well. Beat egg whites until soft peaks form. Fold into corn mixture; spoon into pie shell. Bake in 325° oven 50 to 60 minutes. Remove from oven; cool completely.

For TOPPING:

2/3 c. heavy cream
2 tbsp. powdered sugar

1 tsp. vanilla

Place cream into mixing bowl. Add sugar and vanilla; whip until soft peaks form. Top cooled pie with whipping cream.

Lana Ross, *Indianola*
First Place, 2014 Fresh Corn Cuisine – Desserts

CRANBERRY PIE

2 1/2 c. whole fresh
   cranberries
1/2 c. packed brown sugar
1/3 c. toasted walnuts
1 egg

1/3 c. butter, melted
1/2 c. granulated sugar
1/2 c. all-purpose flour
Pastry for single-crust
   9-inch pie

Pour cranberries on top of unbaked crust. Sprinkle brown sugar over cranberries; sprinkle walnuts over top brown sugar. In small bowl, combine egg, butter, sugar and flour. Spread over cranberry mixture in crust. Bake in 350° oven 30 to 40 minutes or until lightly golden brown.

Linda Spevak, *Urbandale*
First Place, 2014 Machine Shed Pies – One Crust Fruit Other Than Named

APPLE CRUMB PIE

For CRUMB TOPPING:
1/4 c. all-purpose flour
1/4 c. quick-cooking rolled
   oats

Pinch of salt
3 tbsp. light brown sugar
2 tbsp. butter

In small bowl, combine flour, oats and salt; mix in brown sugar. Cut in butter until coarse crumbs form; set aside.

For APPLE FILLING:
6 c. peeled and sliced apples
   (Granny smith and
   golden delicious)
1 tbsp. lemon juice
1/2 c. granulated sugar

2 tbsp. all-purpose flour
1/2 tsp. cinnamon
1/4 tsp. salt
Pastry for single-crust
   8-inch pie

Place apples in large bowl; toss with lemon juice. Combine sugar, flour, cinnamon and salt; toss with apples. Let stand 15 minutes. Spoon apples into crust; sprinkle crumb topping over apples. Bake in 375° oven 45 minutes or until apples are tender.

Marcia G. Miller, *Urbandale*
First Place, 2014 Machine Shed Pies – Apple Crumb

SWEET POTATO PIE

14-oz. can sweet potatoes
3/4 c. evaporated milk
1 c. packed brown sugar
2 eggs
1/2 tsp. cinnamon

1 tsp. almond extract
1/2 tsp. salt
Pastry for single-crust
9-inch pie

Beat together potatoes, milk, brown sugar and eggs. Add cinnamon, almond extract and salt. Pour into pie shell. Bake in 350° oven 40 to 45 minutes.

Patty Hummel, *Allison*
First Place, 2014 Machine Shed Pies – Sweet Potato Pie

CHOCOLATE CREAM PIE

For CHOCOLATE CREAM PIE FILLING:
3 oz. German sweet baking
    chocolate
1/3 c. milk, divided
8 oz. cream cheese
3 tbsp. granulated sugar

1 1/2 c. whipped cream
    (recipe below)
Mini chocolate bar
Baked 9-inch pie crust

Melt baking chocolate with 1 tablespoon milk; set aside. In large bowl, cream the cream cheese and sugar. Add melted chocolate; mix well. Slowly add remainder of milk; mix well. Refrigerate chocolate mixture 10 minutes. Fold in whipped cream. Spoon mixture into baked pie shell. Refrigerate 3 hours or until set. Top with whipped cream and shavings from chocolate bar.

For WHIPPED CREAM:
1 1/2 c. heavy cream
3/4 tsp. vanilla

6 tbsp. granulated sugar

Beat heavy cream, vanilla and sugar until soft peaks form.

Keri Crowley, *Indianola*
First Place, 2015 Machine Shed and Gold Medal Flour Pies – One Crust Cream Pie Other Than Named

LEMON MERINGUE PIE

For LEMON PIE FILLING:

1 1/4 c. granulated sugar
3/4 c. fresh squeezed lemon
   juice
3/4 c. water
1/4 c. cornstarch

1/4 tsp. salt
8 large egg yolks
1 tbsp. finely shredded
   lemon zest
3 tbsp. unsalted butter
Baked 9-inch pie crust

In saucepan, mix together sugar, lemon juice, water, cornstarch and salt. Heat until cornstarch is dissolved. Bring to simmer over medium heat, stirring until mixture becomes translucent and begins to thicken, about 5 minutes. Stir in egg yolks until combined. Stir in lemon zest and butter. Bring to simmer, stirring constantly, 2 minutes. Cool and pour mixture into baked pie shell; chill 10 minutes and top with meringue.

For MERINGUE:

4 egg whites
1 tsp. vanilla

1/2 tsp. cream of tartar
1/2 c. granulated sugar

Bring egg whites to room temperature. Add vanilla and cream of tartar. Beat with electric mixer 1 minute or until soft peaks form. Gradually add sugar; beat until stiff peaks form. Spread over filling. Carefully seal meringue to edge of crust. Bake in 350° oven 15 minutes.

Tanya K. Hardy, *Osceola*
First Place, 2014 Machine Shed Pies – Lemon Meringue

KEY LIME COCONUT PIE

For CRUST:

1 1/2 c. graham cracker
   crumbs

2 tbsp. granulated sugar
1/3 c. melted butter

Combine graham cracker crumbs and sugar. Add melted butter; stir until well blended. Press onto bottom and up sides of 9-inch metal or glass pie dish. Cover and freeze 30 minutes. Bake in 350° oven 8 minutes. Cool completely.

(CONTINUED)

PIES, CAKES AND DESSERTS

For FILLING:

15-oz. can cream of coconut	**2 tsp. unflavored gelatin**
2/3 c. plain low-fat yogurt	**3/4 c. chilled heavy cream**
1/2 c. key lime juice	**2 tbsp. powdered sugar**
2 tsp. grated key lime zest	**1 lime, thinly sliced into**
3 tbsp. cold water	**rounds**

In 4-cup measuring cup or large bowl, whisk together cream of coconut, yogurt, juice and zest. Pour water into small metal bowl. Sprinkle gelatin over water; let stand until gelatin softens, about 10 minutes. Set bowl in small saucepan of barely simmering water. Whisk until gelatin dissolves, about 1 minute. Whisk into coconut mixture. Pour into baked crust (filling will reach top of crust). Chill until set, about 4 hours. (Can be prepared 1 day ahead. Cover and keep refrigerated.) Beat cream and powdered sugar in medium bowl until stiff peaks form. Transfer to pastry bag fitted with large star tip. Pipe around edge of pie. Dip lime rounds into additional powdered sugar; garnish pie with lime slices.

Christine Montalvo, *Windsor Heights*
First Place, 2014 Key Lime Challenge – Dessert
First Place Overall, 2014 Key Lime Challenge

BROWNED BUTTERSCOTCH PIE

2 tbsp. plus 1/4 tsp. unsalted	**2 c. milk**
butter, divided	**1/4 c. half and half**
1 c. packed dark brown sugar	**3 egg yolks**
4 tbsp. cornstarch	**1 tsp. sweet whiskey**
1/4 tsp. salt	**Baked 7-inch pie crust**

In large saucepan, melt 2 tablespoons butter over medium heat. Continue to heat until butter begins to turn brown. Add brown sugar, cornstarch and salt. Whisk in milk, half and half and egg yolks. Cook over medium-high heat, whisking constantly, until thickened and bubbly. Cook and whisk 2 minutes more; remove from heat. Pour filling through strainer; stir in whiskey and remaining butter. Pour filling into crust. Refrigerate until filling is set, at least 4 hours. When cool, garnish with whipped cream.

Marcia G. Miller, *Urbandale*
First Place, 2015 Machine Shed and Gold Medal Flour Pies – Butterscotch

PIES, CAKES AND DESSERTS

MAPLE NUT CREAM PIE

For FILLING:

2 c. whole milk
Pinch of salt
1/2 c. packed brown sugar
1/8 c. pure maple syrup
2 tbsp. cornstarch
2 tbsp. all-purpose flour

3 egg yolks, beaten
1 tsp. pure maple extract
1/2 tsp. vanilla
1 tbsp. butter
1/2 c. toasted pecans
Baked 9-inch pie crust

In saucepan, combine milk, salt, brown sugar, maple syrup, cornstarch and flour. Place over medium heat, bring to a boil. Stir small amount of hot mixture into yolks. Gradually add yolks to hot milk mixture; stir until thick. Remove from heat. Mix in maple extract, vanilla and butter. Sprinkle toasted pecans in bottom of prepared pie shell. Pour filling into baked pie shell; refrigerate.

For TOPPING:

1 c. heavy cream
4 tbsp. granulated sugar
1 tsp. vanilla

1/2 tsp. maple extract
Candied pecans

Combine heavy cream, sugar, vanilla and maple extract. Beat until soft peaks form. Spread over pie; garnish with pecans.

Lana Ross, *Indianola*
First Place, 2014 Puckerbrush Potluck – Dessert

COCONUT CREAM HAUPIA PIE

For HAUPIA FILLING:

3/8 c. granulated sugar
4 tbsp. cornstarch
1/8 tsp. salt
7/8 c. coconut milk

1/2 c. skim milk
1/2 c. water
1 tsp. coconut extract
Baked 9-inch pie crust

In small saucepan, combine sugar, cornstarch and salt. Whisk in coconut milk, skim milk and water. Cook over medium-high heat, whisking constantly, until thick and bubbly. Cook and whisk 2 minutes more; remove from heat. Add coconut extract to mixture. Pour into pie crust.

(CONTINUED)

PIES, CAKES AND DESSERTS

For COCONUT CREAM FILLING:

3/4 c. granulated sugar	3 egg yolks
3 tbsp. cornstarch	1/2 tsp. vanilla
1/8 tsp. salt	1/2 c. coconut, lightly
2 c. skim milk	toasted

In medium saucepan, combine sugar, cornstarch and salt. Whisk in milk and egg yolks. Cook over medium-high heat, whisking constantly, until thickened and bubbly. Cook and whisk 2 minutes more; remove from heat. Pour mixture through strainer; stir in vanilla and coconut. Carefully spoon coconut cream filling on top of haupia layer. Refrigerate until filling is set, at least 4 hours. When set, garnish pie with whipped topping and toasted coconut.

Marcia G. Miller, *Urbandale*
First Place, 2015 Machine Shed and Gold Medal Flour Pies – Coconut Cream
First Place Overall, 2015 Machine Shed and Gold Medal Flour Pies – Cream

BERRY CUSTARD PIE

1 c. granulated sugar	1/2 c. red raspberries
1/3 c. all-purpose flour	1 c. strawberries
2 large eggs	1/2 c. black raspberries
1/2 c. sour cream	1 tbsp. butter
1/2 tsp. cinnamon	1 tbsp. milk
1/8 tsp. freshly grated nutmeg	Sugar
1 tsp. vanilla	Pastry for double-crust
1 c. blueberries	9-inch pie

In large bowl, combine sugar, flour, eggs, sour cream, cinnamon, nutmeg and vanilla; mix well and set aside. Place berries in bottom pie crust. Pour sour cream mixture over berries. Dot with butter; cover with top crust. Press sides of crust around pan to create a ridge. Cut slits in top. Brush crust with milk; sprinkle with sugar. Bake in 350° oven 50 minutes or until crust is golden brown.

Keri Crowley, *Indianola*
First Place, 2014 Machine Shed Pies – Two Crust Cream Other Than Named

SPICED UP SOUR CREAM RAISIN PIE

For FILLING:
2 c. raisins
3/4 c. granulated sugar
1/4 c. cornstarch
1 tsp. cinnamon
1/2 tsp. salt
1/2 tsp. nutmeg
2 c. whole milk
3 egg yolks, beaten
1 c. sour cream
1 tsp. lemon juice
Baked 8-inch pie crust

In saucepan, combine raisins, sugar, cornstarch, cinnamon, salt, nutmeg and milk. Heat slowly, stirring constantly, until mixture boils. Add small portion of hot mixture to egg yolks until warmed. Return egg yolks to hot filling; return to boil. Remove from heat; gradually add sour cream and lemon juice. Pour into baked pie crust.

For MERINGUE:
1/2 c. water
1 tsp. cornstarch
7 tbsp. granulated sugar,
    divided
3 egg whites
1/4 tsp. cream of tartar

In saucepan, combine water, cornstarch and 2 tablespoons sugar. Cook until clear and thick. Beat egg whites in a mixer, gradually add cream of tartar and remaining sugar. Beat until stiff peaks form. Add water mixture; beat until smooth. Place meringue onto pie, spreading evenly to edge of crust. Bake in 350° oven 15 to 20 minutes until lightly browned.

Lana Ross, *Indianola*
First Place, 2014 Machine Shed Pies – Sour Cream Raisin

STRAWBERRY CHIFFON PIE

For GRAHAM CRACKER CRUST:
1 1/3 c. graham cracker
    crumbs
1 tbsp. granulated sugar
5 tbsp. butter or margarine,
    melted
1/8 tsp. salt

Combine all ingredients; tossing until crumbs are evenly moistened. Press into 9-inch pie pan. Bake in 375° oven 8 to 10 minutes. Cool completely; set aside.

(CONTINUED)

For FILLING:

2 3/4 c. hulled and chopped strawberries
3/4 c. water
4 tsp. unflavored gelatin
2 tbsp. powdered egg whites
6 tbsp. warm water
1/8 tsp. cream of tartar
1/4 c. plus 1/3 c. granulated sugar, divided
1/2 c. frozen whipped topping, thawed

Puree strawberries in blender or food processor. Press through sieve to remove seeds. Put puree in medium bowl; set aside. Place 3/4 cup water in microwave-safe dish. Sprinkle gelatin over water; let stand 1 minute. Microwave on high 30 seconds; stir until gelatin is dissolved. Pour into strawberry puree; stir until well combined. Refrigerate until mixture thickens and mounds slightly. Whisk powdered egg whites into warm water. Add cream of tartar. Beat with electric mixer on high speed until foamy. Gradually beat in 1/4 cup sugar, 1 tablespoon at a time, until stiff peaks form. Fold whipped topping into egg whites. Fold in strawberry puree and 1/3 cup sugar until no white streaks remain. Refrigerate approximately 20 minutes, stirring once, until mixture starts to mound. Spoon into crust. Refrigerate at least 4 hours or until set. Garnish with whipped topping and fresh strawberries.

Marcia G. Miller, *Urbandale*
First Place, 2014 Machine Shed Pies – Chiffon

PRECIOUS PEACH PIE

3/4 c. granulated sugar
3 tbsp. all-purpose flour
1/4 tsp. cinnamon
Dash of salt
5 c. sliced fresh peaches
2 tbsp. butter
Pastry for double-crust 9-inch pie

Combine sugar, flour, cinnamon and salt. Add peaches; mix lightly. Spoon into pastry shell. Dot with butter. Cover with top crust; trim dough with 3/4-inch overhang. Fold top edge under bottom crust; press edges together and flute. Cut slits in top crust. Bake in 400° oven 40 to 45 minutes or until crust is lightly browned.

Larry Harker, *Johnston*
First Place, 2014 Machine Shed Pies – Peach
First Place Overall, 2014 Machine Shed Pies – Fruit Pie

PIES, CAKES AND DESSERTS

ZUCCHINI PIE

For ZUCCHINI PIE FILLING:

2 c. peeled, seeded and
    sliced zucchini
2 beaten eggs
2 c. granulated sugar
4 tbsp. all-purpose flour
1/2 tsp. salt

1/2 c. butter
2 c. evaporated milk
2 tsp. vanilla
1/4 tsp. nutmeg
Pastry for single-crust
    9-inch pie

Boil zucchini in water until tender; drain and let stand in cold water 5 minutes. In large bowl, mix eggs, sugar, flour, salt, butter, evaporated milk and vanilla. Drain zucchini; add to egg mixture. Beat on medium speed until mixture is smooth and creamy. Pour filling into unbaked pie crust; sprinkle with nutmeg. Bake in 350° oven 55 to 60 minutes or until knife inserted into center comes out clean; cool.

For WHIPPED CREAM:

1 c. heavy cream
1/2 tsp. clear vanilla

4 tsp. granulated sugar

Mix together cream, vanilla and sugar in chilled bowl. Beat until soft peaks form. Spread on top of cooled pie.

Tanya K. Hardy, *Osceola*
First Place, 2015 Machine Shed and Gold Medal Flour Pies – Zucchini
Second Place Overall, 2015 Machine Shed and Gold Medal Flour Pies – Cream

SWEET CORN PIE

For FILLING:

1/4 c. butter
2 tbsp. corn flour
1 tbsp. all-purpose flour
1/4 c. milk

15-oz. can whole kernel
    corn, drained
1/2 c. granulated sugar
1/2 tsp. salt
1/2 tsp. cinnamon

Melt butter in medium saucepan; stir in flours. Add milk, corn, sugar, salt and cinnamon. Cook 5 minutes; set aside to cool.

(CONTINUED)

PIES, CAKES AND DESSERTS

For CRUST:

1 1/2 c. all-purpose flour	3/4 c. ice cold water
1/2 c. corn flour	1 egg, separated
1 tsp. salt	1 tbsp. coarse sugar
3/4 c. shortening	

Mix together flours and salt; cut in shortening. In separate bowl, combine water and egg yolk. Add enough liquid to flour mixture to make dough stick together. Divide dough into 8 balls. Roll each ball into 6-inch circle. Place 2 to 3 tablespoons filling in center of each. Brush edges with egg white; fold in half and crimp edges with fork. Brush top with egg white; sprinkle with sugar. Bake in 375° oven 20 to 25 minutes.

Anita Van Gundy, *Des Moines*
First Place, 2015 Butter Kernel Corn Creation

TRIPLE CHERRY PIE

1 c. Mt. Rainier cherries	1/4 tsp. salt
1 c. sweet cherries	3 tsp. unsalted butter
2 c. tart cherries	Milk
1 c. granulated sugar	Granulated sugar
2 1/2 tbsp. cornstarch	Pastry for double-crust 9-inch pie

Place cherries in medium saucepan. Add sugar, cornstarch and salt; cook over medium heat until mixture thickens. Pour cherry mixture into unbaked pie crust; dot with butter. Cut top crust into strips and weave across cherries. Press sides of crust around pan to create a ridge. Brush crust with milk; sprinkle with sugar. Bake in 375° oven 30 minutes or until crust is golden brown.

Keri Crowley, *Indianola*
First Place, 2015 Machine Shed and Gold Medal Flour Pies – Triple Cherry
Third Place Overall, 2015 Machine Shed and Gold Medal Flour Pies - Fruit

EGGNOG PUMPKIN PIE

15-oz. can 100% pure
    pumpkin
1 1/4 c. eggnog
2/3 c. granulated sugar

3 eggs
2 tsp. pumpkin pie spice
1/4 tsp. salt
Pastry for single-crust
    9-inch pie

In large bowl, combine pumpkin, eggnog, sugar, eggs, pumpkin pie spice and salt. Pour into pastry shell. Bake in 375° oven 60 to 65 minutes or until knife inserted near center comes out clean. Cool on wire rack; refrigerate until serving.

Larry Harker, *Johnston*
First Place, 2015 Machine Shed and Gold Medal Flour Pies – Pumpkin

---

LEMON SPONGE PIE
WITH LIMONCELLO CRUST

For HOMEMADE LIMONCELLO:
14 lemons
6 c. grain alcohol

6 c. water
4 1/2 c. granulated sugar

Peel lemons separating only the yellow part of the peel from the fruit. Place peels in glass jars. Add alcohol; seal tight and let rest 2 weeks in a dark cool place. Do not expose to sunlight. After 2 weeks, heat water in saucepan; mix in sugar. Let cool about 1 hour, stirring occasionally making sure to incorporate sugar collected on bottom of pan. Remove lemon peels from alcohol; discard peels. Add sugar water to alcohol. Close jar tight and let rest in dark, cool spot 1 month. After a month, bottle and store in freezer.

For LIMONCELLO PIE CRUST:
1 1/4 c. all-purpose flour
1/4 tsp. salt
1/3 c. cold lard

**3 to 4 tbsp. ice cold
    homemade limoncello**

Sift together flour and salt; cut in cold lard. Sprinkle with limoncello, 1 tablespoon at a time, lightly tossing with fork after each addition until

(CONTINUED)

moistened. Gently form into disc. The less the dough is handled the better, similar technique as biscuits. Wrap disc in plastic wrap; chill in refrigerator 2 hours. Roll out disc and place in 9-inch pie pan; set aside.

For FILLING:

1 c. granulated sugar	**1/8 tsp. salt**
1 tbsp. butter, softened	**1/4 c. lemon juice**
2 eggs, separated	**2 tsp. grated lemon zest**
1 c. milk	**1 1/2 tbsp. homemade**
3 tbsp. all-purpose flour	**limoncello**

In large bowl, beat sugar and butter until well blended. Add egg yolks, one at a time, beating well after each addition. Add milk, flour and salt; mix well. Stir in lemon juice and zest; set aside. In small bowl, beat egg whites until stiff peaks form. Gently fold into lemon mixture. Pour into prepared pie shell. Bake in 325° oven 50 to 55 minutes or until lightly browned and knife inserted near center comes out clean; cool. Garnish with whipped cream and lemon if desired. Store in refrigerator.

Jennifer Bartles, *Des Moines*
First Place, 2015 When Life Gives You Lemons – Desserts

MAPLE PECAN PIE

3/4 c. pure maple syrup	**1 tsp. vanilla**
3/4 c. packed light brown	**1 tsp. maple extract**
sugar	**1/4 tsp. salt**
1/2 c. light corn syrup	**1 1/2 c. pecan halves**
1/4 c. unsalted butter	**Pastry for single-crust**
3 large eggs	**9-inch pie**

In medium saucepan over medium heat, stir maple syrup, brown sugar, corn syrup and butter until sugar dissolves and butter melts. Increase heat; boil 1 minute. Cool to lukewarm, about 45 minutes. In 4-cup measuring cup, whisk eggs, vanilla, maple extract and salt. Gradually whisk maple syrup mixture into egg mixture; stir in pecan halves. Pour into crust; bake in 350° oven until filling is slightly puffed around edges and center is set, about 55 minutes. Cool pie completely on rack.

Christine Montalvo, *Windsor Heights*
First Place, 2015 Machine Shed and Gold Medal Flour Pies – Pecan

PIES, CAKES AND DESSERTS

PINEAPPLE CREAM PIE

1 5/8 c. pineapple juice
    (see below)
1 c. granulated sugar
4 tbsp. cornstarch
1/4 tsp. salt

3/4 c. water
3 egg yolks
8 oz. can crushed pineapple,
    drained reserving juice
Baked 9-inch pie crust

In measuring cup, measure juice drained from pineapple. Add additional pineapple juice to equal 1 5/8 cup; set aside. In large saucepan, combine sugar, cornstarch and salt. Whisk in pineapple juice, water and egg yolks. Cook over medium-high heat, whisking constantly, until thickened and bubbly. Cook and whisk 2 minutes more; remove from heat. Pour filling through a strainer; stir in crushed pineapple. Pour into crust. Refrigerate until filling is set, at least 4 hours. When cool, garnish with whipped topping and dried pineapple.

Marcia G. Miller, *Urbandale*
First Place, 2014 Machine Shed Pies – One Crust Cream Other Than Named
First Place Overall, 2014 Machine Shed Pies – Cream Pie

FIVE LAYER LEMON-RASPBERRY PIE

For RASPBERRY CREAM LAYER:
1 c. raspberries, pureed
2 tbsp. orange juice
3 tbsp. granulated sugar

1 tbsp. cornstarch
Graham cracker pie crust

Strain raspberry puree; add orange juice, sugar and cornstarch in a small saucepan. Heat over medium heat until bubbly and mixture is thick and clear. Cool while preparing lemon cream layer.

For LEMON CREAM LAYER:
Fresh squeezed juice from
    1 lemon (1/3 c.)
Grated zest from 1 lemon

14-oz. can sweetened
    condensed milk
2 tbsp. sour cream

Whisk together all ingredients until smooth; add 1/3 cup of mixture to raspberry puree filling. Mix together thoroughly; spread into pie crust. Pour remaining lemon cream layer over raspberry layer. Bake in 350°

(CONTINUED)

oven 10 minutes. Remove to wire rack; cool 15 minutes. Place in refrigerator while making lemon curd layer.

For LEMON CURD LAYER:

**4 egg yolks
1/2 c. plus 2 tbsp. granulated
   sugar
3 tbsp. lemon juice**

**1/4 c. butter, room
   temperature
1/2 tsp. grated fresh lemon
   zest**

In small saucepan, cream together egg yolks and sugar. Add lemon juice, butter and lemon zest, whisking thoroughly. Cook over medium-low heat until mixture is thickened and resembles a thin hollandaise sauce. Do not boil. Remove from heat; immediately strain to remove any lumps. Spread over lemon cream layer. Chill at least 1 hour before adding whipped cream layer.

For WHIPPED CREAM LAYER:

**1 c. heavy cream
1/4 c. powdered sugar**

1/2 tsp. vanilla

Beat cream, powdered sugar and vanilla in large mixing bowl with electric mixer until stiff peaks form. Chill; before serving, spread on top of pie. Garnish with fresh raspberries.

Ann Carter, *Carlisle*
First Place, 2015 Best Pie Using Kellogg Keebler Products

BUTTERMILK PIE

**1 3/4 c. granulated sugar
3 tbsp. all-purpose flour
1/2 c. butter, softened
1 tsp. almond extract
1/2 tsp. clear vanilla
1/2 tsp. butter flavoring**

**3 eggs
1 c. buttermilk
Dash of salt
Pastry for single-crust
   9-inch pie**

Cream together sugar, flour and butter. Beat in flavorings, eggs, buttermilk and salt. Pour into prepared crust. Bake in 425° oven 15 minutes; reduce heat to 350° and bake 35 to 40 minutes more.

Patty Hummel, *Allison*
First Place, 2015 Favorite Tone's Everyday Family Recipe

PIES, CAKES AND DESSERTS

GOOSEBERRY PIE

4 c. gooseberries
1 tbsp. water
1 1/2 c. granulated sugar
1/3 c. all-purpose flour

1/4 tsp. nutmeg
1 tbsp. light cream or milk
Pastry for double-crust
9-inch pie

In medium saucepan, combine gooseberries and water; cook over medium-low heat until berries pop, stirring occasionally. Combine sugar, flour and nutmeg; add to gooseberries. Cook and stir until mixture just begins to bubble. Place mixture in unbaked pie shell; cover with top crust. Seal and flute edges; cut slits in top. Brush top crust with cream or milk; sprinkle with a little sugar. Bake in 375° oven 45 minutes.

Lester Holst, *Indianola*
First Place, 2014 Machine Shed Pies – Gooseberry

MOCHA RUM CHIFFON PIE

For CHOCOLATE GRAHAM CRACKER CRUST:

1 1/8 c. graham cracker
　crumbs
2 1/2 tbsp. unsweetened
　cocoa powder

2 tbsp. granulated sugar
1/8 tsp. salt
5 tbsp. butter or margarine,
　melted

Combine all ingredients. Press into 8-inch pie plate. Bake in 375° oven 9 minutes; cool completely.

For FILLING:

2 1/2 tsp. instant coffee
　granules
3/4 c. boiling water
2 1/4 tsp. unflavored gelatin
2 oz. unsweetened chocolate,
　chopped

1/2 c. milk
1/2 c. granulated sugar
1/4 tsp. salt
2 egg yolks
1/8 c. silver rum
1/2 tsp. vanilla

Dissolve coffee granules in boiling water. Sprinkle gelatin over hot coffee; let stand a few minutes, then stir to dissolve. In medium saucepan, combine chocolate and milk. Place over low heat; stir until chocolate melts. Remove from heat; whisk in sugar, salt and egg yolks.

(CONTINUED)

PIES, CAKES AND DESSERTS

Return to moderate heat; whisk constantly until mixture thickens slightly and barely reaches a simmer. Add coffee mixture; stir over medium heat until mixture simmers, about 2 minutes. Pour chocolate mixture into a bowl; refrigerate, stirring occasionally, until it mounds when dropped from a spoon, about 60 minutes. Stir in rum and vanilla. Prepare egg whites.

For EGG WHITES:

2 tbsp. powdered egg whites   **1 c. nondairy whipped**
3/8 c. water   **topping**
1/4 c. granulated sugar

In medium bowl, stir powdered egg whites into water. Stir 2 minutes, giving powder time to absorb water. Mix on high speed, adding sugar, 1 tablespoon at a time until stiff peaks form. Fold egg whites and whipped topping into chocolate mixture until combined and no white streaks remain. Chill chiffon mixture 30 minutes until chiffon starts to set up. Mound into baked crust. Refrigerate until firm, at least 4 hours. Garnish pie with chocolate shavings.

Marcia G. Miller, *Urbandale*
First Place, 2015 Machine Shed and Gold Medal Flour Pies – Chiffon

PEACH RASPBERRY PIE

4 c. sliced fresh peaches   **2 tsp. butter**
2 c. fresh raspberries   **Half and half**
1/4 c. cornstarch   **Sparkling sugar**
3/4 c. granulated sugar   **Pastry for double-crust**
1 tbsp. lemon juice   **9-inch pie**

Combine peaches, raspberries, cornstarch and sugar; sprinkle with lemon juice. Spoon into prepared pie crust. Dot with butter; cover with top crust. Seal and flute edges. Cut slits in top. Brush with half and half and sprinkle with sugar. Cover edges with foil. Bake in 400° oven 15 minutes. Reduce heat to 350° and bake 40 to 45 minutes, until filling is bubbly and crust is golden. Remove foil for last 25 minutes of baking. Cool on wire rack.

Cynthia Murphy, *Des Moines*
First Place, 2015 Machine Shed and Gold Medal Flour Pies – Peach-Red Raspberry

PIES, CAKES AND DESSERTS

COCONUT CREAM PIE

For FILLING:

3/4 c. granulated sugar
3 tbsp. cornstarch
1/4 tsp. salt
2 c. milk
3 slightly beaten egg yolks

2 tbsp. butter
1 tsp. vanilla
1 c. coconut
Baked 9-inch pie crust

In saucepan, combine sugar, cornstarch and salt; heat and gradually stir in milk. Cook and stir over medium heat until mixture boils and thickens. Cook 2 minutes more; remove from heat. Stir small amount of hot mixture into yolks; return yolks to hot mixture. Cook 2 minutes, stirring constantly. Remove from heat; add butter, vanilla and coconut. Cool to room temperature. Pour into baked shell.

For MERINGUE:

3 egg whites
1/4 tsp. cream of tartar
1/2 tsp. vanilla

6 tbsp. granulated sugar
1/3 c. coconut

Beat egg whites with cream of tartar and vanilla until soft peaks form. Gradually add sugar, beating until stiff peaks form and all sugar is dissolved. Spread on top of pie, spreading to edge of pastry to seal. Sprinkle coconut over meringue. Bake in 350° oven 12 to 15 minutes; cool.

Larry Harker, *Johnston*
First Place, 2014 Machine Shed Pies – Coconut Cream

BLUEBERRY CREAM PIE

For CRUST:

1/4 c. soy flour
3/4 c. all-purpose flour
1/2 c. (8 tbsp.) vegan buttery
   baking sticks

1/2 c. chopped honey
   roasted soy nuts
1/4 c. powdered sugar

Mix together all ingredients using pastry blender. Pat into pan, shaping crust with your hands. Bake in 400° oven 12 minutes; set aside to cool. Reduce oven to 350° after crust is done.

(CONTINUED)

For FILLING:
1/2 c. granulated sugar
1 tsp. almond extract

1 1/2 c. (12-oz.) silken
 firm tofu

Combine sugar, almond extract and tofu in food processor. Puree on low until very smooth. Pour into baked crust. Bake in 350° oven 30 minutes or until filling is set. Cool; cover filling with topping.

For TOPPING:
2 pts. fresh blueberries,
 washed and dried

1 c. apricot jam
Soy whipped cream

Reserve 1/4 cup blueberries and set aside. Spoon remaining blueberries on filling. Puree jam in food processor. Heat in microwave 45 seconds; spoon or brush over blueberries. Refrigerate at least 1 hour before serving. Garnish with soy whipped cream and reserved blueberries.

Jan Trometer, *Jamaica*
First Place, 2015 It's Soy Amazing – Desserts

CHERRY PIE

1 c. juice reserved from
 cherries
1 c. granulated sugar
Pinch of salt
2 tbsp. tapioca
5 tsp. cornstarch

3 c. pitted cherries, drained,
 reserving juice
2 tsp. butter
1 egg beaten with 1 to 3 tsp.
 milk, cream or water
Pastry for double-crust
 9-inch pie

In saucepan, combine juice, sugar, salt, tapioca and cornstarch. Cook until mixture beings to thicken; let cool slightly. After mixture is cooled, add cherries; pour into crust. Dot with butter; cover with top crust. Seal and flute edges. Cut slits in top. Brush with egg wash; sprinkle with sugar. Bake in 350° oven 60 minutes.

Lana Shope, *Indianola*
First Place, 2015 Iowa Orchards Creations – Fruit Pie (adults)
Second Place Overall, 2015 Iowa Orchards Creations

CRANBERRY-RASPBERRY PIE

2 c. chopped cranberries
4 c. raspberries
1/2 tsp. almond extract
1 1/4 c. granulated sugar
1/4 c. quick-cooking tapioca
1/4 tsp. salt
Pastry for double-crust
9-inch pie

In large bowl, combine cranberries, raspberries and almond extract. Combine sugar, tapioca and salt; add to fruit, tossing gently to coat. Let stand 15 minutes. Spoon into crust; cover with top crust. Trim, seal and flute edges. Cut slits in top crust. Bake in 350° oven 45 to 50 minutes or until crust is golden brown and filling is bubbly.

Lorraine Doke, *Indianola*
First Place, 2015 Machine Shed and Gold Medal Flour Pies – Two Crust Berry

STRAWBERRY LEMONADE CHIFFON PIE WITH DONUT CRUMB CRUST

For DONUT CRUST:
40 miniature sugar donuts   3 tbsp. butter, melted

In food processor pulse donuts until crumbled. Spread out onto parchment-lined baking sheet. Toast in 375° oven 8 to 10 minutes, stirring halfway through. Place crumbs into a bowl; stir in melted butter. Press into 9-inch pie pan. Bake 6 to 8 minutes; set aside to cool.

For FILLING:
1 1/2 c. strawberry lemonade,
    divided
1 1/2 c. unsweetened frozen
    strawberries
4 oz. fresh lemon juice
1/2 c. granulated sugar
1 1/2, 1-oz. envs. unflavored
    gelatin
2 egg whites from
    pasteurized eggs
1 c. heavy cream

In saucepan, combine 1/2 cup lemonade, frozen strawberries, lemon juice and sugar. Simmer, stirring occasionally over low heat 20 to 25 minutes. In small bowl, soften gelatin in remaining lemonade. Strain hot

(CONTINUED)

strawberry mixture into large bowl. Add gelatin mixture; stir until gelatin is dissolved. Let stand until cooled to room temperature, about 1 hour. Whip egg whites until stiff peaks form. Gently fold into cooled strawberry mixture. Whip cream until stiff peaks form. Gently fold into cooled mixture. Pour into cooled donut crust. Refrigerate 3 to 4 hours, until set. If desired, garnish with whipped cream.

Jennifer Bartles, *Des Moines*
First Place, 2015 Fair Delicious

KEY LIME PIE

For CRUST:

1/4 c. butter
8 graham cracker sheets,
 crushed

1 1/2 tbsp. granulated sugar

Melt butter in large saucepan. Add graham crackers and sugar. Press into 9-inch pie pan. Bake in 350° oven 15 minutes or until lightly browned. Set aside to cool.

For KEY LIME PIE FILLING:

4 large egg yolks
14-oz. can sweetened
 condensed milk

1/2 c. key lime juice
1 1/2 tbsp. grated lime zest

Beat egg yolks in large bowl until pale yellow and thick. Slowly add condensed milk; beat at low speed. Add lime juice and lime zest; blend well. Pour filling into crust; bake in 350° oven 12 minutes. Chill in refrigerator at least 2 hours. Top with whipped cream, extra key limes and lime zest if desired.

For WHIPPED CREAM:

1 1/2 c. heavy cream
3/4 tsp. vanilla

6 tbsp. granulated sugar

Beat heavy cream, vanilla and sugar until soft peaks form.

Tanya K. Hardy, *Osceola*
First Place, 2015 Machine Shed and Gold Medal Flour Pies – Key Lime

PIES, CAKES AND DESSERTS

PRIZE-WINNING PIE CRUST RECIPES

PIE CRUST

2 c. all-purpose flour
1/2 tsp. salt
2/3 c. shortening

2 tsp. vinegar
5 to 7 tbsp. ice water

Mix together flour and salt; cut in shortening. Add vinegar to water; gradually pour into flour mixture until all sticks together. Divide into 2 equal parts. Roll out to fit 8-inch pie pan. Poke holes in dough; fill with pie weights. Bake in 350° oven 15 to 20 minutes. Cool completely.

Lana Shope, *Indianola*

PIE CRUST

2 c. all-purpose flour
1/2 tsp. salt

1/2 c. butter-flavored
    shortening
4 to 6 tbsp. cold water

Combine flour and salt; cut in shortening with pastry blender until pea-sized crumbs form. Add water, 1 tablespoon at a time, tossing with fork until dough comes together. Roll out half the pastry into 10-inch circle; ease into 7-inch pie plate. Roll out remaining pastry for top crust.

Marcia G. Miller, *Indianola*

PIE CRUST

1 1/2 c. all-purpose flour
1/2 tsp. salt

1/2 c. shortening
4 to 5 tbsp. cold water

Mix together flour and salt; cut shortening into mixture until ingredients resemble small peas. Add water, 1 tablespoon at a time, until dough comes together. Roll out until 1/8-inch thick. Transfer to 9-inch pie plate. Fit loosely onto bottom and sides. Trim 1/2 to 1-inch beyond edge; fold under and flute. Prick bottom and sides well. Bake in 450° oven until pastry is golden, 10 to 12 minutes.

Larry Harker, *Johnston*

PIES, CAKES AND DESSERTS

PIE CRUST

2 1/2 c. all-purpose flour
1 tsp. salt
1 tbsp. granulated sugar

3/4 c. cold butter, cut into
    chunks
1/4 c. cold lard, cut into
    chunks
1/4 c. ice water

Place flour, salt and sugar in food processor. Add butter and lard; pulse until ingredients resemble small peas. Add water; mix until just incorporated. Shape into 2 rounds; wrap in plastic wrap. Refrigerate at least 1 hour prior to rolling out. Roll out to fit 9-inch pie pan.

Linda Spevak, *Urbandale*

PIE CRUST

2/3 c. solid vegetable
    shortening
2 c. all-purpose flour

1 tsp. salt
2 1/2 tbsp. ice water

Using a pastry cutter, combine shortening, flour and salt until mixture is crumbly. Add water; mix with fork until mixture starts to stick together. Depending on humidity, you may need to add additional water. Add water, 1 teaspoon at a time, until mixture can be worked into ball of dough. Roll dough out to fit 9-inch pie pan. Place crust in pan; set aside. Repeat rolling for top crust.

Keri Crowley, *Indianola*

PIE CRUST

3 c. sifted all-purpose flour
1 tsp. salt

1 c. cold lard
6 to 8 tbsp. ice water

Sift together flour and salt; cut in cold lard. Sprinkle with water, 1 tablespoon at a time, lightly tossing with fork after each addition until adequately moistened. Gently form into 2 discs. Wrap discs in plastic wrap; chill in refrigerator 2 hours. Roll out discs to fit 9-inch pie pan.

Jennifer Bartles, *Des Moines*

PIES, CAKES AND DESSERTS

PIE CRUST

2 c. all-purpose flour
2/3 c. lard
1 tsp. salt

1 egg
1/2 c. water
1 tsp. vinegar

Mix together flour, lard and salt until coarse crumbs form. Mix together egg, water and vinegar. Using 5 to 7 tablespoons of egg mixture, sprinkle over dough, 1 tablespoon at a time until mixture holds shape. Divide dough in half; roll out on lightly floured surface to fit 9-inch pie pan.

Lorraine Doke, *Indianola*

PIE CRUST

3 c. all-purpose flour
1 tsp. salt
1/2 c. lard
1/2 c. butter

1 egg
1/3 c. cold water
1 tsp. apple cider vinegar

Mix together flour and salt; cut in lard and butter. In separate bowl, whisk together remaining ingredients. Slowly add to flour mixture; mix until dough just holds together. Divide into 2 portions. Refrigerate at least 1 hour. Roll out to fit 9-inch pie plate. Place in pie dish; fill with pie weights. Bake in 425° oven 10 to 15 minutes.

Christine Montalvo, *Windsor Heights*

GLUTEN FREE SPONGE CUPCAKES WITH BUTTERCREAM FROSTING

For CUPCAKES:

2 eggs
1 c. granulated sugar
1 c. white rice flour

1 tsp. baking powder
1/2 c. milk
2 tbsp. margarine, melted

Beat eggs in bowl 4 minutes on high. Add sugar; beat 4 minutes more. Add flour and baking powder; stir until combined. Stir in milk and margarine until well mixed. Pour into lined muffin tins. Bake in 350° oven 16 minutes.

For FILLING:

1 c. heavy cream
1/3 c. powdered sugar
1 tsp. vanilla

1/3 c. unsweetened cocoa
powder

Beat all ingredients until soft peaks form. Pipe into center of cupcakes.

For FROSTING:

4 oz. granulated sugar,
divided
1 c. whole milk

1 oz. cornstarch
1 1/2 c. butter
1 tsp. vanilla

Place 3 ounces sugar and milk into saucepan; heat until mixture boils. In bowl, mix remaining sugar and cornstarch; whisk into milk mixture. Continue to boil until thick. Refrigerate 2 hours. In large mixing bowl, beat butter and vanilla on high until fluffy. Add chilled mixture; mix until smooth. Frost cupcakes.

Meredith Hodges, *Des Moines*
First Place, 2014 "Smile in Every Aisle" Cakes – Gluten Free

PIES, CAKES AND DESSERTS

BLUEBERRY CREAM CAKE

For CAKE:

3 c. cake flour
3 tsp. baking powder
1/4 tsp. salt
1 c. butter, softened

1 1/2 c. granulated sugar
6 egg whites
1 1/2 tsp. vanilla
1 c. buttermilk

In bowl, sift together flour, baking powder and salt; set aside. In large bowl, cream together butter and sugar until very light and fluffy, 3 to 5 minutes. Add egg whites, one at a time, blending well after each addition. Mix in vanilla. Add one-fourth of flour mixture to creamed mixture; then one-third of the buttermilk. Continue adding flour and buttermilk to mixing bowl ending with flour. Pour batter equally into 3 greased and floured 8-inch round pans. Bake in 350° oven on center rack of oven 25 minutes or until light golden brown and cakes spring back to the touch. Cool 10 minutes in pans; remove to wire racks and cool completely.

For FILLING/FROSTING:

12 oz. fresh or frozen
    blueberries
1/4 c. granulated sugar
1 tbsp. cornstarch
1 tsp. lemon juice

1 tbsp. plus 1 tsp. grated
    lemon zest, divided
3 c. heavy cream
1 c. powdered sugar
1/2 c. lemon preserves
Fresh blueberries

Mix together blueberries and sugar in saucepan; heat over medium-high heat. Bring to boil; reduce heat and simmer 10 minutes. Blend cornstarch and lemon juice; add to blueberry mixture. Allow mixture to thicken about 1 minute. Remove from heat. Stir in 1 teaspoon lemon zest. Place cream in chilled bowl; whip until slightly thickened. Add powdered sugar and remaining lemon zest; continue whipping until stiff peaks form. Place a cake round on cake stand or cake circle. Spread with 1/4 cup lemon preserves and one-third of the blueberry filling. Spread 1/3 cup whipped cream; top with another cake round. Repeat using remaining filling. Top with final cake round. Frost cake with remaining whipped cream. Decorate with blueberries.

Lisa Alessandro, *Winterset*
First Place, 2015 "Smile in Every Aisle" Cakes – Whipped Cream Cake

WALNUT MOCHA SOUR CREAM CAKE

For CAKE:

3 c. all-purpose flour
3/4 c. unsweetened cocoa
** powder**
1 3/4 tsp. baking soda
3/4 tsp. salt
1 3/4 c. granulated sugar

3/4 c. canola oil
3 tbsp. butter, softened
3 eggs
3/4 c. sour cream
1 tsp. vanilla
1 1/2 c. coffee

Sift together flour, cocoa, baking soda and salt; set aside. In large mixing bowl, beat together sugar, oil and butter. Mix in eggs, one at a time. Mix in sour cream and vanilla. Add flour mixture alternately with coffee, mixing until well combined. Pour into 3 greased and floured 8-inch round pans. Bake in 350° oven 20 to 25 minutes or until cake tester inserted in center has moist crumbs when removed. Let cool in pans 10 minutes; remove to cool completely.

For FUDGE LAYER:

1 c. semisweet chocolate
** chips**

4 tbsp. butter
1 tbsp. light corn syrup

Place chips, butter and corn syrup in microwave-safe dish. Heat on full power 45 seconds. Stir until chips are melted and smooth.

For CHOCOLATE FROSTING:

1/2 c. shortening
3/8 c. milk
1 tsp. vanilla
1/2 c. unsweetened cocoa
** powder**

6 c. powdered sugar
3/4 c. chopped walnuts,
** toasted and divided**
Walnut halves

In large bowl, cream together shortening, milk and vanilla. Sift in cocoa and powdered sugar; mix until frosting is smooth. To assemble cake, trim bottom cake layer. Spread half the fudge on cake. Sprinkle with half the toasted walnuts. Trim middle cake layer and stack on top. Repeat with fudge and walnuts. Place top layer on filling. Frost cake; garnish with walnuts.

Marcia G. Miller, *Urbandale*
First Place, 2015 "Smile in Every Aisle" Cakes – Walnut Mocha Cake

HARVEST APPLE CAKE

For CAKE:

1 c. butter, softened
2 c. granulated sugar
2 eggs, slightly beaten
2 c. all-purpose flour
1 tsp. salt
1 tsp. baking soda

1 tsp. cinnamon
1/2 tsp. nutmeg
4 c. peeled and chopped
    Granny Smith apples
1/2 c. chopped pecans

Cream together butter and sugar; mix in eggs. Combine flour, salt, baking soda, cinnamon and nutmeg; add to butter mixture. Stir in apples and pecans. Pour into greased 8x12-inch pan. Bake in 350° oven 50 to 60 minutes.

For TOPPING:

1/2 c. packed brown sugar
2 tbsp. all-purpose flour
1/4 c. melted butter
2 tbsp. water

1 tbsp. quick-cooking
    rolled oats
1/2 c. chopped pecans

Combine all ingredients; mix well. Spread over hot cake; return to oven and bake 5 minutes more.

Tammy Post, *West Des Moines*
First Place, 2014 "Smile in Every Aisle" Cakes – Raw Apple Cake

---

SOUR CREAM CARROT CAKE

For CAKE:

2 5/8 c. all-purpose flour
2 1/4 tsp. baking powder
3/4 tsp. baking soda
3/4 tsp. salt
1 tsp. cinnamon
1 1/2 c. granulated sugar

3/4 c. canola oil
3 eggs
1 c. coarsely pureed cooked
    carrots
3/4 c. sour cream
1/2 tsp. vanilla

Combine flour, baking powder, baking soda, salt and cinnamon; set aside. In large mixing bowl, cream together sugar and oil; mix in eggs. Add carrots, sour cream and vanilla; mix well. Stir in flour until incorporated. Pour batter into 2 greased and floured 8-inch round pans.

(CONTINUED)

Bake in 350° oven 30 minutes or until cake tester inserted in center has moist crumbs when removed. Cool cakes in pans 10 minutes; remove from pans and cool completely on wire racks. When cool, frost with cream cheese frosting.

For CREAM CHEESE FROSTING:

1/2 c. shortening, softened	**1 tsp. vanilla**
4 oz. cream cheese, softened	**5 1/2 c. powdered sugar**
2 tbsp. milk	

In large mixing bowl, cream together shortening and cream cheese. Mix in milk and vanilla. Sift in powdered sugar, 1 cup at a time, mixing until frosting is smooth. Place 1 cake layer on serving plate; top with frosting. Place second layer on top; frost top and sides of cake.

Marcia G. Miller, *Urbandale*
First Place, 2014 2014 "Smile in Every Aisle" Cakes – Carrot Cake

JELLY ROLL

Powdered sugar	**3/4 c. granulated sugar**
3/4 c. all-purpose flour	**1 tsp. vanilla**
3/4 tsp. baking powder	**1/2 tsp. almond extract**
1/4 tsp. salt	**1 heaping c. jam**
4 large eggs, room	
temperature	

Sift powdered sugar over cloth kitchen towel; set aside. In small bowl, sift together flour, baking powder and salt; set aside. Beat eggs until foamy. With mixer running, slowly add granulated sugar. Continue beating 3 to 8 minutes until batter is very thick and light yellow. Beat in vanilla and almond extract. Fold in flour mixture with spatula. Spread into 10x15-inch jelly roll pan lined with parchment paper. Bake in 400° oven 12 to 14 minutes, until golden brown and slightly springy. Turn cake onto prepared towel. Peel off parchment paper. Trim crusty edges if necessary. Starting with short end, roll up cake and towel together. Cool completely on wire rack. Before serving, unroll cake, spread jam on cake and reroll.

Deirdre Scott, *Grimes*
First Place, 2014 "Smile in Every Aisle" Cakes – Jelly Roll

CZECH COFFEE CAKE

5 eggs, separated
1 c. granulated sugar, divided
1 tsp. vanilla
1 tbsp. fresh squeezed lemon
   juice
3/4 c. all-purpose flour

1/4 c. dried fruit mix
1 tsp. finely chopped lemon
   zest
1/2 c. unsalted butter, melted
   and cooled
Powdered sugar for garnish

Beat egg whites until soft peaks form. Gradually add 1/3 cup sugar, beating until stiff peaks form; set aside. In separate bowl, beat egg yolks, 2/3 cup sugar, vanilla and lemon juice until thickened, about 3 minutes. Gently fold one-third of egg whites into yolk mixture until incorporated. Gently fold in half the flour, until incorporated. Repeat, ending with egg whites. Gently fold in dried fruit, lemon zest and butter. Pour into greased and floured 6 to 8 cup Bundt pan. Bake in 350° oven 15 minutes. Reduce heat to 300°. Bake 30 to 35 minutes more or until toothpick inserted near middle comes out clean. Cool in pan 10 minutes; turn out on cooling rack. Before serving, sprinkle with powdered sugar.

Joyce Krause, *Johnston*
First Place, 2014 Eggs Around the World – Breakfast
Second Place Overall, 2014 Eggs Around the World

HONEY OATMEAL CAKE

For CAKE:
1 1/2 c. boiling water
1 c. regular rolled oats
1/2 c. butter
1 1/2 c. honey
2 eggs
1 tsp. vanilla

1 3/4 c. whole wheat flour
1 tsp. baking soda
3/4 tsp. salt
1 tsp. cinnamon
1/4 tsp. nutmeg
1/4 tsp. ginger

Pour boiling water over oats and butter; let stand 20 minutes. Mix together honey, eggs and vanilla. Add to oat mixture. Combine flour, baking soda, salt and spices. Add to oat mixture. Pour into 2 greased round pans. Bake in 350° oven 30 to 40 minutes. Allow to cool completely in pans.

(CONTINUED)

For FROSTING:

1 c. milk	**1/2 c. honey**
1/4 c. all-purpose flour	**1 tsp. almond extract**
1 c. butter	**Pinch of salt**

In saucepan, whisk together milk and flour. Cook over medium heat until thickened; set aside to cool. Beat butter 4 minutes. Add honey; beat 4 minutes more. Add cooled milk mixture; beat 4 minutes. Add almond extract and salt. Place 1 cake layer on serving plate. Frost top of layer; add second layer. Frost top and sides of cake. Garnish with cinnamon and mint leaves.

Natalie Ridgway, *Johnston*
First Place, 2015 Foods Made with Honey – Honey Oatmeal Cake
First Place Overall, 2015 Foods Made with Honey – Honey Creations

---

FABULOUS, FRESH RASPBERRY CAKE

For CAKE:

1/2 c. butter	**1/2 tsp. salt**
2 c. granulated sugar	**1/2 tsp. baking soda**
1/2 tsp. vanilla	**Juice from 1/2 lemon**
2 eggs	**2 c. fresh raspberries**
2 c. all-purpose flour	**Streusel (recipe below)**

Cream together butter, sugar and vanilla. Add eggs, one at a time. In separate bowl, combine all dry ingredients; gradually add to butter mixture. Stir in lemon juice and raspberries. Pour into greased and floured 13x9-inch pan. Sprinkle streusel over top. Bake in 350° oven 40 minutes.

For STREUSEL:

1/3 c. packed brown sugar	**1/8 tsp. cinnamon**
1 tbsp. all-purpose flour	**1 tbsp. cold butter**

Combine all ingredients; mix well.

Mackenzie Branstad, *Des Moines*
First Place, 2015 Adventureland Resort Junior – One Layer Cake from Scratch

MARBLE CAKE WITH CHOCOLATE BUTTERCREAM FROSTING

For WHITE CAKE:

2 egg whites
1 c. all-purpose flour
1/2 tsp. baking powder
1/4 tsp. baking soda
1/4 tsp. salt

1/4 c. unsalted butter,
  softened
7/8 c. (14 tbsp.) granulated
  sugar
1/2 tsp. vanilla
2/3 c. buttermilk

Allow egg whites to stand at room temperature 30 minutes. In medium bowl, stir together flour, baking powder, baking soda and salt; set aside. In large mixing bowl, beat butter with mixer on medium to high speed 30 seconds. Add sugar and vanilla; beat until combined. Add egg whites, one at a time, beating well after each addition. Alternately add flour mixture and buttermilk, beating on low speed after each addition until combined. Spread batter in greased and lightly floured 9-inch round cake pan.

For CHOCOLATE CAKE:

1/2 c. all-purpose flour
3/16 c. unsweetened cocoa
  powder
1/4 tsp. baking soda
3/16 tsp. baking powder
1/8 tsp. salt

3/16 c. unsalted butter,
  room temperature
1/2 c. granulated sugar
1 egg, room temperature
1/2 tsp. vanilla
3/8 c. milk

In medium bowl, stir together flour, cocoa, baking soda, baking powder and salt; set aside. In large mixing bowl, beat butter with mixer on medium to high speed 30 seconds. Gradually add sugar, 1/4 cup at a time, beating on medium speed until combined. Scrape sides of bowl; beat 2 minutes more. Add egg and beat well. Beat in vanilla. Alternately add flour mixture and milk, beating on low speed until combined. Beat on medium to high speed 20 seconds more. Using knife, swirl chocolate cake into white cake, making sure knife does not touch bottom of pan. Bake in 350° oven 35 to 40 minutes, or until toothpick inserted in center comes out clean. Cool in pan on wire rack 10 minutes. Remove from pan; cool thoroughly. Frost with chocolate buttercream frosting.

(CONTINUED)

PIES, CAKES AND DESSERTS

For CHOCOLATE BUTTERCREAM FROSTING:

1 c. shortening	1 lb. powdered sugar
1 tsp. almond extract	3/4 c. unsweetened cocoa
8 to 10 tbsp. water	powder
	1 tbsp. meringue powder

Cream shortening, almond extract and water. Add dry ingredients; mix on medium speed until all ingredients are thoroughly mixed together. Blend an additional minute or so, until creamy.

Jessica Denner, *Polk City*
First Place, 2014 "Smile in Every Aisle" Cakes – Marble Cake

SPICE CAKE WITH APPLE FILLING

For CAKE:

3/4 c. butter	1 1/2 tsp. baking soda
1 1/2 c. granulated sugar	1/2 tsp. salt
3 eggs	3/4 tsp. cinnamon
1/2 c. buttermilk	1/2 tsp. ginger
1 1/2 c. apple butter	1 c. apple pie filling
3 c. all-purpose flour	

In large mixing bowl, cream together butter and sugar. Add eggs; beat well. In small bowl, combine buttermilk and apple butter. In separate bowl, combine flour, baking soda, salt, cinnamon and ginger. Alternately add to creamed mixture the dry ingredients and buttermilk mixture. Grease two, 8-inch cake pans. Line with wax paper. Divide batter evenly between pans. Bake in 350° oven 35 to 40 minutes or until done in center. Remove and cool. Place 1 layer on serving plate. Spread with apple pie filling. Lay second layer on top.

For FROSTING:

1/2 c. butter	1 tsp. vanilla
1/2 c. butter-flavored	Few drops of milk
shortening	3 1/2 c. powdered sugar
4 oz. cream cheese	

In large mixing bowl, beat all ingredients until smooth. Frost entire cake.

Belinda Myers, *Osceola*
First Place, 2015 "Smile in Every Aisle" Cakes – Spice Cake

TOFFEE CRUNCH CUPCAKES

For CUPCAKES:
1 c. all-purpose flour
1 c. plus 2 tbsp. granulated
    sugar
1/3 c. plus 2 tbsp.
    unsweetened cocoa
    powder
1/2 tsp. baking soda
1/4 tsp. salt

1/2 c. unsalted butter,
    melted and warm
2 large eggs
1 tsp. vanilla
1/2 c. hot coffee
1/2 c. chocolate covered
    toffee bits
1/4 to 1/2 c. caramel sauce

In large bowl, combine flour, sugar, cocoa, baking soda and salt; mix thoroughly to combine. In separate bowl, combine butter, eggs and vanilla; beat on medium speed 1 minute. Add butter and egg mixture to dry ingredients; beat 20 seconds. Scrape sides of the bowl; add hot coffee. Beat 20 to 30 seconds until batter is smooth; add toffee bits. Batter will be thin enough to pour. Divide batter evenly among 12 paper-lined cupcake tins. Bake in 350° oven in lower third of the oven 18 to 22 minutes until a toothpick inserted comes out clean. Set pan on rack to cool. To assemble cupcakes, remove the centers; fill with caramel sauce. Fill pastry bag fitted with large round tip. Pipe caramel frosting from outside working in to center to create 1 even layer. Freeze cupcakes 20 minutes. Dip in warm chocolate sauce then rim with chocolate covered toffee bits. Return cupcakes to freezer 5 minutes for chocolate to set. Remove from freezer; finish piping frosting on top.

For CARAMEL FROSTING:
5 large egg whites
1 1/2 c. granulated sugar
2 c. unsalted butter, diced
    and softened

1/4 tsp. salt
1 tbsp. vanilla
1/3 c. caramel sauce

Combine egg whites and sugar in bowl placed over simmering water. Bring mixture to 150° while whisking constantly. Transfer mixture to bowl. Beat on medium speed until mixture cools and doubles in volume. Add butter, one piece at a time, mixing to incorporate after each addition. Mixture may appear clumpy and curdled. Continue mixing until even and smooth. Add salt and vanilla; mix to combine. Add caramel sauce; mix to combine.

(CONTINUED)

For CHOCOLATE DIPPING SAUCE:

| 2/3 c. coarsely chopped dark chocolate | 4 tbsp. powdered sugar, sifted |
| 2 tbsp. heavy cream | 5 to 8 tbsp. warm milk |

Place chocolate and cream in bowl over simmering water. Let chocolate and cream sit 2 to 3 minutes to melt without stirring. Slowly stir mixture to combine. Add powdered sugar and mix to combine. Add milk, 1 tablespoon at a time, mixing after each addition until pouring consistency. Set aside; let sauce cool to warm.

Kathy Ann Gocke, *Bondurant*
First Place, 2015 Calling All Cupcakes

RHUBARB UPSIDE-DOWN CAKE

2/3 c. packed brown sugar	1 tsp. vanilla
3 tbsp. butter, melted	1/4 tsp. almond extract
2 1/4 c. diced fresh or frozen rhubarb	1/2 tsp. grated lemon zest
3/4 c. plus 4 1/2 tsp. granulated sugar, divided	1 c. plus 2 tbsp. all-purpose flour
	1 1/2 tsp. baking powder
	1/2 tsp. salt
6 tbsp. butter, softened	1/4 c. milk
2 eggs, separated	1/4 tsp. cream of tartar

In small bowl, combine brown sugar and melted butter; spread into greased 9-inch round baking pan. Layer with rhubarb; sprinkle 4 1/2 teaspoons granulated sugar over top. Set aside. In large bowl, cream together softened butter and remaining sugar until light and fluffy. Beat in egg yolks, vanilla, almond extract and zest. In separate bowl, combine flour, baking powder and salt; add to creamed mixture alternately with milk, beating well after each addition. In small bowl, beat egg whites and cream of tartar on medium speed until stiff peaks form. Gradually fold into creamed mixture, about one-half cup at a time. Gently spoon over rhubarb (pan will be full, about 1/4-inch from the top of pan). Bake in 325° oven 50 to 60 minutes or until cake springs back when lightly touched. Cool 10 minutes; invert onto serving plate. Serve warm with whipped cream if desired.

Jennifer Bartles, *Des Moines*
First Place, 2014 "Smile in Every Aisle" Cakes – Rhubarb Cake

SOUR CREAM PUMPKIN SPICE CAKE

For CAKE:

3 1/2 c. all-purpose flour	2 c. granulated sugar
1 tbsp. baking powder	1 c. canola oil
1 tsp. baking soda	4 eggs
1 tsp. salt	1 1/3 c. pumpkin puree
1 tsp. cinnamon	1 c. fat-free sour cream
1/2 tsp. nutmeg	1 tbsp. milk
3/8 tsp. cloves	1 tsp. vanilla

Combine flour, baking powder, baking soda, salt and spices; set aside. In large mixing bowl, cream together sugar and oil; mix in eggs. Add pumpkin, sour cream, milk and vanilla; mix well. Mix in flour until incorporated. Pour into 3 greased and floured 8-inch pans. Bake in 350° oven 30 minutes or until cake tester inserted in center has moist crumbs when removed. Cool cakes in pans 10 minutes; remove from pans and cool completely. Place 1 cake layer on serving plate; frost top of layer. Repeat with second and third layer. Frost sides of cake. Garnish with pumpkin seed brittle.

For CREAM CHEESE FROSTING:

1/2 c. shortening, softened	1 tsp. vanilla
4 oz. cream cheese, softened	5 1/2 c. powdered sugar
2 tbsp. milk	

In large mixing bowl, cream together shortening and cream cheese. Mix in milk and vanilla. Sift in powdered sugar, 1 cup at a time, mixing until frosting is smooth.

For PUMPKIN SEED BRITTLE:

4 tbsp. butter	1/2 tbsp. light corn syrup
1/4 c. granulated sugar	1/8 c. pumpkin seeds

In small saucepan, combine butter, sugar and corn syrup. Bring to boil over medium heat, stirring constantly. Cook and stir until mixture is golden brown. Stir in pumpkin seeds. Pour onto parchment-lined baking sheet. Refrigerate until firm; break into pieces.

Marcia G. Miller, *Urbandale*
First Place, 2014 "Smile in Every Aisle" Cakes – Spice Cake
Third Place Overall, 2014 "Smile in Every Aisle" Cakes

MOCHA CHIA CAKE

For CAKE:

1/2 c. plus 1 tbsp. chia seeds
1 1/4 c. Italian roast coffee,
    brewed strong and
    cooled
1/2 c. unsalted butter, cubed
7 oz. dark chocolate chips

5 large eggs, separated
1 c. plus 2 tbsp. granulated
    sugar, divided
1 tsp. vanilla
2 c. ground hazelnuts
1/2 c. instant cappuccino mix

Soak chia seeds in coffee 15 minutes. Melt butter and chocolate chips in double boiler; set aside to cool. Beat egg whites and 1/3 cup sugar until soft peaks form; set aside. Beat egg yolks, vanilla and remaining sugar until pale and creamy. Fold chocolate mixture into egg yolks. Fold in hazelnuts, cappuccino mix and chia seeds into chocolate/yolk mixture. Fold in egg whites. Line bottom of 10-inch nonstick springform pan with parchment paper. Pour batter into pan. Bake in 350° oven 45 to 50 minutes. Allow to cool completely. Remove from pan; using a 2 1/2-inch round cookie cutter, cut out small cakes. Place cakes on wire rack with parchment paper-lined baking sheet underneath. Coat cakes with chocolate; let rest until coating has cooled and set. Garnish with cappuccino cream and chocolate coated espresso beans.

For CHOCOLATE COATING:

12 oz. dark chocolate chips
1 tbsp. shortening

1 tbsp. instant espresso
    powder

Melt all ingredients in double boiler. Pour over cakes, coating top and sides evenly; let coating cool and set.

For CAPPUCCINO CREAM:

1 c. heavy cream
1 oz. coffee flavored liqueur

1 tbsp. instant cappuccino
    powder

Whip cream, liqueur and cappuccino powder until stiff peaks form. Pipe into desired designs on cakes.

Jennifer Bartles, *Des Moines*
First Place, 2015 Cooking with Coffee – Desserts
First Place Overall, 2015 Cooking with Coffee

CHOCOLATE SOUR CREAM CAKE

For CAKE:

1 c. unsalted butter, room
    temperature
3 c. packed dark brown sugar
4 large eggs
2 tsp. vanilla
3/4 c. unsweetened cocoa
    powder

1 tbsp. baking soda
1/2 tsp. salt
3 c. sifted cake flour
1 1/3 c. sour cream
1 1/2 c. hot coffee

In large mixing bowl, cream butter until light. Add brown sugar and eggs, beating until fluffy, about 3 minutes. Add vanilla, cocoa, baking soda and salt; mix well. Add half the flour then half the sour cream. Mix and repeat. Drizzle in hot coffee, mixing until smooth. Batter will be thin. Grease three 9-inch round cake pans; line bottoms with wax paper and dust with flour. Pour batter into pans. Bake in 350° oven 30 to 35 minutes or until cake tester inserted in center comes out clean. Remove to wire racks; cool 10 minutes. Invert pan to release cake; cool completely. To assemble, place 1 cake layer on serving platter; top with 1/2 to 3/4 cup white chocolate frosting. Top with second layer and spread with additional frosting. Top with third layer, frosting top and sides of cake with remaining frosting. Garnish as desired.

For WHITE CHOCOLATE FROSTING:

18 oz. white chocolate,
    chopped
24 oz. cream cheese,
    softened

8 tbsp. butter, room
    temperature
4 tbsp. lemon juice

Melt chocolate in top of double boiler, stirring until smooth; cool slightly. Beat cream cheese in mixing bowl until smooth; slowly add cooled chocolate until combined. Add butter and lemon juice; beat until well blended and smooth.

Sally Kilkenny, *Granger*
First Place, 2015 "Smile in Every Aisle" Cakes – Chocolate Sour Cream Cake
First Place Overall, 2015 "Smile in Every Aisle" Cakes

STRAWBERRY ANGEL FOOD CAKE

For CAKE:

1 c. sifted cake flour
1 1/2 c. sifted sugar, divided
12 egg whites, room
    temperature
1 tsp. cream of tartar

1/4 tsp. salt
1 1/2 tsp. vanilla
1 1/2 tsp. lemon juice
1/2 tsp. almond extract

Whisk flour and 3/4 cup sugar in small bowl. Beat egg whites on low speed until just beginning to froth. Add cream of tartar and salt; beat at medium speed until whites form soft mounds. With mixer running, add remaining sugar, 1 tablespoon at a time. Beat until soft peaks form. Add vanilla, lemon juice and almond extract; beat until blended. Fold in flour-sugar mixture by hand. Gently place mixture in ungreased 10-inch tube pan. Bake in 325° oven 50 to 60 minutes until golden brown and top springs back when pressed. Remove from oven; invert pan over a bottle. Cool completely before removing from pan. Freeze at least 2 hours.

For STRAWBERRY MOUSSE:

2 c. mashed fresh or frozen
    strawberries
1-oz. env. unflavored gelatin

1/4 c. granulated sugar
2 c. heavy cream
1/2 tsp. vanilla

Mix strawberries, gelatin and sugar in microwave-safe bowl; microwave 1 minute. Remove from microwave; chill in refrigerator 30 to 60 minutes or until thickened. Place in bowl with cream and vanilla; whip until thick. Using a serrated blade, cut a channel in the cake leaving inner and outer walls for support. Be careful not to cut through bottom of cake. Fill channel with strawberry mousse. Frost cake with remaining mousse.

For GLAZE:

1/2 c. strawberry jam
7 tbsp. water

1-oz. env. unflavored gelatin

Heat jam and strain through fine mesh strainer. Place water in microwave-safe bowl. Stir in gelatin; allow to stand 5 minutes. Heat in microwave about 1 minute, stirring, until gelatin dissolves. Stir into jam. Refrigerate until thickened slightly; pour over cake, allowing to dribble down sides. Freeze cake again 2 to 3 hours or overnight before serving.

Deirdre Scott, *Grimes*
First Place, 2014 Homemade Angel Food Cake

UN-FRIED MEXICAN FRIED ICE CREAM

5 c. corn flakes cereal
1/2 c. pecan pieces
1/2 c. salted butter
2 tsp. ground cinnamon

Hot chocolate con churros
ice cream
Hot chocolate quatro leches
ice cream
Caramel sauce
Maraschino cherries

Pulse corn flakes and pecans in food processor until finely chopped. Melt butter in nonstick 10-inch fry pan over medium heat. Once butter is melted, stir in crushed corn flake mixture and cinnamon. Increase heat slightly. Cook mixture, stirring constantly until golden brown and fragrant, about 2 minutes. Remove from heat; pour into shallow dish and allow to cool slightly. Scoop out a couple tablespoons of each ice cream flavor and combine into ball. Roll in corn flake mixture to evenly coat while pressing mixture around outer surface for thicker coating. Put into freezer while making more balls. When serving, drizzle with caramel sauce and top with a cherry.

Megan McGuire, *Johnston*
First Place, 2014 Kids Ice Cream Dessert

GERMAN CHOCOLATE CAKE

For CAKE:
4-oz. German sweet
     chocolate bar
1/2 c. boiling water
1 c. butter
2 c. granulated sugar
4 egg yolks, unbeaten

1 tsp. vanilla
2 1/2 c. sifted cake flour
1/2 tsp. salt
1 tsp. baking soda
1 c. buttermilk
4 egg whites, stiffly beaten

Combine chocolate and boiling water in pan over boiling water; stir until chocolate is melted and set aside to cool. Cream together butter and sugar until fluffy. Add egg yolks, one at a time. Beat well after each addition. Add melted chocolate and vanilla; mix well. Sift together flour, salt and baking soda. Add alternately with buttermilk to chocolate mixture, beating well until smooth. Fold in beaten egg whites. Pour into three 8 or 9-inch cake pans lined on bottoms with parchment paper. Bake in 350° oven 30 to 40 minutes; cool.

(CONTINUED)

For COCONUT-PECAN FROSTING:

1 c. evaporated milk	**1/2 c. margarine**
1 c. granulated sugar	**1 tsp. vanilla**
3 egg yolks	**1 1/3 c. flake coconut**
	1 c. chopped pecans

In large saucepan, combine evaporated milk, sugar, egg yolks, margarine and vanilla. Cook and stir over medium heat until thickened, about 12 minutes. Add coconut and pecans. Beat until thick enough to spread. Place 1 cake layer on serving plate; top with frosting. Place second layer on top; frost top of cake.

Terri Treft, *Sioux City*
First Place, 2015 Our Iowa Church Cookbook Favorites – Anything Chocolate

HONEY PECAN TASSIES

For CRUST:

1 c. whole wheat flour	**1 1/2 tbsp. shortening**
1/8 tsp. salt	**3 tbsp. cold water**
4 tbsp. chilled butter	

Mix together flour and salt; cut in butter and shortening. Mix in water and make a dough ball. On lightly-floured surface, knead dough 6 to 7 times. Wrap in plastic wrap. Chill 8 hours or overnight. Roll out on floured surface to 1/8-inch thick. Cut into 2-inch circles; fit into small tassie pans.

For PECAN FILLING:

1 c. honey	**Pinch of freshly ground**
3 eggs, beaten	**nutmeg**
3 tbsp. butter	**1 c. chopped pecans**
1 tsp. vanilla	**Pastry for 9-inch**
	pie (recipe above)

In small saucepan, boil honey; quickly whisk in eggs. Add butter, vanilla and nutmeg. Pour into crusts in tassie pans. Sprinkle with pecans. Bake in 325° oven 25 minutes or until set.

Cassandra Hyatt, *Ankeny*
First Place, 2014 Foods Made with Honey – Pecan Tassies

PIES, CAKES AND DESSERTS

LEMON BUNDT CAKE

18.25-oz. pkg. lemon cake mix
3.4-oz. pkg. instant lemon
   pudding mix
3/4 c. vegetable oil
4 eggs
1 c. lemon-lime flavored
   carbonated beverage

In large mixing bowl, combine cake mix and pudding mix; stir in oil. Beat in eggs, one at a time. Stir in lemon-lime soda. Pour batter into greased and floured 10-inch Bundt pan. Bake in 325° oven 50 to 55 minutes. Allow to cool in pan 15 minutes; transfer to cooling rack.

Marjorie Rodgers, *Indianola*
First Place, 2014 "Smile in Every Aisle" Cakes – Creations with Cake Mixes

---

HUMMINGBIRD CAKE

For CAKE:
3 c. all-purpose flour
1 tsp. baking soda
1 tsp. ground cinnamon
1/2 tsp. salt
1 c. butter, melted and cooled
2 c. granulated sugar
2 tsp. vanilla
3 large eggs
2 c. mashed ripe banana
8-oz. can crushed pineapple
1 c. chopped walnuts or
   pecans
1 c. unsweetened desiccated
   coconut

In medium bowl, whisk together flour, baking soda, cinnamon and salt. In separate bowl, combine butter, sugar and vanilla. Beat until well combined, about 2 minutes. Add eggs, one at a time, beating to combine. Continue beating until mixture is light and pale yellow. In medium bowl, stir together banana, pineapple, nuts and coconut. Add flour and banana mixtures in 3 additions, alternating dry and wet to the butter and sugar mixture. Butter two 9-inch cake pans and line bottoms with parchment paper; dust with flour, tapping out excess. Divide batter between pans. Bake in 350° oven until golden brown, 30 to 40 minutes. When done, remove pans to rack; cool 15 minutes. Remove from pans; cool completely.

(CONTINUED)

PIES, CAKES AND DESSERTS

For CREAM CHEESE FROSTING:

**1 lb. cream cheese, room
    temperature
2 tsp. vanilla extract or paste**

**1 c. butter
2 lb. powdered sugar**

Beat cream cheese and vanilla until light and creamy, about 2 minutes. Gradually add butter until incorporated. At slow speed, gradually add powdered sugar until mixed. Place cake layer on serving plate; frost top. Place second layer on first layer; frost top and sides.

Denise Donald, *Des Moines*
First Place, 2014 "Smile in Every Aisle" Cakes – Layer Cake Other Than Named
First Place Overall, 2014 "Smile in Every Aisle" Cakes

MOCHA MOUSSE

For MOUSSE:

**5 1/4 oz. bittersweet
    chocolate, coarsely
    chopped
14 oz. heavy cream, cold**

**3 large egg whites from
    pasteurized eggs
1 oz. granulated sugar**

Place chocolate in large bowl set over double boiler at low simmer. Stir chocolate until melted. Remove from heat; let stand. Beat cream over ice until soft peaks form. Set aside; hold at room temperature. In mixer, whip egg whites to soft peaks. Gradually add sugar; continue whipping until firm. Scrape chocolate into large bowl and using whisk, fold in egg whites all at once. When whites are almost completely incorporated, fold in whipped cream. Cover and refrigerate 1 hour or until set.

For SWEETENED WHIPPED CREAM:

**1 c. heavy cream
1 tsp. vanilla**

**1 tbsp. powdered sugar
Shaved bittersweet
    chocolate**

In large bowl, whip cream until stiff peaks are just about to form. Beat in vanilla and powdered sugar until peaks form. Do not over beat. Serve with mousse. Garnish with shaved chocolate if desired.

Mick Wise, *Des Moines*
First Place, 2014 Chocolate Mousse

PIES, CAKES AND DESSERTS

SEA SALT AND HONEY ICE CREAM

2 c. heavy cream
14-oz. can sweetened
   condensed milk
1/4 c. plus 1 tbsp. honey,
   divided

1/2 tsp. sea salt
3 tbsp. chopped lavender
   flowers (optional)

Pour cream into bowl. Mix on low speed; slowly increase speed to high. Beat cream until stiff peaks form, about 2 minutes. Gently fold in sweetened condensed milk, 1/4 cup honey, sea salt and lavender. Continue stirring gently until completely combined. Pour into freezer-safe container with airtight lid. Drizzle top with remaining honey; seal. Freeze until solid, at least 6 hours. Drizzle individual servings with honey and a pinch of sea salt.

Natalie Ridgway, *Johnston*
First Place, 2015 Foods Made with Honey – Honey Dessert Other Than Named
First Place Overall, 2015 Foods Made with Honey - Adult

CHOCOLATE SOUR CREAM APPLESAUCE BUNDT CAKE

For CAKE:
2 5/8 c. all-purpose flour
3/4 c. unsweetened cocoa
   powder
2 tsp. baking soda
1 tsp. salt
1 7/8 c. granulated sugar
1 c. canola oil

3 eggs
3/4 c. sour cream
3/4 c. unsweetened
   applesauce
1 tsp. vanilla
1 c. boiling water

Sift together flour, cocoa, baking soda and salt; set aside. In large mixing bowl, beat together sugar and oil. Mix in eggs, one at a time. Mix in sour cream, applesauce and vanilla. Add flour mixture alternately with boiling water, mixing until well combined. Pour batter into greased and floured 12-cup Bundt pan. Bake in 350° oven 45 to 50 minutes or until cake tester inserted in center has moist crumbs when removed. Let cake cool in pan 10 minutes; remove from pan and cool completely. When cool, top with drizzle.

(CONTINUED)

For DRIZZLE:

1 1/4 c. plus 5/8 c. powdered sugar, divided
4 to 6 tsp. water, divided

1 tsp. unsweetened cocoa powder

Sift 1 1/4 cups powdered sugar into bowl; add 3 to 4 teaspoons water to make drizzle consistency. Drizzle onto cake. Sift together remaining powdered sugar and cocoa. Add 1 to 2 teaspoons water to make of drizzle consistency. Drizzle over cake.

Marcia G. Miller, *Urbandale*
First Place, 2014 "Smile in Every Aisle" Cakes – Bundt Cake

WALNUT TORTE WITH COFFEE WHIPPED CREAM

4 large eggs, separated
1/2 c. granulated sugar
1 c. plus 6 tbsp. coarsely grated walnuts, divided
1 c. chilled heavy cream

3 tbsp. powdered sugar
1 tsp. instant coffee crystals dissolved in 2 tsp. heavy cream
3/4 tsp. vanilla
Walnut halves

Beat egg yolks in large bowl until light and fluffy, about 4 minutes. Gradually add granulated sugar, beating until well blended. Reserve 2 tablespoons walnuts; set aside. Stir remaining ground walnuts into yolk mixture. Using clean, dry beaters, beat egg whites in another large bowl until stiff but not dry. Fold whites into nut mixture in 2 additions. Butter bottom (not sides) of 9-inch springform pan. Transfer batter to prepared pan. Bake cake in 350° oven until tester inserted into center comes out clean, about 40 minutes. Cool 5 minutes. Run knife between cake and pan sides to loosen; remove pan sides. Cool cake completely on rack (cake will fall in center). Using electric mixer, beat cream, powdered sugar, coffee mixture and vanilla in large bowl until peaks form. Spread coffee whipped cream onto top of cake. Sprinkle top with reserved ground walnuts. Arrange walnut halves in center of cake.

Emma Whitlock, *Indianola*
First Place, 2014 Trust Your Recipe to Gurley's – Cakes & Muffins
First Place, 2015 Create a Winner with Gurley's – Cakes & Muffins

PEACH ICE CREAM

3 oz. peach gelatin
1 c. boiling water
2 1/2 c. granulated sugar

20 oz. peeled and chopped
peaches (approx. 4 large)
1 qt. half and half

Dissolve gelatin in boiling water. Place dissolved gelatin, sugar, peaches and half and half in a 1 gallon ice cream freezer. Freeze according to manufacturer's directions. If desired, garnish with sprinkle of cinnamon.

Rose Ridgway, *Johnston*
First Place, 2014 Jell-O – Desserts
Second Place Overall, 2014 Jell-O

STUFFED CARROT CAKE WITH ORANGE CREAM CHEESE GLAZE

For CAKE:
2 c. all-purpose flour
1 1/2 c. granulated sugar
1/2 c. packed light brown
    sugar
1 c. finely chopped pecans
2 tsp. baking soda
1/4 tsp. ground nutmeg
1 tsp. baking powder
1/2 tsp. salt

4 tsp. ground cinnamon
1/2 tsp. allspice
4 large eggs
3/4 c. vegetable oil
1/2 c. full fat vanilla Greek
    yogurt
1 tsp. vanilla
2 tsp. orange extract
2 1/2 c. peeled and grated
    carrots

In large bowl, combine flour, sugars, pecans, baking soda, nutmeg, baking powder, salt, cinnamon and allspice. In separate bowl, gently whisk eggs. Stir in oil, yogurt, vanilla and orange extract just until combined. Do not over mix. Stir wet ingredients into dry ingredients until moistened. Stir in carrots until evenly combined. Spoon 3 cups batter into greased and floured 10-inch Bundt pan. Spoon cream cheese filling over batter. Gently smooth; leaving 1/2-inch border from sides of pan. Top with remaining batter. Bake in 350° oven 45 minutes. Cover with foil; reduce heat to 325°. Bake 25 to 30 minutes more or until toothpick inserted near center comes out clean. Cool in pan 10 minutes; transfer to cooling rack to cool completely.

(CONTINUED)

For CREAM CHEESE FILLING:

8 oz. cream cheese, softened **1 tsp. lemon juice**
1/2 c. granulated sugar **1/2 tsp. vanilla**
1 large egg **3 tbsp. all-purpose flour**

Beat cream cheese and sugar until light and creamy. Beat in remaining ingredients until smooth.

For ORANGE CREAM CHEESE GLAZE:

4 oz. cream cheese, softened **1/2 tsp. vanilla**
2 tbsp. butter, softened **2 c. powdered sugar, sifted**
2 tbsp. orange juice **Toasted chopped pecans**
2 tsp. lemon juice **Grated orange zest**
1 tsp. orange extract

Combine cream cheese, butter, orange juice, lemon juice, orange extract and vanilla. Beat on medium speed 1 to 2 minutes or until completely smooth. Add sifted powdered sugar; beat until very smooth. Place frosting in refrigerator 5 to 10 minutes before using. When cake has cooled, drizzle glaze over cake. Whisk in additional orange juice or milk if glaze has become too thick upon standing. Sprinkle with pecans and orange zest. Store in refrigerator.

Rebecca Howe, *Des Moines*
First Place, 2015 Favorite Tone's Recipe That I Love to Bake

PRALINE SUNDAE TOPPING

1/4 c. butter **Dash of salt**
1 1/4 c. packed light brown **1 c. evaporated milk**
    sugar **1/2 c. chopped pecans,**
16 large marshmallows   **toasted**
2 tbsp. light corn syrup **1 tsp. vanilla**
      1/4 tsp. cinnamon

Melt butter in saucepan. Add brown sugar, marshmallows, corn syrup and salt. Cook and stir over low heat until marshmallows are melted and mixture comes to a boil. Boil 1 minute. Remove from heat; cool 5 minutes. Stir in milk, pecans, vanilla and cinnamon. Serve over ice cream. Store in refrigerator.

Phoelisa McGuire, *Johnston*
First Place, 2014 My Favorite Ice Cream Topping – Sauces/Syrups

APPLE PIE CUPCAKES

For CUPCAKES:
3/4 c. diced Granny Smith
   apples
1 1/2 tbsp. cinnamon-sugar
   mix
1/3 c. sifted almond meal
1 2/3 c. all-purpose flour
1 1/2 tsp. baking powder
1/4 tsp. salt
10 tbsp. unsalted butter,
   softened
1 c. granulated sugar
3 large egg whites
1 tsp. vanilla
3/4 c. water

In small bowl, mix together diced apples and cinnamon-sugar mix; set aside. In separate bowl, whisk together almond meal, flour, baking powder and salt. In large bowl, beat butter until smooth. Add sugar; beat until fluffy, about 2 minutes. Add egg whites, one at a time, beating well after each addition. Beat in vanilla. On low, beat in half the flour mixture, then water. Beat in remaining flour mixture until well blended. Stir in diced apples. Place cupcakes liners in muffin tins. Divide batter evenly among prepared cups. Bake in 325° oven 20 minutes. Cool completely.

For FROSTING:
1 1/4 c. heavy cream
3 tbsp. plus 1 tsp. powdered
   sugar
1 tsp. vanilla
Caramel syrup

Beat cream, powdered sugar and vanilla until stiff peaks form. Frost cupcakes; drizzle caramel syrup over frosted cupcakes.

Emily Durbala, *Urbandale*
First Place, 2015 Iowa Orchards Creations – Dessert (kids)

BOOZY BOURBON POUND CAKE

For CAKE:
1 3/4 c. all-purpose flour
1/2 tsp. baking powder
1/2 tsp. baking soda
1/2 tsp. salt
10 tbsp. unsalted butter,
   softened
7/8 c. granulated sugar
1/3 c. packed light brown
   sugar
2 eggs
1/2 c. buttermilk
1/4 c. bourbon

(CONTINUED)

Sift together flour, baking powder, baking soda and salt; set aside. In medium mixing bowl, cream together butter and sugars. Mix in eggs until well combined. Add flour mixture alternately with buttermilk and bourbon, mixing until well incorporated. Pour batter into greased and floured 6-cup Bundt pan. Bake in 350° oven 30 to 35 minutes or until cake tester inserted in center has moist crumbs when removed. Let cake cool in pan 10 minutes. Remove from pan; cool completely and drizzle with glaze.

For BOURBON GLAZE:

1/2 c. powdered sugar
1 tsp. bourbon

1/2 to 1 tsp. water

Stir together all ingredients until smooth.

Marcia G. Miller, *Urbandale*
First Place, 2015 "Smile in Every Aisle" Cakes – Pound Cake (unfrosted)

MOLTEN CHOCOLATE LAVA CAKES

1/2 c. butter
4 squares semisweet
    baking chocolate
1 c. plus 2 tbsp. powdered
    sugar, divided
2 eggs

2 egg yolks
6 tbsp. all-purpose flour
Fresh raspberries or
    strawberries
Chocolate syrup

Place butter and chocolate into large microwave-safe bowl. Microwave 1 minute or until butter is melted; stir until butter and chocolate are smooth. Add 1 cup powdered sugar; stir until smooth. Add eggs and egg yolks; stir until smooth. Add flour; stir until just combined. Spray 4 custard cups with nonstick spray; place onto baking sheet. Pour chocolate batter evenly into cups. Bake in 425° oven 12 to 13 minutes or until sides are set and center is soft but not jiggly. Let cool 2 minutes; invert onto serving plates. Dust with remaining powdered sugar and serve with fresh berries. Garnish with chocolate syrup.

Jessica Rundlett, *Ankeny*
First Place, 2014 Desserts for Christina

CHOCOLATE MOUSSE CHEESECAKE

For CHEESECAKE:

8.5-oz. pkg. chocolate cream-
    filled sandwich cookies
1.5 oz. powdered sugar
6 tbsp. butter
3, 8-oz. pkgs. cream cheese,
    softened
2 tsp. vanilla

2 tsp. lemon juice
1/2 c. granulated sugar
14-oz. can sweetened
    condensed milk
12-oz. pkg. semisweet
    chocolate chips, melted
3 large eggs

Crush cookies; combine with powdered sugar and butter. Press into greased springform pan. Bake in 375° oven 5 minutes. Cool 5 minutes; reduce oven temperature to 250°. In bowl, stir together remaining ingredients; pour over crust. Wrap outside of pan in double-layer of foil, covering the underside and extending all the way to the top. Set wrapped pan in large roasting pan; pour hot water into roasting pan to depth of 2 inches or about halfway up sides of cheesecake pan. Bake in 250° oven 75 minutes. Shut off oven; allow cheesecake to cool in oven 60 minutes. Chill 6 hours or overnight. Remove from springform pan.

For MOUSSE & GARNISH:

1 1/2 c. heavy cream, divided
6 oz. semisweet chocolate
    chips
1/2 tsp. vanilla

Dash of salt
2 tbsp. granulated sugar
3 oz. chocolate chips
1 tbsp. shortening

Heat 1/2 cup heavy cream in saucepan. Pour over 6 ounces chocolate chips; stir until melted. Stir in vanilla and salt. Cool to room temperature. Whip remaining heavy cream until stiff peaks form. Stir in chocolate mixture. Fill piping bag with mousse; pipe onto top of cheesecake. To make chocolate curls, combine remaining chocolate and shortening in microwave-safe bowl. Microwave 30 to 45 seconds or until shortening is melted. Stir together. Spread mixture very thin on back of a baking sheet. Freeze until set. Use a flat metal spatula to curl the chocolate; garnish cake with curls.

Amanda Hagenow, *Windsor Heights*
First Place, 2014 Knapp's Build Your Best Cheesecake

BLACK & WHITE CHOCOLATE CHEESECAKE

For CRUST:

2 c. chocolate cookie crumbs　**4 tbsp. melted butter**
1/4 c. powdered sugar　**Melted chocolate**

In small bowl, combine cookie crumbs with powdered sugar. Add melted butter; stir well. Press into bottom of a 9-inch round springform pan. Bake in 350° oven 10 to 12 minutes until fragrant. Set aside to cool; brush with melted chocolate to keep crust crisp. Reduce oven to 325°.

For FILLING:

3, 8-oz. pkgs. cream cheese,　**1 c. heavy cream**
**　softened**　**1/2 c. (3 oz.) dark chocolate,**
1 c. granulated sugar　**　melted and cooled**
1/4 tsp. salt　**1/2 c. (3 oz.) white chocolate,**
1 tbsp. vanilla　**　melted and cooled**
**　3 eggs**

In bowl of food processor, mix cream cheese and sugar until smooth. Add salt, vanilla and eggs; process until smooth. Add cream; mix well. Divide batter in half; mix dark chocolate into 1 half and white chocolate into other half. Alternate pouring light and dark batter into prepared pan for marbled effect. Wrap outside of pan in double-layer of foil, covering the underside and extending all the way to the top. Set wrapped pan in large roasting pan; pour hot water into roasting pan to depth of 2 inches or about halfway up sides of cheesecake pan. Bake in 325° oven 45 to 60 minutes, until an instant-read thermometer placed 1-inch from edge reads 165°. Turn off oven; prop open door slightly. Let cheesecake rest 1 hour in oven. Remove from oven; refrigerate overnight. Top with whipped cream and garnish with ganache.

For GANACHE:

1/2 c. (3 oz.) dark chocolate　**2 tbsp. heavy cream**

Place dark chocolate and cream in small microwave-safe bowl. Heat in 15 second intervals, stirring, until chocolate is melted. Stir until smooth. Allow to cool slightly.

Deirdre Scott, *Grimes*
First Place, 2014 Black and White Panda Dessert

PIES, CAKES AND DESSERTS

BEST CHOCOLATE CAKE
WITH CHOCOLATE BUTTERCREAM

For CAKE:

2 c. unsifted all-purpose flour
2 c. granulated sugar
1 tsp. salt
3/4 c. water
3/4 c. shortening
1 tsp. vanilla

3/4 c. unsweetened cocoa
   powder
1 tsp. baking soda
1/2 tsp. baking powder
3/4 c. buttermilk
2 eggs

Combine all ingredients in large mixing bowl. Blend 30 seconds on low speed, then mix 3 minutes on high speed. Pour into 2 greased and floured 8-inch round pans. Bake in 350° oven 30 to 35 minutes. Remove to wire racks; cool completely.

For CHOCOLATE BUTTERCREAM ICING:

1 c. shortening
1 tsp. almond extract
6 to 8 tbsp. water
1 tbsp. meringue powder

3/4 c. unsweetened cocoa
   powder
1 lb. powdered sugar

Cream shortening, almond extract and water. Add dry ingredients; mix on medium speed until all ingredients are combined. Blend an additional minute or so until creamy. Place 1 layer on serving plate; frost top. Top with remaining layer; frost top and sides of cake.

Jessica Denner, *Polk City*
First Place, 2015 "Smile in Every Aisle" Cakes – Chocolate Cake (frosted)
Second Place Overall, 2015 "Smile in Every Aisle" Cakes

LEMON-LIME FILLED CAKE ROLL

For CAKE:

7/8 c. all-purpose flour
1 tsp. baking powder
1/4 tsp. salt
1 egg

2 egg whites
7/8 c. granulated sugar
1/4 c. water
1 tbsp. lemon juice
1/4 tsp. grated lemon zest

(CONTINUED)

PIES, CAKES AND DESSERTS

Sift together flour, baking powder and salt; set aside. In separate mixing bowl, beat egg and egg whites until thick and frothy. Mix in sugar, water, lemon juice and zest. Mix in flour mixture until batter is smooth. Pour into parchment-lined 15x10-inch jelly roll pan. Bake in 350° oven 15 minutes or until center of cake springs back when touched. Invert cake onto new sheet of parchment. Peel parchment from cake. Starting with short side of cake, roll up warm cake and parchment together; cool completely. When ready to fill, unroll cake leaving on parchment. Spread lime filling over cake to within 1-inch of edges. Re-roll cake, using parchment to lift and guide cake into an even roll. Cover and chill at least 4 hours. Sift with powdered sugar before serving.

For LIME FILLING:

2/3 c. granulated sugar	1/2 c. water
2 1/2 tbsp. cornstarch	2 egg yolks
1/8 tsp. salt	1 tsp. grated lime zest
1/2 c. lime juice	1/2 tsp. butter

In medium saucepan, combine sugar, cornstarch and salt. Whisk in lime juice, water and egg yolks. Cook over medium heat until mixture starts to bubble. Continue to cook 1 minute, whisking constantly. Remove from heat; stir in lime zest and butter. Chill until ready to use.

Marcia G. Miller, *Urbandale*
First Place, 2015 "Smile in Every Aisle" Cakes – Cake Rolls

DARK CHOCOLATE RASPBERRY SAUCE

1 c. coarsely chopped dark chocolate	1 tbsp. granulated sugar
	1/2 c. English toffee bits
4 tbsp. raspberry preserves, divided	Ice cream of choice

Add dark chocolate to saucepan on low heat; melt completely. Add 2 tablespoons raspberry preserves; blend on low heat. Pour sauce over ice cream of choice and place in freezer. In separate saucepan, heat remaining preserves and sugar on low heat until blended. Remove from heat; chill 1 to 2 hours. Pipe on top of ice cream. Sprinkle English toffee bits for garnish.

Jacqueline Riekena, *West Des Moines*
First Place, 2014 My Favorite Ice Cream Topping – Other Toppings

HARISSA ESPRESSO ICE CREAM

For ICE CREAM:

2/3 c. honey
1 1/2 c. heavy cream
4 egg yolks, beaten
1/3 c. Harissa olive oil

2 tbsp. espresso balsamic
    vinegar
2 tsp. vanilla bean paste
1/2 c. chocolate chips,
    chopped

In saucepan, mix together honey and cream; heat until honey is dissolved. Add yolks very slowly, whisking as you pour. Continue whisking until mixture is thickened and coats the whisk, 8 to 10 minutes. Remove from heat; add olive oil, vinegar, vanilla and chocolate chips. Mix and pour into ice cream maker when cool. Freeze according to manufacturer's directions. Serve with chai spice.

For CHAI SPICE:

2 tsp. ground cinnamon
2 tsp. ground ginger
2 tsp. ground cardamom
1 tsp. ground cloves

1/2 tsp. white pepper
1/2 tsp. ground allspice
3 star anise beans, ground

Mix all ingredients; store in airtight container.

Angela Lawler, *West Des Moines*
First Place, 2015 Allspice Ice Cream – Olive Oil Ice Cream

LIME DREAM ANGEL FOOD CAKE

For CAKE:

1 c. sifted cake flour
1 1/2 c. sifted granulated
    sugar, divided
12 egg whites, room
    temperature

1 tsp. cream of tartar
1/4 tsp. salt
1 1/2 tsp. vanilla
1 1/2 tsp. lime juice

In small bowl, whisk together flour and 3/4 cup sugar. Beat egg whites on low speed until beginning to froth. Add cream of tartar and salt; beat at medium speed until whites form soft mounds. With mixer running, add remaining sugar, 1 tablespoon at a time. Beat until soft peaks form.

(CONTINUED)

PIES, CAKES AND DESSERTS

Add vanilla and lime juice; beat until blended. Fold in flour-sugar mixture by hand. Gently place mixture in ungreased 10-inch tube pan. Bake in 325° oven until golden brown and top springs back when pressed, about 50 to 60 minutes. Remove from oven; invert pan over a bottle. Cool completely before removing from pan. To assemble cake, cut cake in half horizontally and remove top. Pipe a thin "dam" of buttercream around the top edges of bottom layer. Spoon lime curd onto bottom layer. Place top layer. Coat outside and top with buttercream. Using the ganache, pipe decorative border around top of cake. Garnish with lime zest. Keep refrigerated.

For LIME CURD AND GANACHE:

1/2 c. fresh-squeezed lime juice	2 tbsp. butter
1 large egg	4 oz. white chocolate, chopped
3 large egg yolks	1/4 c. heavy cream
1 c. granulated sugar	

To make lime curd, place lime juice, egg, egg yolks, sugar and butter in top of a non-reactive double boiler. Cook, stirring constantly, 15 minutes or until thickened. Set aside to cool. To make ganache, in microwave or top of double boiler, melt white chocolate and cream together until smooth. Let cool.

For ITALIAN BUTTERCREAM:

4 egg whites	2 tbsp. vegetable shortening
1 c. plus 2 tbsp. granulated sugar	1 1/2 tsp. vanilla
	1 1/2 tsp. lemon juice
1/4 c. water	3/4 tsp. salt
1 c. unsalted butter	

Bring all ingredients to room temperature. Place egg whites in bowl. Place sugar and water in small saucepan. Cook, stirring, over medium-low heat until sugar has dissolved and small bubbles start to appear. A few minutes before temperature reaches 242°, turn on mixer. Beat egg whites until shiny with soft peaks. When sugar mixture reaches 242°, remove from heat. Slowly pour into egg whites while mixer is running. Continue to beat until completely cool. Place butter, vegetable shortening, vanilla, lemon juice and salt in separate bowl. Beat until creamy and light-colored. Fold in meringue in 4 parts.

Deirdre Scott, *Grimes*
First Place, 2015 Homemade Angel Food Cake

KANZI'S FRUIT CAKE

For CAKE:

7/8 c. all-purpose flour
1 tsp. baking powder
1/4 tsp. salt
1 egg

2 egg whites
7/8 c. granulated sugar
1/3 c. water
1/2 tsp. vanilla

Sift together flour, baking powder and salt; set aside. In medium mixing bowl, beat egg and egg whites until thick and frothy. Mix in sugar, then add water and vanilla. Mix in dry ingredients until batter is smooth. Pour into 15x10-inch jelly roll pan lined with parchment. Bake in 350° oven 15 minutes or until center of cake springs back when touched. Invert cake on new sheet of parchment. Peel parchment from cake bottom. Invert cake onto serving platter; cool completely.

For CREAM CHEESE & FRUIT LAYER:

4 oz. reduced-fat cream
    cheese, softened
1/4 c. fat-free sour cream
1 tbsp. granulated sugar
Grapes, halved

Apples, sliced (dipped in
    lemon juice and
    blotted dry)
Strawberries, sliced
Raisins

In small mixing bowl, combine cream cheese, sour cream and sugar; mix until smooth. Spread onto cooled cake. Arrange fruit on cake in decorative manner. Store in refrigerator.

Marcia G. Miller, *Urbandale*
First Place, 2014 Kanzi's Favorite Dessert

ALMOND CHEESECAKE

For CRUST:

2/3 c. raw almonds
4 pitted dates
1/2 c. shredded coconut

1 to 2 tsp. water
2 tsp. coconut oil

Blend almonds, dates and coconut in food processor. Add water, 1 teaspoon at a time, while blending. Add oil; blend until mixture forms a ball when pressed in your hand. Press mixture into bottom of 2 mini-cheesecake pans.

(CONTINUED)

For FILLING:

8-oz. pkg. cream cheese	**1 1/8 tsp. almond flavoring**
1 1/8 c. granulated sugar	**1 1/8 tsp. vanilla**
1 egg	

Using mixer; mix all ingredients. Pour evenly between 2 pans. Bake in 350° oven 45 minutes. Remove pans from oven.

For TOPPING:

1 c. sour cream	**1/2 tsp. vanilla**
1/2 c. granulated sugar	**Raspberries**
	Slivered almonds

Blend all ingredients; pour evenly over cheesecakes. Return to oven and bake 5 minutes more. Allow to cool completely. Top with raspberries and slivered almonds.

Nicole Woodroffe, *Des Moines*
First Place, 2014 The Amazing Almond

SMOKIN' CINNAMON ICE CREAM

5 egg yolks	**1/4 tsp. salt**
2/3 c. granulated sugar,	**5 tsp. ground soft stick**
divided	**true cinnamon**
2 c. heavy cream	**1/4 tsp. whole cloves**
1 c. whole milk	**1/8 tsp. chipotle chili brown**
1/3 c. light corn syrup	**powder**
	2 tsp. vanilla paste

Whisk together yolks and half the sugar. In saucepan, combine cream, milk, remaining sugar, corn syrup, salt, cinnamon, cloves and chipotle. Heat to 170°. Pour 1 cup hot cream into yolks to temper. Pour tempered yolks back into hot cream; heat to 180°. Strain mixture; cool in refrigerator. Add vanilla paste. Process in ice cream maker according to manufacturer's directions. Freeze before serving.

Matthew Phoenix, *Ankeny*
First Place, 2015 Allspice Ice Cream – Spiced Flavored Ice Cream
First Place Overall, 2015 Allspice Ice Cream

SWEET ESPRESSO TAPIOCA

2 c. strong brewed espresso
1/2 c. plus 1 tbsp. granulated
    sugar, divided
1/2 c. instant tapioca

1/2 tsp. vanilla
1/4 tsp. salt
1/2 c. heavy cream

In medium saucepan, combine coffee, 1/2 cup sugar, tapioca, vanilla and salt. Stir well; let stand 5 minutes. Bring mixture to full boil over medium heat, stirring constantly. When mixture continues bubbling while being stirred, remove from heat and divide evenly among 4 serving dishes. Chill 2 to 3 hours. Combine cream and 1 tablespoon sugar; whip until peaks form. Divide whipped cream among chilled portions.

Diane Caron-Smith, *Winterset*
First Place, 2014 Cooking with Coffee – Desserts
Second Place Overall, 2014 Cooking with Coffee

PIÑA COLADA CUPCAKES

For CUPCAKES:
1 3/8 c. all-purpose flour
1/2 tbsp. baking powder
1/2 tsp. salt
3/8 c. shredded coconut
1 egg white

3/4 c. granulated sugar,
    divided
5 tbsp. butter, melted
3/4 c. skim milk
1/2 tsp. coconut extract

Combine flour, baking powder, salt and coconut; set aside. In small bowl, beat egg white until frothy. Add 1/8 cup sugar, 1 tablespoon at a time, until soft peaks form; set aside. Cream together butter and remaining sugar. Add flour mixture alternately with milk. Stir in extract. Fold in egg white until no white streaks remain. Place 14 cupcake liners in muffin tins. Pour batter into cupcake liners. Bake in 350° oven 15 to 20 minutes or until cake tester inserted in center has moist crumbs when removed. Remove from tins; cool completely. When cool, frost and fill.

For PINEAPPLE CURD:
1/3 c. granulated sugar
1 tbsp. cornstarch
Pinch of salt
1/4 c. pineapple juice

1/4 c. water
1 egg yolk
1 tsp. butter

(CONTINUED)

PIES, CAKES AND DESSERTS

In small saucepan, combine sugar, cornstarch and salt. Whisk in pineapple juice, water and egg yolk. Cook over medium heat until mixture starts to bubble. Continue to cook 1 minute, whisking constantly. Remove from heat; stir in butter. Cover surface directly with plastic wrap and chill.

For RUM FROSTING:

1/4 c. shortening	2 1/2 c. powdered sugar
2 tbsp. milk	Maraschino cherries
1/2 tsp. rum extract	Dried pineapple
1/2 tsp. vanilla	

In small mixing bowl, cream together shortening, milk, rum extract and vanilla. Mix in powdered sugar, 1 cup at a time, mixing until smooth. To assemble, using pastry bag, squeeze pineapple curd into center of cupcakes until cupcakes bulge slightly. Frost cooled cupcakes. Garnish with maraschino cherries and dried pineapple.

Marcia G. Miller, *Urbandale*
First Place, 2014 "Smile in Every Aisle" Cakes – Filled Cupcakes

MARGARITA DESSERT

50 butter-flavored wheat crackers, crushed	14-oz. can sweetened condensed milk
1/2 c. butter, melted	8 oz. frozen whipped topping, thawed
1/2 c. frozen margarita concentrate	2 to 3 drops green food coloring
1/4 c. key lime juice	

Mix together cracker crumbs and butter. Press into pie plate or 8 dessert glasses. Mix margarita concentrate, key lime juice, sweetened condensed milk, whipped topping and food coloring. Pour into pie crust or dessert glasses; refrigerate. If desired, salt rim of glasses and garnish with lime slices.

Patty Hummel, *Allison*
First Place, 2015 Key Lime Challenge – Key Lime Dessert
First Place Overall, 2015 Key Lime Challenge

BUTTERMILK PUMPKIN DOUGHNUTS WITH BROWN BUTTER MAPLE GLAZE

For DOUGHNUTS:

1 1/2 c. all-purpose flour
1 1/2 tsp. baking powder
1/4 tsp. pumpkin pie spice
1/2 tsp. salt
1/4 c. melted butter
1/4 c. vegetable oil

1/3 c. buttermilk
1 egg
1 egg yolk
1 c. packed brown sugar
1 c. pumpkin puree
1 tsp. vanilla
Chopped pecans

Combine flour, baking powder, pumpkin pie spice and salt. In separate bowl, combine butter, oil, buttermilk, egg, egg yolk, brown sugar, pumpkin and vanilla. Whisk to combine. Add dry ingredients; stir until combined. Spray 2, 6-well doughnut pans with cooking spray. Fill doughnut wells three-fourths full. Bake in 350° oven 15 to 18 minutes. Cool; glaze with brown butter maple glaze. Sprinkle with pecans.

For BROWN BUTTER MAPLE GLAZE:

1/4 c. butter
2 tbsp. maple syrup
1/2 tsp. vanilla

1/2 c. packed brown sugar
2 tbsp. heavy cream
1 1/2 c. powdered sugar

Melt butter in saucepan until butter starts to brown. Add maple syrup, vanilla and brown sugar. Cook until sugar is dissolved, about 3 minutes. Add cream and powdered sugar; stir until smooth.

Anita Van Gundy, *Des Moines*
First Place, 2014 Casey's General Stores' Donut Competition

PEACHES AND CREAM PARFAIT

For CREAM:

1/2, 3-oz. box peach gelatin
4 oz. cream cheese

2 tbsp. powdered sugar
8 oz. whipped topping
6 tbsp. light cream

With mixer, combine gelatin and cream cheese. Add powdered sugar, whipped topping and cream; beat until smooth.

(CONTINUED)

For PEACH LAYER:

1/2, 3-oz. box peach gelatin	1/4 c. granulated sugar
4 peaches, peeled and sliced	2 tbsp. butter

In saucepan, combine gelatin, peaches, sugar and butter. Cook until peaches are soft and gelatin is dissolved. Cool completely.

For CRUMB LAYER:

3/4 c. coconut, chopped	1/4 c. granulated sugar
2 tbsp. sliced almonds, chopped	3 tbsp. butter, melted
1/4 c. all-purpose flour	6 shortbread cookies, broken coarsely

Combine all ingredients on parchment covered baking sheet. Bake in 350° oven 10 to 15 minutes, stirring as needed for even browning. Layer as desired in parfait glasses with crumb, cream and peach layers. Refrigerate before serving.

Pat Felderman, *Pleasant Hill*
First Place, 2015 Jell-O – Dessert
Second Place Overall, 2015 Jell-O

SPICED BANANA ICE CREAM

3 bananas, chopped	1/2 tsp. nutmeg
1/3 c. packed brown sugar	1 1/2 c. whole milk
1 tbsp. butter	2 tbsp. granulated sugar
1 1/2 tsp. cinnamon	1/2 tsp. vanilla
1/8 tsp. cloves	1/4 tsp. salt

In 2-quart glass baking dish, toss together bananas, brown sugar, butter and spices. Bake in 400° oven 40 minutes, stirring after 20 minutes. Remove from oven and place in blender. Add milk, sugar, vanilla and salt; blend until smooth. Refrigerate overnight. Place in ice cream freezer; freeze according to manufacturer's directions.

Larry Mahlstedt, *Des Moines*
First Place, 2014 My Favorite Tone's Recipe – Holiday Recipe
First Place, 2015 Desserts for Jake

PIES, CAKES AND DESSERTS

CHOCOLATE ORANGE CHEESECAKE

20 chocolate wafer cookies,
    finely crushed
1/4 tsp. cinnamon
3 tbsp. butter, melted
4, 8-oz. pkgs. cream cheese,
    softened
3/4 c. granulated sugar
1/2 c. sour cream

1 tsp. vanilla
4 eggs
4 oz. semisweet baking
    chocolate, melted
2 tbsp. orange extract
2 tsp. grated orange zest
1/2 c. orange marmalade

Mix wafer crumbs, cinnamon and butter; press onto bottom of 9-inch springform pan. Beat cream cheese and sugar in large bowl. Add sour cream and vanilla; mix well. Add eggs, one at a time, mixing on low speed after each, just until blended. Transfer 3 cups batter to medium bowl; stir in chocolate. Pour over crust. Bake in 350° oven 30 minutes. Stir orange extract and zest into remaining batter. Refrigerate until ready to use. Reduce oven to 325°. Spoon remaining orange batter over baked chocolate layer in pan. Bake 30 minutes or until center is almost set. Run small knife around rim of pan to loosen. Cool completely before removing rim. Refrigerate 4 hours. Top with marmalade before serving.

Angela Miller, *Des Moines*
First Place, 2015 Egg-ceptional Eggs Cooking Contest – Desserts
First Place Overall, 2015 Egg-ceptional Eggs Cooking Contest

LOMALAGI CHEESECAKE

For CRUST:
1 c. all-purpose flour
1/2 c. powdered sugar
1/4 tsp. salt

6 tbsp. cold butter
1 c. macadamia nuts

Combine flour, powdered sugar and salt in bowl of food processor. Process a few seconds to mix. Add butter, a tablespoon at a time. Process until mixture looks like coarse crumbs. Add nuts; process until nuts are chopped. Press into bottom and sides of greased 9-inch springform pan. Bake in 350° oven 10 to 12 minutes until firm and fragrant. Let cool; reduce oven to 325°.

(CONTINUED)

For MANGO TOPPING:

2 tbsp. granulated sugar
1 tbsp. instant cornstarch
    thickener

15.5-oz. can mango slices
    in heavy syrup
1 tbsp. freshly squeezed lime
    juice

In small bowl, combine sugar and thickener; stir until well blended. Drain mango slices; puree in blender or food processor with lime juice until smooth. Place in small saucepan. Cook over medium heat, stirring until puree begins to boil. Add sugar mixture; heat, stirring constantly, until thickened and no longer cloudy. Set aside to cool.

For CHEESECAKE:

3, 8-oz. pkgs. cream cheese,
    softened
1 1/4 c. granulated sugar
1/4 tsp. salt
4 large eggs
1 tbsp. vanilla

1 tbsp. fresh squeezed lime
    juice
3/4 c. heavy cream
2-oz. env. coconut cream
    powder

In bowl of food processor, mix cream cheese and sugar until smooth. Add salt, eggs, vanilla and lime juice and process until smooth. Do not over process. Add cream and coconut cream powder; mix. Pour cheesecake batter onto crust. Drop half the mango topping by tablespoonfuls into cheesecake. Swirl with a toothpick. Wrap outside of pan in double-layer of foil, covering the underside and extending all the way to the top. Set wrapped pan in large roasting pan; pour hot water into roasting pan to depth of 2 inches or about halfway up sides of cheesecake pan. Bake in 325° oven 45 to 60 minutes, until instant-read thermometer placed 1-inch from edge reads 165°. Turn off oven; prop open oven door slightly. Let cheesecake rest 1 hour. Remove from oven; refrigerate overnight. If desired, top with remaining mango topping.

Deirdre Scott, *Grimes*
First Place, 2015 Dole Cans' Fruit Dessert Competition

JAMMIN' APPLE CROSTATA

For CRUST:

2 c. all-purpose flour
2 tbsp. granulated sugar
1/4 tsp. salt

3/4 c. butter, sliced
1/4 c. shortening
1/3 c. ice water

Combine flour, sugar and salt in large bowl. Cut in butter and shortening until crumbly. Add water; mix quickly with fork. Dough will start to form a ball. Gather, cut in half and wrap each half in plastic wrap. Chill dough overnight. Roll 1 dough into 14-inch round. Reserve other dough for future use. Place on parchment-lined baking sheet. Place filling in middle; fold over edges, partially covering filling. Sprinkle with streusel. Bake in 400° oven 45 minutes or until filling is bubbly and crust is golden. If crust starts to get too dark, lightly cover with foil.

For FILLING:

3 apples, peeled, cored and
    sliced

1/2 c. mixed berry jam
2 tbsp. all-purpose flour

Gently combine ingredients.

For STREUSEL:

1/4 c. granulated sugar
1/4 c. all-purpose flour

1/4 c. butter

Combine all ingredients until crumbly.

Connie Sherman, *Iowa City*
First Place, 2014 Desserts for Jake

BLACK FOREST CREPES

For CREPES:

3/4 c. all-purpose flour
1/2 tbsp. granulated sugar
1/4 tsp. baking powder

1/4 tsp. salt
1 c. skim milk
1 egg

In medium mixing bowl, sift together flour, sugar, baking powder and salt. Whisk in milk and egg. Spray a 6-inch skillet with cooking spray; set

(CONTINUED)

on medium heat. When skillet is hot, pour approximately 3 tablespoons batter into skillet. Immediately rotate pan until batter covers bottom. Cook until crepe is light brown; turn and brown other side. Remove from skillet and repeat. Refrigerate crepes until ready to fill.

For CHERRY FILLING:

1/2 c. granulated sugar	1/8 c. water
2 tbsp. cornstarch	2 c. pitted dark-red tart
Pinch of salt	cherries, drained,
1/3 c. cherry juice (reserved	reserving liquid
from cherries)	1/4 tsp. almond extract

In medium saucepan, combine sugar, cornstarch and salt. Stir in cherry juice, water and cherries. Cook and stir over medium heat until mixture starts to bubble. Cook 1 minute more. Remove from heat; stir in almond extract. Cool at room temperature, stirring occasionally. Set aside 1/4 cup cooked cherry mixture to use for garnish.

For WHIPPED CREAM AND CHOCOLATE:

3/4 c. heavy cream	Cherry filling (recipe above)
2 oz. reduced-fat cream	1/4 c. semisweet chocolate
cheese	chips
1/8 c. granulated sugar	1 tbsp. butter
6 oz. light, fat-free vanilla	
yogurt	

Whip cream until stiff; mix in cream cheese and sugar. Remove 1/2 cup to use for garnish. Mix yogurt into whipped cream mixture; stir in cherry filling until well combined. Place approximately 1/4 cup cherry filling at center top end of each crepe. Overlap bottom ends of each crepe to form a "V" shape. Pipe whipped cream onto each crepe. Combine chips and butter; microwave on high 30 seconds. Stir until melted and smooth. Garnish crepes with reserved 1/4 cup cherry filling; drizzle with chocolate.

Marcia G. Miller, *Urbandale*
First Place, 2014 Dessert Crepes by Le Jardin

PIES, CAKES AND DESSERTS

PEACH COBBLER

For FILLING:

4 c. sliced fresh peaches
1/2 c. granulated sugar
1 tbsp. cornstarch
1/4 c. packed brown sugar

1/2 c. cold water
1 tbsp. butter, melted
1 tbsp. freshly squeezed
lemon juice

Combine peaches and sugar in saucepan; mix gently. Add cornstarch, brown sugar and cold water. Bring to simmer over medium heat. Add butter and lemon juice; simmer 2 to 3 minutes. Pour into greased 12x7-inch baking dish.

For TOPPING:

1 c. all-purpose flour
1/2 c. plus 1 1/2 tbsp.
granulated sugar,
divided
1 1/2 tsp. baking powder

1/2 tsp. salt
1/2 c. milk
1/4 c. butter, softened
1/4 tsp. nutmeg
Mint for garnish
Peach slices for garnish

Combine flour, 1/2 cup sugar, baking powder and salt; mix well. Add milk and butter; beat until smooth. Drop heaping tablespoonfuls of topping over top of filling. Combine remaining sugar and nutmeg; mix well. Sprinkle evenly over topping. Bake in 350° oven 30 to 40 minutes. Garnish with mint and peach slices.

Lana Shope, *Indianola*
First Place, 2015 Iowa Orchards Creations – Dessert (Adults)
First Place Overall, 2015 Iowa Orchards Creations

DOUBLE CHOCOLATE MINT CHOUX PASTRY

For CHOUX PASTRY:

1/2 c. unsalted butter
1 c. water

1 c. all-purpose flour
4 eggs

Place butter and water in large saucepan. Simmer over medium heat until butter is melted; stir in flour. Remove from heat; add eggs, one at a

(CONTINUED)

PIES, CAKES AND DESSERTS

time. Drop 1/4 cup portions of dough onto parchment-lined baking sheet. Bake in 400° oven 20 to 30 minutes or until golden brown and small bubbles are no longer forming on tops of pastry. Remove from oven; poke each with a skewer to release steam. Allow to cool. With pastry tip, fill pastries with pastry cream then dip in ganache. Garnish with herbs or chocolate if desired.

For PASTRY CREAM:

2 c. whole milk	**4 tbsp. unsweetened cocoa**
4 egg yolks	**powder**
1/3 c. granulated sugar	**1 tbsp. unsalted butter**
1/4 c. cornstarch	**1 vanilla bean, split and**
1/8 tsp. salt	**scraped**

In heavy saucepan, warm milk over low heat. In a bowl, cream egg yolks and sugar. Whisk in cornstarch until smooth. Pour 1/2 cup warm milk into yolk mixture; whisk to combine. Pour mixture back into pan with warm milk. Over medium heat, bring mixture to boil, whisking constantly. When mixture starts to boil, whisk continually until cream thickens. Add salt and cocoa; remove from heat. Stir in butter and vanilla. Transfer to plastic wrap-lined baking pan. Cover surface with plastic wrap. Chill in refrigerator at least 2 hours. This can be made ahead and stored in refrigerator up to 2 days.

For GANACHE:

1/2 c. heavy cream	**1/2 c. bittersweet chocolate**
1 tsp. corn syrup	**chips**
	1/2 tsp. peppermint extract

In heatproof bowl, microwave cream and corn syrup on high 1 to 2 minutes. Stir in chocolate chips. Allow to sit 30 seconds to melt chips. Stir in peppermint extract; whisk to combine.

Amber Wagner, *Prairie City*
First Place, 2015 Memories for Myrna

ALMOND VENETIAN DESSERT

1/2 c. almond paste	1/8 tsp. salt
3/4 c. butter, softened	5 drops green food coloring
1/2 c. granulated sugar	4 drops red food coloring
2 eggs, separated	2/3 c. apricot preserves
1/4 tsp. almond extract	3 oz. semisweet chocolate,
1 c. all-purpose flour	chopped

Place almond paste in large bowl; break up with fork. Add butter, sugar, egg yolks and almond extract. Beat until smooth and fluffy. Stir in flour and salt. In separate bowl, beat egg whites until soft peaks form. Stir one-quarter of the whites into dough; fold in remaining whites. Dough will be stiff. Divide dough evenly into 3 portions, about 2/3 cup each. Tint 1 portion green; 1 red and leave remaining portion white. Grease bottoms of three 8-inch square baking dishes; line with parchment paper. Grease parchment paper. Spread each portion into prepared pan. Bake in 350° oven 13 to 15 minutes or until edges are golden brown. Immediately invert onto wire racks; remove parchment paper. Place another wire rack on top and turn over. Cool completely. Place green layer on large piece of plastic wrap. Spread evenly with 1/3 cup apricot preserves. Top with white layer; spread with remaining preserves. Top with red layer. Bring plastic over layers. Slide onto baking sheet and set a cutting board on top to compress layers. Refrigerate overnight. In microwave-safe bowl, melt chocolate. Remove cutting board and unwrap dessert. Spread melted chocolate over top; let stand until set. With sharp knife, trim edges. Cut into 2-inch x 5/8-inch bars.

Charlotte Bowden, *Monroe*
First Place, 2015 Adventureland Resort Intermediate – Bars Other Than Named

---

PUMPKIN CHEESECAKE

For CRUST:

3/4 c. all-purpose flour	1/8 tsp. ginger powder
2 tbsp. granulated sugar	5 tbsp. cold butter

Sift together flour, sugar and ginger. Using fingers, cut in butter. Press into 9-inch springform pan. Bake in 325° oven 13 to 16 minutes or until light brown.

(CONTINUED)

PIES, CAKES AND DESSERTS

For FILLING:

1/2 c. margarine, room temperature	1/3 c. cornstarch
	1/2 tsp. salt
4, 8-oz. pkgs. cream cheese, room temperature	1 tsp. cinnamon
	1/8 tsp. nutmeg
1 1/4 c. granulated sugar	1/4 tsp. ground cloves
1/4 c. packed brown sugar	1/8 tsp. ginger powder
5 eggs	16-oz. can pumpkin puree
1 tbsp. vanilla	

In large bowl, cream together margarine and cream cheese. Add sugar and brown sugar; mix well. In small bowl, mix eggs and vanilla. Add to cream cheese mixture; mix until blended. Do not overmix. In medium bowl, sift together cornstarch, salt and spices. Add cornstarch mixture to cream cheese mixture. Mix; do not overmix. Add pumpkin; mix to blend. Pour into pan on top of baked crust. Wrap outside of pan in double-layer of foil, covering the underside and extending all the way to the top. Set wrapped pan in large roasting pan; pour hot water into roasting pan to depth of 2 inches or about halfway up sides of cheesecake pan. Bake in 325° oven 75 minutes. Turn off oven; let sit in oven 1 hour. Cool on counter; remove outside ring before frosting. Refrigerate.

For TOPPING:

4 oz. cream cheese, room temperature	1 tsp. vanilla
	1/3 c. powdered sugar
1 tbsp. butter, room temperature	1 tbsp. granulated sugar
	1 tsp. pumpkin pie spice

Cream together cream cheese and butter; add vanilla. Mix in powdered sugar. Spoon topping onto each slice of cake. Combine sugar and pumpkin pie spice; sprinkle over top.

Bridget Lottman, *Norwalk*
First Place, 2014 My Favorite Pumpkin Recipe

LEMON MOUSSE CREPES
WITH BLUEBERRY SAUCE

For CREPES:

3/4 c. all-purpose flour	1/4 tsp. salt
1/2 tbsp. granulated sugar	1 c. skim milk
1/4 tsp. baking powder	1 egg

In medium bowl, sift together flour, sugar, baking powder and salt. Whisk in milk and egg. Spray a 6-inch skillet with cooking spray; set on medium heat. When skillet is hot, pour approximately 3 tablespoons batter into skillet. Immediately rotate pan until batter covers bottom. Cook until crepe is light brown; turn and brown other side. Remove from skillet and repeat. Refrigerate crepes until ready to fill. To assemble crepes, place approximately 1/4 cup lemon mousse at center top of each crepe. Overlap bottom ends of each crepe. Spoon blueberry sauce over crepes. Garnish with reserved whipped cream.

For LEMON CURD:

1/3 c. granulated sugar	1/4 c. water
4 tsp. cornstarch	1 egg yolk
Pinch of salt	1/2 tsp. grated lemon zest
1/4 c. lemon juice	

In saucepan, combine sugar, cornstarch and salt. Whisk in lemon juice, water and egg yolk. Cook over medium heat until mixture bubbles. Cook 1 minute more. Remove from heat; stir in lemon zest. Refrigerate 3 hours.

For WHIPPED CREAM:

3/4 c. heavy cream	2 oz. cream cheese,
1/8 c. granulated sugar	softened

Whip cream until stiff. Mix in sugar and cream cheese. Reserve half the whipped cream to use for garnish. To remaining whipped cream, mix in chilled lemon curd. Refrigerate mousse several house before using.

For BLUEBERRY SAUCE:

1/2 c. granulated sugar	3/4 c. water
1 1/2 tbsp. cornstarch	1 1/2 c. blueberries
Pinch of salt	

(CONTINUED)

In small saucepan, combine sugar, cornstarch, salt and water. Stir in blueberries. Cook over medium heat until mixture starts to bubble; cook 1 minute more. Remove from heat; cool to room temperature.

Marcia G. Miller, *Urbandale*
First Place, 2015 Creative Crepes by Le Jardin – Dessert Crepes

---

NOT YOUR BASIC PANNA COTTA

For PANNA COTTA:

1 1/2 c. heavy cream	**1/4 c. white chocolate chips**
1/3 c. granulated sugar	**1 1/2 tsp. gelatin**
1/4 c. chocolate syrup	**1/4 c. water**

In large saucepan, heat cream and sugar. Bring to simmer just until sugar dissolves. Remove from heat; add chocolate syrup and white chocolate chips. Stir until melted. In small bowl, dissolve gelatin in water. Scrape into cream mixture; whisk until dissolved. Fill 6 small glasses. Chill until set, about 1 hour.

For CREAM CHEESE LAYER:

8 oz. cream cheese, room temperature	**2 tsp. unsweetened cocoa powder**
2 oz. butter, room temperature	**1 c. heavy cream**
1/2 c. plus 1 tbsp. powdered sugar, divided	**1/4 c. semisweet chocolate chips**
	1/4 c. grated white chocolate

Mix together cream cheese, butter, 1/2 cup powdered sugar and cocoa; set aside. Whip the cream; spoon half the whipped cream into cream cheese mixture. Spoon over set panna cotta. Process semisweet chips until finely chopped. Spoon on top of cream cheese layer. Add remaining powdered sugar to remaining whipped cream. Spoon on top of semisweet chocolate. Top with grated white chocolate. Drizzle with additional chocolate syrup if desired.

Bridget Lottman, *Norwalk*
First Place, 2015 Innovative Chocolate

PIES, CAKES AND DESSERTS

CHOCOLATE TRUFFLE CHEESECAKE

For CHEESECAKE:

1 1/2 c. crushed toffee
   shortbread sandies
2 tbsp. melted butter
8 oz. bittersweet chocolate,
   chopped
1 c. heavy cream
4, 8-oz. pkgs. cream cheese,
   softened

14-oz. can sweetened
   condensed milk
2 tsp. vanilla
4 large eggs
Ganache (recipe below)
White chocolate drizzle
   (recipe below)
Fresh raspberry for garnish

Combine crushed cookies and butter; press on bottom of 9-inch springform pan. Wrap pan in double layer of heavy foil. Bake in 325° oven 12 to 15 minutes or until set and fragrant. Cool on wire rack. Microwave chocolate and cream on high 1 1/2 minutes or until melted, stirring at 30-second intervals. Beat cream cheese at medium speed 2 minutes or until smooth. Add sweetened condensed milk and vanilla, beating just until combined. Add eggs, one at a time, beating at low speed just until blended after each addition. Add chocolate mixture, beating just until blended. Pour batter into prepared crust. Place cheesecake pan in large roasting pan. Pour enough boiling water into roasting pan to come 1-inch up sides of cheesecake pan. Bake until filling is set and almost golden brown on top, about 1 hour 15 minutes. Set roasting pan on wire rack; loosen cake from sides of pan. Cool until water is just warm, about 45 minutes. Remove springform pan from water bath; discard foil and cool completely. Run a thin knife around sides of pan to loosen. Refrigerate at least 4 hours or overnight until well chilled. Remove sides of pan; place cheesecake on serving plate. Slowly pour warm ganache topping over cheesecake, spreading to edges. Chill at least 1 hour. Drizzle with white chocolate drizzle and garnish with fresh raspberries.

For GANACHE AND WHITE CHOCOLATE DRIZZLE:

1 1/2 c. heavy cream, divided

8 oz. bittersweet chocolate,
   finely chopped
4 oz. white chocolate,
   finely chopped

(CONTINUED)

Bring 1 cup cream to light boil in saucepan over medium heat. Place bittersweet chocolate in microwave-safe bowl. Pour cream over chocolate; let stand 1 minute. Stir gently until fully combined. Let mixture cool until slightly warm, 20 to 30 minutes. Place mixture in resealable plastic bag; snip off a corner. Drizzle over chilled cheesecake as desired. Repeat with remaining cream and white chocolate.

Rebecca Howe, *Des Moines*
First Place, 2015 Best Cheesecake Using Keebler Products

CHOCOLATE CHERRY NO-BAKE CHEESECAKE

For CRUST:

20 chocolate sandwich cookies, filling removed and crushed	**1/3 c. melted butter**

Combine crushed cookies and butter. Press into 8-inch springform pan; chill.

For FILLING:

2, 8-oz. pkgs. cream cheese	**1 pt. heavy cream**
2 tbsp. lemon juice	**1 c. granulated sugar**

Beat together cream cheese and lemon juice. Add cream and sugar. Beat until stiff. Pour into chilled crust. Chill overnight.

For CHERRY TOPPING:

4 tsp. cornstarch	**1 c. granulated sugar**
1/2 c. water	**2 c. cherries**

In medium saucepan, combine cornstarch and water. Stir until cornstarch is dissolved. Stir in sugar and cherries. Bring to boil on medium heat. Stir constantly until sauce is thickened. Cool completely; spoon over cheesecake before serving. Garnish as desired.

Judy Diapico, *Altoona*
First Place, 2015 Tammie's No Bake Desserts – With Crust
First Place Overall, 2015 Tammie's No Bake Desserts

PEACHES AND CREAM CHEESECAKE

For CRUST:

1/3 c. cake flour, sifted
3/4 tsp. baking powder
Pinch of salt
2 extra large eggs, separated
1/3 c. granulated sugar,
    divided

1 tsp. vanilla
2 drops lemon extract
2 tbsp. unsalted butter,
    melted
1/4 tsp. cream of tartar

In small bowl, sift flour, baking powder and salt. In large bowl, beat egg yolks with mixer on high 3 minutes. With mixer running, slowly add 2 tablespoons sugar. Beat until thick, light yellow ribbons form, about 5 minutes. Beat in vanilla and lemon extract. Sift flour mixture over batter; stir in by hand until no more white flecks appear. Blend in butter. Beat egg whites and cream of tartar until frothy. Gradually add remaining sugar and beat until stiff, shiny peaks form. Fold whites into batter. Butter bottom and sides of 9-inch springform pan. Wrap outside of pan with foil, covering bottom and sides. Gently spread batter over bottom of pan; bake in 350° oven until set and golden, about 10 minutes and cool.

For PEACH FILLING:

10-oz. dry pack frozen
    peaches, thawed
1/2 c. apple cider

1 tbsp. cornstarch
1 tbsp. granulated sugar
1/8 tsp. cinnamon

Drain peaches on paper towels; cut into 1/2-inch pieces. In small saucepan, combine cider, cornstarch, sugar and cinnamon. Stir and bring to a boil. Cook 1 minute, until thickened. Fold in peaches; let cool.

For CHEESECAKE:

3, 8-oz. pkgs. cream cheese
1 1/3 c. granulated sugar
1/4 c. cornstarch

1 tbsp. vanilla
2 extra large eggs
2/3 c. heavy cream

(CONTINUED)

Combine cream cheese, sugar, cornstarch and vanilla; beat until fluffy. Add eggs, one at a time. Beat in cream. Spoon batter over crust. Spoon peach filling over the top, almost to the edge of the pan. Place pan in large shallow pan and add hot water to come up 1 inch on sides of cake pan. Bake in 350° oven 80 to 85 minutes until top is slightly browned. Remove from water bath; remove foil and let stand 2 hours. Chill.

For CRUMB TOPPING:

3/4 c. all-purpose flour	**Grated zest of 1 large lemon**
1/3 c. packed brown sugar	**1/2 c. cold unsalted butter**
1/2 tsp. cinnamon	

Mix flour, brown sugar, cinnamon and zest. Cut in butter to make coarse crumbs. Spread crumbs out on greased jelly roll pan. Bake in 350° oven 15 minutes, until golden brown and bubbly. Toss with a spatula 2 or 3 times during baking. Let cool in pan; break into fine crumbs. Sprinkle crumbs on top of cake. Prior to serving, garnish cheesecake with whipped cream and additional peach slices if desired.

For WHIPPED CREAM:

1 c. heavy cream	**1/3 c. powdered sugar**
1 tsp. vanilla	

Place all in bowl; beat until stiff peaks form.

Marianne Carlson, *Jefferson*
First Place, 2015 Knapp's Build Your Best Cheesecake

PEACH CREPES

For CREPE BATTER:
1 c. rice flour
2/3 c. buttermilk
2 eggs
1/2 tsp. salt
1 tbsp. granulated sugar

1 tsp. vanilla
3/4 c. water
1/4 tsp. cinnamon
1 tsp. oil
2 tbsp. melted butter

Mix together all ingredients; whisk until batter is smooth. Let stand 15 minutes. Heat skillet over medium heat. Pour 1/4 cup batter into skillet. Tip and rotate skillet dispersing batter into 8-inch circle. Cook about 1 minute; flip crepe and cook second side 1 minute. To assemble, fill crepes and top with whipped topping. Garnish with pureed peaches.

For FILLING:
3/4 c. sliced peaches
1/8 c. granulated sugar

1/4 tsp. cinnamon
1 tbsp. butter

Combine all ingredients in hot skillet; sauté over medium heat until peaches are tender.

For WHIPPED CREAM TOPPING:
1 c. heavy cream
1/4 c. powdered sugar

1 tsp. cinnamon

Combine all ingredients in large bowl. Beat until soft peaks form.

Daniel Hodges, *Des Moines*
First Place, 2015 Gluten Free for You and Me

Iowa State Fair
COOKBOOK

FIVE LAYER BARS

1 c. all-purpose flour
3/4 c. regular rolled oats
1/2 c. packed brown sugar
1/2 tsp. baking soda
1/4 tsp. salt

3/4 c. butter
8 oz. semisweet chocolate
chips
3/4 c. chopped walnuts
12 oz. hot caramel topping

Combine flour, oats, brown sugar, baking soda and salt. Cut in butter until mixture resembles coarse crumbs. Reserve 1 cup of mixture and press remainder of crumb mixture into 9x13-inch baking pan. Bake in 350° oven 12 minutes. Over hot baked crust, layer chocolate chips, then chopped nuts. Drizzle caramel evenly over all. Top with reserved crumb mixture. Bake 20 minutes until bubbly. Cool at least 2 hours. Cut into bars.

Patricia Malatek, *Ely*
First Place, 2014 Midwest Living Cookies – Five Layer Bars

BUTTERSCOTCH BARS

1/2 c. all-purpose flour
1/2 c. cake flour
1/4 tsp. baking powder
1/4 tsp. salt
3/4 tsp. nutmeg
1/4 tsp. mace
8 tbsp. butter, melted and
cooled

3/4 c. packed brown sugar
2 extra large egg yolks
1 1/2 tsp. vanilla
1/2 tsp. maple extract
1/4 c. maple syrup
1 c. chopped pecans

Sift together flours, baking powder, salt, nutmeg and mace. In large mixing bowl, whisk melted butter, brown sugar and egg yolks. Stir in vanilla, maple extract and maple syrup. Toss pecans with 2 teaspoonfuls of the sifted flour mixture. Stir pecans and sifted mixture into butter mixture, blending just until particles of flour have been absorbed. Spoon batter into lightly buttered and floured 9-inch baking pan. Bake in 350° oven 30 to 35 minutes or until light golden on top and just firm to the touch. Cool in pan on wire rack; cut into bars.

Mary Burr, *Iowa City*
First Place, 2014 Midwest Living Cookies – Butterscotch Bars

COOKIES, CANDIES AND SNACKS

PUMPKIN CHOCOLATE CHIP BARS

1 c. all-purpose flour
1 c. white whole wheat flour
3/4 c. granulated sugar
1/2 c. finely chopped pecans
　　or walnuts (optional)
2 tsp. baking powder
1 tsp. cinnamon
1/2 tsp. baking soda
1/2 tsp. salt
4 eggs, slightly beaten

15-oz. can pumpkin puree
1/2 c. vegetable/canola
　　oil blend
1/4 c. 2% milk
1/2 c. plus 2 tbsp. miniature
　　semisweet chocolate
　　pieces, divided
2 oz. each melted white and
　　chocolate almond bark

In large bowl, stir together flours, sugar, nuts, baking powder, cinnamon, baking soda and salt. In separate bowl, combine eggs, pumpkin, oil and milk. Add pumpkin mixture to flour mixture along with 1/2 cup chocolate pieces; stir just until combined. Spread batter evenly in lightly greased 15x10-inch baking pan. Sprinkle top with 2 tablespoons chocolate pieces. Bake in 350° oven 25 minutes or until toothpick inserted in center comes out clean. Drizzle melted bark over bars.

Kay Smith, *Des Moines*
First Place, 2014 Midwest Living Cookies – Single Layer Pumpkin Bars

FUDGY CHOCOLATE CHUNK BROWNIES

1/2 c. butter, room
　　temperature
1 c. granulated sugar
1 tsp. vanilla
2 eggs

1/2 c. all-purpose flour
1/2 c. dark cocoa powder
1/4 tsp. salt
1/4 tsp. baking soda
2 c. chocolate chunks

Beat together butter, sugar and vanilla. Add eggs, one at a time, mixing well. Stir together flour, cocoa powder and salt. Gradually add to butter mixture. Mix in baking soda; add chocolate chunks. Batter will be thick. Scrape into parchment-lined 9x9-inch baking dish; spread evenly. Bake in 350° oven 25 minutes and brownies begin to pull away from sides.

Clarissa Ridgway, *Johnston*
First Place, 2015 Adventureland Resort Intermediate – Chocolate Brownies (no nuts)

ALMOND BUTTER – JAM THUMBPRINTS

3/4 c. almond butter
1/2 c. butter, softened
1/2 c. packed brown sugar
1/4 c. granulated sugar
1/2 tsp. almond extract
1 egg
1 1/2 c. all-purpose flour

1/2 tsp. baking powder
1/2 tsp. baking soda
1/2 tsp. salt
1/2 c. slivered almonds,
    finely chopped
1/2 c. strawberry jam

In large bowl, beat almond butter, butter and sugars on medium speed 1 minute until light and fluffy. Beat in almond extract and egg until blended. On low speed, beat in flour, baking powder, baking soda and salt until soft dough forms. Place chopped almonds in small bowl. Shape dough into 1-inch balls; roll in almonds. Place 2 inches apart on parchment-lined baking sheet. Bake in 350° oven 8 to 10 minutes until edges are almost set. Using thumb or backside of small melon ball scoop, make indentation in center of each cookie; bake 5 minutes more until browned and edges are set. Cool 2 minutes; remove from baking sheets to wire racks. Cool completely. Place strawberry jam into sealable bag, snip off corner of bag. Squeeze to pipe jam into indentations.

Angela Miller, *West Des Moines*
First Place, 2015 Midwest Living and Gold Medal Flour Cookies –
Thumbprint

SPRITZ

1 1/2 c. butter, softened
1 c. granulated sugar
1 tsp. baking powder
1 egg

1 tsp. vanilla
1/4 tsp. Fiori di Sicilia
3 1/2 c. all-purpose flour
Colored sugar

Beat together butter, sugar and baking powder. Add egg, vanilla and Fiori di Sicilia; mix well. Gradually add flour; mix well. Spoon dough into cookie press. Press cookies onto ungreased baking sheet. Sprinkle with colored sugar. Bake in 375° oven 8 to 10 minutes, until edges are firm but not brown. Cool on wire racks.

Hester Derscheid, *Ellston*
First Place, 2014 Midwest Living Cookies – Spritz

PEANUT BUTTER BARS

1 c. butter, melted
1 c. packed dark brown sugar
1 tsp. baking soda
2 1/4 c. quick-cooking rolled
    oats
1 1/2 c. all-purpose flour
1 tsp. salt

1/2 c. creamy peanut butter
14-oz. can sweetened
    condensed milk
2.8-oz. peanut butter cup
    candy bar, roughly
    chopped
1 c. milk chocolate chips

In medium mixing bowl, stir together melted butter, brown sugar, baking soda, oats, flour and salt; mix until crumbly. Set aside approximately 1 cup of mixture. Press remainder into lightly greased pan. Bake in 350° oven 10 minutes. While crust is baking, stir together peanut butter and sweetened condensed milk. Once crust is done baking, evenly spread peanut butter mixture over baked crust. Be gentle so you do not pull up warm crust. Evenly sprinkle reserved crumbs on top of peanut butter mixture. Bake in 350° oven 15 minutes. Remove from oven; sprinkle chopped candy bars and chocolate chips evenly over top. Return to oven; bake 5 to 10 minutes or until topping is light golden brown and candy bars and chips are melting.

Peri Halma, *West Des Moines*
First Place, 2014 Midwest Living Cookies – Peanut Butter Bars

BLONDE BROWNIES

2/3 c. butter
2 1/4 c. packed brown sugar
3 large eggs
2 tsp. vanilla
2 1/2 c. all-purpose flour

2 1/2 tsp. baking soda
1/2 tsp. salt
1 to 2 c. chocolate chips
1/2 c. chopped walnuts
    (optional)

Cream together butter and sugar until smooth. Add eggs, one at a time, beating thoroughly. Blend in vanilla. In separate bowl, combine dry ingredients; stir into butter mixture until well blended. Add chocolate chips and walnuts. Smooth out into lightly greased 9x13-inch baking pan. Bake in 375° oven 25 minutes.

Triniti Conlan, *Pleasant Hill*
First Place, 2014 Adventureland Resort Junior – Blonde Brownies

ORANGE AND ALMOND COCONUT MACAROONS

1/2 c. unsalted butter,
   room temperature
3/4 c. granulated sugar
1/8 tsp. salt
1/2 tsp. almond extract
2 tsp. finely grated orange
   zest

3 large eggs
24 oz. sweetened flake
   coconut (approx. 6 c.
   firmly packed)
6 oz. bittersweet chocolate,
   melted

Line 3 large rimmed baking sheets with parchment; set aside. Using electric mixer, beat butter in large bowl until smooth. Add sugar and salt; beat until blended. Mix in almond extract and orange zest; then eggs, one at a time. Mix in coconut. Drop batter onto prepared baking sheets by tablespoons, spacing 1 1/2-inches apart. Bake on center rack of 325° oven until golden on bottom and browned in spots, 25 to 30 minutes. Cool completely on baking sheets. Using fork, drizzle chocolate over macaroons. Chill on baking sheets until chocolate is firm, about 30 minutes.

Eileen Gannon, *Des Moines*
First Place, 2014 Midwest Living Cookies – Coconut Macaroon

HONEY BARZZZZ

1 c. honey
3 eggs, well beaten
1 tsp. baking powder
1 1/3 c. all-purpose flour
1 c. chopped nuts

1 c. raisins
1 tsp. vanilla
Pinch of salt
1/4 tsp. grated orange zest
1/2 c. crushed, roasted nuts

Mix together honey and eggs. Sift together baking powder and flour; add to honey mixture. Stir in chopped nuts, raisins, vanilla, salt and zest. Spread into lightly greased 8x8-inch baking pan. Bake in 350° oven 20 minutes. Let cool; sprinkle with crushed nuts.

Grace Whitlow, *Johnston*
First Place, 2015 Foods Made with Honey – Youth Entries
First Place Overall, 2015 Foods Made with Honey – Overall Youth

COCONUT KEY LIME MACAROONS

3 1/2 c. sweetened coconut
flakes
1/4 c. all-purpose flour
1/8 tsp. salt

2 tbsp. grated lime zest,
divided
3 tbsp. key lime juice
14-oz. can sweetened
condensed milk

Combine coconut, flour, salt and 1 tablespoon lime zest in bowl; mix thoroughly. Add key lime juice and sweetened condensed milk. Mix well with spatula. Scoop cookie dough balls onto greased or parchment paper-lined baking sheet. Sprinkle tops with remaining zest. Bake in 350° oven 12 to 15 minutes or until edges and bottoms are just slightly browned.

Natalie Ridgway, *Johnston*
First Place, 2014 Key Lime Challenge – Cookies
Second Place Overall, 2014 Key Lime Challenge

DIVINE CHOCOLATE TOFFEE COOKIES

8 oz. 72% dark chocolate,
coarsely chopped
4 tbsp. butter
2 2/3 c. all-purpose flour
1/2 tsp. baking powder
1/2 tsp. salt
2 large eggs, room
temperature

3/4 c. packed dark brown
sugar
1 tsp. vanilla
3/4 c. brickle toffee chips
1 c. chocolate chips
1/2 c. finely chopped toasted
pecans
White chocolate for garnish

In double boiler, melt together chocolate and butter; cool to room temperature in mixing bowl. Mix together flour, baking powder and salt; set aside. Place chocolate mixture in bowl of stand mixer. Add eggs and brown sugar; beat well. Add vanilla. Slowly add dry ingredients until blended. Add toffee chips and chocolate chips; stir by hand until evenly mixed. Roll into 3/4 to 1-inch balls; roll balls in toasted pecans. Place on parchment paper-lined baking sheets; bake in 350° oven 11 to 12 minutes. Cool on baking sheets. Garnish with white chocolate.

Michelle Burgmeier, *Lockridge*
First Place, 2015 Land O'Lakes Best Butter Cookie

COOKIES, CANDIES AND SNACKS

SALTED CARAMEL BROWNIES

1/2 lb. unsalted butter
14 oz. semisweet chocolate
   chips, divided
3 oz. unsweetened chocolate
3 extra large eggs
1 1/2 tbsp. instant coffee
   granules
1 1/2 tbsp. vanilla

1 c. plus 2 tbsp. granulated
   sugar
1/2 c. plus 2 tbsp. all-purpose
   flour, divided
1 1/2 tsp. baking powder
1/2 tsp. kosher salt
5 to 6 oz. caramel sauce
2 to 3 tsp. flaked sea salt

In saucepan over low heat, combine butter, 8 oz. chocolate chips and unsweetened chocolate. Heat until melted; remove from heat and let cool 15 minutes. In large bowl, stir together eggs, coffee, vanilla and sugar. Add chocolate mixture; stir well. Combine 1/2 cup flour, baking powder and kosher salt. Add to chocolate mixture. Combine remaining chocolate chips with 2 tablespoons flour; add to chocolate mixture. Spread in greased and floured 9x12-inch pan. Bake in 350° oven 35 minutes. Remove from oven; let stand 15 minutes. Warm caramel in microwave; drizzle over brownies. Sprinkle with sea salt.

Mary Cownie, *West Des Moines*
First Place, 2014 Midwest Living Cookies – Brownies (unfrosted)

RASPBERRY CHOCOLATE BARS

2 1/2 c. all-purpose flour
1 c. granulated sugar
3/4 c. finely chopped toasted
   pecans
1 c. butter, softened

1 large egg
12 oz. seedless raspberry jam
1 2/3 c. chocolate raspberry
   chips

Stir together flour, sugar, nuts, butter and egg until coarse crumbs form; set aside 1 1/2 cups mixture. Press remaining crumbs on bottom of greased 9x13-inch pan. Spread jam over the crust; sprinkle chips over jam. Add remaining crumb mixture to top. Bake in 350° oven 40 to 45 minutes until lightly browned. Cool completely before cutting into bars.

Marianne Carlson, *Jefferson*
First Place, 2015 Midwest Living and Gold Medal Flour Cookies – Four or More Layer Bars – Other Than Named

CHOCOLATE CHIP OATMEAL CHIA COOKIES

4 tbsp. water
2 tbsp. flax meal
1 c. granulated sugar
1 c. packed brown sugar
1 c. coconut oil
1 tsp. vanilla
2 eggs
1 tsp. cinnamon
2 c. all-purpose flour
1 tsp. baking soda
1 tsp. salt
3 tbsp. brewer's yeast
1 c. nuts
1 c. coconut
1 c. chocolate chips
3 tbsp. chia seeds
3 c. old-fashioned rolled oats

Mix water and flax meal in small cup; set aside 5 minutes. Combine sugars, oil, vanilla, eggs and flax mixture in large bowl. In separate bowl, combine cinnamon, flour, baking soda, salt and yeast; add to wet ingredients; mix thoroughly. Mix in nuts, coconut, chocolate chips, chia seeds and oats. Drop by spoonful onto baking sheets. Bake in 350° oven 13 minutes. Store in airtight container when cool.

Lindsey Pepper, *Boone*
First Place, 2014 Midwest Living Cookies – High Fiber

BLUEBERRY BARS

1/2 c. margarine
1 c. packed light brown sugar
1 1/2 c. all-purpose flour
1/2 tsp. baking soda
1/4 tsp. salt
1 1/2 c. regular rolled oats
1/4 c. water
2 c. blueberry jam
1 tsp. lemon juice
1/2 tsp. grated lemon zest

Cream together margarine and brown sugar until light and fluffy. In separate bowl, combine flour, baking soda and salt. Add flour mixture to margarine mixture; combine until crumbly. Add oats and water; mix until combined. In small bowl, combine jam, lemon juice and zest. Spread half the crumbled mixture into greased 9x13-inch baking dish. Spread jam mixture over top. Sprinkle remainder of crumbled mixture evenly over jam mixture. Bake in 350° oven 25 to 30 minutes or until set. Cool completely; cut into bars.

Jennifer Leeper, *Altoona*
First Place, 2015 Adventureland Resort Intermediate – Jam Bars

ULTIMATE DOUBLE CHOCOLATE COOKIES

11.5 oz. bittersweet chocolate
  chips
6 tbsp. unsalted butter
3 eggs
1 c. granulated sugar

1/3 c. all-purpose flour
1/2 tsp. baking powder
12 oz. semisweet chocolate
  chips
1 c. chopped walnuts

In double boiler over hot water, melt bittersweet chocolate chips and butter. In large bowl, beat eggs and sugar until thick; stir in melted chocolate mixture. In small bowl, stir together flour and baking powder; stir into chocolate mixture. Gently fold in semisweet chips and walnuts. Using plastic wrap, form into 2 logs, 2 inches in diameter and 8 inches long (dough will be soft; wrap tightly). Refrigerate at least 1 hour or until firm. Unwrap and using sharp knife, cut into 3/4-inch slices. Place on baking sheets; bake in 375° oven 12 to 14 minutes or until shiny crust forms (interior should be soft). Drizzle with additional melted bittersweet chocolate.

Rose Ridgway, *Johnston*
First Place, 2014 Nan's Nummiest Cookies – Chocolate Cookies

SOFT MOLASSES COOKIES

1/2 c. butter, softened
1/2 c. solid vegetable
  shortening (not
  margarine)
1 1/2 c. granulated sugar
1/2 c. molasses
2 eggs, lightly beaten

4 c. all-purpose flour
1/2 tsp. salt
2 1/4 tsp. baking soda
2 1/4 tsp. ground ginger
1 1/2 tsp. ground cloves
1 1/2 tsp. ground cinnamon
Additional sugar

In large bowl, cream together butter, shortening and sugar until light-colored and fluffy. Beat in molasses and eggs; set aside. In separate bowl, combine flour, salt, baking soda, ginger, cloves and cinnamon. Blend well with wire whisk. Gradually mix dry ingredients into wet mixture until dough is blended and smooth. Roll dough into 1 1/2-inch balls. Roll balls in additional sugar; place 2 1/2 inches apart on greased baking sheets. Bake in 350° oven 11 minutes.

Shari Bral, *Eddyville*
First Place, 2014 Midwest Living Cookies – Molasses

GRANOLA BARS

1 c. finely chopped dates
1 c. coarsely chopped
    almonds

1 1/2 c. regular rolled oats
1/4 c. honey
1/4 c. nut butter

In medium bowl, combine dates, almonds and oats; stir to combine. In microwave-safe bowl, combine honey and nut butter. Heat until warm. Pour over almond mixture. Stir until combined; pour into parchment paper-lined 8x8-inch pan and press down firmly. Cover with plastic wrap and refrigerate at least 15 minutes.

Jennifer Leeper, *Altoona*
First Place, 2014 Five Alive – Ages 11-17

SPICED ROSEMARY CHOCOLATE CHIP COOKIES (VEGAN)

2 c. all-purpose flour
1/2 tsp. salt
1 tsp. baking soda
1/2 tsp. smoked paprika
1/2 tsp. cayenne pepper
1 tsp. Saigon ground
    cinnamon
1 1/2 tbsp. snipped fresh
    rosemary
2/3 c. non-dairy margarine
1/3 c. vegetable shortening

1/2 c. packed dark brown
    sugar
1/3 c. granulated sugar
2 tbsp. smoked maple syrup
1/2 tsp. vanilla
1 c. chopped and toasted
    pecans
3/4 c. semisweet or
    bittersweet vegan
    chocolate chips

Combine flour, salt, baking soda, paprika, cayenne, cinnamon and rosemary; set aside. In large bowl, cream margarine, shortening and both sugars. Mix in maple syrup and vanilla. Mix flour into margarine, a little at a time. Mix in pecans and chocolate chips. Drop spoonfuls of dough onto baking sheets lined with parchment paper. Flatten each cookie slightly. Bake in 350° oven 10 to 15 minutes or until barely dry on top and lightly golden on edges. Cool 1 minute; move to wire racks.

Sara Woolery, *Grinnell*
First Place, 2014 Allspice Cookie Contest – Spiced Cookie
First Place Overall, 2014 Allspice Cookie Contest

CHOCOLATE ALMOND BISCOTTI

2 1/2 c. all-purpose flour
2 c. granulated sugar
3 sq. unsweetened chocolate,
   melted
5 eggs
1/2 tsp. vanilla
1/4 tsp. almond extract
1 tsp. baking soda
1/2 tsp. salt
1 c. slivered almonds

In large mixing bowl, combine all ingredients except almonds. Mix well; stir in almonds until well blended. Dough will be thick and sticky. Place half the dough on parchment-lined baking sheet. Form 4x12-inch log. Form second loaf on another sheet. Bake in 350° oven 30 minutes. Remove from oven; reduce heat to 325°. Allow loaves to cool 20 to 25 minutes. Cut into 1/2-inch thick slices. Lay slices flat on baking sheets. Bake 15 minutes more. Turn slices over; bake 15 minutes or until very crisp. Allow to cool; store in airtight container.

Charlotte Bowden, *Cedar Rapids*
First Place, 2014 Adventureland Resort Intermediate – Chocolate Almond Biscotti

CHEWY FRUIT & OATMEAL BARS

3/4 c. packed brown sugar
1/2 c. granulated sugar
8 oz. non-fat vanilla yogurt
2 egg whites
2 tbsp. canola oil
2 tbsp. skim milk
2 tsp. vanilla
1 scoop whey protein
1/4 c. wheat germ
3/4 c. all-purpose flour
3/4 c. wheat flour
1 tsp. baking soda
1 tsp. cinnamon
1/2 tsp. salt
3 c. old fashioned rolled oats
1/4 to 1/2 c. sunflower seeds
1/2 c. dried pineapple
1/2 c. dried sweetened
   cranberries
1/4 c. miniature semisweet
   chocolate chips

Combine sugars, yogurt, egg whites, oil, milk and vanilla. Add protein, wheat germ, flours, baking soda, cinnamon and salt. Stir in oats, seeds, fruits and chocolate chips. Spread into 9x13-inch pan. Bake in 350° oven 30 minutes.

Rose Ridgway, *Johnston*
First Place, 2015 Snack Time with Live Healthy Iowa – Pack Your Snack

SUGAR COOKIES

3/4 c. granulated sugar
1/2 c. lard
1 egg
1 tsp. clear vanilla
3/4 tsp. lemon extract
1 tsp. grated lemon zest

1 1/4 c. plus 2 tbsp. all-
    purpose flour
1 tsp. cream of tartar
1/2 tsp. baking soda
1/4 tsp. salt
Sugar for sprinkling

Cream together sugar and lard. Add egg, vanilla, lemon extract and zest. Combine remaining dry ingredients in separate bowl. Gradually add dry ingredients to creamed mixture. Cover bowl and chill 1 to 2 hours; shape into balls. Sprinkle with sugar. Place on baking sheet; bake in 350° oven 9 minutes.

Judy Kiburz-Harrison, *Mount Ayr*
First Place, 2015 Make It with Lard – Cookies Other Than Named
Second Place Overall, 2015 Make It with Lard – Desserts

RASPBERRY ALMOND THUMBPRINTS

For COOKIES:
1 c. butter, softened
2/3 c. granulated sugar
1/2 tsp. almond extract

2 c. all-purpose flour
1/4 c. raspberry jam

In large glass bowl, cream together butter, sugar and almond extract. Add flour; blend until well mixed. Cover and chill at least 1 hour. Shape into 1-inch balls; place on baking sheet. Make imprint in each ball; fill with 1/4 teaspoon jam. Bake in 350° oven 14 to 18 minutes. Cool on baking sheet for a few minutes; transfer to cooling rack.

For DRIZZLE:
1 c. powdered sugar
3/4 to 1 tsp. almond extract

2 to 3 1/2 tsp. water

Combine all ingredients. Add enough water and almond extract to make drizzle consistency. Drizzle over cooled cookies.

Dana Edleman, *Cambridge*
First Place, 2014 Adventureland Resort Intermediate – All Butter Cookies

CHOCOLATE CHIP AND BUTTERSCOTCH GLUTEN FREE COOKIES

1 c. creamy peanut butter
1/4 c. granulated sugar
1/2 c. packed dark brown
    sugar
1 large egg, beaten
1/2 tsp. baking soda
1/4 tsp. Himalayan rock salt
1/2 tsp. vanilla
1/2 c. milk chocolate chips
1/4 c. butterscotch chips
Pinch of Himalayan rock salt

Stir together peanut butter, sugars, egg, baking soda, salt and vanilla. Once stirred to even consistency, stir in chocolate and butterscotch chips. Using small melon baller, place 12 evenly-spaced scoops on ungreased baking sheet. Bake in 350° oven 10 to 12 minutes. Let cookies stand a few minutes on baking sheets before moving to wire racks to finish cooling.

Kevin Fisher, *Ankeny*
First Place, 2015 Hotel Pattee Cookie of the Year

DONNA AND LINDA'S PUMPKIN BARS

For BARS:
2 c. all-purpose flour
2 c. granulated sugar
1/2 tsp. salt
2 tsp. baking soda
2 tsp. cinnamon
4 eggs, slightly beaten
2 c. pumpkin puree
1 c. vegetable oil

Sift together dry ingredients into mixing bowl; add eggs, pumpkin and oil. Mix 3 minutes. Spread in ungreased jelly roll pan; bake in 350° oven 25 minutes.

For CREAM CHEESE FROSTING:
6 oz. cream cheese
1/2 c. margarine, softened
2 1/2 c. powdered sugar
2 tsp. milk
1 tsp. vanilla paste

Blend together cream cheese and margarine. Add remaining ingredients; mix until smooth. Spread over cooled bars.

Diane Rauh, *Des Moines*
First Place, 2015 Midwest Living and Gold Medal Flour Cookies – Pumpkin Bars

CHOCOLATE ALMOND BARS

2 c. cake flour
4 tbsp. cornstarch
1 c. butter
1/2 c. granulated sugar
1/2 c. packed brown sugar

1 beaten egg yolk
1 tsp. vanilla
12 oz. milk chocolate chips
1 c. sliced almonds, coarsely
  chopped

In medium bowl, whisk together flour and cornstarch; set aside. Cream together butter, sugar and brown sugar. Add beaten egg yolk, vanilla and flour mixture. Pat dough into bottom of lightly greased 9x13-inch baking dish. Bake in 350° oven 15 to 20 minutes until edges are light brown. Let cool slightly. In microwave-safe dish or double boiler, melt milk chocolate. Pour chocolate on top of cookie crust; spread evenly. Sprinkle nuts on top.

Peri Halma, *West Des Moines*
First Place, 2015 Midwest Living and Gold Medal Flour Cookies – Two-Layer Bars Other Than Named

RASPBERRY MASCARPONE-FILLED BROWNIES

For BROWNIE BASE:
4 oz. unsweetened chocolate,
  coarsely chopped
2/3 c. unsalted butter
2 c. granulated sugar
4 large eggs, lightly beaten

1 tsp. vanilla
1 1/4 c. unbleached all-
  purpose flour
1 tsp. baking powder
1 tsp. salt

Melt chocolate and butter in medium saucepan over low heat, stirring to blend. Remove pan from heat; whisk in sugar, eggs and vanilla. Stir in flour, baking powder and salt until just blended. Pour half the batter into greased and floured 9x13-inch baking dish and smooth out. Drop raspberry-mascarpone filling by spoonfuls atop batter in pan. Spread gently to cover chocolate batter. Spoon preserves over filling. Drop remaining chocolate batter by spoonfuls over filling. Spread chocolate batter gently and evenly so it reaches edges of pan. Bake in 350° oven 40 to 50 minutes or until toothpick inserted in center comes out clean. Cool pan completely on wire rack. Cut into bars.

(CONTINUED)

For RASPBERRY-MASCARPONE FILLING:

8 oz. mascarpone cheese,
softened to room
temperature

1/3 c. superfine sugar
1 large egg, lightly beaten
3/4 c. seedless red raspberry
preserves

In small mixing bowl, beat together mascarpone, sugar and egg until light, fluffy and well blended.

Amy Smith, *Winterset*
First Place, 2015 Kids, the King and Brownies

APPLESAUCE BARS WITH PECAN PRALINE TOPPING

For BARS:

1/4 c. butter, softened
1/2 c. packed brown sugar
1 egg
1 tsp. vanilla
1 c. applesauce
1 1/2 c. all-purpose flour
1 tsp. cinnamon

1/2 tsp. baking powder
1/2 tsp. baking soda
1/4 tsp. ground cloves
1/4 tsp. salt
1/2 c. chopped pecans
1 1/2 c. peeled, chopped
Granny Smith apples

Beat together butter and brown sugar until light and fluffy. Add egg and vanilla; beat until blended. Stir in applesauce until blended (mixture will look curdled). Sift together flour, cinnamon, baking powder, baking soda, cloves and salt. Stir into butter mixture until just blended. Fold in pecans and apples. Spread in lightly greased 9x13-inch baking pan.

For PRALINE TOPPING:

2/3 c. packed brown sugar
1 tbsp. all-purpose flour

3 tbsp. butter, softened
1 c. chopped pecans

Combine brown sugar, flour and butter; blend with fork. Stir in pecans until blended. Crumble mixture evenly over top of batter. Bake in 350° oven 30 to 35 minutes or until edges begin to pull away from sides of pan. Cool on wire rack; cut into bars. Garnish with caramel and pecans if desired.

Natalie Ridgway, *Johnston*
First Place, 2014 Midwest Living Cookies – Apple Bars

ORANGE & CRANBERRY GINGER OAT BARS

For FILLING:

12-oz. pkg. whole cranberries	1 tbsp. ginger
3/4 c. water	1 tbsp. grated orange zest
3/4 c. granulated sugar	

In saucepan, heat cranberries, water, sugar, ginger and orange zest until boiling. Cook over medium heat until all cranberries pop and mixture is thickened, about 10 minutes. Remove from heat; transfer to shallow plate or bowl. Refrigerate until cooled and very thick.

For CRUST AND TOPPING:

1 3/4 c. all-purpose flour	1 c. butter, softened
2 tsp. ginger powder	1 c. packed light brown sugar
1 tsp. baking powder	2 large eggs
1/2 tsp. salt	1 1/2 c. regular rolled oats

Sift together flour, ginger, baking powder and salt; set aside. Beat butter and brown sugar until light and fluffy. Add eggs, one at a time, beating well. Beat in sifted mixture and oats until just blended. Reserve about 1 1/2 cups of dough. Spread remaining dough in even layer into lightly greased 9x13-inch pan. Spoon cranberry filling over dough; spread in even layer. Using floured hands, sprinkle small clumps of reserved dough over cranberries. Bake in 350° oven 35 to 40 minutes.

Joseph Ridgway, *Johnston*
First Place, 2014 Adventureland Resort Junior – Cranberry Orange Bars

---

LUSCIOUS LEMON BARS

For CRUST:

1 c. all-purpose flour	1/2 c. powdered sugar
1/8 tsp. salt	1/2 c. butter, melted and cooled

Spray 8x8-inch baking pan with vegetable spray. Fit 8x16-inch piece of foil across pan bottom and up 2 sides as foil overhangs. Spray foil with vegetable spray. Mix flour, salt and powdered sugar in medium bowl; stir in butter to form dough. Press dough into pan. Bake in 325° oven on middle rack until pale golden, about 20 minutes.

(CONTINUED)

COOKIES, CANDIES AND SNACKS

For FILLING:

2 large eggs	1 tsp. finely grated lemon
3/4 c. granulated sugar	zest
1 1/2 tbsp. all-purpose flour	1 tsp. finely grated orange
6 tbsp. fresh lemon juice	zest

In medium bowl, whisk eggs, sugar, flour, lemon juice and zests. Add lemon mixture to crust; continue to bake until just set, about 20 minutes. Let cool in pan a few minutes. Using foil handles, lift bars from pan. Set on wire rack. Cool to room temperature. Cut into squares.

Diane Rauh, *Des Moines*
First Place, 2015 Midwest Living and Gold Medal Flour Cookies – Lemon Bars

WHITE CHOCOLATE ORANGE DROP COOKIES

For COOKIES:

3 c. all-purpose flour	3 tbsp. cream or whole milk
1 c. granulated sugar	1 tbsp. orange flavoring
1 1/2 tsp. baking powder	Orange food coloring
1/2 tsp. salt	(optional)
1 c. butter	12-oz. pkg. white chocolate
1 egg	chips

In large bowl, sift together dry ingredients. Cut in butter until evenly mixed. Add egg, cream, flavoring and food coloring if desired. Stir in white chocolate chips. Refrigerate at least 1 hour; scoop onto baking sheets. Bake in 350° oven 5 to 7 minutes, do not brown.

For FROSTING:

1/2 c. butter	1 tsp. vanilla or orange
4 c. powdered sugar	extract (if desired)
	Cream or milk

Beat together all ingredients, adding enough cream or milk to make spreading consistency. Frost cooled cookies.

Natalie Ridgway, *Johnston*
First Place, 2014 Midwest Living Cookies – Orange Drop

ORANGE BROWNIES

For BROWNIES:

1/2 c. butter
1/4 c. unsweetened cocoa
 powder
2 large eggs, beaten
1 c. granulated sugar
3/4 c. all-purpose flour

1/2 c. chopped pecans,
 toasted
2 tbsp. thawed orange juice
 concentrate
1 tbsp. grated orange zest
1/8 tsp. salt

In small saucepan, melt butter. Stir in cocoa until smooth; add eggs. Without stirring, add sugar, flour, pecans, orange juice concentrate, zest and salt. Pour cocoa mixture over top; mix well. Transfer to greased 8x8-inch baking pan. Bake in 350° oven 28 to 32 minutes or until edges begin to pull away from sides of pan. Cool completely on wire rack.

For FROSTING:

1 1/2 c. powdered sugar
3 tbsp. butter, softened

2 tbsp. thawed orange juice
 concentrate
1 tbsp. grated orange zest

Combine all ingredients; mix well. Spread over cooled brownies. Cut into bars; garnish with toasted pecans and grated orange zest if desired.

Missy Johansen, *Urbandale*
First Place, 2014 Midwest Living Cookies – Brownies (frosted)
Third Place Overall, 2014 Midwest Living Cookies

TRIPLE CHOCOLATE BROWNIE DELIGHT

For BROWNIES:

3 c. all-purpose flour
1 1/2 tsp. salt
1 c. unsweetened cocoa
 powder
3 c. granulated sugar

1 c. packed brown sugar
4 eggs plus 2 egg yolks
1 2/3 c. vegetable oil
1 c. water
1 tbsp. vanilla

Combine flour, salt, cocoa and sugars; set aside. In separate bowl, combine eggs, oil, water and vanilla; mix well. Pour wet ingredients into dry mixture; mix just until combined. Pour into foil-lined 9x13-inch pan. Bake in 350° oven 38 minutes; cool but do not cut.

(CONTINUED)

For WHIPPED GANACHE & TOPPINGS

1 c. heavy cream
2 c. semisweet chocolate
   chips
24-oz. pkg. almond bark

3 tbsp. plus 2 tsp. shortening,
   divided
1/2 c. milk chocolate chips

Heat cream and pour over semisweet chocolate; mix until melted and smooth. Cool to room temperature; whip until fluffy, about 2 minutes. Spread on cooled brownies. Freeze brownies 2 hours or overnight. While still frozen, remove from pan; cut to desired size. Return to freezer 1 hour. Melt almond bark and 3 tablespoons of shortening; mix until smooth. Dip brownies in almond bark; let set up and repeat. Melt milk chocolate chips and remaining shortening. Drizzle over almond bark.

Bridget Lottman, *Norwalk*
First Place, 2015 Midwest Living and Gold Medal Flour Cookies – Brownies (frosted)

PECAN PIE BARS

For CRUST:

3 c. all-purpose flour
3/4 c. granulated sugar

1/2 tsp. salt
1 c. cold butter, cubed

In large bowl, combine flour, sugar and salt. Cut in butter until crumbly. Press mixture into bottom and up sides of greased 10x15-inch baking pan. Bake in 350° oven 18 to 22 minutes or until crust edges begin to brown.

For FILLING:

4 eggs
1 1/2 c. granulated sugar
1 1/2 c. light corn syrup

1/4 c. butter, melted
1 1/2 tsp. vanilla
2 1/2 c. chopped pecans

Combine eggs, sugar, corn syrup, butter and vanilla. Stir in pecans. Pour over baked crust. Bake 25 to 30 minutes or until edges are firm and center is almost set. Cool on wire racks; cut into bars. Refrigerate before serving.

Jacob Van Patten, *Indianola*
First Place, 2015 Midwest Living and Gold Medal Flour Cookies – Pecan Bars

DARK CHOCOLATE BROWNIES

1/2 c. butter
4 oz. bittersweet chocolate
1/2 c. granulated sugar
1/2 c. packed dark brown
    sugar
2 eggs, beaten

1/2 c. all-purpose flour
1/2 tsp. baking powder
3/4 c. chopped walnuts
1/4 c. miniature semisweet
    chocolate chips

In double boiler or medium saucepan over water, melt butter and bittersweet chocolate. Stir until melted; remove from heat. Using a wooden spoon, stir sugars into chocolate mixture until smooth. Add eggs, beating with spoon until combined. In small bowl, combine flour and baking powder. Stir into chocolate mixture until smooth. Add nuts and chips. Spread in greased and floured 7x11-inch baking pan. Bake in 350° oven 25 minutes until top is set but still soft. Cool on wire rack.

Rita Johannsen, *Des Moines*
First Place, 2015 Midwest Living and Gold Medal Flour Cookies –
Brownies (unfrosted)

RICH BUTTERSCOTCH BARS

For BARS:
1/3 c. unsalted butter
12-oz. pkg. butterscotch
    chips
2 c. graham cracker crumbs
1 c. chopped and toasted
    unsalted nuts

8-oz. pkg. cream cheese,
    softened
15-oz. can sweetened
    condensed milk
1 tsp. vanilla
1 egg
1/4 c. all-purpose flour

In microwave-safe bowl, melt butter and butterscotch chips on high in 30 second intervals; stir until smooth. Stir in graham cracker crumbs and nuts; save one-fourth of the mixture and set aside. Press remainder into greased 9x13-inch baking pan. In large mixing bowl, beat cream cheese until fluffy; beat in sweetened condensed milk, vanilla, egg and flour. Pour over prepared crust. Top with remainder of graham cracker crumb mixture. Bake in 350° oven 25 to 30 minutes or until knife inserted in center comes out clean. Cool completely on wire rack. Cut into bars. Store in refrigerator in airtight container.

(CONTINUED)

COOKIES, CANDIES AND SNACKS

For ICING:

1/2 c. unsalted butter, softened	1/4 c. milk
3 1/2 c. powdered sugar	1 tsp. vanilla

In large mixing bowl, beat butter until fluffy. Beat in powdered sugar, milk and vanilla until smooth. Fill small resealable plastic bag. Cut a small hole in one corner; pipe onto bars in desired pattern.

Carolyn Maschmann, *Hartwick*
First Place, 2015 Midwest Living and Gold Medal Flour Cookies – Butterscotch Bars

DARK CHOCOLATE & MINT GANACHE STOUT BROWNIES

For BROWNIES:

1 c. Irish dry stout beer	3 large eggs
1/2 c. unsalted butter	1 tsp. vanilla
2 c. granulated sugar	3/4 tsp. salt
3/4 c. unsweetened cocoa powder	1 1/2 c. all-purpose flour
	Mint sprig (optional)

In saucepan, simmer beer over medium heat until reduced by half, about 20 minutes. Melt butter in microwave-safe bowl on high 2 minutes or until melted. Add sugar, cocoa, eggs, beer, vanilla, salt and flour, stirring after each addition. Pour into greased muffin tins. Bake in 350° oven 15 to 20 minutes until toothpick inserted in middle comes out clean. Cook for less time for chewier brownies. Remove from pan; dip half in ganache when cooled. Garnish with mint sprig if desired.

For CHOCOLATE MINT GANACHE:

1/2 c. heavy cream	1 tsp. peppermint extract
1/2 c. white chocolate chips	Green food coloring

In heatproof bowl, microwave cream on high 1 minute. Add chocolate chips; let stand 30 seconds to melt chips. Add peppermint extract and food coloring; stir together to combine.

Amber Wagner, *Prairie City*
First Place, 2015 World's Tallest Leprechaun St. Patrick's Treats

MOLASSES CRACKLES

2/3 c. vegetable oil
1 1/3 c. granulated sugar,
    divided
1 large egg
1/4 c. molasses

2 c. all-purpose flour
2 tsp. baking soda
1 tsp. cinnamon
1 tsp. ginger

In large bowl, combine oil and 1 cup of sugar. Add egg; beat well. Stir in molasses, flour, baking soda, cinnamon and ginger. Shape dough into 1 1/4-inch balls. Roll balls in remaining sugar. Place 3 inches apart on ungreased baking sheet. Bake in 350° oven 12 minutes.

Michael Kephart, *Carlisle*
First Place, 2015 Midwest Living and Gold Medal Flour Cookies – Crackles/Crinkles (any flavor)

PEANUT BUTTER CRUNCH BARS

For BARS:
1/3 c. margarine
1 1/2 c. granulated sugar
2 eggs
1/2 c. milk

1 1/2 c. all-purpose flour
1/2 tsp. salt
2 tsp. baking powder

Melt margarine in saucepan; remove from heat. Add sugar, eggs and milk; blend well. Add flour, salt and baking powder; mix well. Pour into greased and floured 10x15-inch sheet pan. Bake in 350° oven 15 to 20 minutes; cool.

For TOPPING:
2 c. (11 oz.) butterscotch
    chips

1 c. peanut butter
2 1/2 c. crushed corn flakes

Melt butterscotch chips in saucepan; remove from heat. Add peanut butter; stir until melted. Mix in crushed corn flakes; spread over top of bars. Cut into squares.

Angela Miller, *West Des Moines*
First Place, 2015 Midwest Living and Gold Medal Flour Cookies – Peanut Butter Bars

OLD FASHIONED SOUR CREAM COOKIES

For COOKIES:

1 c. shortening	6 1/2 c. all-purpose flour
2 c. granulated sugar	1 tsp. baking powder
2 eggs	1 tsp. salt
2 tsp. vanilla	1 c. sour cream
2 tsp. grated lemon zest	Walnut halves

Cream together shortening and sugar until light and fluffy. Add eggs, vanilla and lemon zest; beat well. Combine dry ingredients. Add dry ingredients in thirds with sour cream to sugar mixture; beating until smooth. Cover; chill dough 30 minutes. Drop onto baking sheets; sprinkle with sugar and lemon zest. Top with walnuts; flatten slightly. Bake in 375° oven 10 to 12 minutes or until lightly brown around edges.

For ICING:

1/4 tsp. lemon extract	1 to 1 1/2 c. powdered sugar
2 tbsp. milk	

Mix together all ingredients, adding powdered sugar to make desired consistency to drizzle over cooled cookies.

Natalie Ridgway, *Johnston*
First Place, 2014 Midwest Living Cookies – Sour Cream

GLUTEN FREE DUTCH LETTER BARS

1 c. softened butter	1 c. almond paste
2 eggs plus 1 egg yolk, reserve egg white	1 1/2 c. granulated sugar
	2 tsp. almond extract
2 c. gluten free flour	Sliced almonds
1/2 tsp. vanilla	Coarse sugar

Combine butter, eggs, egg yolk, flour, vanilla, almond paste, sugar and almond extract; mix well. Spread in 9x13-inch pan. Brush with beaten egg white. Sprinkle with sliced almonds and coarse sugar. Bake in 325° oven 30 minutes until light brown. Do not over bake.

Peri Halma, *West Des Moines*
First Place, 2014 Midwest Living Cookies – Gluten Free

LITTLE ALMOND BITES

1/2 c. granulated sugar
1/4 c. all-purpose flour
1/4 tsp. salt

7 oz. almond paste, crumbled
2 egg whites, room
    temperature
32 whole toasted almonds

In medium bowl, whisk together sugar, flour and salt; set aside. Combine almond paste and egg whites in large bowl; beat at medium speed about 3 minutes or until mixture is smooth. Gradually beat in sugar mixture. Drop mounds of dough onto parchment paper-lined baking sheets. Place an almond into each cookie. Bake in 350° oven 12 to 14 minutes. Cool cookies on baking sheets on wire racks 2 minutes; remove from baking sheets and cool on wire racks.

Kim Van Patten, *Indianola*
First Place, 2015 Midwest Living and Gold Medal Flour Cookies – Drop Cookies Other Than Named

CRANBERRY STREUSEL SHORTBREAD BARS

For CRUST AND STREUSEL:
10 1/2 oz. (1 c. plus 5 tbsp.)
    unsalted butter, melted
    and cooled to lukewarm
1 c. granulated sugar, divided
3/4 tsp. salt

2 large egg yolks
14 1/4 oz. (3 c. plus 3 tbsp.)
    unbleached all-purpose
    flour

Line a straight-sided 9x13-inch baking pan with aluminum foil, letting ends create an overhanging edge for easy removal. In medium bowl, stir together butter, 3/4 cups sugar and salt. Whisk in egg yolks. Stir in flour to make stiff dough. Transfer about 2 cups of dough to prepared pan; press mixture evenly into bottom. Prick dough all over with a fork. Refrigerate pan 30 minutes or freeze 5 to 7 minutes until dough is firm. Position a rack in center of oven and another rack near top. Bake dough in 325° oven on center rack until crust begins to set but does not brown on edges (center will not yet be firm), about 20 minutes. While crust bakes, prepare streusel and cranberry topping. For streusel, combine remaining sugar with reserved dough until crumbly. Mixture should hold together when pressed, but readily break into smaller pieces.

(CONTINUED)

For CRANBERRY TOPPING:

12-oz. pkg. fresh or frozen cranberries, rinsed and drained

1 c. granulated sugar
1/4 c. water

In medium saucepan, bring cranberries, sugar and water to boil over high heat. Reduce heat to medium high; continue to boil until liquid is reduced to thick syrup, 5 to 8 minutes. Remove from heat; let mixture cool 5 to 10 minutes. Syrup will continue to thicken as mixture cools. Spread evenly over hot crust; scatter streusel over cranberries. Do not crumble streusel too much or texture will be sandy. Increase oven to 350°; bake bars near top of oven until streusel is golden and set, about 25 minutes. Baking bars at top of oven helps streusel brown faster without overbrowning crust. Cool on wire rack until crust is completely firm, at least 1 hour. When bottom of pan is cool, carefully lift bars from pan using foil sides; transfer to cutting board. Separate foil from bars by sliding a spatula between bars and foil. Cut into bars.

Heidi Carter, *Clarinda*
First Place, 2014 Midwest Living Cookies – Three Layer Bars
Second Place Overall, 2014 Midwest Living Cookies

WHITE CHOCOLATE RUBY ROADS

3 1/2 c. all-purpose flour
1 tsp. baking soda
1 tsp. salt
1 c. butter, softened
1 c. granulated sugar
1 c. packed brown sugar
1 c. corn oil

1 egg
1 tsp. vanilla
1 c. crispy rice cereal
1 c. quick-cooking rolled oats
1 c. white chocolate chips
4 oz. dried cranberries

In medium bowl, whisk together flour, baking soda and salt. In large mixing bowl, cream together butter and sugars. Add oil, egg and vanilla. Add flour mixture, a little at a time, until combined. In separate bowl, combine cereal, oats, white chocolate chips and cranberries. Slowly add to cookie batter until combined. Drop by small cookie scoop onto parchment-lined baking sheet. Bake in 350° oven 10 to 12 minutes.

Claire Roorda, *Waukee*
First Place, 2015 Adventureland Resort Junior – White Chocolate Chip Cookies

LEMON PIE SANDWICH COOKIES

1 c. unsalted butter, room
  temperature
4 c. powdered sugar, divided
1/2 tsp. salt
2 tbsp. plus 1 tsp. fresh
  lemon juice, divided
  (1 to 2 lemons)

2 tbsp. grated lemon zest,
  divided
2 c. unbleached all-purpose
  flour
4 oz. cream cheese, room
  temperature
Powdered sugar for garnish

Beat butter, 2 cups powdered sugar and salt until smooth. Add 2 tablespoons lemon juice and 1 tablespoon zest. On low speed, add flour, one-half cup at a time, until just incorporated. Turn dough out onto board; roll dough into a log. Cover with plastic wrap. Refrigerate at least 1 hour and up to 24 hours. Remove from refrigerator; cut into thin 1/4-inch thick discs. Arrange discs on two silicone or parchment-lined baking sheets 1-inch apart. Bake in 350° oven until edges are just golden, about 20 minutes. Remove cookies from oven; transfer to wire rack to cool completely. Using mixer, mix cream cheese with remaining powdered sugar, 1 teaspoon lemon juice and remaining zest. Top half the cookies with cream cheese mixture; cover with another cookie to make a sandwich. Dust top of cookie sandwiches with powdered sugar and serve.

Trent Gilbert, *West Des Moines*
First Place, 2015 Adventureland Resort Intermediate – Sandwich Cookies

PEANUT BUTTER SHORTBREAD COOKIES

For SHORTBREAD:
1 1/2 c. butter
3/4 c. sifted powdered sugar
3/4 c. cornstarch

2 c. all-purpose flour
1/4 c. powdered peanut
  butter

In mixing bowl, beat butter until softened. Add powdered sugar, cornstarch, flour and peanut butter; mix well. Place dough on large piece of wax paper. Roll into square or a rectangle 3/4-inch thick; cover and refrigerate 30 minutes. Unwrap dough; cut into squares. Place on ungreased baking sheet about 1 inch apart. Bake in 350° oven 10 to 12 minutes or until bottoms turn brown. Cool on wire rack.

(CONTINUED)

For PEANUT BUTTER CREAM:

6 oz. cream cheese, room temperature

6 tbsp. butter, room temperature

3/4 c. natural creamy peanut butter

1 tsp. vanilla

1/2 c. powdered sugar

Beat cream cheese and butter until well blended. Add peanut butter and vanilla; mix well. Add powdered sugar; blend well. Place in quart freezer bag. Snip one corner off bag; pipe cream onto shortbread cookies.

For CHOCOLATE AND PEANUT BUTTER DRIZZLE:

1/3 c. semisweet chocolate chips

1/3 c. peanut butter chips

Place chocolate chips in small freezer bag; microwave about 1 minute. Snip small hole in corner of bag; pipe over peanut butter cream. Repeat with peanut butter chips. Refrigerate cookies.

Bridget Lottman, *Norwalk*
First Place, 2014 Midwest Living Cookies – Refrigerator (sliced)

DUTCH LETTER CIRCLES

1 c. butter, melted
8-oz. can almond paste
2 eggs
1 egg, separated
1 1/2 c. granulated sugar

2 c. all-purpose flour
2 tsp. almond extract
1/2 tsp. vanilla
Sliced almonds
Coarse sugar

Combine butter, almond paste, 2 eggs, 1 egg yolk, sugar, flour, almond extract and vanilla; blend well. Spread dough in 9x13-inch pan. Press dough into pan until it covers the bottom of pan. Brush with beaten egg white; sprinkle sliced almonds and coarse sugar over dough. Bake in 325° oven 25 to 30 minutes or until golden brown. Do not overbake. When cool, cut with circle cookie cutter and transfer to wire rack.

Olive Jean Tarbell, *Centerville*
First Place, 2014 Midwest Living Cookies – Unfrosted Other Than Named

PINEAPPLE DROP COOKIES

For COOKIES:
1/2 c. butter, softened
1 c. granulated sugar
2 eggs
1/4 c. crushed pineapple
1/2 tsp. vanilla

1/2 tsp. pineapple flavoring
2 c. all-purpose flour
1/2 tsp. baking soda
1/4 tsp. salt
1/2 c. finely chopped pecans

By hand, cream together butter and sugar; beat in eggs. Add pineapple, vanilla and pineapple flavoring; mix well. Add flour, baking soda and salt; mix well. Fold in nuts. Drop by spoonfuls onto parchment paper-lined baking sheet. Bake in 350° oven 10 to 12 minutes. Cookies will not brown on top. Cool completely before frosting.

For PINEAPPLE FROSTING:
3 tbsp. butter
1 tsp. pineapple flavoring

1 c. powdered sugar, sifted

Melt butter in saucepan; remove from heat. Stir in flavoring. Add powdered sugar; beat by hand until smooth. Frost cooled cookies.

Laura Wingler, *Cedar Rapids*
First Place, 2015 Midwest Living and Gold Medal Flour Cookies – Frosted Drop Cookies

---

MOM'S SUGAR COOKIES WITH A LEMON TWIST

For COOKIES:
1/2 c. butter
1/2 c. shortening
1 c. granulated sugar
3 eggs

3 1/2 c. all-purpose flour
1 tsp. baking soda
1 tsp. cream of tartar
1 1/2 tsp. vanilla

Cream together butter, shortening and sugar. Add eggs, one at a time. Blend in dry ingredients and vanilla; cover and chill dough. Roll out dough to 1/4-inch thickness; cut with cookie cutters. Place on parchment paper-lined baking sheets. Bake in 375° oven 8 to 10 minutes.

(CONTINUED)

For LEMON TWIST FROSTING:

4 tbsp. butter, softened
4 oz. cream cheese, softened
1/4 tsp. lemon extract
Zest of 1 lemon

Juice from 1/2 lemon
    (about 3 tsp.)
Pinch of salt
2 c. powdered sugar

Combine all ingredients except powdered sugar. Blend together; gradually add powdered sugar. Mix until smooth; spread on cooled cookies.

Connie Sherman, *Iowa City*
First Place, 2015 Midwest Living and Gold Medal Flour Cookies – Rolled Sugar (frosted)

SCANDINAVIAN ALMOND BARS

For ALMOND BARS:

1 3/4 c. all-purpose flour
2 tsp. baking powder
1/4 tsp. salt
1/2 c. butter, softened
1 c. granulated sugar

1 egg
1/2 tsp. almond extract
Milk
1/2 c. sliced almonds,
    coarsely chopped

Stir together flour, baking powder and salt; set aside. Beat butter with sugar until combined; add egg and almond extract. Stir in flour mixture. Divide dough into 4 equal parts; form each into 12-inch roll. Place about 5 inches apart on baking sheet. Using hands, slightly flatten each to approximately 3 inches wide. Brush with milk; sprinkle with almonds. Bake in 325° oven 12 to 15 minutes or until edges are lightly browned. While warm, slice diagonally into 1-inch pieces. Transfer to wire rack to cool. Drizzle with almond icing.

For ALMOND ICING:

1 c. powdered sugar
1/4 tsp. almond extract

3 to 4 tsp. milk

Beat together all ingredients, adding enough milk to make drizzle consistency.

Natalie Ridgway, *Johnston*
First Place, 2014 Midwest Living Cookies – Scandinavian
First Place Overall, 2014 Midwest Living Cookies

BLUE CHEESE SUGAR COOKIES

For COOKIES:
2 c. butter
2 c. granulated sugar
2 eggs
2 tsp. vanilla

4 tsp. baking powder
6 c. all-purpose flour
1/4 c. crumbled blue cheese

Mix together butter and sugar. Add eggs, vanilla and baking powder; mix well. Add flour; fold in blue cheese. Cover and chill dough 20 minutes. Roll out to 1/4-inch thickness; cut into desired shapes. Place on baking sheets. Bake in 400° oven 6 to 8 minutes.

For MAPLE FROSTING:
2 1/2 c. powdered sugar
4 tbsp. water
1 1/2 tbsp. meringue powder

1/2 tsp. maple extract
Food coloring

Mix together powdered sugar, water, meringue powder and maple extract. Add desired food coloring; mix well. Pipe on cookies.

Brooke Mickelson, *West Des Moines*
First Place, 2015 Midwest Living and Gold Medal Flour Cookies – Rolled Cookies Other Than Named

WHITE CHOCOLATE CRANBERRY BLONDIES

For BARS:
3/4 c. butter, cubed
1 1/2 c. packed light brown
    sugar
2 eggs
3/4 tsp. vanilla
2 1/4 c. all-purpose flour

1 1/2 tsp. baking powder
1/4 tsp. salt
1/8 tsp. ground cinnamon
1/2 c. dried cranberries
6 oz. white chocolate,
    chopped or chips

Melt butter; stir in brown sugar. Transfer to large bowl; set aside to cool to room temperature. Beat in eggs and vanilla. In separate bowl, combine flour, baking powder, salt and cinnamon. Gradually add to butter mixture. Stir in cranberries and chocolate. Spread in greased 9x13-inch pan. Bake in 350° oven 18 to 21 minutes. Cool on wire rack.

(CONTINUED)

For FROSTING:

8-oz. pkg. cream cheese, softened	6 oz. white chocolate, melted and divided
1 c. powdered sugar	1/2 c. dried cranberries, chopped
1 tbsp. grated orange zest	

Beat cream cheese, powdered sugar and orange zest until blended. Gradually add half the melted chocolate, beating until blended. Frost brownies. Sprinkle with cranberries and drizzle with remaining melted chocolate. Cut into bars; store in refrigerator.

Sophia Ridgway, *Johnston*
First Place, 2015 Midwest Living and Gold Medal Flour Cookies – Bar Cookies (age 12 and under)

PINEAPPLE JEWELS

3/4 c. butter, softened	1 tsp. vanilla
1/2 c. powdered sugar	1 1/2 c. all-purpose flour
2 large egg yolks, reserve whites	1 c. pineapple preserves
	Coarse sugar

Cream butter; add sugar and beat until smooth. Add egg yolks and vanilla; beat at medium speed until light and fluffy. Add flour; blend at low speed until thoroughly combined. Gather dough into ball; flatten to form disk. Wrap in plastic wrap; refrigerate 1 hour. Roll dough on floured board; cut out circles and place on baking sheets. Drop pineapple preserves by spoonful onto center of half of cookies. Brush outer edges of cookies with whisked egg whites; top with another circle of dough. Seal cookie edges with a fork. Brush tops of cookies with whisked egg whites; sprinkle with coarse sugar. Bake in 325° oven 15 to 17 minutes or until edges begin to brown.

For ICING:

1/4 tsp. vanilla	1 to 1 1/2 c. powdered sugar
2 tbsp. milk	

Mix together all ingredients, adding powdered sugar to make desired consistency to drizzle over cooled cookies.

Natalie Ridgway, *Johnston*
First Place, 2014 Midwest Living Cookies – Filled Cookies

GRANDMA'S ITALIAN COOKIES

For COOKIES:

1 c. butter, room temperature
4 oz. cream cheese
3/4 c. granulated sugar
3/4 c. packed brown sugar
2 tsp. anise extract
1/2 tsp. anise seed, crushed
3 eggs

2 1/2 c. all-purpose flour
2 tsp. baking powder
1 tsp. baking soda
1/2 tsp. salt
1 c. chopped and toasted
   macadamia nuts

Cream together butter, cream cheese, sugars, anise extract and anise seed. Add eggs, one at a time, mixing well. Combine dry ingredients; add to creamed mixture gradually. Stir in nuts. Spray and sugar 2 springform pans; place parchment paper on bottoms. Divide dough into pans. Bake in 325° oven 20 to 22 minutes just until golden brown. Cut into wedges; drizzle.

For DRIZZLE:

1 c. powdered sugar
1 tsp. anise extract

Water

Mix powdered sugar with extract; stir in water to make drizzle consistency. Drizzle cookies and let set before serving.

Bridget Lottman, *Norwalk*
First Place, 2014 Midwest Living Cookies – Bar Cookies Other Than Named

---

NO-BAKE PEANUT BUTTER CUP BARS

For CHOCOLATE CRUST:

2 tbsp. unsweetened cocoa
   powder
3 tbsp. pure maple syrup

1 tbsp. melted coconut oil
Pinch of salt
3/4 c. almond flour

In medium bowl stir together all ingredients until moist dough is formed. Press dough evenly into bottom of parchment paper-lined loaf pan. Place in freezer to set.

(CONTINUED)

For PEANUT BUTTER FILLING:

1/2 c. creamy peanut butter	1 tbsp. coconut oil
4 tbsp. pure maple syrup	Pinch of salt

Stir together all ingredients. Remove crust from freezer. Spread filling evenly over crust with spatula. Return pan to freezer to set.

For CHOCOLATE TOPPING:

1/4 c. unsweetened cocoa powder	1/4 c. melted coconut oil
	5 tbsp. maple syrup

Combine all ingredients; whisk well. Once mixture is smooth, pour over peanut butter layer. Return pan to freezer for 1 to 2 hours. Once bars are firm, use parchment paper to easily lift bars from pan. Use sharp knife to slice bars. Store in airtight container in refrigerator up to two weeks or in freezer for up to a month.

Holly Houg, *Urbandale*
First Place, 2015 Eating without Heating – Raw Vegan Dessert
First Place Overall, 2015 Eating without Heating

CHOCOLATE CRACKLE COOKIES

3/4 c. vegetable oil	2 tsp. vanilla
1 c. unsweetened cocoa powder	2 1/3 c. all-purpose flour
	2 tsp. baking powder
2 c. granulated sugar	1/2 tsp. salt
4 eggs	1 c. powdered sugar

Mix together oil, cocoa and granulated sugar. Blend in eggs, one at a time, until well mixed. Add vanilla; stir in flour, baking powder and salt. Chill several hours or overnight. Drop by teaspoonfuls into powdered sugar; roll in powdered sugar to shape into ball. Place on baking sheet. Bake in 350° oven 10 to 12 minutes. Do not overbake. Cool on wire racks; store in airtight container.

Charlotte Bowden, *Monroe*
First Place, 2015 Adventureland Resort Intermediate – Chocolate Crackle Cookies

JACKED-UP JALAPENO COOKIES

1 1/4 c. granulated sugar, divided
Zest of 3 limes, divided
2 1/2 c. all-purpose flour
1 tsp. baking soda
1 tsp. salt
1 tsp. cinnamon
1 1/2 tsp. ground cayenne
1/4 tsp. cumin
1/2 lb. butter, room temperature
3/4 c. packed brown sugar
1/2 c. powdered sugar
3.4-oz. pkg. cheesecake-flavored instant pudding
2 large eggs
2 tsp. lime juice
1 large jalapeno, seeded and finely chopped (about 1/4 c.)

For lime sugar, combine 3/4 cups granulated sugar with zest of 2 limes. Process well in food processor. Once blended, stir in remaining granulated sugar. Spread on rimmed baking sheet; allow to dry 1 hour. Can be refrigerated in airtight container for up to 1 month. Sift together flour, baking soda, salt, cinnamon, cayenne and cumin; set aside. In large bowl, beat together butter, brown sugar and powdered sugar until light and fluffy. Add instant pudding; mix well. Add eggs, lime juice, remaining lime zest and jalapeno, mixing until well blended. Slowly add flour mixture, mixing well. Using melon baller, scoop dough; roll in lime sugar. Drop dough onto ungreased baking sheet. Bake in 350° oven 10 to 12 minutes or until golden around edges. After one minute, transfer to wire rack to cool.

Sharon Krause, *Waukee*
First Place, 2015 Allspice Cookie Contest – Spiced Cookie (adult)
First Place Overall, 2015 Allspice Cookie Contest

CHOCOLATE MINT BROWNIES

For BROWNIES:
1 c. all-purpose flour
1 c. granulated sugar
1/2 c. melted butter
4 eggs
16 oz. chocolate syrup

In large bowl, beat flour, sugar, butter, eggs and chocolate syrup until smooth. Pour into greased and floured 9x13-inch pan. Bake in 350° oven 30 minutes; cool.

(CONTINUED)

COOKIES, CANDIES AND SNACKS

For MINT LAYER:

2 c. powdered sugar
1/2 c. melted butter
1 tbsp. water

1/2 tsp. wintergreen
flavoring
3 drops green food coloring

In small bowl, combine all ingredients; beat until smooth. Spread over cooled brownies.

For CHOCOLATE FROSTING:

3 c. powdered sugar
1/3 c. milk
1/4 c. butter, softened
2 tsp. vanilla

2 oz. unsweetened baking
chocolate, melted
5 oz. crème de menthe thins,
chopped
Melted semisweet chocolate

In small bowl, beat powdered sugar, milk, butter, vanilla and melted unsweetened chocolate until smooth. Spread over mint layer. Sprinkle chopped mint thins on top of brownies. Drizzle melted semisweet chocolate over top of brownies.

Robin Tarbell-Thomas, *Centerville*
First Place, 2015 Midwest Living and Gold Medal Flour Cookies – Brownies (flavored)

CREAMY DARK CHOCOLATE MOCHA FUDGE

1 1/3 c. granulated sugar
2/3 c. evaporated milk
7-oz. jar marshmallow creme
1/4 c. butter
1/4 c. coffee liqueur

2 tbsp. instant coffee
granules
12-oz. pkg. dark chocolate
chips
1 tsp. vanilla

In 2-quart saucepan combine sugar, milk, marshmallow creme, butter, liqueur and instant coffee. Heat to boiling over medium-high heat, stirring constantly. Boil 5 minutes; remove from heat. Stir in chocolate chips until melted. Stir in vanilla. Spread fudge into 8x8-inch baking pan lined with aluminum foil. Refrigerate until firm.

Emma Whitlock, *Indianola*
First Place, 2015 Chocolate Storybook Candies – Dark Chocolate

COOKIES, CANDIES AND SNACKS

KEY LIME COOKIES

For COOKIES:

2 2/3 c. unbleached all-
    purpose flour
1 tsp. baking soda
1/2 tsp. baking powder
1/2 tsp. salt

1 c. butter or vegan
    replacement, softened
1 1/2 c. granulated sugar
1 egg or egg replacer
1/2 tsp. vanilla
2 tbsp. lime juice
Zest of 1 large lime

Combine flour, baking soda, baking powder and salt in bowl; set aside. Cream butter and sugar. Prepare egg replacer if using. Add egg, vanilla, lime juice and zest to butter mixture. Add dry ingredients to wet ingredients in batches and blend. Drop tablespoon-sized dough balls on nonstick baking sheet. Bake in 350° oven 8 to 10 minutes or until lightly browned. Let stand on baking sheet several minutes before cooling on wire rack.

For ICING:

1/2 c. butter or vegan
    replacement, softened
4 c. powdered sugar

3 tbsp. key lime juice
1/8 tsp. salt
1 tsp. vanilla

Combine butter, powdered sugar, lime juice, salt and vanilla. Beat until fluffy. Frost cookies.

Jacqueline Riekena, *West Des Moines*
First Place, 2015 Key Lime Challenge – Key Lime Cookies

CINNAMON VANILLA SUGAR NUTS

2 tbsp. water
1/4 c. granulated sugar
1/2 tsp. cinnamon

1 1/2 c. raw nuts (any variety)
1 tsp. vanilla

In saucepan, bring water, sugar and cinnamon to a boil. When sugar dissolves, add nuts and vanilla; continue stirring 2 minutes. Remove from heat; stir vigorously until coated. Pour onto plate to cool.

Clarissa Ridgway, *Johnston*
First Place, 2015 Adventureland Resort Intermediate – Sugared Nuts

FALL FANTASY FLAVORED COOKIES

For COOKIES:

1/2 c. granulated sugar	2 tsp. baking soda
1/2 c. packed brown sugar	1/8 tsp. salt
3/4 c. butter	1 tsp. Ceylon true ground
1 egg	cinnamon
1/4 c. molasses	1/2 tsp. ginger powder
1 tsp. vanilla paste	1/4 tsp. ground cloves
2 1/4 c. all-purpose flour	Cinnamon-sugar

Cream together sugars and butter; add egg, molasses and vanilla paste. In separate bowl, combine flour, baking soda, salt, cinnamon, ginger and cloves. Slowly add flour mixture to sugar mixture until completely combined. Form into balls; roll balls in cinnamon-sugar. Place on greased baking sheet. Bake in 350° oven 10 minutes. Frost cookies.

For CREAM CHEESE FROSTING:

1/2 c. butter, softened	2 tbsp. maple sugar powder
8 oz. cream cheese, softened	3 1/2 c. powdered sugar
1 tbsp. vanilla paste	

Cream together butter and cream cheese until smooth. Add vanilla paste, maple sugar powder and powdered sugar. Beat until smooth.

Diana Bedwell, *Norwalk*
First Place, 2015 Allspice Cookie Contest – Frosted Cookie (adult)

CHIPOTLE PEANUT CLUSTERS

12-oz. pkg. semisweet	10-oz. can chipotle peanuts
chocolate chips	1 oz. vanilla candy coating

In heavy medium saucepan over low heat, heat chocolate, stirring constantly until melted. Stir in peanuts; spoon by rounded teaspoons onto wax paper-lined baking sheet. Heat vanilla candy coating in heavy small saucepan over low heat, stirring constantly until melted. Drizzle small amount of coating atop each cluster. Chill candy 30 minutes or until firm.

Megan McGuire, *Johnston*
First Place, 2014 Adventureland Resort Junior – Peanut Clusters

SUNBUTTER CRUNCH SHELL

1/2 c. coconut oil
1 c. sunflower seed butter
1/3 c. honey
1/16 tsp. salt

1 1/2 c. crispy rice cereal, finely chopped into crumbs

Place coconut oil in microwave-safe bowl. Melt oil, about 30 seconds. Add butter to oil; microwave 30 seconds more. Stir until smooth and creamy. Add honey and salt; stir and microwave 30 seconds. Add cereal; stir again. Pour onto cold ice cream and it will create a shell.

Holly Houg, *Urbandale*
First Place, 2015 My Favorite Ice Cream Topping – Sauces/Syrups

---

DARK CHOCOLATE ESPRESSO COOKIES

COOKIES:
1 1/4 c. all-purpose flour
1/4 c. unsweetened dark cocoa powder
1/4 c. unsweetened cocoa powder
1 tsp. instant coffee granules
1 tsp. baking soda
1/8 tsp. salt
1/2 c. salted butter, room temperature
1/2 c. packed dark brown sugar

1/2 c. granulated sugar
1 large egg
1 tsp. vanilla
1/4 c. coarsely ground dark chocolate espresso beans
1/3 c. semisweet or bittersweet chocolate chips
1 tbsp. milk
1/4 c. coarsely chopped pecans

In medium bowl, whisk together flour, dark cocoa, cocoa, coffee granules, baking soda and salt; set aside. Cream together butter and sugars; beat until fluffy. Add egg and vanilla; beat 2 minutes. Add dry ingredients to creamed mixture; stir until combined. Add ground espresso beans and chocolate chips. Stir in milk and pecans. Drop by tablespoonfuls onto parchment paper-lined baking sheet. Bake in 350° oven 9 to 10 minutes. If desired, top each cookie with a chocolate covered espresso bean prior to baking. When cool, drizzle with milk chocolate drizzle.

(CONTINUED)

For MILK CHOCOLATE DRIZZLE:

1/2 c. milk chocolate chips   **2 to 3 tbsp. milk**

Heat chips and milk in microwave until chips are melted; drizzle over cookies.

Luann Sutter, *Ankeny*
First Place, 2015 Midwest Living and Gold Medal Flour Cookies –
Chocolate Base

JAM BARS

2 1/2 c. all-purpose flour
2 c. granulated sugar
1 tsp. grated orange zest
1/2 tsp. salt
3/4 c. cold butter, cut into
    pieces

2 large eggs
1 tsp. vanilla
1 c. peach jam
Powdered sugar

Combine flour, sugar, zest and salt in bowl of food processor. Add butter, a few pieces at a time, until mixture is crumbly. Beat together eggs and vanilla until blended. While mixing, add eggs in steady stream. Process until mixture forms a dough. Turn out onto floured surface; shape into disk. Cut in half; roll out half between wax paper into 9x13-inch rectangle. Place into lightly greased 9x13-inch pan. Refrigerate until ready to bake. Roll out remaining dough to a strip at least 13 inches long and at least 5 inches wide. Slide dough onto baking sheet and freeze 30 minutes or until very cold. Just before assembling, remove pan from refrigerator and spread with thin layer of jam. Remove pastry from freezer; lift off top sheet of wax paper. Working quickly, cut dough into 1/2-inch-wide strips. Peel strips off wax paper, one at a time, and carefully arrange 5 strips lengthwise over jam, spacing about 1 1/2-inches apart. Trim edges to fit. Lay remaining strips about 1-inch apart to form a diamond pattern. Cut ends to fit pan. Bake in 350° oven 25 to 30 minutes or until edges are golden. Cool on wire rack. Garnish with sprinkle of powdered sugar or mixture of powdered sugar, vanilla and milk to drizzle or glaze.

Rose Ridgway, *Johnston*
First Place, 2015 Midwest Living and Gold Medal Flour Cookies – Jam Bars

COOKIES, CANDIES AND SNACKS

SWEET & SPICY PECANS

3/4 c. granulated sugar
1 tbsp. kosher salt
1 tbsp. chili powder
2 tsp. cinnamon

2 tsp. cayenne pepper
1 large egg white
4 c. pecan halves

In small bowl, whisk sugar, salt, chili powder, cinnamon and cayenne. In large bowl, beat egg white until frothy. Add pecans and spiced sugar; toss to coat. Spread nuts on baking sheet sprayed with nonstick cooking spray; bake in 300° oven 45 minutes, stirring once, until browned. Let nuts cool on baking sheet, stirring occasionally. Spiced nuts can be stored in airtight container up to 2 days or frozen 1 month.

Sharon Krause, *Waukee*
First Place, 2015 Chocolate Storybook Candies – Sweetened Nuts
Second Place Overall, 2015 Chocolate Storybook Candies – Variations

CHERRY BROWNIE COOKIES

For COOKIES:
18.3-oz. pkg. fudge brownie
　mix
1/4 c. water
1/4 c. vegetable oil
1 egg
1 tsp. cherry flavoring

Chocolate fudge filling
　(recipe below)
2, 10-oz. jars maraschino
　cherries, with stems
1/2 c. powdered sugar

In medium bowl, combine brownie mix, water, oil, egg and flavoring. Use spoon and beat until well blended (about 50 strokes). Fill greased 1 3/4-inch miniature muffin cups two-thirds full with batter. Bake in 350° oven 15 minutes or until wooden toothpick inserted into center comes out with fudgy crumbs (do not overbake). Cool slightly in pans; loosen edges with tip of knife; remove from pans. Turn each brownie onto wax paper-lined tray while warm. Make 1/2-inch indentation on top of each brownie with end of wooden spoon; cool completely. Prepare chocolate fudge filling. Drain cherries, reserve liquid. Let cherries stand on paper towels to dry. Combine powdered sugar with enough reserved liquid to form thin glaze. Spoon or pipe about 1 teaspoon chocolate fudge filling into indentation of each brownie. Gently press cherry into filling; drizzle with powdered sugar glaze.

(CONTINUED)

For CHOCOLATE FUDGE FILLING:

3 oz. cream cheese,
    softened
1 tsp. vanilla
1/4 c. light corn syrup

3 squares unsweetened
    chocolate, melted and
    cooled
1 c. powdered sugar

Beat cream cheese and vanilla in small bowl until smooth. Slowly pour in corn syrup, beating until well blended. Add chocolate; beat until smooth. Gradually add powdered sugar, beating until well blended and smooth.

Olive Jean Tarbell, *Centerville*
First Place, 2014 Midwest Living Cookies – Drop or Shaped

SICILIAN LEMON & FIG TRUFFLES

10 oz. white chocolate
8-oz. pkg. cream cheese
2 tsp. grated lemon zest
10 to 20 drops lemon oil
    (to taste)

3 c. powdered sugar
4 tbsp. fig preserves
12 oz. dark chocolate
    coating

Melt white chocolate in double boiler; set aside to cool slightly. Blend cream cheese, lemon zest, lemon oil and powdered sugar in bowl. Add melted chocolate to cream cheese mixture; mix until completely combined. Add fig preserves; mix well. Scoop mixture into 1-inch balls for large candies or melon baller for smaller bite-size chocolates. Chill truffle balls 45 minutes, then roll into rounded shape. Freeze truffle balls 15 minutes. They should be as solid as possible before dipping in melted chocolate. Melt coating chocolate in double boiler over simmering water or in microwave. Using fork, dip and cover truffles in warm chocolate. Work quickly so they do not melt. Place on nonstick surface. Decorate by drizzling any leftover coating over chocolates. Chill overnight to set chocolate.

Lisa Alessandro, *Winterset*
First Place, 2014 Chocolate Storybook Candies – Truffles
First Place Overall, 2014 Chocolate Storybook – Chocolate Works
First Place 2014 Piper's Homemade Candies – Candies Other Than Named
Second Place Overall, 2014 Piper's Homemade Candies

SALTY CHURRO TOFFEE SNACK MIX

5 c. oyster crackers
1 c. butter
1 c. packed brown sugar
1 tsp. vanilla

2 1/2 tsp. Korintje ground
cinnamon, divided
2 tbsp. vanilla sugar
1 tsp. kosher salt

Line baking sheet with foil; spread crackers evenly on baking sheet; set aside. In medium saucepan, combine butter and brown sugar. Stirring constantly, bring mixture to boil; boil 2 minutes. Remove from heat; stir in vanilla and 1 1/2 teaspoons cinnamon. Pour immediately on top of crackers. Using rubber spatula, stir and coat crackers evenly with mixture. Bake crackers in 350° oven 10 minutes, until crackers appear bubbly all over. While crackers are in oven, combine vanilla sugar, remaining cinnamon and salt. Remove crackers from oven; sprinkle immediately with salt/cinnamon mixture. Let crackers cool; break into pieces. Serve immediately or store in airtight container for up to 1 week.

Katherine Kilkenny, *Grimes*
First Place, 2015 Allspice Snack Mix – Sweet 'n Salty

APPLE HAZELNUT BLONDIES

For COOKIES:
1 c. hazelnuts
3/4 c. granulated sugar
3/4 c. packed light brown
 sugar
1/2 c. butter, melted
2 eggs, lightly beaten
1 tsp. vanilla

1 c. whole wheat flour
1 c. all-purpose flour
2 tsp. baking powder
1/4 tsp. salt
2 c. peeled, cored and
 chopped Fuji apples

Place nuts on rimmed baking sheet. Bake in 350° oven 10 minutes. Cool slightly; rub with fingers to remove skin. Chop nuts and reserve. In large bowl, combine sugars, butter, eggs and vanilla. In separate bowl, whisk together flours, baking powder and salt; stir into sugar mixture until dry ingredients are just moistened. Fold in apples and 1/2 cup chopped nuts. Spoon batter into greased 12-cavity brownie pan, about 1/3 cup into each cavity. Bake in 350° oven 30 minutes or until toothpick inserted into center comes out clean. Cool on wire rack 30 minutes; turn out onto rack to cool completely.

(CONTINUED)

For MAPLE ICING:

8 oz. cream cheese, softened   **2 tbsp. maple syrup**
1 c. powdered sugar   **3/4 tsp. vanilla**

In large bowl, beat cream cheese until smooth. Gradually beat in powdered sugar; add maple syrup and vanilla. Beat until smooth. Frost each brownie with generous 2 tablespoons icing. Sprinkle with remaining 1/2 cup chopped hazelnuts.

Cassandra Hyatt, *Ankeny*
First Place, 2015 Midwest Living and Gold Medal Flour Cookies – Blondies

---

CHOCOLATE COVERED CARAMELS

For CARAMELS:

2 c. granulated sugar   **1/4 tsp. sea salt**
1 1/2 c. light corn syrup   **1 c. heavy cream**
1 c. half and half   **2 tsp. vanilla**
1 c. butter

In heavy saucepan, bring sugar, corn syrup, half and half, butter and sea salt to rolling boil. Gradually add cream, making sure boil is not disturbed. Cook until mixture reaches hard ball stage (260°). Remove from heat; add vanilla. Stir; pour into greased 8x8-inch pan. Cool; cut into squares.

For DIPPING CHOCOLATE:

8 oz. dipping chocolate   **Roasted pecans with sea salt**
10 Caramels (recipe above)

Melt dipping chocolate over low heat in double boiler. Using dipping fork, dip each piece of caramel; place on wax paper to set up. Place pecans on each piece before completely dry.

Harold Magg, *Spirit Lake*
First Place, 2014 Chocolate Storybook Candies – Candy Other Than Named
First Place Overall, 2014 Chocolate Storybook Candies – Variations of Candy

FRENCH MACAROONS

For COOKIES:
1 2/3 c. powdered sugar
1 c. almond flour
3 egg whites, room
    temperature

1/4 tsp. cream of tartar
1/4 c. granulated sugar
Food coloring

Sift together powdered sugar and almond flour. Beat egg whites and cream of tartar until foamy. Beat in granulated sugar until shiny, stiff peaks form. Add coloring if desired. Quickly fold in sifted sugar and almond flour. Spoon into pastry bag with 1/2-inch tip and pipe 1 1/2-inch circles onto parchment paper-lined baking sheets. Sharply tap baking sheet three times on the counter; let macaroons set 30 minutes to form hard skin on top. Bake in 295° oven 10 to 11 minutes. Let cool; fill with Italian buttercream. These are best if refrigerated in an airtight plastic container a few days then served at room temperature.

For ITALIAN BUTTERCREAM:
4 egg whites
1 1/4 c. granulated sugar

1 1/2 c. unsalted butter, room
    temperature
1 tsp. vanilla

In heatproof bowl set over saucepan of simmering water, combine egg whites and sugar. Cook, whisking constantly until sugar dissolves and mixture is at 160°. Remove from heat. Beat on high speed until stiff peaks form. Continue beating until mixture is fluffy and cooled, about 6 minutes. On low-medium speed, add butter, several tablespoons at a time, beating well after each addition. Beat in vanilla. Beat on lowest speed to eliminate any air bubbles. Stir with rubber spatula until smooth. Spread 2 tablespoons buttercream on flat sides of half the macaroons; sandwich with other halves.

Marianne Carlson, *Jefferson*
First Place, 2015 Midwest Living and Gold Medal Flour Cookies –
Macaroons
First Place Overall, 2015 Midwest Living and Gold Medal Flour Cookies

TOFFEE

3/4 c. chopped pecans
2 c. butter
2 2/3 c. granulated sugar

1/3 c. water
1/4 c. light corn syrup
1 lb. milk chocolate, chopped

Toast pecans by spreading on baking sheet. Place in 325° oven approximately 10 minutes. Stir every 3 to 4 minutes. Remove from oven; let pecans cool. Line 12x16-inch cookie sheet with aluminum foil; spay foil with nonstick spray. In large, heavy saucepan over medium heat, combine butter, sugar, water and corn syrup. Stir constantly to dissolve sugar and melt butter. Insert candy thermometer. Bring candy to boil; continue to cook, stirring frequently until mixture reaches 300°. Remove from heat; pour into prepared pan. Cover with chocolate. Allow to melt then spread with offset spatula. Sprinkle pecans on top of chocolate. When set, break into pieces. Store in airtight container.

Cynthia Murphy, *Des Moines*
First Place, 2015 Chocolate Storybook Candies – Toffee

MILK CHOCOLATE ALMOND TOFFEE

1 c. butter
1 1/4 c. granulated sugar
2 tsp. honey
1/4 tsp. cream of tartar

1 c. chopped and toasted
  slivered almonds,
  divided
1 tsp. almond extract
1 c. milk chocolate chips

Line 9x13-inch pan with aluminum foil; butter foil. Melt butter in medium saucepan over medium heat. Add sugar, honey and cream of tartar; stir until sugar dissolves. Increase heat to medium-high. Cook until mixture registers 310° on candy thermometer, stirring occasionally, about 11 minutes. Stir in 1/2 cup almonds and almond extract. Immediately pour toffee into prepared pan. Let stand 1 minute. Sprinkle with chocolate. Let stand 2 minutes to soften. Spread chocolate with back of spoon over toffee until melted and smooth. Sprinkle with remaining almonds. Refrigerate until firm; break into pieces.

Emma Whitlock, *Indianola*
First Place, 2015 Piper's Homemade Candies – Candies
Second Place Overall, 2015 Piper's Homemade Candies

CHOCOLATE FUDGE

4 c. granulated sugar
2 1/2 oz. unsweetened cocoa
    powder
4 c. heavy cream
2 tbsp. light corn syrup
1/4 tsp. sea salt

1 1/2 tsp. vanilla
2 tbsp. butter
1/2 tsp. black walnut flavoring
1 c. chopped roasted black
    walnuts

Sift together sugar and cocoa. In saucepan, combine cream and sugar mixture. Stir over medium-high heat until sugar is dissolved. When boiling, add corn syrup. Cook to firm ball stage (242° to 248°). Pour into large bowl; add salt, vanilla, butter and black walnut flavoring. Do not stir. Cool 30 minutes. Add nuts; beat with mixer until thick and loses gloss. Pour into 9x13-inch pan.

Harold Magg, *Spirit Lake*
First Place, 2015 Piper's Homemade Candies – Fudge
First Place Overall, 2015 Piper's Homemade Candies
First Place, 2015 Chocolate Storybook Candies – Chocolate

BACON & CHOCOLATE BRITTLE BITES

3 c. granulated sugar
1 c. light corn syrup
1 c. water
1 lb. apple wood smoked
    bacon, cooked and
    coarsely chopped*

16-oz. pkg. raw peanuts
    with skins
1/4 tsp. sea salt
1 tsp. vanilla
2 tbsp. butter
1 tbsp. baking soda

Coat inside of cooking pan with butter to keep sides clean. Bring sugar, corn syrup and water to a boil on medium-high heat. Do not stir. Boil to hard ball stage (250°). Add bacon and raw peanuts. Stir continually as you continue to heat until temperature reaches caramel stage (342°). Remove from heat; add salt, vanilla, butter and baking soda; mix well. Pour onto greased pan. Let stand until mixture begins to set. When edges begin to become firm pull up and out to stretch. It will be hot but become brittle as it cools. Continue to stretch and then carefully snap into smaller pieces. Pack together then pour chocolate topping over pieces. *If desired, the bacon may be omitted from this recipe.

(CONTINUED)

For CHOCOLATE TOPPING:

| 1 c. dark chocolate baking chips | 1/4 c. heavy cream |
| | 1 tsp. chopped bacon or sea salt |

Combine chocolate and cream in double boiler or bowl. Heat on stove or microwave 1 to 2 minutes, stirring every 15 seconds, until chocolate is melted. Spread over arranged Bacon and Peanut Brittle. Cool 5 minutes; sprinkle with chopped bacon or sea salt if desired. Refrigerate until completely cooled.

Phil Dicks, *Grundy Center*
First Place, 2015 Chocolate Storybook Candies – Chocolate & Bacon
First Place Overall, 2015 Chocolate Storybook Candies – Chocolate Works

BAKED BUTTERMILK CORN DONUTS

For DONUTS:

1/2 c. butter, melted	3 c. all-purpose flour
1/2 c. vegetable oil	1 tbsp. baking powder
2/3 c. buttermilk	1/2 tsp. baking soda
3 eggs	1 tsp. salt
2 c. granulated sugar	1 tsp. cinnamon
1 c. applesauce	12-oz. pkg. frozen golden
2 tsp. vanilla	sweet corn, thawed

In large bowl, combine butter, oil, buttermilk, eggs, sugar, applesauce and vanilla. In separate bowl, stir together flour, baking powder, baking soda, salt and cinnamon. Add to butter mixture; stir to combine. Stir in corn. Fill greased doughnut pans. Bake in 350° oven 15 to 18 minutes. Remove from pan and cool.

For FROSTING:

| 2 c. powdered sugar | 1 tsp. vanilla |
| 1/4 c. butter, softened | 3 to 4 tbsp. milk |

Mix together all ingredients, adding enough milk to make spreading consistency. Frost donuts while slightly warm.

Leeah Hartman, *Des Moines*
First Place, 2015 Locally Grown – Kids (ages 7-12)

COOKIES, CANDIES AND SNACKS

TRUFFLES

2/3 c. heavy cream
12 oz. dark Belgian chocolate
1 tsp. butter rum extract
1 c. sweetened coconut
flakes

Heat cream in heavy 2-quart pan just until boiling. Remove from heat; stir in chocolate. Stir until chocolate is melted; add extract and whisk until smooth. Pour into medium bowl. Chill 3 hours or until firm. Form into teaspoon-size balls; roll in coconut. Chill.

Jeanene Peiffer, *Sigourney*
First Place, 2015 Chocolate Storybook Candies – Truffles
Second Place Overall, 2015 Chocolate Storybook Candies – Chocolate
Works

OLD FASHIONED PEANUT BRITTLE

2 c. granulated sugar
1 c. light corn syrup
1/2 c. water
1 c. butter
3 c. raw peanuts
1/4 c. shredded coconut
1 tsp. baking soda

In large saucepan, combine sugar, corn syrup and water. Cook over medium heat, stirring, until sugar dissolves. Bring to boil; blend in butter. Begin to stir frequently when syrup reaches thread stage (about 230°). When temperature reaches 280° (soft-crack stage), add peanuts. Stir constantly until hard-crack stage (300°) is reached. Remove from heat; stir in coconut and quickly stir in baking soda. Mix well. Pour onto 2 buttered baking sheets or jelly roll-size baking pans. As peanut brittle cools, stretch it out thinner by lifting and pulling at edges with forks. Loosen from pans as soon as possible and turn over. Break hardened candy into smaller pieces; store in airtight container.

Susan Schultz, *Haverhill*
First Place, 2015 Iowa's Best Peanut Brittle

TOFFEE PECAN CREAM FUDGE

2 c. granulated sugar
1 c. packed brown sugar
1 c. heavy cream
1/2 c. butter
7-oz. jar marshmallow creme

11 oz. white chocolate chips
1 tsp. vanilla
1 c. toffee chips
2/3 c. chopped and toasted
pecans

In heavy saucepan, combine sugars, cream and butter. Heat until sugar is dissolved. Bring to full boil; boil 4 minutes. Stir in marshmallow creme, chocolate chips and vanilla. Add toffee chips and pecans. Pour into greased 9x9-inch pan. Cut when cool.

Carole Miller, *Otley*
First Place, 2014 Chocolate Storybook Candies – Fudges Other Than Named

ALMOND RUM TRUFFLES

16 oz. extra dark 70%
chocolate, divided
1/3 c. heavy cream
2 tbsp. amaretto

2 tbsp. rum cream liqueur
2 tbsp. powdered sugar
1/4 c. finely chopped
blanched almonds

Place half the chocolate in large mixing bowl. Put cream in saucepan; bring to boil over medium heat. Stir in amaretto and rum liqueur. Pour over chocolate in mixing bowl; let stand 1 minute. Whip until thoroughly blended; allow to cool slightly. Whip again until mixture has lightened. Chill in refrigerator 6 hours or in freezer 2 hours. Line baking sheet with parchment paper. Scoop 1-inch diameter mounds; place on baking sheet. Cover with plastic wrap; chill 6 hours or in freezer 2 hours. Dust hands with powdered sugar; roll mounds into balls. Cover; return to freezer 2 hours. Remove from freezer; allow to come almost to room temperature. Melt remaining chocolate. Dip each ball in melted chocolate, coating completely; shake off excess. Place on baking sheet lined with parchment paper. Sprinkle finely chopped almonds on top immediately after dipping. Chill until firm. Store in sealed container in refrigerator. Serve at room temperature.

Rebecca Howe, *Des Moines*
First Place, 2014 Chocolaterie Stam Chocolates – Truffles

COOKIES, CANDIES AND SNACKS

TOFFEE

1/2 c. butter
3/4 c. packed brown sugar

2 oz. Belgian dark chocolate
2 tbsp. pecan pieces

Butter 9x9-inch baking pan; set aside. In heavy saucepan, heat butter and sugar to boiling, stirring constantly. Boil over medium heat, stirring constantly, 7 minutes. Immediately spread mixture into prepared pan. Melt chocolate 1 minute in microwave on high. Spread over toffee mixture while hot; sprinkle nuts over top. Cut into pieces.

Jeanene Peiffer, *Sigourney*
First Place, 2014 Chocolate Storybook Candies – Toffee

MAPLE PECAN FUDGE

3 c. packed light brown sugar
1 c. heavy cream
2 tbsp. butter

1 tsp. maple flavoring
1/3 c. chopped toasted
pecans

In heavy saucepan, combine brown sugar, cream and butter. Heat and cook to soft ball stage (234° to 241°). Remove from heat; allow to cool until lukewarm. Add flavoring; beat until candy loses its gloss and has creamy appearance. Stir in pecans. Spread into buttered 8x8-inch pan. Cut into desired size pieces when cool.

Carole Miller, *Otley*
First Place, 2015 Chocolate Storybook Candies – Maple Nut

SALTED HONEY CRISPY CEREAL TREATS

3 tbsp. butter
1/3 c. honey
1 tsp. salt

9 oz. marshmallows
6 c. crispy rice cereal

Melt butter over low heat in large saucepan. Add honey, salt and marshmallows; stir continuously over low heat until marshmallows are completely melted. Add cereal; remove from heat, stirring until combined. Spread into greased 8x8-inch pan; set aside to cool and cut.

Natalie Ridgway, *Johnston*
First Place, 2015 Foods Made with Honey – Rice Krispie Bars

CREAMY CARAMELS

2 c. granulated sugar
1 1/2 c. light corn syrup
1 c. half and half
1 c. butter
1/4 tsp. sea salt

1 c. heavy cream
2 tsp. vanilla
4 oz. chopped roasted
   pecans

In heavy saucepan, bring sugar, corn syrup, half and half, butter and sea salt to rolling boil. Gradually add cream, making sure boil is not disturbed. Cook until mixture reaches hard ball stage (260°). Remove from heat; add vanilla and nuts. Pour into greased 8x8-inch pan. Cool and cut into squares. Wrap each square individually.

Harold Magg, *Spirit Lake*
First Place, 2014 Chocolate Storybook Candies – Caramels
Second Place Overall, 2014 Chocolate Storybook Candies – Variations of Candy

---

OLD FASHIONED FUDGE

4 c. granulated sugar
3/4 c. unsweetened cocoa
   powder
1/8 tsp. salt

2 tbsp. light corn syrup
1 1/3 c. half and half
1/2 c. butter
2 tbsp. vanilla

In saucepan, combine sugar, cocoa, salt and corn syrup. Mix in half and half. Bring to boil, stirring constantly, over medium heat. Add candy thermometer, stop stirring. Cook until temperature reaches 234°. Pour into greased bowl; add butter and vanilla. Do not stir. Let cool to 110°. Beat with wooden spoon until fudge loses its gloss. Pour into greased 8x8-inch pan. Cool; cut into squares.

Marianne Carlson, *Jefferson*
First Place, 2014 Chocolate Storybook Candies – Basic Fudge (no marshmallow creme)
Third Place Overall, 2014 Chocolate Storybook Candies – Fudge

NUTTY TOFFEE POPCORN

11 c. popped popcorn
1 c. toasted pecans
1 c. toasted slivered almonds
1 1/3 c. packed brown sugar
1 c. butter

1/2 c. light corn syrup
1/2 tsp. cream of tartar
1 tsp. vanilla
1/2 tsp. baking soda

In large bowl, combine popcorn and nuts. In heavy saucepan, combine brown sugar, butter, corn syrup and cream of tartar. Stir until sugar dissolves. Cook, without stirring, over medium heat until thermometer reaches 311°. Remove from heat; stir in vanilla and baking soda. Immediately pour over popcorn and mix. Spread out onto 2 greased 10x15-inch pans. Cool completely; break into pieces.

Marianne Carlson, *Jefferson*
First Place, 2015 Chocolate Storybook Candies – Popcorn
Third Place Overall, 2015 Chocolate Storybook Candies – Variations

SPECIAL DARK FUDGE

4 c. granulated sugar
2 1/2 oz. unsweetened dark
    cocoa
4 c. heavy cream
2 tbsp. light corn syrup

1/4 tsp. sea salt
1 1/2 tsp. vanilla
2 tbsp. butter
1 c. roasted chopped mixed
    nuts with sea salt

Sift sugar and cocoa. In saucepan, combine cream and cocoa mixture. Stir over medium-high heat until sugar dissolves. When boiling, add corn syrup. Boil until firm ball stage (244° to 248°). Pour into large bowl. Add salt, vanilla and butter. Do not stir. Cool 30 minutes. Beat with mixer until thick and loses gloss; add nuts. Pour into greased 9x13-inch pan. Cool and cut pieces as desired.

Harold Magg, *Spirit Lake*
First Place, 2015 Chocolate Storybook Candies – Dark Chocolate

MAPLE NUT FUDGE

1 c. granulated sugar
2 c. packed brown sugar
3/4 c. heavy cream
1/4 c. light corn syrup

1 tsp. maple flavoring
3 tbsp. butter
Pinch of salt
1/2 c. chopped pecans

In heavy saucepan, combine sugars, cream and corn syrup. Cook until sugar is dissolved. Bring to full boil; cook to soft ball stage (234° to 241°). Cool in pan until lukewarm. Add maple flavoring, butter and salt; beat until smooth and fudge loses its gloss. Add nuts; pour into buttered 8x8-inch pan. Cut when cool.

Carole Miller, *Otley*
First Place, 2014 Piper's Homemade Candies – Fudge
First Place Overall, 2014 Piper's Homemade Candies

CHOCOLATE DIPPED CHERRIES

30 maraschino cherries with
    stems
1 1/2 tbsp. butter, softened
1 1/2 tbsp. light corn syrup

1 tsp. almond extract
1 1/3 c. powdered sugar
1/2 lb. chocolate coating

Drain cherries on paper towels several hours. Combine butter, corn syrup and almond extract. Stir in powdered sugar; knead until smooth. Cover and chill 1 hour. Shape about 3/4 teaspoon mixture around each cherry. Place upright on wax paper-covered baking sheet. Chill until firm. Melt chocolate; dip cherries into chocolate coating. Place on wax paper-lined baking sheet until coating is firm. Store in cool, dry place.

Penny Murphy, *Des Moines*
First Place, 2014 Chocolate Storybook Candies – Chocolate Dipped Fruit or Nuts

CARAMELS

1 c. butter
2 1/4 c. packed brown sugar
1/8 tsp. salt
1 c. light corn syrup

15-oz. can sweetened
    condensed milk
1 tsp. vanilla

Melt butter in heavy 3-quart saucepan. Add brown sugar, salt and corn syrup; mix well. Gradually add milk, stirring constantly. Cook and stir over medium heat to firm ball stage (245°), 12 to 15 minutes. Remove from heat; stir in vanilla. Pour into greased 9x9-inch pan. Cool; cut into squares.

Robin Tarbell-Thomas, *Centerville*
First Place, 2014 Chocolaterie Stam Chocolates – Caramels
First Place Overall, 2014 Chocolaterie Stam Chocolates

VANILLA FUDGE

4 c. granulated sugar, sifted
4 c. heavy cream
2 tbsp. light corn syrup
1/4 tsp. sea salt

1 1/2 tsp. clear vanilla,
    divided
2 tbsp. butter
2 oz. white chocolate
1 c. chopped roasted pecans

In saucepan, combine sugar and cream. Stir over medium-high heat until sugar is dissolved. When boiling, add corn syrup. Boil until firm ball stage (242° to 248°). Pour into large bowl; add salt, vanilla and butter. Do not stir. Cool 30 minutes or until lukewarm. Add white chocolate. Before beating with mixer, add pecans. Beat until thick and loses gloss. Pour into greased 9x13-inch pan. Cool and cut into squares.

Harold Magg, *Spirit Lake*
First Place, 2014 Chocolate Storybook Candies – Vanilla

ON THE GO SNACK MIX

1 1/2 c. unsalted jumbo cashews
1 1/2 c. natural whole almonds
1 c. dried cranberries
1 c. golden raisins
1/2 c. dark chocolate blueberries

Mix together cashews, almonds, cranberries and raisins. Scoop 1/2 cup portions into individual snack-size zipper bags. Sprinkle a few chocolate pieces into each bag.

Angela Miller, *West Des Moines*
First Place, 2015 Favorite Harvest Time Snack

SOUR CREAM FUDGE

2 c. granulated sugar
3/4 c. sour cream
1/2 c. butter
12 oz. white chocolate
7-oz. jar marshmallow creme
3/4 c. diced dried apricots
3/4 c. chopped walnuts

In large heavy saucepan, combine sugar, sour cream and butter. Bring to boil; boil 7 minutes, stirring frequently. Add white chocolate and marshmallow creme; stir until melted. Add apricots and nuts. Pour into greased 8x8-inch pan. Cool and cut.

Cynthia Murphy, *Des Moines*
First Place, 2014 Chocolate Storybook Candies – Fudge with Nuts

MY FAVORITE CHOCOLATE FUDGE

13-oz. can evaporated milk
4 c. granulated sugar
1/2 c. butter
12-oz. pkg. chocolate chips
7-oz. jar marshmallow creme

In saucepan, combine evaporated milk, sugar and butter. Bring to boil, stirring constantly to medium soft ball stage (234° to 241°). Remove from heat; fold in chocolate chips and marshmallow creme. Stir until blended. Pour into greased 9x13-inch pan. Cool and cut into desired shape. Store, covered, at room temperature.

Jenny Petersen, *Knoxville*
First Place, 2014 Adventureland Resort Intermediate – Chocolate Fudge

SURPRISE CHOCOLATE FUDGE WITH NUTS

15-oz. can pinto beans,
    rinsed and drained
1 c. baking cocoa powder
3/4 c. butter, melted

1 tbsp. vanilla
7 1/2 c. powdered sugar
1 c. chopped walnuts, toasted

Line 9x9-inch baking pan with aluminum foil; butter foil and set aside. In microwave-safe dish, mash beans with fork until smooth. Cover; microwave 1 1/2 minutes or until heated through. Add cocoa, butter and vanilla (mixture will be thick). Slowly stir in powdered sugar; add walnuts. Press mixture into prepared pan; cover and refrigerate until firm.

Missy Johansen, *Urbandale*
First Place, 2015 Create a Winner with Gurley's – Non-Baked Items

---

APPLE SURPRISE BITES

1 egg white
3 tbsp. unsweetened
    applesauce
2 tbsp. steamed, pureed
    cauliflower
1 tbsp. minced kale
6 tbsp. apple pie Greek yogurt
1/2 tsp. almond flavoring
1/2 medium apple with peel,
    finely chopped
1/4 c. raisins

3/4 c. white whole wheat
    flour
2 tbsp. artificial sweetener
3 tbsp. brown sugar
1 1/2 tsp. reduced-sodium
    baking powder
1/2 tsp. cinnamon
1 tbsp. bran (1/2 oat & 1/2
    wheat)
1 tsp. chia seeds
1 1/2 tbsp. ground flax seed

Mix egg white, applesauce, cauliflower, kale, yogurt, almond flavoring, apple and raisins; set aside. In separate bowl, combine remaining ingredients. Add yogurt mixture to dry mix. Stir until moistened but still lumpy. Do not over stir. Coat mini-muffin pan with canola spray. Fill cups with mini ice cream scoop. Bake in 375° convection oven 9 1/2 to 10 minutes. Frost when cool.

(CONTINUED)

For ICING:

1 1/2 oz. fat-free cream cheese, room temperature	1 tsp. vanilla
	1/2 c. sifted powdered sugar
	1/2 c. artificial sweetener

Beat together all ingredients until smooth. Frost cooled bites. If desired, top with cinnamon and raisin.

Lydia Davis, *Pleasant Hill*
First Place, 2015 Snack Time with Live Healthy Iowa – Kid-Friendly, Mom Approved

TRUFFLE FUDGE

16 oz. semisweet chocolate, divided	3 tbsp. heavy cream
	2 tsp. vanilla
14 oz. sweetened condensed milk	

Melt 4 ounces of chocolate in microwave. Spread onto bottom of 8x8-inch pan lined with aluminum foil. Refrigerate 10 minutes or until firm. Microwave remaining chocolate and milk in same bowl on high 2 to 3 minutes or until chocolate is almost melted; stir until completely melted. Add cream and vanilla; mix well. Spread over chocolate layer in pan. Refrigerate 2 hours or until firm. Cut into squares.

Emma Johansen, *Urbandale*
First Place, 2014 Adventureland Resort Junior – Fudge (no nuts)

BROWN SUGAR CRISPY ICE CREAM TOPPING

1/2 c. butter, melted	1 1/4 c. sweetened flake coconut
1 c. packed brown sugar	
2 c. crispy rice cereal	1 c. chopped pecans

Mix all ingredients together in large bowl. Spread mixture over 2 foil-lined baking sheets. Bake in 300° oven 30 minutes. Serve warm over ice cream.

Daphane Trevillyan, *Kelley*
First Place, 2015 My Favorite Ice Cream Topping – Other Topping

CHOCOLATE FUDGE WITH NUTS

3 c. granulated sugar
3/4 c. butter
5-oz. can evaporated milk
2 c. dark chocolate melting
    wafers

1 tsp. vanilla
7-oz. jar toasted marshmallow
    creme
1 c. chopped toasted pecans

In heavy saucepan, combine sugar, butter and milk. Cook to soft ball stage (234° to 241°), stirring constantly. Add wafers, vanilla and marshmallow creme; beat well. Add pecans; mix well. Pour into greased 8x8-inch pan. Cool; cut into pieces.

Olive Jean Tarbell, *Centerville*
First Place, 2014 Fudge

APPLE PIE CANDIED APPLE

6 lollipop sticks
6 medium apples, washed
    and dried
1 2/3 c. white chocolate
    wafers, melted

2 drops cinnamon flavoring
1/8 tsp. mace
1/2 c. red chocolate wafers,
    melted
1/2 c. blue chocolate wafers,
    melted

Insert lollipop stick into each apple. Pour white chocolate wafer, cinnamon flavoring and mace in microwave-safe bowl. Melt at 50% power in microwave 1 minute then 10 second intervals, stirring after each time, until wafers are softened. With pastry brush, brush apples with chocolate mixture. If chocolate becomes too thick, reheat until softened. Repeat until apples are all coated; set aside on parchment-lined baking sheet. Melt red and blue chocolate separately; place in sandwich bags and clip corner of bag. Twirl apples and squeeze red line around apple, using pastry brush, brush strokes downward on apple. Repeat same process for blue chocolate.

Triniti Conlan, *Pleasant Hill*
First Place, 2014 Adventureland Resort Junior – Candied Apple

PEANUT BUTTER FUDGE

1/2 c. butter
2 1/4 c. packed brown sugar
1/2 c. milk

3/4 c. peanut butter
1 tsp. vanilla
3 1/2 c. powdered sugar

Melt butter in medium saucepan over medium heat. Stir in brown sugar and milk. Bring to a boil; boil 2 minutes, stirring frequently. Remove from heat; stir in peanut butter and vanilla. Pour over powdered sugar in large mixing bowl; beat until smooth. Pour into 8x8-inch dish. Chill until firm; cut into squares.

Gabby McCoy, *Hartford*
First Place, 2015 Chocolate Storybook Candies – Any Fudge
First Place Overall, 2015 Chocolate Storybook Candies – Youth

---

CHOCOLATE SPICE SNACK MIX

7 c. chocolate flavored rice
    cereal squares
1 c. caramel funnel shaped
    corn cereal
1 c. peanuts
1/2 c. caramel bits
1 c. packed brown sugar
1/2 c. margarine

1/4 c. light corn syrup
1/2 tsp. baking soda
2 tbsp. unsweetened cocoa
    powder
1/2 tsp. five spice powder
1/2 c. miniature candy coated
    chocolate pieces

Mix together cereals, peanuts and caramel bits in large bowl; set aside. Heat brown sugar, margarine and corn syrup in saucepan over medium heat until bubbly on edges. Bring to rolling boil; boil 2 minutes, stirring constantly. Remove from heat; stir in baking soda. Mix until frothy. Mix in cocoa and five spice powder; pour over cereal mixture. Stir until mixture is covered. Pour onto baking sheet. Bake in 250° oven 15 minutes. Stir and add candy pieces. Set aside to cool using spatula to loosen mixture from baking sheet. Once cool; store in airtight container.

Larry Mahlstedt, *Des Moines*
First Place, 2015 Allspice Snack Mix – Chocolate

CINNAMON BUN POPCORN

12 c. popped popcorn
1 c. roughly chopped pecans
1 c. packed brown sugar
1 tsp. Vietnamese cinnamon
1/2 c. salted butter

1/4 c. light corn syrup
1 tsp. vanilla
1/2 tsp. baking soda
3, 2-oz. squares vanilla
  almond bark

Place popcorn and pecans in very large bowl; set aside. In 2-quart microwave-safe bowl, combine brown sugar and cinnamon. Chop butter into chunks; place on top of sugar mixture. Pour corn syrup over top; microwave on high 30 seconds. Stir to combine. Return to microwave; heat 2 minutes. Remove and stir. Microwave 2 minutes more. Remove from microwave; add vanilla and baking soda. Mix well. Pour over popcorn and pecans; stir until coated. Spread onto foil-lined baking sheet. Bake in 250° oven 30 minutes, stirring every 10 minutes. Melt almond bark in microwave. Spread out caramel corn on sheet of freezer paper. Drizzle melted almond bark with fork over popcorn; cool. Once cool and almond bark hardened, break into pieces.

Andrea Spencer, *Stanton*
First Place, 2015 Snappy Popcorn Creations – Sweet Treats
First Place Overall, 2015 Snappy Popcorn Creations

SORGHUM GRANOLA

4 c. old fashioned rolled oats
3/4 c. chopped pecans
1/3 c. shredded coconut
1/2 c. packed light brown
  sugar

1/2 tsp. salt
1/2 tsp. cinnamon
1/2 c. sorghum
1/4 c. canola oil
1 tsp. vanilla

In large bowl, combine oats, pecans, coconut, brown sugar, salt and cinnamon. In small saucepan, heat sorghum and oil; stir in vanilla. Pour sorghum mixture over oat mixture; stir until oat mixture is evenly moistened. Divide between 2 greased 15x10-inch baking pans. Bake in 300° oven 30 minutes, stirring every 10 minutes. When granola is cool, transfer to airtight containers.

Marcia G. Miller, *Urbandale*
First Place, 2015 Cooking with Sorghum – Sorghum Challenge

QUICK SALTED CARAMEL ROLLS

5 oz. chopped pecans
8 oz. semisweet chocolate
   chips

1/4 tsp. coconut or vegetable
   oil
6 to 8 oz. caramels
4 to 5 ultragrain tortillas
Sea salt

Roast pecans in 300° oven 5 minutes, until lightly toasted; set aside. In small microwave-safe bowl, combine chocolate and oil. Melt in microwave 20 seconds, then stir. Repeat until chocolate is nearly melted; finish by stirring until smooth. Melt caramels in microwave in separate bowl. Be careful to not boil. Lay out tortilla on cutting board. Use spoon to coat lightly with caramel, spread over whole side of tortilla. Sprinkle with chopped pecans and sea salt. Roll up tightly; place on wax paper. Continue with each tortilla, reheating caramel when it becomes hard to spread. Put rolled tortillas in refrigerator 10 minutes to cool so they are easier to slice. Cover flat pan with wax paper. Slice 1/2-inch off ends of each roll. Slice rest of roll into 5 pieces. Dip one end of each slice into chocolate; place chocolate-end up on wax paper. Pour rest of chopped nuts in bowl. Dip each chocolate end into nuts then stand it up on pan. Sprinkle cut ends with additional sea salt. Refrigerate to firm chocolate before serving.

Cathy Stahlman, *Ames*
First Place, 2014 It's A "Wrap" with Azteca Tortillas

SPICY SUGAR CORN

1/3 c. corn oil
1/2 c. yellow popcorn
1/2 c. granulated sugar
1/2 tsp. ground chipotle chili

1/4 tsp. ground cinnamon
1/4 tsp ground cardamom
1/4 tsp. salt

Place corn oil in stir-popper; heat over medium-high heat until oil is hot. Add popcorn, sugar, chipotle chili, cinnamon and cardamom all at once. Stir continuously until popcorn has popped. Pour into large serving bowl; sprinkle with salt. Stir to mix.

Marianne Carlson, *Jefferson*
First Place, 2014 My Favorite Tone's Recipe – Casual Appetizers

KICKIN' AND KRUNCHY SNACK MIX

1 c. pretzels
1 c. corn chips
1 c. oyster crackers
1 c. pumpkin seeds, roasted
    and salted
1 c. honey roasted, dry
    roasted peanuts
2 tbsp. butter, melted

2 tbsp. dark brown sugar
1 tsp. chili powder
1 1/4 tsp. Worcestershire
    sauce
1/2 tsp. onion salt
1/2 tsp. cumin
1/8 tsp. ground red pepper

In large bowl, toss together pretzels, corn chips, oyster crackers, pumpkin seeds and peanuts. In separate bowl, whisk together remaining ingredients. Pour over pretzel mix; stir well to coat. Spread in roasting pan. Bake in 300° oven 25 minutes, stirring after 10 minutes. Cool completely; store in airtight container.

Amy Fuson, *Indianola*
First Place, 2014 Allspice Snack Mix – Salty
First Place Overall, 2014 Allspice Snack Mix

PUMPKIN PIE SPICE MIX

3 c. corn cereal squares
3 c. round oat cereal
1 c. honey roasted peanuts
1 c. cashews
2 c. pretzels
1 1/2 c. chopped graham
    crackers

1/2 c. butter
1/2 c. maple syrup
2 tbsp. pumpkin pie spice
1 tbsp. vanilla
1 c. dried cherries
1 c. dried cranberries

In large bowl, mix cereals, peanuts, cashews, pretzels and graham crackers. In separate bowl, melt butter in microwave. Once melted, mix in maple syrup, pumpkin pie spice and vanilla. Pour over cereal mixture. Spread on baking sheet lined with parchment paper. Bake in 250° oven in 15 minute intervals. Do not bake more than 45 minutes. Once out of oven, add cherries and cranberries.

Jennifer Leeper, *Altoona*
First Place, 2015 Adventureland Resort Intermediate – Party Mix-Sweet

MAPLE SUGAR CHAI MACADAMIA NUTS

5 chai tea packets
3 c. macadamia nuts
3/4 c. packed brown sugar,
    divided

1/3 c. pure maple syrup
1/2 c. unsweetened coconut
1/16 tsp. salt
2 tbsp. coconut oil

Remove contents from tea packets into bowl. Add nuts, 1/2 cup brown sugar, maple syrup and coconut. Line baking sheet with aluminum foil; grease foil with coconut oil. Spread nut mixture on prepared pan. Bake in 400° oven 4 minutes. Stir; bake 4 minutes more. Immediately place in bowl; toss with remaining brown sugar and salt. Let cool before serving.

Carson Houg, *Urbandale*
First Place, 2015 Gridiron Goodies, Favorite Super Bowl Snack (ages 8-12)
First Place, 2015 Kids' Favorite Party Foods/Snacks (ages 11-15)

CINNAMON APPLE HARVEST SNACK MIX

5 c. wheat or corn cereal
    squares
1 c. lightly salted nuts
1 c. pretzel twists
1/4 c. butter

1/3 c. packed brown sugar
2 tbsp. light corn syrup
1 tsp. cinnamon
1 c. dried apples
1/2 c. vanilla yogurt-covered
    raisins

Mix cereal, nuts and pretzels in roasting pan; set aside. Melt butter, brown sugar, corn syrup and cinnamon together. Pour over cereal. Bake in 250° oven 1 hour, stirring every 15 minutes. Cool; add apples and raisins.

Sophia Ridgway, *Johnston*
First Place, 2015 Gridiron Goodies – Favorite Super Bowl Snack (ages 13-17)

TOFFEE POPCORN

12 c. popped popcorn
1 c. slivered almonds
1 c. packed brown sugar
1/2 c. salted butter

1/4 c. light corn syrup
1 tsp. vanilla
1/2 tsp. baking soda

Place popcorn and almonds in large bowl; set aside. Place brown sugar in 2-liter capacity microwave-safe bowl. Chop butter into chunks and place on top of sugar. Pour corn syrup over top; microwave on high 30 seconds. Stir to combine. Return to microwave; heat 2 minutes. Remove and stir; microwave 2 minutes more. Remove from microwave; add vanilla and baking soda. Stir to combine. Mixture will foam and rise. Pour over popcorn and almonds; stir very well. Spread popcorn mixture onto foil-lined jelly roll pan. Bake in 250° oven 30 minutes, stirring every 10 minutes. Remove from oven; spread on large piece of parchment, wax paper or foil. Allow to cool.

Andrea Spencer, *Stanton*
First Place, 2014 Chocolate Storybook Candies – Popcorn

WHITE CHIP SNACK MIX

1/2 c. butter, melted
2 tbsp. unsweetened cocoa
   powder
2 tbsp. granulated sugar
4 c. round oat cereal

4 c. wheat cereal squares
1 c. slivered almonds
1 c. golden raisins
2 c. white chocolate chips

Stir together butter, cocoa and sugar. In large bowl, combine cereals and almonds; stir in butter mixture. Toss until ingredients are well coated. Pour into 9x13-inch pan. Bake in 250° oven 1 hour, stirring every 15 minutes. Cool completely; stir in raisins and white chips. Store in tightly covered container in cool, dry place.

Triniti Conlan, *Pleasant Hill*
First Place, 2015 Adventureland Resort Junior – Snack Mix

GRANOLA

1/2 c. butter
1 1/2 c. old fashioned rolled
    oats
1 1/2 c. quick-cooking rolled
    oats
1/3 c. honey

1 c. toasted pecans
1 c. coconut
1 tsp. cinnamon
1/2 tsp. salt
2/3 c. raisins

Melt butter in 9x13-inch pan. Mix in all remaining ingredients except raisins. Bake in 350° oven 25 minutes, stirring every 5 minutes. When done, stir in raisins. Store in airtight bag.

Cynthia Murphy, *Des Moines*
First Place, 2015 Foods Made with Honey – Honey Granola

SWEETENED NUTS

2 c. pecans
1/2 c. granulated sugar
1/2 c. packed brown sugar

1/2 c. water
1 tsp. vanilla
1/4 tsp. hot sauce

Spread pecans on baking sheet; toast in 350° oven 6 to 8 minutes. Stir several times. Combine sugars and water in heavy saucepan. Stir over medium heat until melted. Boil until soft ball forms when mixture is dropped in cold water (238°); add vanilla and hot sauce. Add pecans; stir until fully coated. Spread on wax paper; let stand until firm.

Jeanene Peiffer, *Sigourney*
First Place, 2014 Chocolate Storybook Candies – Sweetened Nuts
Third Place Overall, 2014 Chocolate Storybook Candies – Variations of Candy

SUGARED NUTS

1 egg white
1 tbsp. water
1 c. granulated sugar
3/4 tsp. salt

1/4 tsp. cinnamon
1 lb. nuts (pecans, almonds,
  macadamia nuts)

In mixing bowl, whip together egg white and water until frothy. In separate bowl, mix together sugar, salt and cinnamon. Add nuts to egg whites; stir to coat nuts evenly. Remove nuts; toss in sugar mixture until coated. Spread nuts out on greased baking sheet. Bake in 250° oven 1 hour, stirring every 15 minutes.

Megan McGuire, *Johnston*
First Place, 2015 Adventureland Resort Junior – Sugared Nuts

RASPBERRY LEMON CREAM CHEESE WHOOPIE PIES

For COOKIES:
1/2 c. unsalted butter, room
  temperature
3/4 c. granulated sugar
1 large egg
1 large egg white
1 vanilla bean, split
  lengthwise or
  1 tsp. vanilla

1 tsp. grated lemon zest
2 1/4 c. all-purpose flour
1 1/2 tsp. baking powder
3/4 tsp. salt
1/2 c. buttermilk

Combine butter and sugar; beat on medium-high speed until light and fluffy, about 2 to 3 minutes. Blend in egg and then egg white, scraping down bowl between additions. Scrape beans from vanilla pod into bowl; blend in with lemon zest. In separate bowl, whisk together flour, baking powder and salt. With mixer on low speed, beat in half the dry ingredients, mixing just until incorporated. Mix in buttermilk. Beat in remaining dry ingredients. Transfer batter to large pastry bag fitted with large round tip. Pipe batter into 1-inch or 1 1/2-inch rounds onto parchment-lined pans. Bake in 350° oven 7 to 12 minutes or until puffed

(CONTINUED)

COOKIES, CANDIES AND SNACKS

and set, rotating halfway through baking time. Let cool on pan at least 10 minutes; transfer to wire rack to cool completely. To assemble cookies, match cookies up in pairs by size. Pipe dollop of filling onto flat side of one cookie of each pair. Sandwich cookies together pushing filling to edges. Place in airtight container; refrigerate until set, at least 1 hour.

For FILLING:

4 oz. cream cheese, chilled	**2 tbsp. raspberry preserves**
2 1/2 tbsp. unsalted butter,	**1 1/4 c. powdered sugar**
room temperature	**Red food coloring (optional)**
1/4 tsp. vanilla	

Beat cream cheese and butter on medium-high speed until well combined and smooth. Mix in vanilla and raspberry preserves. Gradually beat in powdered sugar until totally incorporated. Increase speed; beat until smooth. Add food coloring, if desired. Transfer to pastry bag fitted with large tip.

Peri Halma, *West Des Moines*
First Place, 2015 Midwest Living and Gold Medal Flour Cookies – Filled Cookies

---

CASHEW CEREAL SNACK MIX

7 c. crispy rice/corn cereal	**1/2 c. butter**
8 oz. salted cashews	**1/2 tsp. vanilla**
1/2 c. light corn syrup	**1/2 tsp. baking soda**
1/2 c. packed brown sugar	

Put cereal and cashews in large bowl; set aside. In saucepan, combine corn syrup, brown sugar and butter; bring to boil. Boil 5 to 6 minutes. Remove from heat; stir in vanilla and baking soda. Stir well. Pour over cereal and cashews; mix well. Spread on silicone mat-lined baking sheet. Bake in 220° oven 2 hours, stirring occasionally. Remove to wax paper to cool completely.

Megan McGuire, *Johnston*
First Place, 2014 Adventureland Resort Junior – Snack Mix

HONEY AND NUTS GRANOLA

4 c. quick-cooking rolled oats
1/2 c. steel cut oats
1 c. whole almonds
1 c. pecan halves
1 c. sunflower seeds

1 c. vegetable oil
2 c. honey
1 tbsp. vanilla bean paste
2 tsp. cinnamon

Stir together oats, nuts and seeds in large bowl. In separate bowl, mix together remaining ingredients. Add to dry ingredients; mix well. Spread mixture onto 2 parchment paper-lined baking sheets. Bake in 300° oven 40 minutes, stirring every 10 minutes. Let cool completely; store in non-plastic airtight container.

Cassandra Hyatt, *Ankeny*
First Place, 2014 Foods Made with Honey – Honey Granola

A

Almond
  Bars, Scandinavian, 289
  Bites, Little, 284
  Bread, Poppy Seed, 166
  Butter-Jam Thumbprints, 263
  Cheesecake, 240
  Chocolate Bars, 274
  Cinnamon Nut Bread, 160
  Rum Truffles, 309
  Venetian Dessert, 252
Amish Bread, Old Order, 141
Anadama Bread, 115
Angel Food Cake
  Lime Dream, 238
  Strawberry, 223
Appetizer
  Meatballs, 22
  Risotto Balls (Arancini) Parmesan
    Pesto, 19
  Shrimp, Madam Mary Small Batch, 3
  Teriyaki Hawaiian, 12
Apple
  Bites, Surprise, 316
  Blondies, Hazelnut, 302
  Cake, Harvest, 212
  Candied, 318
  Crostada, Jammin', 248
  Cupcakes, Apple Pie, 232
  Muffins, Maple Drizzled, 168
Apple Pie
  Crumb, 186
  Cupcakes, 232
Applesauce
  Bars with Pecan Praline Topping, 275
  Salsa, 21
Apricot
  Bread, 165
  Bread, Nut, 164
  Pie, 180
  Scones, Mango, 176

B

Bacon
  Baked Potatoes, 68
  Bites, and Chocolate Brittle, 306
  Soup, Cheeseburger, 43
Baked Beans
  Picnic, 47
  Rockin' Rowan, 34
Balls, Flaming, 11

Banana Bread, 156
  Best Ever, 154
  Chocolate Chip and Coconut, 157
Banana Nut Bread
  Cream Cheese, 166
  Ginger, 157
  Honey, 142
  Nutty, 178
  Strawberry Walnut, 156
Banana Spiced Ice Cream, 245
BBQ Sauce
  Bourbon Whiskey, 2
  Honey, 4, 7, 97
Bean and Kale Soup, 42
Bear Claws, Cinnamon, 140
Beef
  Curry in Sweet Peanut Sauce with
    Coconut Rice, 84
  Tenderloin, Rubbed, 73
Beer Bread, 117, 120
Beet Salad, Mom's, 44
Berry Custard Pie, 191
Biscotti, Chocolate Almond, 271
Biscuits
  Baking Powder, 175
  Buttermilk, 155
  Onion Herb, 155
  Sausage Gravy, 108
Bites
  Apple Surprise, 316
  Bacon and Chocolate Brittle, 306
  BLT, 9
  Polenta Sweet Corn Edamame, 1
  Sausage Pretzel, 14
  Sweet n' Spicy, 12
Black Forest Crepes, 248
Blonde Brownies, 264
Blondies
  Apple Hazelnut, 302
  White Chocolate Cranberry, 290
Blue Cheese Sugar Cookies, 290
Blueberry
  Bars, 268
  Cream Cake, 210
  Cream Pie, 202
  Muffins, Lemon, 175
Borscht
  Classic Ukrainian, 26
  Real Russian, 41
Bourbon
  BBQ Sauce, 2
  Pound Cake, 232

Braid
  Cherry Rhubarb, 130
  Harvest, 75
Brown Sugar Crispy Ice Cream
    Topping, 317
Brownie Cookies, Cherry, 300
Brownies
  Chocolate Mint, 294
  Dark Chocolate, 280
  Dark Chocolate & Mint Ganache, 281
  Fudgy Chocolate Chunk, 262
  Orange, 278
  Raspberry Mascarpone-Filled, 274
  Salted Caramel, 267
  Triple Chocolate, 278
Bruschetta Toppers, Mini, 3
Burger
  Rice and Black Bean, 95
  Walnut, 70
Burrito, Breakfast, 59
Butter Pecan Bread, 144
Butterhorns, 133
Buttermilk
  Biscuits, 155
  Corn Bread, Grandmother's, 147
  Donuts, 244, 307
  Pie, 199
Butternut Squash
  Pie, 184
  Soup, Roasted, 42
Butterscotch
  Bars, 261, 280
  Pie, Browned, 189
  Rolls, 152

C
Caesar
  Dressing, Mayonnaise, 50
  Kale, 27
Cake Roll, Lemon-Lime Filled, 236
Caramel(s), 314
  Chocolate Covered, 303
  Creamy, 311
  Rolls, Salted, Quick, 321
Carrot
  Noodles in Chimichurri Sauce, 32
  Soup, 48
Carrot Cake
  Sour Cream, 212
  Stuffed, with Orange Cream
    Cheese Glaze, 230
Cashew Cereal Snack Mix, 327

Casserole
  Chicken, Garlic Butternut Squash, 57
  Kielbasa, Rockin' Rowan, 58
  Potato, Twice Baked, 49
  Sausage, Spiced Pasta, 58
  Taco, Gluten Free, 99
Cheddar Bread
  Savory, 143
  Sesame, 124
Cheddar Cheese Cornbread, 174
Cheese Ball
  Buffalo Chicken Cheese, 9
  Edamame, 26
Cheese Bread, Taco, 150
Cheeseburger Pockets, Dill Pickle, 66
Cheesecake
  Almond, 240
  Chocolate Black & White, 235
  Chocolate Cherry No-Bake, 257
  Chocolate Mousse, 234
  Chocolate Orange, 246
  Chocolate Truffle, 256
  Lomalagi, 246
  Peaches and Cream, 258
  Pumpkin, 252
Cheesy
  Bacon Party Mix, 10
  Chili Dip, 10
  Pasta, 72
  Potato Bread, 129
Cherry(ies),
  Braid, Rhubarb, Cream Cheese, 130
  Brownie Cookies, 300
  Chocolate Dipped, 313
  Danish, Raspberry Almond, 134
  Pie, 195, 203
  Salsa, Sweet, Hot, Chopped, 28
Chicken
  Casserole, Garlic Butternut Squash, 57
  Cheese Balls, Buffalo, 9
  Chocolate Fried, 80
  Citrus Glazed, Grilled with Mixed-
    Grain Salad, 90
  Enchilada Mac n' Cheese, 91
  Kabobs, 92
  Lettuce Wraps, Jamaican Jerk, 78
  Quinoa Al Fresco, Garlic, 61
  Rub, 94
  Salad, 31, 38
  Wings, Grilled Sweet and Spicy, 13
Chicken and Noodles
  Bessie's, 74
  Grandma's, 69

Chili, 68
  Game Day, 83
  Iowa Sweet Corn, 100
  My Favorite, 88
Chipotle Peanut Clusters, 297
Chocolate
  Bars, Raspberry, 267
  Bread, Zucchini, 159
  Biscotti, Almond, 271
  Caramels, Chocolate Covered, 303
  Cherries, Dipped, 313
  Chicken, Fried, 80
  Choux Pastry, Mint, 250
  Pie, Cream, 187
  Snack Mix, Spice, 319
Chocolate Brownies
  Fudgy, Chunk, 262
  Mint, 294
  Triple, Delight, 278
Chocolate Cake
  Applesauce Sour Cream Bundt, 228
  Lava, Molten, 233
  Sour Cream, 222
  with Chocolate Buttercream Icing, 236
Chocolate Cheesecake
  Black-and-White, 235
  Cherry No-Bake, 257
  Orange, 246
  Mousse, 234
  Truffle, 256
Chocolate Chip Cookies
  and Butterscotch, Gluten Free, 273
  Oatmeal Chia Cookies, 268
  Spiced Rosemary, 270
Chocolate Cookies
  Crackle, 293
  Toffee, Divine, 266
  Ultimate Double, 269
Chocolate Fudge, 306
  My Favorite, 315
  with Nuts, 316, 318
Chowder, Corn, Creamy Double, 31
Christmas Wreath (Holiday Bread), 124
Cinnamon
  Bear Claws with Milk and
     Honey Glaze, 140
  Ice Cream, 241
  Nuts, 296
  Popcorn, 320
  Rolls, 136
  Snack Mix, 323
Cinnamon Bread, 130
  Raisin, 142, 153

Cobbler, Peach, 250
Cocktail Cookies, Rosemary, Almond
     and Parmesan Shortbread, 25
Coconut
  Coffee Cooler, 50
  Macaroons, Key Lime, 266
  Muffins, 151
  Wings, Chutney, 6
Coconut Cream Pie, 202
  Haupia Pie, 190
Coffee Cake
  Apple-Nut, 172
  Braided 145
  Chocolanutty Banana, 169
  Czech, 214
  Honey Glazed Buttermilk, 171
  Honey Oatmeal, 173
  Honeycomb, 168
  Sour Cream Pumpkin, 170
Corn
  Chowder, 31
  Pie, Nothing Compares to Iowa
     State Fair, 185
  Pudding, 49
  Salsa, Chorizo, 15
  Soup, Spicy Southwest, 30
Corn Bread
  Buttermilk, Grandmother's, 147
  Cheddar Cheese, 174
  Chipotle Cheddar, 153
  Sweet Potato, 146
Corn Muffins
  Corn-ucopia, 170
  Salsa, 163
  Raspberry, 174
Cranberry
  Bread, Whole Wheat, 154
  Meatballs, Apple Spicy, 88
  Salsa, Waiting for the Turkey, 7
  Streusel Shortbread Bars, 284
Cranberry Pie, 186
  Raspberry, 204
Crepes
  Black Forest, 248
  Lemon Mousse with Blueberry
     Sauce, 254
  Peach, 260
Crescent Rolls, Halle's Honey, 146
Croissants, 151
Crostada, Apple, Jammin', 248
Curry, Beef in Sweet Peanut Sauce
     with Coconut Rice, 84

Custard Pie
  Berry, 191
  Rhubarb, 183

D

Danish, Cherry Raspberry Almond, 134
Dark Chocolate
  Cookies, Espresso, 298
  Ice Cream Sauce, Raspberry, 237
Dark Chocolate Brownies, 280
  and Mint Ganache, 281
Dark Chocolate Fudge
  Creamy, 295
  Special, 312
Date Nut Loaf, 161
Deviled Eggs
  Cinnamon Mango, 46
  Sicilian 28
Dill Pickle Cheeseburger Pockets, 66
Dip
  Best Tailgate, 14
  Cheesy Chili, 10
  Coffee Liqueur, 21
  Honey, 13
  Mango, Honey, 11
  Nacho, Robin's Cheesy, 6
  Pumpkin Pie, 2
  Spinach and Artichoke Cream
    Cheese, 5
Dipping Sauce
  Raspberry Chipotle, 8
  Sweet n' Spicy Boom Boom, 33
Donuts
  Baked Buttermilk Corn, 307
  Buttermilk Pumpkin, 244
Dressing
  Caesar Mayonnaise, 50
  Parmesan, Creamy, 29
Dutch Letter
  Bars, Gluten Free, 283
  Circles, 287

E

Edamame Cheese Ball, 26
Egg(s)
  Bread, Braided, 137
  Deviled, 28, 46
  Weekend, 94
  Wrap, Curry, 51
Egg Salad, 65
  Sandwich, Grandpa Bob's Favorite, 93
Eggnog Pumpkin Pie, 196

Empanadas
  Chorizo and Corn, 59
  Jalapeno Pizza with Jalapeno
    Pesto Dipping Sauce, 16
Enchilada Pie, 89
English Muffin Bread, 116
Espresso Tapioca, Sweet, 242

F

Five Layer Bars, 261
Foccacia, 144
French Bread, White, 126
French Toast Bake, Peaches and
    Cream, 79
Fruit
  and Oatmeal Bars, 271
  Bread, Holiday, 164
  Cake, Kanzi's, 240
  Cream, 34
  Pizza, 18
Fudge
  Chocolate, 306, 311, 315
  Chocolate with Nuts, 316, 318
  Dark, Special, 312
  Maple Nut, 310, 313
  Mocha, Dark, 295
  Peanut Butter, 319
  Sour Cream, 315
  Toffee Pecan Cream, 309
  Truffle, 317
  Vanilla, 314

G

German
  Apple Pancake, 74
  Chocolate Cake, 224
  Chocolate Pie, 181
Gingerbread, Honey, 160
Gluten Free
  Chocolate Chip and Butterscotch
    Cookies, 273
  Dutch Letter Bars, 283
  Sponge Cupcakes with Buttercream
    Frosting, 209
  Salisbury Steak, French Onion, 114
  Taco Casserole, 99
Gooseberry Pie, 200
Granola, 325
  Bars, 270
  Honey and Nuts, 328
  Sorghum, 320
Grilled Cheese, Grown Up, 105

Guacamole, 18
Gyoza, 20

H

Ham Loaf
 Cupcakes with Sweet Potato Tops, 85
 Potato-Covered & Swiss Surprise, 100
Hamburger Soup, 37
 with a Kick, 39
Harissa Espresso Ice Cream, 238
Honey
 Barzzzz, 265
 BBQ Sauce, 4, 7, 97
 Blueberry Muffins, 159
 Butter Rolls 128
 Crescent Rolls, Halle's, 146
 Dinner Rolls, 148, 150
 Dip, 13
 Gingerbread, 160
 Granola, 328
 Mango Dip, 11
 Mocktail, Tropical, 41
 Oatmeal Cake, 214
 Pecan Tassies, 225
 Pie, 179
 Sangria, Sweet, 44
 Scones, Star-Spangled, 161
 Wheat Bread, 118, 133
Honey Coffee Cake
 Honeycomb, 168
 Oatmeal, 173
Hummingbird Cake, 226

I

Ice Cream
 Banana, Spiced, 245
 Cinnamon, Smokin', 241
 Harissa Espresso, 238
 Mexican UnFried, 224
 Peach, 230
 Sea Salt and Honey, 228
Ice Cream Sauce, Dark Chocolate
 Raspberry, 237
Italian
 Bread, Artisan, 125
 Cookies, Grandma's, 292
 Crusty, 129
 Pita, 103

J

Jalapeno
 Cookies, Jacked Up, 294

Pizza Empanadas with Jalapeno
 Pesto Dipping Sauce, 16
Jam Bars, 299
Jelly Roll, 213

K

Kabobs, Chicken, Pineapple Rum, 91
Key Lime
 Cookies, 296
 Pie, 188, 205
Kielbasa Casserole, Rockin' Rowan, 58
Kolaches, 120
 Raspberry, 115

L

Lasagna
 Seafood Alfredo, 113
 White, 104
Lavender Walnut Scones, 177
Lemon and Fig Truffles, Sicilian, 301
Lemon
 Bars, Luscious, 276
 Cookies, Sandwich, 286
 Crepes, Mousse with Blueberry
  Sauce, 254
Lemon Cake
 Bundt, 226
 Filled, Roll, 236
Lemon Pie
 Meringue, 188
 Raspberry, Five Layer, 198
 Sponge with Limoncello Crust, 196
Lemon Scones
 Chai Cranberry Orange, 162
 Ginger, 162
Lime Dream Angel Food Cake, 238
Lobster Fra Diavolo, 86

M

Mac n' Cheese
 Beer, 67
 Candy Corn Bacon, 70
 Chicken Enchilada, 91
 with a Zing, 71
Macaroons
 Coconut Key Lime, 266
 French, 304
 Orange and Almond, 265
Mango Fire Wing Sauce, 5
Maple Nut
 Cream Pie, 190
 Fudge, 310, 313

I-5

Maple Sugar Chai Macadamia
   Nuts, 323
Marble Cake with Chocolate
   Buttercream Frosting, 216
Margarita Dessert, 243
Meatball(s)
   Appetizer, 22
   Cranberry Apple, Spicy, 88
   Moroccan, 110
   Pie, Tex-Mex, 81
   Ricotta with Chianti Sauce, 112
   Sour Cream and Onion Turkey, 102
Meatloaf, 60
   Farmer, 83
   Grandma Ostendorf's, 84
   Smokey, 76
Millet Bread, Oat Sunflower, 128
Mincemeat Pie, Orange and Spice, 182
Mocha Chia Cake, 221
Mocha Rum Chiffon Pie, 200
Molasses
   Cookies, Soft, 269
   Crackle Cookies, 282
Mousse, Mocha, 227
Muffins
   Apple, Maple Drizzled, 168
   Blueberry-Lemon, 175
   Caramel Apple, 158
   Coconut, 151
   Corn, Salsa, 163
   Corn-ucopia, 170
   Honey-Blueberry, 159
   Raspberry Corn, 174
Multi Grain Sunflower Bread, 148
Mushroom
   Portobello, Pizza, 52
   Sam's Stuffed Spicy, 17

N

Nacho Dip, Robin's Cheesy, 6
No-Bake Peanut Butter Cup Bars, 292
Nut Bread
   Almond Cinnamon, 160
   Apricot, 164
   Cream Cheese Banana, 166
   Honey Banana, 142
   Pumpkin, 176
Nuts
   Cinnamon Vanilla Sugar, 296
   Macadamia, Maple Sugar, Chai, 323
   Sugared, 326
   Sweetened, 325

O

Oat Bars, Orange and Cranberry
   Ginger, 276
Oat Sunflower Millet Bread, 128
Oatmeal Bread, 119
   Honey-Mustard, 143
Oatmeal Pecan Raisin Pie, 179
Olive Bread, Pesto, Black, 118
Onion
   and Garlic, Caramelized Pasta, 66
   Biscuits, Herb, 155
   Pie with Country Sausage, 108
Orange
   Bars, Cranberry Ginger Oat, 276
   Brownies, 278
   Macaroons, Almond Coconut, 265
   Mincemeat Pie, 182
   Tea Bread, Pecan, 172
Ostrich Stroganoff, 53

P

Pancake, German Apple, 74
Pane Bianco, Tomato, Basil, Garlic, 122
Panini
   Cheese, Grilled, 105
   Turkey, Basil Cream Cheese, 60
Panna Cotta, Not Your Basic, 255
Parfait, Peaches and Cream, 244
Pasta
   Caramelized Onion and Garlic, 66
   Casserole, Sausage, Spiced, 58
   Cheesy, 72
   Penne, Dreams Are Made Of, 64
   Sausage and Butternut Squash in
      Roasted Red Pepper Sauce, 62
Peach
   Cheesecake, 258
   Cobbler, 250
   Crepes, 260
   French Toast Bake, 79
   Ice Cream, 230
   Parfait, 244
   Salsa, 20
Peach Pie
   Precious, 193
   Raspberry, 201
Peanut Brittle, Old Fashioned, 308
Peanut Butter
   Bars, 264
   Cookies, Shortbread, 286
   Crunch Bars, 282
   Cup Bars, No-Bake, 292

I-6

Fudge, 319
Pie, 182
Peanut Clusters, Chipotle, 297
Pecan Pie
  Bars, 279
  Maple, 197
Pecans, Sweet and Spicy, 300
Pesto Bread, Black Olive, 118
Pickle Pizza Pie, 52
Pie Crusts, 206 - 208
Piña Colada
  Cupcakes, 242
  Zucchini Bread, 165
Pineapple
  Cream Pie, 198
  Drop Cookies, 288
  Jewels, 291
Pinwheel Bread, 121
Pita, Italian, 103
Pizza
  Alfredo Garlic Thai, 102
  Fruit, 18
  Pickle, 52
  Portobello Mushroom, 52
  Yummy Party, 96
Pizza Rice Pie, 53
Polenta Sweet Corn Edamame 1
Popcorn
  Cinnamon Bun, 320
  Nutty, Toffee, 312
  Spicy Sugar, 321
  Toffee, 324
Pork Rub, 109
Pork Loin
  Stuffed, 64
  with Ginger-Maple Sauce, Spicy, 78
Pork Tacos
  and Provolone, 94
  Tamarind with Grilled Corn Crema
    and Corn and Bacon Slaw, 54
Pot Pie, Wild Game, 111
Potato(es)
  Bacon Baked, 68
  Bake, Hearty for Supper, 72
  Bread, 129, 147
  Buns, 123
  Casserole, Twice Baked, 49
  La "Causa" De Tita Denegri, 77
  Salad, Hot, 47
  Soup, Cheesy Hashbrown, 36
  Tartlets, 32
  Twice Baked, Stuffed, 36
Pound Cake, Bourbon, Boozy, 232

Praline Sundae Topping, 231
Pudding, Corn, 49
Puff Pastry, Stuffed, 76
Pumpkin
  Bars, Chocolate Chip, 262
  Bars, Donna and Linda's, 273
  Dip, 2
  Cake, Spice, Sour Cream, 220
  Cheesecake, 252
  Coffee Cake, Sour Cream, 170
  Snack Mix, 322
Pumpkin Bread
  Nut, 176
  Rustic, 167
Pumpkin Pie, Eggnog, 196

Q
Quiche
  Cheesy Zucchini, 98
  Iowa State Fair Corny Crabby, 65
Quinoa, Chicken, Garlic, Al Fresco, 61

R
Raisin Bread
  Cinnamon, 142, 153
  Glazed, 139
Raisin Pie
  Oatmeal Pecan, 179
  Sour Cream, Spiced Up, 192
Raspberry
  Almond Thumbprints, 272
  Brownies, Mascarpone-Filled, 274
  Cake, Fabulous, Fresh, 215
  Chipotle Dipping Sauce, 8
  Chocolate Bars, 267
  Kolaches, 115
  Lemon Cream Cheese Whoopie
    Pies, 326
Rhubarb
  Cake, Upside-Down, 219
  Pie, Custard, 183
  Pie, Strawberry, 184
  Slush, Overnight, 37
Rice and Black Bean Burgers, 95
Rice Cakes, Shrimp with Chili Plum
    Sauce, 23
Ricotta Meatballs, Chianti Sauce, 112
Rosemary, Almond and Parmesan
    Shortbread Cocktail Cookies, 25
Rye Bread
  Brewer's, 117
  New York Deli, 127
  Swedish, 135

I-7

S

Salad
  Beet, Mom's, 44
  Chicken, 31, 38
  Kale, Caesar, 27
  Pasta, Crab, 40, 46
  Potato, Hot, 47
  Salmon Chipotle, 29
  Salmon, Smoked Maple-Wine, 35
  Salsa, Layered, 48
  Spinach, Super Seven, 44
  Sweet Potato, 30
  Taco, 98
  Tuna, Charlie's, 35
  Wild Rice, 40
Salisbury Steak, Gluten Free, 114
Salmon
  Glazed with Crispy Skin Topping, 86
  Salad, Chipotle, 29
  Salad, Smoked Maple-Wine, 35
Salsa
  Applesauce, 21
  Cherry, Sweet, Hot, Chopped, 28
  Corn and Chorizo, 15
  Cranberry, Waiting for the Turkey, 7
  Cruda, 16
  Fresh from My Mom's Garden, 22
  Peach, Sunshine Spicy, 20
  Pico De Gallo, 8
  Salad, Layered, 48
  Sauerkraut, Summer's Garden, 23
Salted
  Caramel Brownies, 267
  Caramel Rolls, Quick, 321
  Honey Crispy Treats, 310
Sandwich
  Bread, 132
  Calla Lilly, 97
  Egg Salad, Grandpa Bob's Favorite, 93
  Garden, 87
  Garden Girl's Pep and Veggie, 101
  Sweet Corn Cob, 63
Sangria, Sweet Honey, 44
Sauerkraut, 56
  Salsa, Summer's Garden, 23
Sausage
  Biscuit Gravy, 108
  Pretzel Bites, 14
  Taquitos, 4
Scones
  Apricot Mango, 176
  Lavender Walnut, 177
  Lemon-Chai Cranberry Orange, 162

Lemon Ginger, 162
  Star-Spangled Honey, 161
Sea Salt and Honey Ice Cream, 228
Seafood Alfredo Lasagna, 113
Sesame Cheddar Bread, 124
Shortbread
  Bars, Cranberry Streusel, 284
  Cookie, Peanut Butter, 286
Shrimp
  and Pickle Tea Sandwich, 51
  Appetizer, Madam Mary, 3
  Rice Cakes with Chili Plum Sauce, 23
Snack Mix
  Cashew Cereal, 327
  Chocolate Spice, 319
  Cinnamon Apple Harvest, 323
  Kickin' and Krunchy, 322
  On the Go, 315
  Pumpkin Pie Spice, 322
  Salty Churro Toffee, 302
  White Chip, 324
Sorghum Granola, 320
Soup
  Bacon Cheeseburger, 43
  Bean and Kale, 42
  Bean, Vegan, Vibrant, 39
  Butternut Squash, Roasted, 42
  Carrot, 48
  Corn-Cheese, Southwest Spicy, 30
  Hamburger, 37
  Hamburger with a Kick, 39
  Potato, Cheesy Hashbrown, 36
  Shrimp, Thai Curry, 38
  Tortilla, Low-Fat, 45
Sour Cream
  Cookies, Old Fashioned, 283
  Fudge, 315
  Raisin Pie, Spiced Up, 192
  Spice Cake, Pumpkin, 220
Sourdough, Spelt, 122
Spaghetti and Meatballs, My
    Grandma's Whole Hearty, 107
Spice Cake
  with Apple Filling, 217
  Sour Cream Pumpkin, 220
Spinach
  Dip, Artichoke Cream Cheese, 5
  Salad, Super Seven, 44
Sponge Cupcakes, Gluten Free, 209
Spritz, 263
Steak
  Rub, 92
  Wrap, BBQ, 104

Stöllen, Christmas, 138
Strata, Classic with Crispy Bacon, 69
Strawberry Angel Food Cake, 223
Strawberry Pie
  Chiffon, 192
  Double, 180
  Lemonade Chiffon, 204
  Rhubarb, 184
Stroganoff with Ostrich, Classic, 53
Sugar Cookies, 272
  Blue Cheese, 290
  Mom's with a Lemon Twist, 288
Summer Squash Seven Grain Rolls, 132
Sunflower Bread, Multi Grain, 148
Sweet Corn
  Chili, 100
  Cob Sandwiches, 63
  Pie, 194
Sweet Potato
  Corn Bread, 146
  Pie, 187
  Salad, 30

T
Taco(s)
  Cheese Bread, 150
  Flarin' Southwest Style, 82
  Pork and Provolone, 94
  Pork, Tamarind with Grilled Corn
    Crema & Corn & Bacon Slaw, 54
  Salad, 98
Tapioca, Sweet Espresso, 242
Taquitos, Sausage, 4
Tartlets, Potato, 32
Tassies, Honey Pecan, 225
Tea Bread, Orange Pecan, 172
Tea Sandwich, Shrimp and Pickle, 51
Thumbprints
  Almond Butter-Jam, 263
  Raspberry Almond, 272
Toffee, 305, 314
  Cupcakes, 218
  Fudge, Pecan Cream, 309
  Milk Chocolate Almond, 305
  Popcorn, 312, 324
Topping
  Brown Sugar Crispy, 317
  Praline Sundae, 231
  Sunbutter Crunch, 298
Torte, Walnut with Coffee Whipped
    Cream, 229
Tortilla
  Appetizers, Corn & Sausage Fritter, 24

Soup, Low-Fat, 45
Truffle(s), 308
  Almond Rum, 309
  Fudge, 317
  Lemon and Fig, Sicilian, 301
Tuna
  Burgers, Sweet and Spicy, 80
  Salad, Charlie's, 35
Turkey
  Meatballs, Sour Cream & Onion, 102
  Panini, Basil Cream Cheese, 60
Twice Baked Potatoes, Stuffed, 36

U, V
Vanilla Fudge, 314
Vegan Bean Soup, Vibrant, 39

W
Walnut
  Burger, 70
  Cake, Sour Cream Mocha, 211
  Torte with Coffee Whipped
    Cream, 229
White Chocolate
  Blondies, Cranberry 290
  Cookies, Orange Drop, 277
  Ruby Roads, 285
Whole Wheat
  Rolls, 126
Whole Wheat Bread, 116
  Cranberry, 154
Wild Rice Salad, 40
Wing Sauce, Mango Fire, 5
Wings
  Chicken, Sweet & Spicy, 13
  Coconut Chutney, 6
Wrap
  Chicken Lettuce, Jamaican Jerk, 78
  Egg, Curry, 51
  Lunch, 61
  Steak, BBQ, 104

X, Y, Z
Zucchini
  Bread, Chocolate, 159
  Bread, Piña Colada, 165
  Quiche, Cheesy, 98
Zuppa with Asparagus and Cannellini
    Beans, Zippy, 33
Zucchini Pie, 194
  Italian with Venison Salami, 106

I-9